# A Woman's Place

# CHATELAINE

# *A Woman's Place*

SEVENTY YEARS IN THE LIVES OF CANADIAN WOMEN

EDITED BY SYLVIA FRASER

INTRODUCTION BY RONA MAYNARD

KEY PORTER  BOOKS

**Canadian Cataloguing in Publication Data**

Main entry under title:

A woman's place : seventy years in the lives of Canadian women

Extracts from Chatelaine.
Includes index.
ISBN 1-55013-910-X

1. Women – Canada – History – 20th century.     2. Women – Canada – Social conditions.     I. Fraser, Sylvia.

HQ1453.W577      1997      305.4'0971'0904      C97-931303-1

THE CANADA COUNCIL | LE CONSEIL DES ARTS
FOR THE ARTS | DU CANADA
SINCE 1957 | DEPUIS 1957

The publisher gratefully acknowledges the support of the Canada Council for the Arts and the Ontario Arts Council for its publishing program.

Key Porter Books Limited
70 The Esplanade
Toronto, Ontario
Canada  M5E 1R2

Design: Jean Lightfoot Peters
Electronic formatting: Heidi Palfrey
Permissions editor: Julie Crysler
Printed and bound in Canada

97 98 99 00 6 5 4 3 2 1

# Contents

# Introduction

I

N 1928, THE YEAR *Chatelaine* was born, middle-class Canadian wives served Scotch eggs for breakfast and knew how to use finger bowls. The novels of L.M. Montgomery, whose fans included the Prince of Wales, fired their national pride. On the face of things they led enviable lives: husbands paid their bills and maids kept their homes shipshape. But they still did not qualify as persons, according to the Supreme Court of Canada. If they lived in Quebec, they could not vote in a provincial election. And bearing children still threatened their survival, especially in rural areas. That year, poor medical care claimed the lives of more than 1,500 Canadian mothers.

*Chatelaine* captured all this and more. If Canadian women were thinking about it, their fledgling magazine was talking about it, creating a nationwide conversation in which readers set the tone from the start. The Maclean Hunter Publishing Company had thought of calling its new creation *Better Housekeeping*, but wisely decided to solicit ideas from the public. A contest announced in *Maclean's* drew 75,000 entries, and Hilda Paine, a rancher's wife from Eburne, B.C., won the $1,000 prize for "The Chatelaine." The name recalled the ring of keys worn by housewives long ago—keys to every part of the house, from the linen closet to the wine cellar. *Chatelaine* has kept the keys to women's lives ever since, although they now unlock the office as well as the home.

From the Jazz Age to the New Age, *Chatelaine* has belonged to its readers. The first issue contained activities for children, but Canadian women put a stop to that. They wanted a meeting place where grown women could connect as friends do when husbands and kids are not around—a Canada-wide kitchen table where no-holds-barred conversation ranged from what's wrong with health care to what's for dinner. Although kids' games made a brief reappearance in the Baby Boom era, this woman-centered focus has defined *Chatelaine* for seventy years. The magazine was their decorator, cooking coach and beauty adviser. In the sixties, one dollar bought a personal makeover plan, complete with diet and exercise tips, from resident style expert Eveleen Dollery.

Above all, *Chatelaine* was women's confidante, dispensing straight talk about subjects ignored or hushed up almost everywhere else. "How to go to university at home," an unassuming 1959 article, sparked more than a thousand inquiries from readers hungry for learning. "The pill that shook the world," a 1953 cause célèbre, provoked both cancelled subscriptions and heartfelt thanks. (As a Saskatchewan reader lamented, "Here in Canada we may as well be living in the middle ages as far as birth control goes.") In 1956, the January issue sported no cover art and a deliberately provocative coverline, "Woman's greatest hazard: another challenging article." Inside, Dr. Marion Hilliard, chief of obstetrics and gynecology at Women's College Hospital and a *Chatelaine* mainstay, endorsed women's right to sexual pleasure and demolished macho myths. Complaints bombarded *Chatelaine*, but the issue sold out within days.

Through *Chatelaine*, women followed the most famous people of the day—and for years, royalty topped the hit parade. Marion Crawford, much-loved former nanny to the Queen and Princess Margaret, shared her memories in story after story. (Promised a 1952 coverline: "Crawfie tells how a princess can be a prisoner in the palace.") As recently as 1983, the year's hottest-selling cover featured Princess Diana, whose own trials in the palace had not yet come to light. Canadian celebrities boosted sales too, from Joyce Davidson in the fifties to Shania Twain in the nineties. When Elizabeth Taylor graced a 1962 cover, outraged readers called her a "homewrecker"—and demanded a return to Canadian subjects. There was no mistaking the allure of home-grown notoriety: Margaret Trudeau smiled from two blockbuster covers.

Of the ordinary mortals who at times achieved cover status, none created more excitement than journalist Terry Poulton, whose appearance celebrated a sixty-five-pound weight loss. *Chatelaine* readers had cheered Poulton on while she sweated and dieted her way to slimness, chronicling her struggle in a series of articles. Thirteen years later, *Chatelaine* published a follow-up story in which Poulton revealed that she'd regained every pound and then some. At last she had accepted her size and sworn off diets for good. Women applauded Poulton's candor, but gave *Chatelaine* mixed reviews: the cover featured a model, not Poulton, because years had passed since the diet series. Some readers accused the magazine of hypocrisy.

Enraptured, enraged or somewhere in between, readers have always spoken from the heart to *Chatelaine*. They have inspired some of the magazine's defining traditions: recipe contests in the fifties, the Mrs. Chatelaine contest in the sixties and seventies. Every year, thousands of home-makers vied for the title of Mrs. Chatelaine—and every year a few women lampooned the whole affair. One self-described "overweight, pear-shaped and bowlegged" reader, Beatrice Maitland of Chatham, N.B., nominated herself as "Mrs. Slob." When *Chatelaine* published Maitland's letter proclaiming her slapdash cooking and junk-shop decor, she became an instant celebrity.

*Chatelaine*'s bond with readers has had a lot to do with its editors, all but one of them female. Unlike most U.S. magazines for women, which men edited until very recently, *Chatelaine* has been shaped by women for sixty-five of its nearly seventy years.

Elizabeth Anne Wilson, the founding editor, launched *Chatelaine* while editing another Maclean Hunter magazine, *Mayfair*. Yet she somehow found time to write for the new magazine on topics as diverse as home design ("What is this modernist movement?") and social issues ("The problem of the missing girl") before passing the torch to Byrne Hope Sanders in 1929.

There was no mistaking Sanders' tough-mindedness. When she married her art director, company policy dictated that one of them would have to quit. The art director went home to freelance while his wife pursued a stellar career. As editor of *Chatelaine* for more than twenty years, from the heyday of corsets and cocktails through the coming of TV and nylon stockings, the South African-born Sanders became one of the few women in Canada with a public profile. Seconded to Ottawa during the war years to head the Wartime Prices and Trade Board, she implemented food rationing and set up a consumer council of women—an accomplishment that made her a Companion of the Order of Canada. Soon after her return to *Chatelaine*, she recruited an employee whose place in Canadian life would one day rival her own. She hired Doris Anderson to work in the advertising department. In her memoir, *Rebel Daughter*, Anderson recalls that Sanders never began her work day without greeting each employee personally to "make sure we were all right, like a mother checking on her children."

When Sanders left the magazine in 1952 to help bring the Gallup poll to Canada, former newspaper reporter and longtime *Chatelaine* contributor Lotta Dempsey took over. She had turned out more than three hundred articles for the magazine (no wonder she used three pseudonyms). As editor, she came up with so many story ideas that her staff could barely keep up with her. "With relief, we would work through the editor's lunch hour while she met with fascinating scientists and visiting celebrities," said art director Stan Furnival in *The Lady Was a Star*, a biography of Dempsey by Carolyn Davis Fisher. "But we would dread her inevitable return with another six great ideas for *Chatelaine*." Dempsey soon decided she would rather write articles than assign them to others. After less than a year, she returned to newspapers.

*Chatelaine*'s only male editor, former war correspondent John Clare, kept a low profile in the job, writing editorials so seldom that many readers thought a woman still ran the show. He once confided to his audience, "We don't suppose we shall ever become completely accustomed to being addressed by letter as 'Dear Madam.'" Meanwhile, editor-in-waiting Doris Anderson was working her way up through the ranks, honing her sense of language under Clare's astute direction but chafing at his traditional story ideas. As she writes in *Rebel Daughter*, "Any suggestion that every woman wasn't jubilantly happy as a housewife and mother was, like most other unseemly matters, simply not discussed."

All that began to change in 1957, the year Anderson got her break. *Chatelaine* questioned the satisfaction of housework, exposed the battering of babies, investigated sex discrimination in the workplace and criticized restrictive divorce laws. In 1963, when galleys of a provocative book on women reached *Chatelaine*, the editors saw little new in it. Missing out on what she later called "the scoop of the century," Anderson turned down an excerpt from Betty Friedan's *The Feminine Mystique*. She would continue to champion women's quest for equality in *Chatelaine* before striking out for new territory in 1977 (she has headed the National Advisory Council on the Status of Women, served as president of the National Action Committee on the Status of Women and written 5 books).

Just as Anderson anticipated and interpreted the rise of the women's movement, so her successor captured the spirit of the roaring eighties. Mildred Istona had created *Miss Chatelaine* (which later evolved into *Flare*). She brought style to *Chatelaine*'s ever-popular services pages, and cheek to celebrity profiles. She preserved the magazine's tradition of monitoring women's roles and rights, while breaking ground with innovations that flourish to this day. Ask a *Chatelaine* reader what part of the magazine she turns to first, and she'll likely mention "Free for the Asking," in which professionals answer questions about everything from child support to vitamins.

And each December, readers and news media alike watch for another Istona legacy— *Chatelaine*'s Woman of the Year. From barrier-breakers like Barbara Frum to unstoppable mavericks like k.d. lang, the Women of the Year have helped to shape the spirit of their time. But they haven't always won readers' hearts. Controversy flared when *Chatelaine* chose former Prime Minister Kim Campbell, for having "crashed through the political glass ceiling and made history." "Someone who proudly led her party to the most humiliating defeat in Canadian political history is not worthy of such a title," said a Manitoba reader. "Mistake of the year, maybe."

In her *Miss Chatelaine* days, Istona hired a copy editor whose only qualification for the job was a passion for magazines. I was that beginner—one of countless editors, writers and photographers who owe their first break to Mildred Istona. She later kept me busy writing dozens of *Chatelaine* articles about the changing lives of women. I would often start my phone interviews before breakfast to catch women in the Maritimes before they left for work, then keep the phone at my ear until after 11 p.m., when mothers in B.C. had put their kids to bed. I remember how they'd ask me, "What did the other women say?"

Now it's my turn to moderate the cross-Canada conversation that unfolds every month in *Chatelaine*. These days, our typical reader barely has time to pour a bowl of cereal for breakfast, much less prepare Scotch eggs. She can't count on a husband to support her (in these days of downsizing, she may well be supporting her mate). Household help? She's happy if the family pitches in. But as I read Sylvia Fraser's telling selections for this book, what struck me was not how much has changed in seventy years but how much remains the same. Women still want to know what other women are saying about every aspect of their world, from what's new at the bookstore to what's wrong with health care, just as they did in 1928 and will do for decades to come.

—RONA MAYNARD

# A Note on the Process

Last September, a seven-hundred-pound archive was delivered to my door. For the next several months I lived retrospectively within the covers of seven decades of *Chatelaine* magazines. What began as a daunting task turned addictive: my right thumb acquired repetitive stress syndrome from flipping pages.

Since I'd personally experienced all but one of those decades, I wasn't voyaging into the unknown, but I was exchanging a worm's-eye view for a bird's-eye one. What surprised me first was how smart, how informed, how passionate and compassionate the feminists of the twenties were, and how completely we Canadian women fell asleep on feminist issues during the next thirty years. Second, I noted how often the same social battles were refought, with writers and readers vociferously expounding points of view they believed to be uniquely their own, but which were merely historical rematches pitting those who were ahead of their times against those who wanted to apply the brakes; and since social attitudes are as subject to fashion as shoes, it was often difficult to decide who was ahead and who was behind.

Finally, I was struck by how clearly and vividly the story of women emerged from the pages of *Chatelaine*: those decades *did* measure significant shifts in values, even though they didn't necessarily begin on the zero and end on the nine; and since women are the chameleon sex, every social change dramatically colored female lives.

As reflected in the pages of *Chatelaine*, the twenties were defined by the conflict between parents and their coming-of-age children: youth—especially women—used boom times to seize greater personal freedom. In the thirties, the Depression abruptly cut young women out of the job market, returning them to the unskilled marital one; simultaneously, the spotlight shifted from the concerns of youth to an ironic, resentful dialogue between husbands and wives.

During the forties, Canadians of both sexes projected their energies and anxieties overseas, placing many domestic conflicts on hold; as pinch-hitters, women enjoyed unprecedented job opportunities, buoyed by a fantasy life about what would happen when "the boys" came marching home. In the postwar fifties, the focus was once more on nesting couples, now attempting to live out the romantic myth created by separation. Again in lock step, they found themselves divided by a mute and restless discontent that seemed a replay of the thirties, but with one striking difference: pampered by peace, progress and prosperity, they could find no one to blame but themselves.

In the sixties, partnership issues were again overshadowed by an outbreak of hostilities between parents and their teenage offspring: though this resembled the youth revolt of the twenties, the political issues—war and capitalism—centered more on sons than daughters. It took the seventies for women's greater personal freedom to revive the feminist movement of the twenties. Individually and in groups, women turned inward, rediscovering female history and an identity apart from familial relationships. During the eighties, women's increased sense of "personhood" and earning power forced the patriarchy to give up some of its darker secrets—sexual harassment, violence, rape. Though the resulting male-female alienation continues into the nineties, couples high on hope continue to set up camp in the "no combat" zone, often with a passel of offspring from earlier liaisons. Simultaneously, a new battlefront has opened between parents and their still-dependent children—the flotsam and jetsam of too many partnership experiments—now seeking legal control of their own lives.

Does *Chatelaine* accurately reflect Canadian women's lives?

Unlike U.S. women's publications, which can afford to appeal to a narrow segment and still remain mass-market, Canadian magazines have always had to be free-ranging to survive. Though *Chatelaine* cannot be said to have equally reflected the experiences of minority or impoverished women throughout its seventy years, I believe it does credibly reflect the collective Canadian female psyche at any given time: when Canada was ethnocentric and complacent, so was *Chatelaine*, but as the country grew more inclusive, so did the pages of *Chatelaine*. The magazine also took as common ground the domestic territory of women and women's curiosity about each other's lives.

In many ways, *Chatelaine* can be described as Everywoman's diary—seventy years of successes and stalemates, fads and fantasies, enthusiasms and regrets. During this time, the clearest gains have been in the employment field: though universal equity still eludes us, it is no longer legal to fire a woman when she marries; to ban, banish or refuse to promote her because of gender; to sexually harass or insult her. And in contrast to the thirties, when twice as many women worked as domestics than as stenographers or teachers, these gains manifest themselves across a broad professional spectrum.

By contrast, the political equality of women has not been translated into power: success, in this arena, is still played out in breakthroughs and by trailblazers.

On the domestic front, though more men are willing to help with housework and children, these remain essentially female responsibilities—especially after divorce. Though politicians pay lip service to universal day care, no government has dared to fund it. Though more women "have it all," they're often too tired to enjoy it (however, before we blame women's dual roles, take note that full-time housewives in the fifties also named chronic fatigue as their most persistent enemy).

On the personal front, each of us must mark her own scorecard. Though women no longer wait on tenterhooks to see if the lowering of a hem will wipe out a winter wardrobe, good looks are more important than ever as collateral in today's fluid, high-turnover mating mart. Though women have thrown away their boned corsets, the "never-too-thin" rule has converted our own skeletons into straitjackets. Though women have learned to prolong youth, the age of optimum sexual attractiveness, as reflected in popular culture, has plummeted. Though single women are now allowed to have a sex life, fear of pregnancy has been replaced by fear of death (no gender bias here!). Though more women are climbing the corporate ladder, surveys indicate that career success dramatically increases a man's choice of potential mates, while decreasing a woman's: even while paying lip-service to sexual equality, most men continue to insist on financial dominance.

Despite the feminist movements of the twenties and seventies, most young women continue to lead their lives without a sense of history. At the time of their coming of age, when one generation traditionally conveys its wisdom to the next, young women appear most in need of their illusions, most blithely confident of their own strength, most desirous of separating from their mothers and most awash in the admiration and flattery of men. In the pages of *Chatelaine*, single young women were typically the ones who clung most stubbornly, in any decade, to the prevalent romantic myth, to the desire to recast themselves to please a nonexistent mate and to the Cinderella belief in imminent rescue.

Despite these caveats, if you flip the corners of seventy years of *Chatelaine*, as I have done, you will find that we Canadian women *have* been traveling toward greater freedom and equality, and if you listen to *Chatelaine*'s collective voice, you'll find it tends to be a moderate feminist one.

A footnote on the process of selection and editing: the articles in this collection were chosen primarily as an historical record of issues concerning women during the past seventy years. Though skillfully crafted by Canada's best-known writers, they were selected more to reflect attitudes than to showcase literary talent. To provide the widest possible sampling, most have been excerpted from much longer articles. Since this was accomplished without bridging, reorganizing or updating, blame the process and not the writer if some transitions seem abrupt, or important side issues remain unaddressed. The same must be stressed as regards views and language now judged outmoded or even prejudiced. This is not a computer-enhanced portrait. *Chatelaine*'s readers, writers, photographers and editors were there. This is the way it was.

—SYLVIA FRASER

# CHAPTER ONE

# Herself: Woman's Changing Image

**W**ESTERN SOCIETY'S IMAGE of the ideal woman is a portrait drawn on sand, subject to revision at the turn of the next tide. Though this image has often been played out in superficial details, such as the length of a skirt or the slant of a hat, it has accurately projected what each age expected of women—or would allow.

In the 1920s, young women flaunted their postwar independence with the boyish look: bobbed or shingled hair, no waists, chests flattened by breast suppressers, short skirts, bare legs, bare arms. When a woman wanted to look like a woman, she added long strings of beads, dabs of rouge, smoldering eyeshadow, beestung Clara Bow lips, and perhaps a touch of the just-introduced Chanel No. 5.

During the Depression of the thirties, women went under cover: colors darkened, day-time hems plunged, necklines rose, arms vanished under fitted sleeves, and faces under veiled hats. Yet, the figure inside all this mystery was an indisputably female one with waist and breasts shaped by corset and brassiere (now available in cup sizes from A to D). But at least one fashion feature undercut the decade's reclamation of femininity: the defiant introduction of slacks.

Because of World War II, the forties demanded from women a completely different set of qualities. As soldiers marched off to battle, once again the spotlight was on youth, action and extroversion. The wholesome girl-next-door became society's new ideal. Energetic, optimistic, she was expected to help save her country as a farmerette, as Rosie the Riveter, or even to don a military uniform. In daywear, padded shoulders, conspicuous hats and low-heeled walking shoes gave "civvies" a military flavor.

During the war, women were praised for their self-reliance; after the war, that quality came under fierce attack. Dior's New Look, unveiled in 1947, projected the fifties' ideal: ultra-femininity, played out in mid-calf ballerina skirts exaggerated by crinolines, wasp waists cinched with elastic, full breasts with cleavage supplied by the new pushup bras. Dependent, demure and decorous, the fifties woman reflected society's revised priorities for her: as helpmate, wife and mother.

By the sixties, the girlishness of crinolines and peplums had given way to a more understated, more sophisticated silhouette: the sheath, accessorized with white gloves, pointed-toe pumps with Queen Anne heels and pillbox hat afloat on bouffant hair. Inspired by Jacqueline Kennedy, this was the perfect uniform for the upwardly mobile corporate wife as well as the princess of Camelot. Though poodle and Italian boy cuts favored dark hair, Clairol's puckish ad campaign, promising "Only her hairdresser knows for sure," was making it possible for women to confess to their secret bathroom alchemy: turning dross into gold. The new ideal was the sun-streaked status blonde epitomized by Grace Kelly—a real princess.

Like the twenties, the late sixties were a time of youthful revolt—no more Mrs. Nice Wife. For serious fashion dropouts, street wear now meant unisex or peasant clothes from Army Surplus or the

# *Once upon a time ... everyone had a dressmaker or could sew*

Vogue chiffon dress patterns

local Thrift shop—tattered jeans, long gathered skirts, fringed shawls, worn with hip-length ironed hair parted in the middle, army boots, sandals or bare feet.

For the more affluent woman, Italian designers like Pucci or British "Mod" ones like Mary Quant had usurped leadership from Paris. As with Thriftwear, psychedelic fashion challenged convention: mini-skirts with knee-high vinyl boots, pant suits with tunics, bell-bottoms, the tent and—at last!—pantyhose. To create the total look, you needed false eyelashes (sometimes applied one at a time), black liner, luminous eyeshadow, candy-colored matte lipstick and fake hairpieces twisted into Marie Antoinette retros. For brunettes, Sassoon's geometric creations provided the coolest cut, while blondes in frankly altered shades from ash to golden more often chose the gravity-defying beehive (a triumph of the new hairsprays plus a weekly trip to the hairdresser) or the shoulder-length flip-up.

At heart, the psychedelic woman was a rebellious child at play. Though bras were being defiantly discarded as a gesture of emancipation, and the bikini had become standard beachwear, what to make of Twiggy, both the decade's icon and its chief anomaly? Was she, with her coat-hanger body, a symbol of liberation as in the twenties, or the forerunner of today's misogynistic, anorexic models imprisoned inside their own rib cages?

The seventies began with a fashion insurrection: when Paris, in the fall of 1970, arrogantly decreed that women must give up the mini in favor of the midi, most adamantly refused, permanently breaking haute couture's dictatorial hold on the consumer. They even staged a counter-revolution by opting, briefly and spontaneously, for hot pants. What women were ready to discard was their high-upkeep fakery. This evolved into an entirely new image—the natural look with faces framed in wind-blown brown hair, often pushed back by a pair of out-sized Margaret Trudeau sunglasses. Colors were muted, in natural fibers that created softly flowing layers without waists or shoulders. Once again, women's bodies had gone undercover—this time while their psyches absorbed the lessons of the women's movement. Though maxi coats hit their stride in winter, bathing suits continued to be skimpy as if to flaunt the fact that women didn't mind revealing themselves when they chose.

Focus of eighties' fashion was the career woman. By day, power suits in primary colors with piled-high football shoulders served notice that women were out to compete on what they intended to turn into a level playing field. On weekends, they pumped iron or jogged in pursuit of the fatless, well-contoured body, possessed and marketed by Jane Fonda. In the gym—the new center of haute couture—they sported tank tops, with shiny spandex tights ending in designer running shoes. For evening, they hit the hot spots in glittery, metallic fabrics reflecting their self-acquired affluence, yet often concealing a seductive layer of silk and lace. It was this paradox that Madonna exploited by audaciously converting innerwear to outerwear, then calling herself the Material Girl.

By the nineties, many boomers were exchanging diets and gym work for the contemplative glories of the garden. Instead of emulating the ever-more-anorexic, computer-enhanced models, they were protesting them with graffiti scrawled across posters. They were also demanding fashion inclusion, even on the runway—mature models, over-sized models and the disabled. Meanwhile, Generation Xers took to grunge: a deliberate mismatch of patterns and styles, often deceptively expensive, assembled with a code only they could crack.

But boomers, who'd established every major fashion trend since the sixties, still weren't quite ready to give up youth or the spotlight: instead of naturally gray hair and country casuals, many were choosing short skirts with patterned tights and red hair—what *Chatelaine* dubbed any-age dressing.

February
1929

10¢

January
1932

10¢

# Sending Claire to College

*Actual budgets of expenses, and practical suggestions for the girl of moderate means at university*

By Constance K. Seton

**SEPTEMBER 1929** Not only Claire went to college, but Audrey, too, as it turned out! At first, we told ourselves that a bachelor's hood for the older girl would be all that we could possibly afford, and we quite expected to tighten our belts an inch or two each year before the coveted rabbit-skin hung in the family wardrobe. That was in 1920, when potatoes at a dollar a peck still haunted the halls—or was it the cells?—of memory.

Our circumstances were in that dubious condition miscalled "moderate"; but ambition soared within us. So when Claire was graduated, we asked ourselves if it were quite fair to expect Audrey to bask in the academic aura surrounding her older sister. Audrey had brains, too. For her, too, libraries and little theatres, choral clubs and "gym" facilities had their appeal.

Perhaps we couldn't have done it but for the fact that, a year after her graduation in 1924, Claire began to earn almost twice as much as she could have made on entering any career from the secondary schools. She helped us out with Audrey, whose degree is due in 1929.

We are methodical souls. Instead of idly wondering how we had accomplished the feat, and how much it had "set us back" in dollars and cents, we took down nine of the little diary and account books which stretch back in an unbroken row, and we did some figuring.

First, we marshalled the various items of college expenditure into four main columns: Fees—Pocket-money—Books—Clothes. On striking an average for Claire's wardrobe during the four important years, we found that $164 was the modest sum that met her needs. What was our surprise to discover that $164 yearly supplied Audrey's outfit also! Books were not so clearly accounted for. Yet for each girl,

buying judiciously at secondhand book bureaus, a sum of $10 to $17 expended in October purchased the requisite. Claire's annual supply of pocket-money averaged $101; Audrey's, $86.

The University of Toronto fee—formerly $40—is now $75, and additional college fees have nearly doubled the former total; so that, adding the charge for final examinations payable in March, Claire's average annual fee bill was $58 and Audrey's, $106.

A yearly expenditure of approximately $360 to $400 will now provide for the upkeep of a girl at college, when the student lives at home. For the out-of-town girls who live, two in a room, at a college residence, something over $300 must be added for board and lodging.

Undoubtedly, this very modest budget could be reduced still further by the very serious or elderly maiden, to whose dogged ambition a degree represents the cultural apex of a pyramid of earnest economy. But we do not recommend a cut in our estimates. For to the average co-ed a class-pin or two, a crest on her blazer-pocket, pennants interspersed with the team photos on her bedroom wall—and perchance a ukulele!—mean very much.

In the final year the expense of college life is undoubtedly somewhat higher, in spite of the fact that the seniors are feted by all the other years. For there are the graduation photographs which must be exchanged between "pals" of the class; there is rather more need for ornate apparel, culminating in the live question of a graduation frock. And whether or not the maiden acquires a mortarboard and gown of her own in this, her senior year, she must pay the charge for her degree—a charge that varies from $5 in Saskatchewan and Nova Scotia to $20 in British Columbia with $10 as a fair average obtaining in Ontario and Manitoba.

Also, though bouquets at some colleges no longer grace the procession of graduates across the campus, they are seen to flourish very prettily at the post-ceremonial garden party. Therefore, proud parents throng the florists' shops, regardless of the fact that hothouse roses in early June are nearly worth their weight in gold.

The courses in Household Science, Social Service, and a few others, fit directly for the chosen occupation, but to enter teaching another year of training is necessary. The graduate who desires to enter the business world is wise if she takes the orthodox business course. To the thoughtful parent, one of the most encouraging signs of the age is that labor has become not only a fashion but a passion.

Claire and Audrey have acted as farmerettes, wielding the hoe. Claire has helped to harvest strawberry crops and the peach crop, employing the intervening weeks at filing in a city office. Audrey has picked raspberries and cherries, has spent months waiting on table in a large summer hotel, and has done a great deal of social service work at the Fresh Air camps.

Earned money in our case paid for some of those unsought luxuries known as "supps," for private tuition, and for such extras as skis, a portable gramophone, a folding camera, a good desk lamp and tennis needs.

Claire inherits a turn for dressmaking. Audrey pos-esses a "nose" for bargains. If Audrey finds a beige crêpe satin—regularly $3.25 for $1.98—and Claire or her mother makes it up on modish lines in some simple style, what have we? An afternoon frock for eight dollars or so, that would have cost $19.75 at least in the ordinary way.

A general rule is that the least practicable of all considered garments is the elaborate two-piece suit. Separate coats and dresses spell economy. Similarly, for the girl who attends few actual evening affairs, it is better to have two afternoon frocks, one much "fussier" than the other—preferably sleeveless—for the latter will be suitable for the smaller evening entertainment, as well as for the more formal afternoon engagement. But one actual evening dress is really de rigueur.

As for sports—no longer is the college outfit represented by one middy and a pair of gym bloomers, both calculated to do time for four years and then descend unimpaired to a younger sister! One bathing suit no longer fills the bill. A light-grey cotton suit is required for tank use, a gaily-colored woollen one for general wear—both together bulking less largely than the one complicated garment of yesteryear. Considering knickers, a light pair of khaki drill serves many a need; and one heavier pair of corduroy answers for cool weather "hikes," or for horseback riding, to the joys of which many a college maiden succumbs sooner or later.

Audrey's inclination would impel her to put all of her allowance into handsome sports garb if she were not restrained. It was Claire, however, who bought, with earned money, a lustrous suede windbreaker. The family thrift fainted at sight of the price-tag. Twenty-five dollars—and a bargain to boot! But that windbreaker has wonderful warmth and endurance—and style. It has shed splendor at several hockey matches; it graces the rink and appears regularly on horseback.

A clannish spirit pervades residence life for girls a spirit that fosters fun and builds up esprit de corps. Most houses provide facilities for piano practice, for the entertainment of relatives and for the medical supervision of the students. The "freshie" obeys a somewhat stricter law than the older girls. Each year some extra liberty or a few extra "late leaves" are added to the list of indulgences.

In conclusion it is scarcely necessary in these days to dwell on the advantages of a college training. Contact with another level of thought, and glimpses of cultural vistas beyond the ken of a girl who enters work from the secondary school, are the privileges of her college-bred sister. Libraries and little theatres, speakers and stars of the musical world lend their attainments and their art. Nor does the wave of culture recede at this point; through the agency of the student herself it enters the home and the community.

No, we were not entirely disinterested when we sent Claire, and Audrey, too, to College. We meant to "get a look in" ourselves behind those doors of learning. And we have!

# The Undercover Story

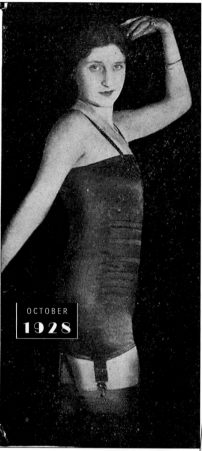

MARCH 1928

**FEBRUARY 1943**

**NOVEMBER 1972**

**OCTOBER 1943**

**JUNE 1946**

## Holeproof Luxsheer Rayons

● Sheerer! Duller! Holeproof's new High-Twist process is the secret of increased elasticity, greater resistance to snagging.

*At Leading Stores Everywhere*

HOLEPROOF HOSIERY CO. OF CANADA LIMITED LONDON, ONT.

HOLEPROOF *Fine Stockings*

Chatelaine, June, 1940 —

More beautiful than ever . . . in

*Velva Leg Film*

*Don't* YOU BELIEVE IT THAT FIGURES DON'T LIE!

"I don't mean my figure; it always looked years younger and pounds lighter under a HICKORY Pantie.***But I do mean all the facts and figures about rubber shortages that were supposed to put us back in whalebones and laces. I had a hunch that HICKORY had the answer— and they did. Sure, they're made with less elastic—but you don't miss it, 'cause HICKORY Panties are just as comfortable, wearable and even more controlling than those pre-war numbers I'd never be without.***They're $5 at leading stores. And ask to see PERMA-LIFT Brassieres with 'The lift that never lets you down'." ***A. Stein & Company, Ltd., Toronto, Canada.

HICKORY PANTIES and *Perma·lift* BRASSIERES

# *Urban Luxury*

## THE HACKING SUIT, UN-SUIT & UN-COAT

**Far left:** An unmannish, man-tailored jacket with suede elbow patches, $75, teams with an easy-moving pleated skirt, $40. Both Hudson Sportswear. Giant cowl, $62, by Mondi. Stridy canvas and leather boots from Boutique Quinto, Eaton Centre, Toronto. **This page, left:** A soufflé-light mohair jacket, $125, gives a

# Hair

A turban offers a stylish way to counter hair loss.

APRIL
1932

MAY
1934

# I Confess I'm a Bleached Blonde

## *"I'm so tired of pretending, and ducking those powder-room insults."*

BY ANGELA BURKE

**MARCH 1952**

I BLEACH MY HAIR. THERE— I've said it and I'm glad. And I'm not hiding behind any pen name. I'm Angela Burke of Toronto. I've gone to schools in Montreal, New York and Paris, France. I belong to a golf club, a tennis club, a sorority. I've reported for newspapers in Timmins, Toronto, New York, and I'm known in dozens of editorial, advertising and radio offices where I try to sell what I write. And all my friends and acquaintances will be chortling heartily when they read this.

But I'm so deathly tired of the barbed, catty remarks a blonde has to put up with, and the pretense she has to resort to in every powder room and over every bridge table that I've decided to confess.

I bleach my hair and—I may as well take the whole sisterhood down with me—so do ninety-five per cent of all blondes over the age of nineteen. If you don't believe me ask your hairdresser.

Oh—we hate those words "peroxide" and "bleach." Every blonde I know cowers before them, and even in my present defiant state I further confess I have to force myself to look at them squarely.

I'M A PEROXIDE BLONDE! There—I've said it again. But I've never admitted it before this moment. My hairdresser and I observe all the Emily Post niceties; my monthly visits to her are "treatment appointments," my hair is "retouched," "brightened" or "highlighted."

But it is never "bleached." I'm calling it that now, though, and I'm calling the bluff of every hypocritical brunette who's ever gasped in sugar-coated tones, "My, your hair is such a pretty color . . ." with all the emphasis on color.

There's only one reason for such cracks—jealousy. It's twenty-seven years since Anita Loos wrote in a world-shaking novel that "Gentlemen Prefer Blondes," but the brunettes have never got over it. Even if they have to dye their hair to stay brunette!

I can't decide which is worse—the sly digs of cunning females or the blunt and devastating attacks of gleeful males. For the men I could murder in cold blood almost equal in number the ladies on Angela Borgia's little list.

One typically female manoeuvre is the use of the suspended sentence. "My," a girl friend will say with a disarming smile in a crowded powder room, "is your hair really natural-"—she pauses dramatically at this point to apply powder to her nose, but her eyes are fixed to your face—"ly curly?" As she finishes the sentence you convulsively sigh your relief—and before you've said a word she's discovered exactly what she's wanted to know.

The back-handed compliment is another favorite of the girls. "Your hair is awfully pretty"— the voice drips honey—"but how have you managed to stay so blond?"

Yet no matter how extreme the provocation a blonde will scarcely ever admit to bleaching. Many husbands, even, are unaware their wives' golden tresses are a marvel of science. Peroxide is something like strong drink—it sneaks up on you gradually.

I began mastering all the standard alibis and a new set of facial expresions to go with them. It was a new shampoo, a new rinse, a sunlamp, or a combination of the three, that were doing "simply wonders for my hair." I hit upon the happy idea of carrying around a portrait of Angela Burke, aged six, with hair of almost albino whiteness, as Exhibit A for the defense.

Just why do we blondes act as though bleaching were one crime removed from drowning babies? And just why does everyone who discovers our guilty secret act as though they've finally found the body in the closet? Nobody pays much attention if a brunette dyes her hair black or auburn—but eyebrows jump at any whisper that a blonde is hitting the peroxide bottle. Well, I for one am sick of pretense and tired of cats. Yes, I'm a bleached blonde!

# *Hats with Everything*

**MAY 1934**

**OCTOBER 1946**

**APRIL 1929**

**APRIL 1952**

**MARCH 1948**

# Do's and Don'ts of Picking a Hat

**APRIL 1952**

DON'T REPEAT A BAD LINE. For example, don't let the brim follow the line of a too-large nose, or repeat the upturn of a too-tilted one. An irregular brim or soft trimming that projects a little over the forehead is helpful in either case.

DO avoid centre trimming if your nose is not your best feature. The eye travels down from it to take in the feature you would prefer to minimize.

DO avoid gaudy, flowery, or multicolored hats if your skin is coarse or blotchy. Rich, solid materials will compliment your complexion.

DON'T match the fabric of your hat with that of your suit. A tweed suit is enough tweed.

DO be sure your hat is as wide as the widest part of your face. Otherwise, your face will bulge out underneath.

DON'T wear a cartwheel if you are under five feet two. It will dwarf you, and your tall companion sees nothing but hat. Pick a bonnet scaled logically to your dimensions.

DON'T wear hats with high crowns or vertical lines if you are taller than you wish.

DO avoid a strictly symmetric hat if your features are irregular. Instead, pick creations with asymmetric lines and off-centre trimming.

DO reject any hat that must be clamped on with elastic or bristle with hatpins. The right hat clings to your head even on windy days.

DON'T wear elaborate earrings when your chapeau is elaborate.

DON'T try to bluff through a mistake. If in an unwary moment you bought a hat that reproaches you every time you look in the mirror, give it up.

DON'T wear a hat with tired band, veil or flowers. Replacing them will revive your hat and your looks. Remember, too, how fresh a veil looks after pressing under waxed paper.

DO choose an eye veil instead of a full one if you would like to look younger. It's prettier and less matronly, and wonderful camouflage for any little lines and puffs under your eyelashes.

DON'T wear a tight face veil—if it clashes with the batting of your eyelashes—OR if you feel awkward about removing it when eating.

DON'T choose a wide-brimmed or drooping hat if your neck is short and thick.

AND DON'T, WHATEVER YOU DO, underestimate the importance of a hat. Without a hat, a street costume is unfinished and flavorless.

# Trousseau Budgets

*Fifty-Dollar Trousseau*

| | |
|---|---|
| Suit | $12.95 |
| Blouse | 2.98 |
| Shoes | 4.00 |
| Hat | 2.98 |
| Bag | 1.98 |
| Gloves | 1.50 |
| Slips (2) | 3.18 |
| Nightie | 1.98 |
| Hosiery (2) | 1.18 |
| Panties (2) | 1.18 |
| Brassiere | 1.00 |
| Girdle | 1.00 |
| House Dress | 2.98 |
| Coat | 12.50 |
| **TOTAL** | **$51.39** |

# The Pursuit of Fitness

GREAT
MAKEOVERS

APRIL
**1977**

APRIL
**1966**

CHATELAINE

Color..*The Style Note*

## 40SOMETHING

"I don't *want* to dress like my 20-year-old daughters. Young trendy clothes look great on them, but I'm very happy to look like *me!*" says Darlene Schwartz, a 40something dynamo who works for a Toronto modeling agency, teaching women her age how to update their look and boost their self-esteem. Her fashion philosophy—"if you're not comfortable wearing it, it's not suitable." Near left: for an up-to-the-minute (but far from uptight) work-day look, Darlene wears a stylish tomato-red vest, $149, and matching skirt, $69. Both Triangle. Jewelry, Chenessa II. Hose, Phantom. Handbag, Adrienne Vittadini.

# Don Becomes Angela

*Most of us experience life either as a woman or as a man. Transsexuals, however, experience life both ways. Meet Angela Wensley, whose name used to be Don*

BY EVE ROCKETT

FEBRUARY 1993

MACMILLAN BLOEDEL, British Columbia's forest products giant, has a corporate image that steams with macho. When men at one of the mills gathered for a meeting in the spring of 1989, the last thing they expected to hear from a head-office executive was that he was going to become a woman.

Don Wensley, then 41, a widely respected metallurgical engineer and corrosion specialist, had a reputation as a powerful and confident speaker, but as he began, the mill workers could see that his entire body was quaking.

"Not many people question the gender they were born into," Don began, his voice rattling gently, "but I am one of those people." The room was so quiet you could have heard sawdust flake. Transsexuals, as Don explained, are not necessarily transvestites, who dress like the opposite sex, nor homosexuals. What obsesses and overwhelms them is their desire to change their sex—man into woman, or woman into man.

When Don had finished his explanation, there was an ovation. Big guys put their arms around his shoulders. Said engineer Ted Dorocicz, "It was very personal and tragic, one of the most moving and dramatic experiences I can remember."

Said project analyst Ron Greenough, "I had a big problem with it but, because it was Wensley, I couldn't dismiss it as the product of a sick mind."

It was believed at one time that the root cause lay in family history but, according to Dr. Diane Watson, medical director of the department of psychiatry at the Vancouver General Hospital and director of its Gender Dysphoria Clinic, "We feel now that gender identity problems may be caused by hormone fluctu-ations at a critical time in the development of the brain before birth."

The transsexual's unshakable belief that he or she has been born into the wrong body develops early in life. For Don Wensley, the realization came when he was 6, living with his parents in Penticton, B.C. "An overwhelming awareness hit me, and I asked my mother to buy me a doll. When I was 8, I went out in my sister Connie's clothes, terrified someone would see me. I used to pray every night I'd wake up as a girl."

Don didn't confide this to his mother, Gladys, a bank teller, or his father, Wes, a manager of a car dealership, or to either of his two younger siblings, Connie and Elaine. As he grew older, he buried his feelings and lived vigorously as a male. When he was 19, he met Darlene Horton on a beach and was immediately smitten. Two years later, they were married. After 10 years, he told Darlene of his compulsion to wear women's clothes. She humored him, and he began to wear them at home. Darlene nicknamed this feminine version of Don "Angela," and they both assumed that he was a transvestite. But Don's desire to be a woman went beyond clothes.

Darlene was hurt, angry and bewildered at what was happening to their marriage. In an attempt to save it, they took a romantic trip to France in early 1968. "Angela" was banished to the closet and Don was welcomed home. But three weeks later, Angela was back.

The strain became too much. The couple divorced the following year, two weeks after their 20th anniversary.

Don was officially diagnosed as a transsexual in the fall of 1988 at Vancouver General's Gender Dysphoria Clinic. He began the hormonal therapy that would change his secondary sex characteristics into a woman's. The operation that would complete the change was, to his knowledge, unavailable in Canada at that point. He booked himself into a clinic in London, England, for December 1989.

When Don first told his mother his intention, she took it with stunning sympathy and grace. His father sat in the living room staring blankly for hours. Today, they are very close.

The hormonal changes were gradual, softening his skin, thickening his hair and slightly enlarging his breasts. After a while, he swapped his suits for androgynous slacks and shirts, and began to let his hair and nails grow.

His secretary at the time, Karen Davidson, says she noticed a few subtle changes but said nothing. However, the company's supervisor of library information services, Judy O'Mara, wondered if she should tell Don long hair wasn't in style for men anymore.

Light makeup followed, and when Don started to wear mascara, a few men thought it was more than interesting. With the growing buzz around the office that he was gay, Don decided it was time to meet with senior VP Otto Forgacs. Forgacs told him, "If you go through this transition and decide you want to become a ballet dancer, I can't be sure we'll have a job for you. But if you want to continue to be an engineer, we'll support you all the way."

On April 24th, 1989, soon after he had told his coworkers, Don Wensley ceased to exist and Angela Wensley walked down the hall to her office in a sleek white suit and green silk blouse, acutely conscious of the clattering of her high heels.

Former secretary Karen Davidson recalls, "We were all curious and intimidated. I had been worried that she would look silly, but she looked fabulous."

Says Ron Greenough, "I was walking down the stairs and noticed these great legs by the elevator. When I got closer, I saw it was Angela, and I thought 'Oh, no!'"

To get rid of Don's beard, Angela went through more than 300 hours of electrolysis.

She also had collagen injected into her upper lip to make it fuller.

At first, Angela self-consciously took pains to comport herself in the way she thought a woman would. Unfortunately, this conformed to the worst female stereotype folding her hands submissively in front, and ending every sentence tentatively, as if it were a question. Judy O'Mara advised her that she was doing herself harm, and Angela assumed a more assertive stance.

The final change came in December 1989, in the London clinic, where Don's sex organs were removed, and parts of his penis used to construct a vagina. His mother accompanied him on the trip and was present when her son came out of the anesthetic. "Say hello to your new daughter," said Angela.

Back in Canada, Angela began to experience life as a woman. Earlier in 1989, she had met Kris Lord, a video producer, and it was "love at first sight."

A less pleasant discovery, Angela says, was a subtle loss of power at work. "I definitely had my wish. I was treated like a woman. When I was Don, the other executives listened to me. They believed they listened to me as Angela, but I don't think they did."

In 1992 she set up as a consulting engineer on her own. She was, she says, "Glad to be out of a male-dominated organization. The joy of finally being who I have known I was all my life transcends everything."

# CHAPTER TWO

# Partnerships

RADITIONALLY, THE GOAL OF THE heroine in *Chatelaine*'s fiction was marriage. When she was already married, the plot usually reconfirmed her choice, i.e., a restless wife is tempted by an old/new love until crisis reminds her of why she married her husband in the first place. By contrast, the magazine's articles functioned as a problem-solving forum in which marriage, its participants and their grievances could be analyzed, surveyed, supported and scolded. In this sometimes grim, always provocative task, *Chatelaine* editors managed to be alternately progressive and conservative. And when they slipped up, readers were swift to supply the corrective.

During 1928, conservatives paused in their celebration of the Dominion's most prosperous year to decry the country's rising divorce rate—748 in 1927, almost double that of 1920. "Until Love Dies" (November 1928) traced this phenomenon to women's new freedom as expressed by the use of prepared food, along with a lack of privacy in apartments. Yet, in "Wages and Wives" (April 1929), *Chatelaine* came out squarely in favor of wives having money of their own.

In March 1935, a spirited young socialist explained why she'd chosen a civil marriage over being "churched." To ward off predictable outrage, an editorial note advised: "*Chatelaine* does not necessarily endorse the opinions expressed." Meanwhile, judging by a string of male-authored putdowns, thirties wives strove to be indulgent helpmates to insufferably patronizing husbands. Out of a field that included "Things That Get on a Husband's Nerves" and "Men Don't Want Clever Wives," we've chosen "What Did Your Husband Give Up for Marriage?" (August 1938).

World War II brought prosperity and dislocation. The ocean became a two-way superhighway—soldiers over, refugees back. Two results of this high-energy flux were hasty, youthful marriages and unions between persons of diverse backgrounds ("I Married a Jew," August 1946). At war's end, wives who'd been sending homebaked cakes and cheery letters to "hubbies" overseas discovered that many of their returned men secretly yearned for the euphoria of battle and their easy liaisons with European women ("Nostalgia," November 1946). But, housewives, too, had their fantasies: confined to their kitchens, they stifled their craving for romance with radio soap operas because "it makes married life easier" ("Why Do Some Women Like Soap Opera?" September 1948).

To the pressures of peace and procreation, the fifties housewife added her own goal: the pursuit of perfection. While he went off in a gray flannel suit to fight the corporate wars, she devoted herself to keeping an immaculate house and the chauffeuring of upwardly mobile children. Though this was supposed to be the decade of Togetherness, the divorce rate was steadily climbing—up to 6,053 in 1955. According to public opinion, reinforced by psychiatrists who'd replaced ministers as society's reigning authorities, all marital discord, including a husband's infidelity, was the wife's responsibility. Despite a houseful of labor-saving devices, she cited her enemies as fatigue and guilt, while he often considered his rivals to be their children and her shiny floors. No matter what the diagnosis, the solution was always the same: *she* must reform. And often she did ("The True Story of One Woman's Fight to Save Her Marriage," November 1952).

Yet, something was stirring deep in the female psyche. As the revolutionary sixties took hold, wives began to look outside of themselves for answers. Nevertheless, it wasn't until the seventies that feminist insights assaulted traditional values to produce some knockout punches. One of these was "A Rap on Marriage" (January 1972), in which Dr. Jessie Bernard declared marriage wonderful for men but lousy for women.

It took the eighties to reveal marriage's dirtiest secret: violence, usually male, coupled with denial, usually female ("Violence in the Home," May 1981). By 1994 the divorce rate stood at 78,880—more than one hundred times that of 1927! Increasingly, the buzz word describing nineties partnerships was "dysfunctional"—including those in high places ("Your Majesty, Can We Talk?" April 1993).

# "Until Love Dies"

## *Or the courts us do part*

BY MADGE MACBETH

**NOVEMBER 1928**

THERE SEEMS TO BE A WHOLE volume of indictment against the existing institution of marriage. All over the world, people are charging it with failure. In a general way, the trend of thought is toward making legal separation simpler and more natural. The possibility of securing "relief" from marital bondage by divorce is claimed by many students of the subject to be the very means of keeping couples yoked together.

An experiment is being tried to take the "divine" principle out of marriage and make it like any other legal contract. Not long ago, in a certain college-town south of the border, a youthful couple approached the altar to the strains of a jazz band; boys wearing girls' dresses acted as bridesmaids; and the words "until love dies" were substituted for the familiar "till death us do part."

In Canada as elsewhere, divorce is on the increase.

The first application for divorce to the Parliament of Canada was made in 1868. It was granted. The following year another successful plea was made; then all went well for some time. But in 1873 and 1875, two more discontented couples brought their differences to Ottawa; after which the country seemed to go to the dogs, for three divorces were asked in 1877 . . . two by wives, no less, and three a year became the normal rule after that. Final decrees granted in 1913 amounted to 60, but it was in 1920 that the real increase set in with a total of 429, and the number has almost doubled since then. In 1927 there were 748, and this year's figures will go higher.

A good many people in British Columbia, for some reason that does not appear, make an unfortunate selection in choosing their life-partners, as this province leads the others (with but two exceptions since 1913) in her pleas for divorce. Prince Edward Island, on the other hand, would seem to be the home of felicitous unions, a place like Heaven where they are made; for since 1868, the number of divorces granted makes the grand total of ONE!

Marriage, apparently, is still considered the ideal state, and people continue to fall in love. Why, then, can't they live more happily together?

First, *because we Canadians are suffering from the universal sense of impermanence that prevails.* Within the memory of most readers of this article, a different condition existed. One's mother—certainly, one's grandmother—bought a sealskin coat to last a lifetime. One built a house for one's descendants. One married for eternity. Secondly, *divorce is no longer regarded as a questionable proceeding.* Time was when a woman, especially, preferred respectable misery to disreputable freedom. A divorcee was an outcast, a pariah, no matter how just had been her cause for separation. Why, even a divorced man was suspect, and kept as far as possible from the society of young maidens!

*Woman's economic independence* is responsible in Canada, as in the United States, for this increase in divorce. In an era when her earning capacity was small, when man was her provider and the protector of her children, he had stout chains by which to bind her. Women were forced to make the best of a bad bargain.

Would it surprise you to learn that in the opinion of a prominent barrister who hears the troubles of dozens of dissatisfied couples during the year, *apartment houses constitute a salient reason for the increase of divorce?* Physical crowding is bad enough, but more serious is the spiritual buffeting that is inevitable. The average apartment offers no privacy. There is no corner into which one may creep to battle and triumph over the angry moment; there is no screen behind which one may change a scowl into a smile, and put the best foot forward. Sugary though it sounds, love holds an element of mystery, and mystery is murdered in any modern flat.

The tendency to use prepared foods, the temptation to serve paper-bag-meals is affecting the character of our people. The old-fashioned housewife would be horrified to discover how many young couples in—let us say Montreal—eat sketchy breakfasts out of a cardboard box, a piece of pie for luncheon, and dine from the products, sometimes not even heated, of the corner delicatessen! Granting that our forebears ate too much, many of us are not sufficiently fed. Not in quantity, perhaps, but in the quality of our daily menus. The craze for dieting has made the nervous body as tenuous as the physical form is desired to be. Nerves lack sufficient nourishment. Nobody can "stand" anybody else. The result is bad temper—and divorce.

Which sounds very logical when you realize that most of the divorces granted in Canada are not the outcome of infidelity (which must be proven whether it exists or not), or cruelty, or non-support, but of the rather loose term "incompatibility."

> **The average apartment offers no privacy. There is no corner into which one may creep to battle and triumph over the angry moment**

Also, another interesting point comes to light when one learns from those intimately associated with the Divorce Court that women seek "relief" from the annoyances of everyday existence more often than men. When a man asks for divorce, it is generally for some cogent reason—infidelity on the part of his wife, neglect of the children, or because he has fallen in love with another woman. But the wife wants "relief" from the ennui of little things—the awfully great little things, and sometimes she knows it.

Said a recent divorcee to me: "John will make a splendid husband for some other woman. There was no fault I could lay my finger on. He just had a way of rasping my nerves past endurance. That's all!"

And returning to the subject of food, I must tell the story of my conversation with a Toronto milkman, the gist of which seems to have some bearing on the subject of divorce. My hostess being ill, and the maid out, I volunteered for duty, one item of which was buying tickets from the milkman. He caught me just preparing to dress; very ungroomed, very déshabillé. He was such a young and good-looking milkman, I was embarrassed, even annoyed; but snatching at the bright side of things, as is ever my custom, I apologized and observed:

"You are probably used to seeing women in unbecoming regalia—early in the morning on your rounds."

"Lord love us, lady!" he exclaimed. "I never see a *woman*! In all this district" (it was one of the new developments, very popular with brides and grooms), "it's the men I see getting their own breakfasts—and likely a tray to take upstairs in the morning!"

Women like that, who have no conception of the

fairness of a bargain, could not possibly make a happy marriage.

And the man, who has no conception of a woman's passionate desire for an identity of her own, will find himself at last sitting in the midst of domestic ruin.

We are rather bewildered by all this divorce business. But shall we deny our women their independence, or move in a body to Prince Edward Island?

# Wages—and Wives

### *Professional women are not content to let their brains rust from disuse*

By Nancy Leigh

**APRIL 1929**

ALL OVER THE WORLD THE economic questions of marriage are receiving more and more attention. Should wives have to be dependent on their husbands for every cent they get? Should wives have wages? Is it economically desirable that a wife should earn money outside the home? My mail-bag bulges with letters from both husbands and wives along these lines. One agitated youth writes:

"My girl says she won't marry me unless I let her keep on with her work. She has a very interesting job which she loves and she gets just about the same money as I do. She argues that we can get an apartment in the neighborhood we like, keep up with our world, even have a little car if we pool our salaries. She says I'm old-fashioned and a reactionary because I say I'd rather live in a poorer neighborhood, do without a car and have my wife all to myself. She says the work of a modern apartment isn't enough to keep an able-bodied intelligent woman busy for more than an hour or two a day, and that she doesn't like embroidering, pink teas or bridge, and what is she to do with herself all day? What am I to do? I always looked forward to having my wife dependent on me and thought what fun it would be to save up for little 'doo-dads' for her. You can't have much fun giving to somebody who has as much as you."

You have the absolutely traditional masculine viewpoint with which I have a great deal of sympathy. In the present transitional stage of this whole question, the situation is much harder on the husband than it is on the wife. She is doing what she wants and getting paid for it. He is getting blamed by the outside world for allowing her to do it, and while recognizing the fact that her salary will make a tremendous difference to their comfort, he frankly doesn't like it.

In Canada we are very slow to adopt the double wage idea, although in the United States it is estimated there are nearly four million married women workers. Even in conservative England, the after-war depression, the huge taxes and the high cost of living have combined to send many women of gentle birth into the wage-earning classes.

There it is the professional women who are forcing the pace. They are not content to let their brains rust from disuse. They have received expensive educations. They have work they enjoy and they have a certain sense of responsibility for their intelligence.

And yet they are not always happy in their choice. A woman who conducts a very successful shop in a large city writes me: "I am beginning to wonder if I have made a mistake in keeping up my business career. We have a nice house, a car, and not only comfort, but even luxury—and yet, I think I have deprived my husband of something, the right every man has to feel he is the controlling factor in the home. He has always been rather delicate, so I have assumed most of the responsibilities of our household management. Now he is perfectly satisfied to let me do so. He has no responsibility for me or my expenses and never assumes any. In any emergency it is always my savings account that is depleted—he doesn't have one. I feel that I have been all wrong and, if I could, I would go back and settle down to being just an ordinary housewife."

Then there is the woman who writes: "What am I going to do about my husband's meanness? He never gives me a cent without a row. I am almost in rags before I can nerve myself to the point of asking him for money for clothes because I know there will be a battle royal before I get it. As for the children,

they dread to tell him they even need schoolbooks; he flies into such a rage. I have begged and pleaded with him to give me an allowance but he gets so furiously angry that I have ceased even to mention the subject. I know now why women get dressmakers to send bills for a few dollars more than the dress and ask for the difference. I haven't descended to that yet, but I think I will if things don't improve. Can you suggest some way out?"

First of all, I think you are afraid of him. He sounds like a bully and bullies are nearly always cowards. I think I should try a little bullying myself. I would tell him that I would leave and keep house for somebody; that you would get good wages as a housekeeper and not have to ask for them. Ask him how he would run his business if he didn't have money for supplies. If he won't give you an allowance, get what you want for the house, the children and yourself and send him the bills. If he protests, tell him to provide you with a fair allowance and you won't run any bills. Make an estimate of what amount you need in accordance with your social and financial standing, and give him a clear-cut business statement.

Don't let his shouting and anger terrify you. Brace up; your happiness and that of your children depends on getting this question settled.

# Why I Had a Civil Marriage

By Gloria Queen

*Editor's note: In presenting this article,* Chatelaine *does not necessarily endorse the opinions expressed.*

MARCH
*1935*

IN THE SUMMER OF 1931, A perfectly sane and perfectly charming young gentleman persuaded me it would be a bright idea if we walked down the aisle—pardon me—I mean faced the judge, together. Since the proposition seemed very bright indeed (to me), we were duly married in one of the large court rooms, at the Law Courts building in Winnipeg, November, 1931.

When *Chatelaine* wrote and wanted to know "Why did you have a civil marriage?" I could think of a million reasons. But they did not all affect me alone. So I went into a spirited huddle with my husband, for I could hardly write about my own marriage and not about his. We came to one important conclusion, namely: that in order to understand our reasons for a civil marriage, it is essential that readers have some inkling of our ideas on social organization and sex.

Being socialists, our approach to life is closely related to ideals for a new social order. We believe in placing human rights before property rights. Therefore we believe that human beings should have the fullest, freest and happiest sort of life it is possible for our present civilization to offer. And when we married we wanted the sort of ceremony that would best express these ideals.

We were conscious of the fact that, today, marriage implies a superiority of the male over the female. Generally speaking the pretty, new bride is expected to don a pretty, new apron and waste no time in getting busy on the carpets or the egg beater. There is usually a wide howl of protest if she decides to continue with her business or professional work, and along with her husband bring home a monthly cheque. Conservative citizens scream that she is displacing another breadwinner and so on, until, particularly in years like these, her employer will suggest that one income is enough for one family. And then we hear ballyhoo about emancipated women! I believe that woman will never be free until she is economically free, until she has the same social standing as a man, until she has the right to choose her life occupation, until it is socially accepted that a wedding ring should not be a hindrance to business responsibilities. And so, my husband agreeing fully with me, we had a civil marriage. We felt it implied this principle more than a church marriage would, so that was reason number one.

In spite of the eyebrow-raising and head-shaking that went on, we have no patience with silly conventions. And that was another reason for a civil marriage; it was not bound up with superstitions.

This antipathy to custom, convention, superstition, brought with it an attitude to sex. But our attitude to sex was not born in a minute. It rather developed after much thought and some reading. We knew that many marriages which go wrong do so because of misunderstandings about sex, and we were anxious to make our marriage go right.

Never for the life of me could I understand why sexual problems were not handled in school, and sex taken as much a part of child life and education as music. Why tell children the stork brought them, when it is to their advantage and beauty of thought to tell them they were born because two people loved each other? Why not begin from the cradle to teach honesty in sex, trust and loyalty in sex as in other things? And believing in honesty in sex, in the single standard for both men and women, my husband and I again decided in favor of a civil marriage.

Honesty in sex is perhaps the most difficult mental hurdle to take. It was the first thing we tackled. We did not want to underestimate it, neither did we want to overemphasize it. We discussed our problems until they vanished. We understood each other's emotions and mental attitudes before marriage. And after three years of living together we are enthusiastic about our success. And let me say right here, in case of any misunderstanding, that we are firm believers in the single standard and self-control. So again we decided in favor of a civil marriage: it was free from the taint of hypocrisy.

∾

Neither my husband nor myself is an advocate of the present rigid divorce laws in Canada. In the first place, it is a pretty poor home that is only held together because of the difficulty in procuring a divorce. Can any earthly reason be given why people who have ceased to love each other should be forced to live under the same roof and share the same name? I call it legalized prostitution.

Naturally, children should have first claim and consideration in any home. They are brought into the world without their own consent and at the desire of their parents. They cannot be left to the whims of adults and particularly in the act of making divorce easy should responsibility for children be made rigid and definite. I believe that the old order should be reversed and that parents owe their children everything. Love, respect and loyalty are natural feelings developed by the child for its parents through careful upbringing. But for parents to sit back and demand them, and for parents to declare that children should be thankful they are alive, is another story.

So we come back to the third case for divorce. It is for you to decide whether it is to a child's advantage to be reared in an unhappy home. I don't think it is.

So my husband and I believe that marriage without love is immoral. We felt we were on the right track when we stood before the judge, but who can tell what changes time will bring? Perhaps that young, charming gentleman will leap ahead of me, intellectually. Then I would not blame him for wanting to get rid of me. We wanted the fact of our marriage simply recorded without any superfluous "do you's." We just wanted to share our lives together for as long as we could be happy, and when happiness ceases we will call it quits.

So many people consider it a "duty" to have children, regardless of the family purse. We do not. We both want children, but we do not want to see them denied opportunities which we consider their inherent right. We do not feel justified in having children when their food, clothing and education are uncertain quantities.

When our position, like thousands more, is so insecure, and when there is no assurance of security in the future, then we have no business to involve more innocent people in our struggle. And the big problem arose, "How *not* to have children?" We were desirous of finding a scientific, harmless and healthy method of birth control, so we went in search of information. There was no such information to be had in an open way. As a matter of fact we had to rely on the good graces of an American friend who had been in touch with modern birth control clinics in his own country.

It can be understood how we felt resentment at this. We were two healthy young people, very much in love. We had decided to get married. We could not possibly afford to have children. We did not want to waste the best years of our lives, waiting. And we wanted to be in the position of choosing and planning our children when the time arrived that we could afford a family.

We are in favor of birth-control clinics being set up by the government and of medical information being properly handled. And we were forced to admit again that a civil marriage had won the day. A civil marriage was at least free from anti–birth control entanglements.

Before entering our new home together, we did two things which puzzled a number of people. We had a double ring ceremony, and we joined our names together. While it was, in our case, really essential that I wear a ring, there was no reason why I should be marked as "housewife," or "married," and my life partner not. He agreed. So we exchanged the tokens.

Practically the same principle guided our actions in regard to our names. Why should I be expected to throw my identity to the winds because I wanted to get married? Why should my future children be known only by their father's name? And so he took my name, and I took his, and in private life we are Mr. and Mrs. R. W. Queen-Hughes.

I must say the family bore the strain well, although many friends who should have known better thought we were just plain "high-hat." As a matter of fact one acquaintance said he thought that hyphenated names were an English custom which should be banned by the government of Canada!

In the face of more unconventionality, we had to decide again on a civil marriage. Through a maze of conflicting whispers, smiles of toleration, murmurs of disapproval and the occasional hearty applaud, we marched into our new life. We had certain aims and objects and enough enthusiasm to sink a battleship. We would not have changed places then, and would not now, with any other couple in the world.

# What Did Your Husband Give Up for Marriage?

Small Caps: James Wedgwood Drawbell

AUGUST 1938

I DINED WITH THE HAPPIEST woman I know the other evening. I happened to be on her right at a small party. We had been carrying on our discussion under the hum of talk about the table, and I had just said to her—after glancing down the table to her husband—"I don't know how you do it!"

She leaned nearer. "I try never to forget," she answered, "what Keith gave up to marry me."

Now this may sound dramatic. It may suggest that in this woman's case her husband had made all kinds of sacrifices to achieve his bride. At the very least, you might gather he had married beneath him, defied his own family for love, been cut off without a cent, and married the girl of his choice.

---

**The world smiles indulgently at the old bachelor, but has only a smirk and a cruel joke for the old maid**

.......................................

As far as I knew, Keith had made no tremendous sacrifices to marry Eileen. They were just a couple of nice, ordinary people who fell in love—actually it was at the tennis club—got engaged, and were duly married.

She saw that I was a little surprised at her remark, and she went on to elaborate. "If only every woman would ask herself why any man should marry her at all, there would be less discontent among women, more happiness among men, and many more successful marriages. When a man marries, he gives up everything. The woman gains everything. We all know this, if we just think of it for a moment, but so many women forget it."

❧

What a biff in the eye, from one of their own sex, for all that pack of discontented women who fill the cafés for eleven o'clock coffee each morning! What a reversal of the grand old romantic idea, engendered by hundreds of novelists, that men should pursue their women to the ends of the earth, work like Trojans for them when they've nailed them down to the altar, and leave them "well provided for" when they die through premature old age!

It *is* true that a man gives up that freedom of mind and body that are his till he marries. He can roam where he pleases, do as he likes. Freedom is his, as it never is a woman's. He earns enough for his needs. The world smiles indulgently at the old bachelor, but has only a smirk and a cruel joke for the old maid.

A man alone, wherever he is, can always seem complete; a woman never. A woman needs always the company, the background, of a man.

A man can have his work, his friends, his drinks, his pipe, his round of golf, his nights-out, his week-ends out of town, his books, his apartment. There are always plenty of women ready to sew and darn and run and fetch for the bachelor. There are always plenty of girls ready to be amused and amuse. He can summon this help by just saying, "Oh, Mrs. Thing, I wonder if you would be so kind—" He can still his loneliness by picking up the telephone.

❧

A woman's lot is a vastly different affair, and I, for one, think it is a shame. But I cannot alter it, nor can you.

Woman's instinct is to find her mate. It is not a matter of choice. It is the whole sum and substance of her existence. It is like that because life must go on, children must be born, homes must be provided for.

Woman's gain is marriage. That is her completion, her fulfillment. It would be idle to pretend that women give up something, too, when they marry— "the best years of their life," for instance.

Why, then, should any man marry? What madness is it in a man that can renounce the joys of liberty for the cares and worries of an unequal partnership? A partnership that makes him the wage slave, the early morning train-catcher, the house-insurer, the open chequebook, the eternal provider?

Just ahead of him lie the trials, as well as the joys, of parenthood. Another mouth to feed. Perhaps also another person in the house to look after the growing child. And ahead of that—school fees, illness, expense piled on expense. No relief, except the beggarly and ironical concession in the income tax.

Deep down in her heart, every married woman must wonder what madness it was that came over the man who asked her (if he did) to marry him.

Well, it isn't quite madness. It's the way men are made. There comes a moment in the life of even the luckiest man when it seems that everything must end if one particular woman passes beyond his reach. It is useless, then, to tell a man that he is a fool. It is the law of life that you must experience things to realize them. Twenty men could pin a man down and tell him the most harrowing tales of marriage and its Awful Results. He may listen to them. He will not hear them. Ah, this is different, his soul tells him. This is different, the woman's eyes tell him.

And, of course, he is lost. Almost laughingly he throws away all these rich possessions that women themselves have always envied and are always fighting for—freedom, economic liberty, independence. He joins his lot with the woman. In doing so he may gain, in other things, much more than he has renounced. That, however, has little to do with him. That depends on the woman.

And that is why my hostess is a particularly happy woman. She is wise. But above all she is honest.

After all, you've got to be pretty honest with yourself to ask why your husband should ever have married you, and to remind yourself how much of himself he surrendered to do so.

Mr. Drawbell's devious system of reckoning I give up two hundred merry-go-round rides or three Shirley Temple dolls every time I buy myself a new pair of shoes. I don't feel martyred on that account. I have passed the stage of life where I can happily go barefoot, and merry-go-rounds haven't the appeal they once had.

"What then did my husband give up to marry me?"

He gave up diapers and kiddy-kars, and bicycles and footballs, and dates with blonde flappers, none of which would be particularly becoming to him at his age anyway.

## Chatelaine *Readers Reply to...*

# What Did Your Husband Give Up for Marriage?

*This letter won the $25 prize*

BY EDITH HUNTER, CALGARY

**OCTOBER 1938** "**W**HAT DID MY HUSBAND give up to marry me?" Nothing! Nothing, that is, that the normally developed twenty-six-year-old male isn't ready to give up.

Were I to fall into Mr. Drawbell's erroneous line of reasoning I might say, "I gave up my business career to marry. My husband continued his. I gave up economic independence. My husband still holds his own purse strings. Marriage and its resultant babies have forced me to give up eighty per cent of my contacts with the world. My husband has given up practically none of his. Marriage has limited my opportunities for coy adventure to the milkman, the baker and the sixteen-year-old paper boy. It has in no wise limited my husband's."

To say I "gave up" these things in the sense of exchanging them for marriage is misleading. I simply reached another stage in my jaunt along the allotted three score and ten, and the rules don't allow taking all the good and interesting things all of the way. These things had to be left behind. Others equally excellent are taking their place. Every stage of life has its advantages and drawbacks. It is puerile and illogical to weigh the advantages of one stage against the disadvantages of another. According to

# I Married a Jew

*It isn't easy to mix two completely different backgrounds of race, religion, language, but here is the report of one such marriage that succeeded . . .*

BY ISOBEL RAPPAPORT

**AUGUST 1946** "**W**E MET ONE SUNDAY AFTER-noon in winter. He arrived late. With his formal bow of the Austrian and his accent-tinged "how-do-you-dos," he presented a slightly exotic figure in that roomful of Anglo-Saxons drinking tea.

Presently I cornered our host. "Tell me about the new arrival, Ralph. He looks nice. Is he Jewish?"

"Oh, I imagine so," said Ralph. "Why else would he leave all his friends and a good job in Vienna, to come here in 1938?"

"What about his family?"

"I don't know," said Ralph. "He never mentions them. Probably the war came before he could arrange to get them out. Rotten business. He's nice. Nadine and I like him very much."

As the only words the Austrian and I exchanged that afternoon were "How do you do" and "Goodby," I was surprised a few weeks later when Nadine informed me, by telephone, that "Ralph's friend, the Austrian, often asks about you."

So a foursome for the movies was arranged.

We arrived, separately, at Nadine's and Ralph's, where we were informed that since no sitter was available, they would have to stay home to mind the child.

We didn't go to the movies. We decided to have a cup of coffee "before the show," and two hours later we were still sitting at the restaurant table swapping such urgent information about each other as "how many" brothers and sisters, "what" favorite books, plays, music, people, jobs, etc. He was doing a war job, as a designing engineer.

He came to see me a few evenings later. But this time he was not gay, as he had been at Nadine's and Ralph's.

Presently he said: "I was wondering whether it is a good idea for us to become friends?"

"Why?" I said. "Are you married?"

"Oh, no," he said, "it's something else. Do you know why I came to Canada?"

"I think so. You are Jewish, aren't you?"

"Yes. You don't mind?"

"Do you mind that I am Gentile?"

"No," he said. "Hello."

"Hello," I said.

That was the beginning of a new kind of companionship for me. For the first time I knew someone with whom it was not only fun to go to shows and parties, but who was an equally gay companion for a walk in the country. A Sunday afternoon at the art gallery with him was for me a lesson in the enjoyment and appreciation of pictures. He knew the great art collections of Europe. He had travelled widely, with open eyes and an open mind, and shared with me, over restaurant tables or on country walks, the vivid recollections of a remarkable memory.

One Sunday afternoon we had visited the museum after visiting the butterfly collection. As we strolled toward the park, two women approached us along the sidewalk. One of them said, in a clearly audible voice: "Well! Did you see? a *white* girl with a *Jew!*"

Feeling a little sick, I walked on, carefully avoiding what I thought would be humiliation in his face.

Presently I heard him chuckle. "Do you suppose," he said, "that she would believe it if someone told her that Jews have green and white checked skin under their bathing trunks?"

"Oh, probably!" I said, laughing with relief that the woman's stupidity and bad manners had not (apparently) hurt him and spoiled our afternoon.

> **Jews. It was almost a new word. The only Jew I'd heard of was Jesus.**

"But you know," he said, taking my hand as we walked along, "I saw your face when it happened. Try not to let things like that affect you too deeply. If some people are so unintelligent, there is nothing we can do about it."

We strolled on into the park. He was silent for a little while and then he said: "I wonder if it would be too difficult for you? Do you think you would be happy married to me?"

"I don't know," I said. "But I do know that I won't be happy if I *don't* marry you."

The problem of how a Christian and a Jew might be married, without compromising the traditions of their separate upbringings, was solved when we met a young rabbi who agreed to marry us in a ceremony suitable to both.

Whatever fun there might have been in looking for the home we hoped to share was considerably dampened after two potential landladies said: "Oh! In that case, I'm sorry—" when I informed them that my fiancé was Jewish. He had insisted on my doing this in order "to avoid any future unpleasantness."

One Saturday morning, at the end of that long cold January, I found the apartment of our dreams. With a flourish, in spite of slightly shaking hands, I signed my name (unquestionably Anglo-Saxon) to the cheque for the first month's rent. Then I went to meet him for lunch.

"And *everything* was all right?" he said, when I finished my ecstatic description.

"Oh absolutely!" I said.

He looked at me keenly. "Well, come along, dear."

"Where are we going?"

"To see our apartment and to call on our new landlord."

"Oh—" I said, "Are you going to tell them?"

"My poor darling," he said, "don't you know me well enough yet to realize that I could never go where I am not welcome because of my race?"

The landlord and his wife were obviously puzzled by my fiancé's accent, his un-Anglo-Saxon features and name. But when, after a 15-minute visit with them, he had them laughing at one of his stories, I began to hope. Then, as we left, the landlord said:

"Oh yes, you'll want the keys." The hard-boiled egg in my throat disappeared.

Recently I was asked how my family and friends reacted to my marriage with a Jew. To which I replied that my three brothers and their wives, who constitute my only immediate family, have never expressed an opinion. They seem quite content in the fact that I am obviously happy.

A number of acquaintances dropped from my list, but my friends remained to become our friends. And since our marriage our circle of friends has been enriched by the addition of fine people of my husband's race.

Now, in the fourth year of our marriage, I can say that it has been good. He remembers our wedding anniversary—not just once a year—but on the 25th of every month! And brings me flowers, or a little gift! And on the evening of the 25th there is always a special dinner party (for two).

These are some of the little things that make one say: "I wouldn't change places with any other woman in the world." They are also part of that bulwark behind which one takes refuge from unpleasant incidents like the one that occurred last spring.

I was returning from my marketing. As I turned the corner of our street a group of neighborhood children, who had apparently seen me with my husband on other occasions, greeted me with:

"Dirty Russian Siberian Jew!"

I was too surprised to speak, even if I could have thought of something wise and calm to say. I walked on, and presently found myself thinking of another day, a long time ago.

I was five. I had bustled across the street to call on an elderly neighbor whose conversational talents were augmented by a store of homemade taffy.

"New people moving in at the corner, I see," Mrs. Pogley said, as she handed me a sticky bit. "I wonder if they are Jews. I hope not."

Jews. It was almost a new word. The only Jew I'd ever heard of was Jesus. Wouldn't Mrs. Pogley like me, or let me come for conversation and taffy, if I were a Jew?

This called for consultation with the Fount of All Knowledge. I found the Fount in the kitchen. I rested my chin on the table, where she was mixing a cake.

"Mother, what's a Jew?"

There was a pause, while the Fount gathered her thoughts together.

"Jews are people," she said.

"Are we Jews?"

"No, we are called Gentiles."

"Is Mrs. Pogley like us?"

"Yes, Mrs. Pogley is Gentile too."

Relief at this indisputable evidence that nothing could ever come between me and conversation and taffy with Mrs. Pogley almost precluded my next question.

"What's the difference?"

The Fount sighed patiently. "There really isn't any, you know. They're people. All different kinds of people. Good and bad, clever and stupid, rich and poor. Just like us. But they go to a different church. They call it Temple. Now go out and play."

The one whose judgment I respected above all others had spoken.

# Nostalgia

*It's the new postwar homesickness for far places, for English pubs, for Dutch domesticity and Paris glamour. It's the ex-serviceman's personal problem . . . and his wife's most persistent headache*

BY MARGARET ECKER FRANCIS

**NOVEMBER 1946**

THE SUN IS WARM ON THE fields of Devon. In Yorkshire there's a high lonely wind that twists at your heart. Near Canterbury you can hear the bells of the cathedral as you walk across the downs. In London the pubs are opening. There's a fire on the hearth at the Lord Nelson, and Eve, the barmaid, has kept a couple of doubles of Scotch hidden away for you.

This is the stuff that dreams are made of, but if most of the men and women of the Canadian armed forces don't stop keening their song of remembrance, their wives and parents and sweethearts will probably rise up and commit mayhem.

Let's hear from the pretty young wife who stayed home somewhere in Canada to take a war job by day, and knit, write letters and pack parcels by night.

"John's home now," she said. "I thought he'd be glad to get back to his civilian job, but now he hates it. I thought he'd come home Saturday afternoon and we'd work in the garden like we used to. But he doesn't seem to care about that any more. We used to play bridge with the Smiths every Saturday night, but he can't be bothered now. Bill Smith couldn't help it if he had an essential job and couldn't get in the Army, but somehow John seems to resent it.

"When we go out with my friends (and naturally they're all people who stayed in Canada during the war) he sits still and doesn't say a thing. But nights when some of the men he was overseas with come to the house, why, he talks a blue streak, and all about things I don't understand.

"But worst of all," she said unhappily, "is that John's attitude toward me is different. I guess he thought I was just about perfect when we got married and when he went overseas. But now, I'm sure, he sometimes thinks of me as a jailer. Sometimes I resent him buying a bottle when his friends come in, because after all we can use the money for the house and save for the day when the baby arrives.

"He doesn't think I'm as gay as I should be. But it's hard to be gay after five years of sitting home, talking to women. He thinks my hair is all wrong and my clothes aren't smart enough. Well, I paid for the refrigerator with money I might have spent at the hairdresser. I made old clothes do, so that I could buy that dining room suite we've always wanted.

"I know John had a girl friend in England. I guess she was always gay, a good sport ready for a party. But after all, she wasn't spending the money that might buy her a home. She was spending the money for *my* home."

That's the tale of the girl who was left behind, and her story can be heard from Halifax to Victoria.

Excuse me a minute—my doorbell's ringing. It's the brush salesman. He stands a little way down the steps. "Okay, lady, tell me to go away if you want to. I'm selling bathroom brushes, and I don't suppose you want any. Your next-door neighbor just threatened to kick me down his steps. He said he was sick of returned men coming back begging. Well, I'm not begging. I'm selling something, and it's a good product.

"I had a business of my own before the war," he continued, mounting the last two or three steps. "But I was overseas four years and when I got back it had folded. I wish I were back in the Army, in England or France or Holland, or anywhere. I was a captain in the Army, and at least nobody ever threatened to kick me downstairs for doing what he called begging."

In a few minutes we were perched on stools in my kitchen, having a cup of coffee, and I'd ordered all the brushes my husband could afford for months to come. We talked about England. "The pubs sure were nice," he said. We talked about Holland. "Remember how swell the Dutch people were in the winter of 1944. They'd ask you into their homes and offer you the last bite they had to eat."

When he left he said, "Well, this has been swell, talking about old times again. I don't get much chance to talk about it. You see, my wife doesn't like it."

In a grocery store in mid-August, I complained in the usual housewife's tone that corn cost five cents a cob. The young man behind the counter remarked, "I paid a shilling in England and was glad to get it." I had done that, too, so we got to talking about things over there.

He'd been an NCO in the Air Force and a year ago had been pulling strings to get home.

"Lady, I was a sucker," he said. "I'd give anything to be back in the Air Force now. But most of all, I'd like to be back in the good old United Kingdom. Back here, working for a grocery store, I work twice as long hours as I did in the Air Force, for less money. In the Air Force there was always a chance of promotion. You can't get any place in a grocery store."

Canada, this is your nostalgia. It makes the men who came back, and the women who waited for them, bitter with disillusionment. There wasn't much nostalgia abroad in the land a year ago. Men and women in uniform in Europe were too busy pulling strings to get home, cursing the lack of shipping space for Canadians. When the day arrived for them to sail for home, it was more exciting than V-E day itself. Lines of khaki, lines of blue with duffel bags on shoulders, snaked along English quays and up gangplanks pointed to Canada. There was a twinge in your heart when England dropped behind the Atlantic rim and strange things suddenly seemed dear, like the rumbling bus that took you home in London, the Cockney accent of the waitress in your favorite café, or St. Paul's rising through the rain at the top of Ludgate Hill. There was a wistful thought, "I'll never see them again."

But next morning there were oranges and Canadian bacon and eggs for breakfast, and anyone could see that life at home would be good.

At Quebec (and it was the same at Halifax) people lined the promontories and docksides to wave. A little harbor boat with a band on board came out to meet us. I'm naturally sentimental myself, but I saw a couple of husky, tough-looking privates wiping their eyes, too, with the sleeves of their tunics.

That's the way it was: Canada through rose-colored glasses. Automobiles looked like limousines after the jeeps, the French taxis and the tiny British cars.

People cheered when you walked off the boat, and you could tell by the way the veterans walked that they each felt like something pretty special. Walking down the street in your uniform, beside the folks, you knew they were proud of you and that they hoped people would notice your campaign ribbons. People stopped and shook hands and said, "Welcome home," as if they meant it.

Those were the days when the small things you didn't usually notice were big and important, being able to buy Canadian cigarettes or gloat over a magazine stand, or fill a grocery basket with oranges and bananas and cheese, or order a milk shake at a drugstore counter.

When you bumped into some of the men off your ship they said, in those days, "I'd forgotten how beautiful my wife was or what it was like to live in a modern house. I'm going back to civvy street. I've got my old job back and it's going to be swell."

Some of them did get their old jobs back, and some of them still think it's swell. But a lot of others are bored and restless. A wing commander who went back to his old job of selling shoes finds his thoughts going back to the days when he led bomber attacks on Germany from Yorkshire airfields. A tank corps corporal who saw action in Sicily, Italy and Germany finds his heart isn't in the factory routine at home.

It's a world of mundane jobs; of 44-hour weeks, doing the same thing day after day, week after week. There are no 48-hour-leave jaunts to Rome or Brussels or Edinburgh. A two weeks' vacation at the family cottage by the lake is pretty small potatoes

when excitement and travel and adventure have been your meat for half a decade. But even danger, remembered in retrospect, often becomes exciting adventure, something to be taken out and turned over on a drab Canadian autumn evening.

As one veteran who lost an arm in Sicily said, "At least we were living then, we weren't mildewing like we are at home."

The veterans have forgotten how Canadians overseas gathered in groups to criticize the English and the Dutch and the Belgians, to complain about their food, their beer and their way of doing things generally. The high prices, it was generally concluded, were designed purely to fleece Canadians.

My husband and I had a flat in London, and it was the scene of scores of bitter talkfests when Canadians were in town. Back in Canada we get together with many of the same people, and we're still complaining, only this time it's about Canada, while Britain or France is the place everybody wants to go back to.

**A wing commander who went back to his old job of selling shoes finds his thoughts going back to the days when he led bomber attacks on Germany from Yorkshire airfields**

∞

But in fairness I'll admit that this does not apply to every Canadian son and daughter who came back from the war. Some swear they would not go back to Europe if it were the last place above water on the earth. They like Canadian family life and the same solid food they were used to always. The men like fresh-faced Canadian girls, the cold winters and hot summers.

They're lucky to see it all that way. It gives them a peace of mind which the nostalgic majority do not have. Or do the others just seem to be the majority because they talk more of the things of Europe which they miss?

In Britain, where women far outnumber men, the Canadian male found himself on a pedestal for the first time in his life. No fiddle-faddle did he hear about women being the equal of men.

When he took a girl on a date in England he didn't have to splash his money around to impress her more than somebody else who was rushing her. Likely as not she insisted on paying her own way, and maybe even his too, if payday was a long way off. Chances are, the girl didn't even force him to the mental exhaustion of remembering her telephone number. Probably after the first date, she'd call him. If she was a girl with a home she'd invite him for week ends, and her family would help her give him the time of his life.

British women, according to men who have devoted some time to the study (and practically everyone back from overseas has), are more affectionate and at the same time more intelligent.

"It's swell to meet a girl who's read a few books in her life, and who knows what's going on in the world," one man remarked to me, in England. "All my wife talks about in her letters is how hard it is to get a maid and how she wishes she could have a new fur coat this winter. My girl over here will go without something she really wants to buy me a present. She'd clean my boots if I'd let her. Can you see a Canadian girl doing that?"

So all these things rolled into one make up the nostalgia Canadian veterans feel.

It's all tough on the little woman who stayed behind, or the parents who thought their boy would be happy just to be home again. They think, with justification, that they fought a pretty good war on the home front, and they'd like a little understanding from the veterans who, though certainly they faced more of the dangers of war, had more fun and excitement too.

A cartoonist summed it up. He pictured a discharge centre, with an officer giving a farewell message to the brand-new civilians. "Don't force civilians to talk about their war experiences," he was saying, "but if they want to, let them. It will be good for them."

# Why Do Some Women Like Soap Opera?

*"It makes married life easier"*

BY MARY JUKES

IT WAS A WARM SPRING DAY. THE windows in the apartment were flung wide. Voices—male and female—mingled in what sounded like familiar domestic bickerings.

Words, demanding, beseeching, agonizing, almost

embarrassing in the *tone confidential*, sparked the morning air. They seemed to echo in the apartment well, coming from all the open windows. Almost in unison the housewives in that particular apartment had tuned their dials and were treating themselves to a slice of throbbing domestic life, via soap opera.

How many Canadian women actually listen to and enjoy that kind of radio entertainment?

In the U.S.A. 58.3% of the American women listen regularly to daytime serials; of which there are 45.

"Takes mind off troubles"

Of these, seven are released over the Canadian network. They are "Road of Life," "Big Sister," "Lucy Linton," "Life Can Be Beautiful," "Ma Perkins," "Pepper Young's Family" and "Right to Happiness." Another, "Laura Ltd.," originates in Montreal, making eight. These daytime serials occupy two hours daily of Canadian broadcasting time.

*Chatelaine* went to its Consumer Council of 2,000 women, which gives an authentic cross-section of the thinking of Canadian women, from British Columbia to Prince Edward Island, drawn as it is from rural and urban groups of all ages and incomes.

The question was, "As you know, the radio has quite a few daytime serial stories, frequently dealing with domestic problems. Do you enjoy them or not?"

Of all the replies, only 10% confessed to enjoying them. But 35% said they enjoyed *some* of them, which makes a total of 45% enjoying one or more daytime serial.

More than a third of the women who enjoy soap opera give as their reason, "It takes one's mind off one's own problems and troubles." Murder mysteries probably do the same for the doctor who's glad to tear his thoughts away from Mrs. X's cardiogram. The president of the stock exchange who reads murder mysteries as an escape, might be able to agree with another third of *Chatelaine* Councilors who say, "It makes married life seem easier."

Over a fifth feel that soap opera adds the sentimental and romantic excitement lacking in the lives of so many women.

A tenth mention "the sound of a human voice in a lonely house."

Reasons favoring soap opera were stated in a straightforward unemotional kind of way. But when women *don't* approve of soap opera, their vehemence rises to a crusading height.

Over a quarter deplore the sob stuff, and the melodrama. Some even go so far as to call them immoral. More than a seventh complain that they don't resemble what goes on in everyday life. But the women who feel the strongest say, "They are a waste of time and an insult to the intelligence." A small group give as their reason for not listening a cryptic, "Trouble enough of my own."

But what would women do, if they were in a position to dictate radio-program policy?

To our astonishment "Daily News" got the highest number of votes. Over three fifths of the women were in favor of this type of program. The next highest vote went to light opera or musical comedy tunes.

From there on preference was: Plays (good plays, not crime or soap opera); quiz programs; news commentators; Sunday church services; symphonic music; discussion forums; weekday religious programs; women commentators; Canadian historical events; Canadian stars; book reviews; barn dance music. Those polling the least number of votes were crime plays and jazz music.

# The True Story of One Woman's Fight to Save Her Marriage

*Celia wanted one thing above all—to rescue her tottering marriage. For that she had to face the hardest truth any woman is ever called upon to endure—the truth about herself*

### Anonymous

*Note: This story of the near breakup and the restoration of a marriage is true in every fundamental detail. The remarkable honesty with which it is written makes it essential that the author as well as her friend "Celia," remain unidentified—The Editors.*

 **NOVEMBER 1952**

IN THIS AGE OF COMMON DIvorce we have become callous about the breakup of marriage. I happen to know the intimate story of a marriage that didn't break, although it got into the worst difficulties you can imagine.

In a way it did break—but never officially—and now it is almost mended. You can't shatter a shimmering lustre bowl and put it together again with the iridescence unimpaired. But the bowl, lovingly pieced together, will have the same shape and color and, in time, when the cement has fused into the material it will be useful again.

Celia had come from a broken home at the poverty level, and had grown up in children's shelters and cheap boardinghouses. She knew first-hand all the miserable experiences that happen to little girls without a home, particularly without a father. She didn't want this to happen to her own two little girls, or her son.

Celia's marriage had begun with great love and admiration. Mark had been so protective and devoted that after the long years of loneliness and shabby times in other people's houses she felt she had reached the end of the rainbow. When his strangeness began—his brooding silences, his long absences from home, his harsh criticisms of her housekeeping, her manner with the children, her handling of money—and later of her appearance, her behavior, her very breathing—she could not believe it.

As in so many of our marriages today, the war had intervened. The man who hated to be away from his wife for a day had been away for years. He had been a boy when they married. He had known no other woman and had never dreamed of comparing Celia with anyone. She had been incomparable. But, away from her, lonely and in a strange country with time on his hands, and under the anonymity of khaki, he found that there were lots of lonely girls and women willing to offer themselves.

By the time he came home from the war, he had made a number of alliances, and in each one he had found something pleasant that did not carry the weight of responsibility which marriage and fatherhood entailed.

It is the old familiar story. Homecoming was very difficult, and Celia was not prepared. Anxious to lay down the burden of making all the decisions for the children and the home, she was too quickly demanding. The children were small and she had been lonely. She had been carrying a double load and she hadn't had any fun. She had no idea that her husband had been unfaithful to her. That sort of thing might happen to other men, but not Mark.

As for Mark, he compared his tired, demanding wife with his wartime companions who had always been eager to see him, dressed in their best, demanding nothing from him, meeting his moods.

"If you don't pull yourself together," he told her regularly, "I will find somebody else to be in love with." And he wasted no opportunities.

This incredible situation persisted literally for years.

At last, the last step in the breakup of the marriage was taken and at last, one woman *was* brought out into the open. By this time Mark's guilt was more than he could bear. He spent all his time attempting to prove to his wife in every way possible, by neglect, by words, by deeds, that she was responsible for everything he had done, that she had forced him to fall in love with the other woman. His black callousness in the face of her misery, his brutal taunting, finally broke her and her nervous collapse seemed just a matter of time.

Now, how could this marriage possibly be repaired? For Celia, who had been a woman of some stature, it was shamefully humiliating.

Her close friends stepped in. I was one of them. We said, "There is no use any longer. You *must* leave him. He is destroying you."

Under pressure, Celia went at last to a lawyer, who repeated her friends' advice. She was entitled to the house and furnishings, half Mark's salary, and various other settlements. She would be able to keep her home going and educate the youngsters. From everybody's point of view, except hers, this was good.

She tried psychiatrists, groping dimly toward a deeper understanding, a possible solution. One doctor, a man, said, "The trouble is, you simply will not admit defeat. Your marriage is gone, but you are too vain to admit it."

The woman doctor said, "He doesn't want divorce. He has told you he wouldn't be true to any other woman. He doesn't want to give up the children. All he wants is to have his cake and eat it, too. Well, let him. He'll get over this period. They all do. Spruce yourself up, keep quiet, take care of things and wait."

But Celia was not satisfied. She went away for a while. It was a little like going up on a mountain alone. She took with her a thick pad of paper with blank sheets. She began to write down on it all the things her husband had said about her. All the accusations against which she had defended herself.

*I am not a tidy housekeeper.* (Never mind saying that I've often neglected my house to do other things you asked of me. Just write . . . *I am not a tidy housekeeper.*)

*I do insist on being the centre of attraction.*

*I do make decisions for the whole family.* (I tell Mark what he can and can't eat. I tell him when he should or shouldn't get the car washed.)

The paper filled up fast.

Mark had said, "The thing I like about this other woman is that she is honest. You are a liar."

She wrote, "I am a liar. I don't tell how much I pay for things. I juggle the money around so I can get what I want without telling. I polish the surface of life and sometimes the corners are pretty sketchy."

How can I let you know how very painful Celia's task was? I wouldn't want to face doing what she did.

The little faults, the small easy sins went down first on Celia's paper, but there was much worse to come. She was so bitter at Mark because of his sexual wanderings, but what about her own flirtations at parties? What about the ensuing telephone calls from men who found her charming and wanted to do something about it? If she had had a chance at the free life her husband had led overseas, would she have been any better than he had been?

> **I have always failed you. Whatever you did, I caused you to do. I have not been the woman a good man has a right to expect as his wife"**

Celia wrote, "I think I would have been worse."

Her rebirth was a long process. When she had finished, it was a long time before she could summon up courage to do what had to come next.

She went back to Mark. He had not mended his ways during her absence. He had, if anything, become worse.

She said, "Mark, you were right about me. I was wrong. I'm sorry."

Perhaps she hoped for kindness. Instead she got further vilification. He said, "I told you so. Why didn't you listen to me?"

But she persisted. She said, "I have always failed you. Whatever you did, I caused you to do. I have not been the woman a good man has a right to expect as his wife."

He retorted angrily, "Certainly you failed me! Do you think any man really wants that sort of dishonest life?"

He was right. He was absolutely, utterly right.

Celia begged him. "If you want us to separate, we'll have to do it. But give me time to prove I can be different."

It hurt terribly to beg. But her humility was sincere. He was difficult, unbelieving, scornful. It was as if her humility, her real acceptance of his burden

had loosed in him all his bitterness toward her, and he poured it out over her unsparingly.

Celia persisted. And she did not defend herself.

A month passed and he told her angrily one day, "I've given up the other woman. She was nothing. I didn't want her anyway. I'm relieved."

In three months—three long, aching, painful months, in which he watched every move she made, stood ready to pounce upon the least deviation in the pattern she *said* she had chosen—he said, "I have given up all other women. I don't want that kind of life anymore."

In six months he said cautiously, "I think I may love you."

I don't think I could do what Celia did. I get indignant when I think of her humbling herself so completely, taking the whole fault on herself.

But Celia says, "Who are you to judge? I had the power to take the load of his guilt from him, to accept it myself and so to free him." She says that a woman who does not set these standards for her husband fails him utterly.

Dare to be a Celia?

# A Rap on Marriage with Jessie Bernard

By Catherine Breslin

 **JANUARY 1972**

**T**HE LADY WAS HARD AT WORK on a book due to go to the press in three weeks, but she said on the apartment house phone, "Well, all right, come on up."

The lady is Dr. Jessie Ravage Bernard, sociologist and research scholar, age sixty-eight, widowed twenty-one years, a mother of three. She serves on the boards of a clutch of academic journals and professional societies; after years of teaching at Penn State University, she now lives and writes in what she calls a "geriatrics compound" in Washington, D.C. The lady is so much a scholar that the year after she got her MA at the University of Minnesota she married her professor, Luther Lee Bernard, who was twenty-one years older, and began to turn out books like *Social Problems at Mid-Century: Role, Status and Stress in a Context of Abundance.*

In 1968 she published *The Sex Game*, an improvement in titling, but replete with stuff that would set a bra-burner's teeth to gnashing. (Sample: "A considerable amount of space in the literature of marital sex is devoted to the unhappy wife who is denied orgasm by either an inconsiderate or an unskilled husband. Very little is said of the loving wife who practices thoughtful deceit to please her husband.") Her new book is called *The Future of Marriage*.

Answering her apartment door, Jessie Bernard proved to be a short, smiling woman, a little dumpy and bespectacled, wearing a rumpled button-up housedress. An inch of grey showed under her caramel-colored hair. We sat in a book-lined living room with faded Mexican antimacassars and comfortable slip-covered furniture. Letters, magazines, reports were everywhere and, outside, there was a pleasant eleventh-floor view of trees along the Potomac.

*Catherine Breslin:* Do you see marriage now as being more satisfactory?

*Dr. Bernard:* If you're judging marriage in terms of adjustment, which in the past we have tended to do—you can get adjusted to almost anything if you have to, but the point is why should we? Marriage is wonderful for men but it's very bad for women. If you compare married women with unmarried women, they show up very poorly.

*Breslin:* How did you *get* liberated?

*Dr. Bernard:* I belonged to the first wave of feminism in this century; my teachers were feminists. When I was in college we had a campaign for the Corsetless Coed—we didn't even *have* brassieres in those days. So we got rid of corsets and we cut our hair and we rolled our stockings. I was writing in that feminist vein, too, then. But what's terribly interesting is that here I was, a sociologist who should have known better, also being sidetracked by this feminine mystique, this whole regression in the forties and fifties. I *regressed* along with everybody else—I had my three children in my late thirties. Then, about 1968, I asked a woman I knew to invite me to one of her lib groups—and it was very interesting. You can get quite antagonized by the behavior of a lot of these women, but their message is so true you can't miss it. The girls were going back to college, the birthrate was going down—all those things were already changing.

*Breslin:* Was your marriage happy?

*Dr. Bernard:* Well, as my son's psychiatrist says, it was a very stormy one. [She laughs.] But you see, my husband was my professor, and he was much older than I. I'd say on the whole it was happy. It was a very creative relationship. He was the one who insisted that I accomplish and achieve, and I worked on his research with him for many years. So it really was a very complex kind of relationship. He was a very unusual man—he was a poet, and a very charming person. He cooked better than I and he sewed on the sewing machine better than I; there wasn't any of this domesticity bit.

*Breslin:* Why *do* women marry? I don't quite understand.

*Dr. Bernard:* Well, it's because, as these women say, they're programmed to. Of course, the marriage rate is going down; this I think is very exciting. I can't get anyone to get as excited about it as I am, but a year ago I began to notice it, and I said, look, look what's happening. There were *more* unmarried people in 1970 than 1960, and also the actual rate is going down. It may not be a permanent thing, but abortions are so much easier now, so they don't *have* to get married. And we've known that at any age, if the girl is working, the marriage rate is lower, especially if she has a good job. A lot of people mind the isolation and exclusiveness of the relationship. That it cuts you off from so much. In a good marriage, it's true, you do get this intimacy that lots of people crave, but at the expense of other genuine contacts. Your relationships outside the marriage are usually rather superficial. Marriage traditionally has meant two things. One, it was permanent, till-death-do-us-part sort of thing; and the other, it was exclusive, it's just you and me. But that's changing. They're now talking in terms of a three-, a five- or a ten-year contract.

*Breslin:* What do you think of that?

*Dr. Bernard:* If you want it, that's okay. The breakdown of any relationship is terrible. It's painful if they both want it and it's especially painful if only one wants it. If you're going to have a nonpermanent marriage you have to be strong, the women especially—and the dependencies that women have been reared into make any kind of breakdown twice as hard. We're going to have to rear women to have much more independence—emotional as well as these other ways.

*Breslin:* In accepting adultery?

*Dr. Bernard:* They don't call it adultery any more. It's comarital sex or swinging. But swingers look like losers to me. To be able to make it worthwhile to invest so much time and energy—they go hundreds of miles, and then they have a convention and, oh, sometimes the men find that they can't perform, and they feel terrible. Usually, you know, the husband initiates it and the wife is taken along, if not screaming at least reluctant, and then she gets to liking it. Then there are these group marriages or comarital relationships. You have to figure out who's going to sleep with whom tonight, and it can take all night, practically, to figure out. It's silly to judge them wrong or right. In a way we ought to be grateful to people who will go through all these agonies to work out these new forms.

In my new book I call them the prophets. The male prophets are prophesying all kinds of sexual varietism, that's their thing. But the women, the women's liberation, they want better—not more—sex. And what they want is a different life-style, and some of them are arguing for celibacy.

*Breslin:* And there seems to be a heavy defense of lesbianism.

*Dr. Bernard:* My experience with the lesbian women's liberation is that as yet they are *extremely* hostile. Since they think that they represent the logical outcome of the women's liberation philosophy, that they are the archetypes, if others don't follow them, they become very hostile. I wouldn't be concerned about lesbianism itself, if it were a loving thing.

*Breslin:* How about the business of protection of women? Within the marriage form as it exists today there's a good deal of protection of women, quote unquote—or is there?

*Dr. Bernard:* Women's liberation calls it exploitation. Surely, if half the world is in a cash nexus and you're not, you're at a terrible disadvantage. Everybody says the housewife's work is terribly important, absolutely essential. She's feeding the work force, so I think she should be paid for her contribution.

*Breslin:* Who will pay her?

*Dr. Bernard:* Something like the social security system, where employers would pay into some kind of fund; then out of this fund the housewife would be paid—it wouldn't go through the husband, it would go directly to her.

*Breslin:* If the forms of marriage loosen up so much, how will men be held to their responsibilities?

*Dr. Bernard:* How are they now? It seems to me that the commitment is to the child primarily—that's the test, every child should have *assurances* of the care and concern of two parents. But there's *absolutely* no way to enforce it on a person who's determined to escape it. The family as it has been in the past has not been doing a good job, and when women devote their entire careers to raising children they are devastating.

*Breslin:* Oppressive, castrator mothers, smother-mothers.

*Dr. Bernard:* I just read an article for *Sexual Behavior* in which a rap session is reported, and it seems if women don't put up a fight, the men can't perform. These were, I think, unmarried women. The men are so used to overpowering women and overcoming their resistance that this is part of the game. Actually we hardly know a *thing* about female sexuality. Men have been defining female sexuality for lo, these millennia. I tend to think a lot of the reaction that goes under the name of sex is a power and status thing. A man could have a thousand orgasms with his wife and it wouldn't give him any status down at the tavern, but if he overcomes this reluctant woman, that's what he gets points for. So there's something about *sex-just-as-power* that may be even more important than physical pleasure.

*Breslin:* I was just reading in this chapter you wrote in *Women in a Sexist Society*, where you say could it be that marriage itself is sick, and could it be that women are happily married because they're mentally sick to begin with.

*Dr. Bernard:* My new book, *The Future of Marriage*, is built around the idea that there are two marriages in every union: his is great and hers is bad. I'm a sociologist. I didn't start out to *prove* this. I put together the data and it just hit me. The mental health of married women is terrible. There are lots of studies of mental health—national surveys, California studies, Manhattan studies. They all show the same thing. Unmarried men are the worst. Then married women. Unmarried women and married men are about equal. It's so contrary to all our clichés. But there's hardly any sympathy for married women who complain of their lot. They're told, you've got it made, you're taken care of. I think women want love so much that they're willing to pay an awfully big price. It infuriates me that everybody thinks women should make all the adjustments.

# Violence in the Home

***The one place we should all be sure of love and understanding is for many people a crucible of violent emotions that sometimes erupt in violent behavior. What can be done to help the victims and deter the victimizers?***

By Philip Marchand

MAY
**1981**

**P**EOPLE WHO BATTER THEIR spouses, children or aged parents seldom appear monstrous or deranged. They're people who,

in many cases, are charming company while watching the Grey Cup or chatting on the church steps Sunday morning.

"The people who work with him like him, they think he's a swell guy," one woman told me about her husband. An intelligent, well-educated woman, Laurie had taken her son and left her husband, Mark, a year and a half ago, after six years of an intolerable and brutalizing marriage. She is not alone. Researcher Linda McLeod of the Canadian Advisory Council on the Status of Women estimates that one of every 10 Canadian women who lives with a man—married or common law—is abused every year. A smaller, but significant, proportion of husbands are also abused by their wives every year. Some of these husbands are not violent themselves; others are, and end up badly hurt or even killed by wives who, tormented beyond endurance, finally take a kitchen knife to them.

In this country, there are also an estimated 5,000 to 9,000 abused children who are deliberately burned, scalded, starved, beaten by their parents until their bones break or their bodies are covered with bruises. This does not include children who are sexually abused, a group which may well be more numerous. (In 1979, the first year of the Ontario Child Abuse Register, more than 30 percent of reported child-abuse cases were cases of sexual abuse, a crime which is usually far more concealed and underreported than the crime of physical abuse of children.)

The violence is not limited to any social class. Laurie and Mark, for example, both came from affluent, upper-middle-class families. Laurie knows that his mother regularly beat Mark with a shoe when he was a young child. She was not restrained by his father who, when he was not at work, tended to sink into the newspaper every night and ignore what was going on around him. He did not seem to be aware, for example, when Mark began viciously beating his younger brother. Asked to do an essay as punishment by a female teacher in high school, Mark wrote a grotesquely obscene piece about the teacher having intercourse with a monkey. The teacher, stunned, could only recommend to Mark's parents that they get professional help for their son—a recommendation no one acted on.

Laurie did not have the most promising start in life either. Her father was not a brute, but he was capable of "teasing" her, by tickling her and, when angered, holding her head under a pillow. The pillow would come off when she stopped struggling. Horseplay or teasing is often a polite name for the infliction of pain on a child, or the subverting of the child's dignity. "I thought that's how people loved each other," Laurie recalls.

Laurie met Mark in university. Mark was not rough with her, not during their courtship. He became violent toward other people occasionally during this period, however. And once at dinner he said to her, "You don't butter your bread that way." Laurie was astonished. "I beg your pardon—you don't *what*?" Mark repeated his statement. "But, Mark," Laurie said, "this is the way I've always buttered my bread." Mark was adamant. "It's not the way you're going to butter your bread after we're married," he insisted.

This should have been a clue to Laurie that the man she was marrying was not completely rational. Shortly after the wedding, Mark threw the first of his scenes. "Initially, he said something like, 'If you don't do what I want, I'll throw the stereo out the window.' And I believed him. After that, he had me. I was afraid of him."

As Terry Davidson, researcher into the problem of battered wives, states in her book *Conjugal Crime*, "All the evidence is that when the first or second assault is not firmly dealt with, there will be more. And the assaults will become more frequent and more severe." That was what happened in Mark and Laurie's marriage.

Despite, or perhaps because of, the worsening reality, Laurie decided to have a child. At one point, during her pregnancy, Mark threw her off the bed— fortunately, he did nothing more to endanger her pregnancy, like actually hitting her in the abdomen, a horrific practice frequently indulged in by men who beat their wives.

After their son, Jonathan, was born, Mark made it a habit continually to tell Jonathan how stupid his mother was. At times, he seemed almost jealous of the care and attention Jonathan got from his mother. But then, a major ingredient of Mark's rage was that quality of temper tantrum appropriate to young children. Once, Laurie recalls, he even lay on the floor kicking and screaming like a two-year-old. "I realized then," she says, "that his rage and violence didn't have anything to do with me. It had to do with his feelings toward his mother and how he felt about himself."

Laurie, her self-esteem sunk just about as far as it could go, began to look for help from psychiatrists and social workers. She and Mark would go together. At these sessions, Mark suddenly became Mr. Rational. "I was excitable and upset and I sounded like a madwoman," Laurie recalls.

She finally left when a dispute over something or other resulted in Mark uttering some gratuitously foul-mouthed insults. And then, in a deliberate and cold-blooded fashion, he gave her a beating.

So, Laurie left with Jonathan, and was fortunate to have a sister who could help her out.

She finds it hard to understand why her father and her husband abused her. "Why did they abuse me?" she asks. "They abused me because I was a woman."

Parenting is without doubt the most important influence on the emotional growth of the child. And the child of violent or negligent parents has little chance to differentiate between rage and simple anger (an emotion aroused by specific wrongs, the expression of which often has a healing and cleansing effect). He has little chance to feel natural and non-violent aggression. And he has little chance to lose that profound sense of infantile helplessness, to shake the conviction that people who annoy or restrict him are malicious figures who deserve vengeance. Particularly, he has little chance to shake the conviction that only his bottomless unsatisfied needs are real, and that other people are not real.

The violence of Laurie's husband, then, is not an example of "aggressive behavior" so much as infantile temper tantrums made deadly because the infant is now a physically strong adult. And the object of these tantrums is often not the real person suffering from them but what psychiatrist Dr. Bernard Chodorkoff, who was a consultant to the National Commission on Causes and Prevention of Violence in the United States, calls the "primary target"—usually a parental figure.

Deborah Sinclair works for a Domestic Violence Project for the Family Service Association of Metropolitan Toronto in the suburb of Scarborough, examining violence in the families referred to the project. "The most important resource that we have is our attitude," Sinclair says. "When a woman calls in and says she's been beaten, we act like *that*. We believe her."

The law is at best a clumsy instrument, however. A seriously beaten wife can have her husband arrested on an assault-causing-bodily-harm charge; if she's just been slapped around, she can have him charged with common assault, although witnesses are often required in order for a police officer to arrest a husband on those grounds. The law is least effective when a woman wants legal protection for herself and her children against future attacks from her husband; under present legal remedies, women have to count more on the assistance of friends and neighbors than on anything else.

Sinclair's approach necessarily de-emphasizes wife-beating as a "symptom" of a diseased relationship. It also de-emphasizes the traditional social-work approach of trying very hard to keep a given marriage and family together. Sinclair and other workers in the Domestic Violence Project emphasize the woman "taking control of her life" ahead of keeping her marriage going.

The question of what kind of woman ends up a battered wife and what kind of man ends up a battering husband, is not easy to answer. Abused children or children who have witnessed violence in the home, are certainly high risks for this fate. Linda MacLeod, author of *Wife Battering in Canada: The Vicious Circle*, estimates that one in two wife-beaters is unemployed. But other high-risk husbands, according to her research, are doctors and police officers—men who work under great pressure and receive considerable deference to their authority. Nevertheless, the authors of *Behind Closed Doors* conclude that "the rate of violence between husbands and wives was twice as high in the families of blue-collar workers than for white-collar workers." Partly this may be because such families are more subject to stress of different kinds, particularly economic stress. Partly this may be because violence in general is more taboo among the middle classes. A "good husband" is often defined by a blue-collar wife as one who holds down a steady job, doesn't drink and doesn't hit her. (The last two are closely linked. A great deal of wife-beating is precipitated by the husband's heavy drinking—which most observers see as an excuse for, and not a cause of, the actual violence.) A middle-class wife has somewhat higher expectations of a "good husband." In many cases, however, this only means that a middle-class wife feels more shame and more disgrace about episodes of conjugal violence than her working-class counterpart.

# Your Majesty, Can We Talk?

*Facing a never-ending run of bad-news stories, the Queen stands helpless and hapless before the family firm's shattered image of conventional rectitude*

By Robert Collison

**APRIL 1993**

**A**S JOAN RIVERS IS WONT TO say, Your Majesty, "Can we talk?" Forgive our colonial impudence but we decided you could use some advice. The subject: damage control.

The Queenly images that linger from 1992 are hardly victorious, happy or glorious. Trudging through the charred remains of Windsor Castle last November. Peering through the windows of a Range Rover after the wedding of your divorced daughter. Bowing to raucous demands from your subjects that you pay taxes like the rest of us. And, of course, firing up the front pages of tabloids that first trumpeted the indiscretions and alleged infidelities of your daughters-in-law, then ultimately announcing both women's separations from your sons.

As you informed a luncheon crowd in the year's dying days, it was, indeed, an *annus horribilis*. Such regal understatement, Ma'am. Such uncharacteristic candor. Thank heaven for your youngest child, Prince Edward, the family's confirmed bachelor, a status whose only downside is the occasional need to proclaim he's straight.

Well, that's all water under

**CHUCK AND DI: THE BIG SPLIT**
Seen together but apart—body language tells the story—amid rumors of other loves: his Camilla Parker-Bowles and her James Gilbey.

Tower Bridge. The question is: what now? Obviously, a massive public relations job is in order. The trouble is, PR is not the Palace's strong suit. Strictly speaking, there is no "spin"—i.e., upbeat angle—to the Dallas-at-the-Palace soap opera of failed royal marriages. Too much has happened: "Squidgy" Diana taped talking coquettishly to James Gilbey, a motor-trade executive; Charles recorded talking dirty to his supposedly platonic friend Camilla Parker–Bowles about his desire to be reincarnated as her pants; Fergie shamelessly flaunting her prime Texas beefcake lovers Steve Wyatt and John Bryan—and her so-suckable toes—for the world's lenses.

So, take the leap, Ma'am. Seek out the best family therapist on Harley Street—and haggle on the fees. After all, that's quite a line you'll be offering for the old shingle: "By Appointment to Her Majesty the Queen."

Your plan to save the monarchy should not neglect a careful look at your own health. Are you avoiding fats and salts, Ma'am? Are you working out? We all hope your mom's longevity is in your genes. "Long live the Queen."

**ANNE'S SPRING DIVORCE**
Come December, she tied the knot again, to Commander Tim Laurence.

**FIE! FERGIE**
Her topless frolic sullied her image.

**RANDY ANDY**
His anger at Fergie's follies confirmed their split.

**BURNOUT**
The crowning disaster was the fire at Windsor Castle.

# CHAPTER THREE

# Her Home, Her Castle

**A** MODEST HOUSE IN THE late twenties would probably consist of two furnished floors with a single bathroom, an attic for storage and an unfinished basement with furnace and a wringer washing-machine. Its wood or linoleum floors would be scattered with area rugs, its walls likely papered. Breakfast and lunch would be eaten in the kitchen, with dinner served in the adjoining dining-room. Though avant-garde couples might be influenced by the New Modernism, most young marrieds would choose a rolled-arm chesterfield suite for which the wife might crochet doilies. The focus of the room would be a console radio.

When building supplies became available following World War II, many homes underwent extensive renovations. Attics were dry-walled as extra bedrooms. Pantries were converted into downstairs bathrooms. Kitchens were redesigned with built-in appliances. Basements were turned into rec rooms where teenagers foxtrotted to LPs spun on portable players.

By the fifties, upwardly mobile couples were moving to suburban ranch-style houses with double garages, open floor plans, picture windows and fireplaces. The traditional chose Italian provincial suites, while the more adventurous experimented with sectional furniture. A black-and-white television set and a hi-fi now replaced the radio as focus of the living-room.

For sixties' apartment-dwellers, Scandinavian teakwood furniture and bamboo imports offered style, affordability and mobility. A card table with folding chairs might serve as a starter dining suite, supplemented by the ubiquitous brick-and-board bookcase, a standard-issue rubber plant (later upgraded to benjamina) and shag carpets cut the austerity of parquet flooring. Of course, the really cool "pad" would possess that accessory beloved of swingers: the waterbed.

Throughout the sixties and seventies, the pilgrimage of families back to the city resulted in the stylish reclamation of old neighborhoods. Plexiglass or chromium-and-leather furniture, mirror cubes and Eskimo sculptures contrasted boldly with the house's retro features—brick walls and stained-glass windows. In the newly furbished kitchen, opened by skylights and sliding patio doors, tile had replaced Formica, and appliances might include an automatic dishwasher.

By the eighties, the combination of ready cash, custom-designers and exotic imports turned the furnishing of many urban spaces into a narcissistic adventure. While kitchens grew sleeker and more compact, bathrooms became ever more opulent: even toilet paper became a fashion statement. In the living-room, the style was International Idiosyncratic: Victorian chairs upholstered in contemporary fabrics, lacquered chinoise cabinets, oriental carpets, beaded curtains.

The nineties produced a counter trend: this time for self-assembled, contemporary furniture, uncluttered, open spaces and—replacing the family room or library—a computerized home office.

# What's a Housewife's $ Worth?

**JULY 1972**

**A** STUDY PREPARED FOR THE ROYAL Commission on the Status of Women determined that the work of housewives amounted to eleven percent of the GNP. Since Canada's 1971 GNP was stated at just over $92 billion, housewives' work amounted to over $10 billion. But more likely it was over $19 billion.

Another method of measuring the housewife is by determining how much her skills are worth on the open market. Even this is not a good determinant because peripheral duties such as cleaning have traditionally been low-status, low-paying jobs, while there is no real indication of the value of child care.

With this in mind, it is still an interesting exercise to determine how much a housewife would make per week if all her skills were employed. Sharon Blacktop, an Ajax mother of two, Carol Franke, a Toronto mother of three, and Mary Belle Bird, a Toronto mother of four children who range in age from five to twelve, were asked to break down their working day. An average number of hours for each chore was determined.

It's interesting to note that the average number of hours these housewives allot to their various duties is seventy-six and a half a week. Several studies, including one mentioned in the Status of Women report, found that a housewife with two or more children works on the average of eleven hours a day, seven days a week, or seventy-seven hours a week.

## HEAVY CLEANING $15.40 A WEEK

A good cleaning lady who washes floors, windows, stoves and fridges can expect about $2.20 an hour. Our housewives spent seven hours a week performing these chores.

## LIGHT CLEANING $24.50

A housekeeper whose main job is to dust, make beds, do dishes and vacuum, makes about $1.75. Fourteen hours spread over seven days was the average for our participants.

## BOOKKEEPER, HOME ECONOMIST, SHOPPER $14

This category lumps together juggling family expenses, planning nutritious meals, finding recipes and shopping. Our housewives averaged four hours a week at this. A professional in any of these categories would be paid at the very least $3.50 an hour.

## COOK $35

A cook in a medium-priced restaurant who manages short orders as well as more complicated meals can expect $2.50 an hour. Our housewives cooked about fourteen hours a week, including the odd gourmet meal.

## LAUNDRY $4.50

A skilled laundress makes about $1.80 an hour. Our housewives say they spend two and a half hours sorting, washing, drying and ironing.

## BABY-SITTING $12.10

This is the period when housewives do nothing else but communicate with their children. This is the most valuable aspect of homemaking, so the $1.10 an hour charged by professional babysitters isn't very realistic. But unless the housewife has a diploma in child care there's no other way of measuring it. The average amount of time per week was eleven hours.

## HANDYMAN $4.95

Our homemakers spend about three hours a week fixing the children's toys, putting out the garbage, repairing the eaves trough. The general handyman would get the minimum wage of $1.65.

## CHAUFFEUR $31.50

Taking Johnny to his hockey game or Mary to the dentist is one of the most time-consuming chores for the housewife. Economists tend to ignore this job but there are men who earn a good wage at it. In our urban society it's become a major chore. A part-time chauffeur makes about $3.50. Our homemakers spent a minimum of nine hours a week as a taxi service.

## SEAMSTRESS $5.40

Most women perform simple seamstress chores such as replacing buttons or patching jeans. Other make their own and children's clothes, saving a great deal of money. Our ladies averaged three hours a week. $1.80 is a fair wage for a working seamstress.

## PAINTING AND DECORATING $8

Painting or wallpapering, antiquing or upholstering furniture is part of the work week for many housewives. Ours averaged two hours a week. A nonunion painter won't enter your house for less than $4 an hour.

## GROUNDKEEPER $15

This category includes gardening, snow shoveling, leaf-raking and keeping the bird feeder full. Our housewives say they spend an average of five hours a week as groundkeeper, especially in spring and summer. Average wage for this type of work (not a professional gardener) is $3.

## HOSTESS $4.50

When a husband brings home business associates his wife acts as a hostess, serving drinks, cooking special meals. A hired maid makes about $2.25 an hour. Our housewives said they worked two hours a week extra entertaining.

## TOTAL $174.85

# Mechanical Helpers

The "modern" laundry.

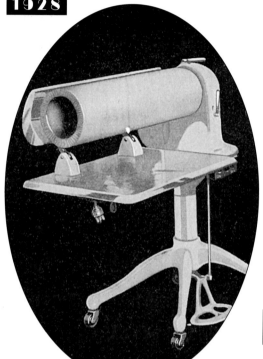

Maxwell Perfection Ironer.

The Cinderella washing machine promised to wash and *vacuum clean* your clothes.

A real boon for homes without electronic wiring—an iron that stayed hot.

Tools for spring cleaning.

# Our Questions and Your Answers

*Three thousand Chatelaine house-keepers answered our questionnaire*

BY HELEN G. CAMPBELL

**OCTOBER 1935**

TWO OR THREE MONTHS AGO, Chatelaine Institute invited seven thousand women—neighbors of ours and yours—to take part in a bit of shop talk with housekeeping as the topic of conversation. Many questions occur to us, from time to time, as we plan each month's articles, and in order to find the right answers we turned to this representative group of readers—chatelaines in city, town and country homes in every province and in widely different circumstances.

Three thousand, or over forty-two percent, accepted our invitation—a grand response, especially when you consider that housekeepers are busy people and that every little thing takes time.

"What kind of cooking utensils do you use?" was one question, and the summary of answers is enlightening. It appears that aluminum is the favorite with an impressive figure to its credit. Enamel ware and granite ware together total quite a count, while the popularity of oven glassware is shown in the fact that over half the number are proud possessors of at least some pieces.

"What kind of a stove do you use in your kitchen?" Answers to this question showed wood the fuel used by about one third with electricity a close second, coal third and gas in fourth place. As you might expect, however, this order is changed when we take cities alone: and is quite different in different provinces. For instance, of the total number of electric range owners over half are in Ontario, and of this number about twenty per cent live in Toronto. Most of the gas ranges—two thirds of the total—are used in Ontario and Alberta. In Montreal gas ranges outnumber electric ones twelve to one, while in Toronto they are about even and in the Maritimes the position is reversed in favor of electricity.

"Do you also use auxiliary cooking equipment?" Rather less than one quarter of the three thousand do. Hot plates are by far the most numerous, then rangettes and cookers next.

"What kind of a refrigerator do you use?" Ice is still at the top; but electric makes a good showing, with a few gas in Ontario, Alberta and B.C.

"What kind of washing machine do you use?" Here the electric washer has almost all its own way—nine out every ten reporting. A few people use water-power and others a hand power machine. But there are still a lot who use their strong right arm.

"Do you use an ironing machine?" Comparitively few answered this question in the affirmative—only one hundred and forty-three.

"Do you use a floor waxer, carpet sweeper vacuum cleaner?" The order is reversed according numbers reported, the count showing that you would hear the whirr of a vacuum cleaner in almost half the three thousand homes that a carpet sweeper is used in close to one quarter had a floor waxer in something over one sixth. Does this meanthat elbow grease gives the polish to a lot of floors? Or that floors are not as bare as they used to be?

"What other electric equipment do you use?" Almost everybody has an iron, it seems, and almost as many a radio. Considerably over half the number enjoy the convenience of a toaster at the table, but a percolator is rather a lame fourth in this list. Of course, there are other good ways of making coffee; perhaps you filter it? Water heaters supply hot water in five hundred cases out of the three thousand a waffle iron performs its duty in three hundred and fifty homes, a fan helps to keep two hundred and cool air heaters two hundred and fifty warm and a food mixer service in one hundred and fifty of these homes.

"What do you plan to buy next?" The refrigerator is the headliner here—a great many women yearfning for one. Four hundred and twenty intend to purchase new cooking utensils to add to their stock or replace those the worse off for wear. A stove and a washing machine nearly tie for third choice—four hundred and ten against four hundred and five with the former leading by a nose or whatever stoves have instead of noses. Vacuum cleaners rank next then floor waxers, ironing machines and carpet sweepers, in this order.

Above: Facing the bed, two Bali paintings on cotton hang above a pair of tortoiseshell bamboo tub chairs, flanked by bamboo end tables with ginger jar, astrological figurines.

# What's the Matter with Housework?

*If the general help problem is acute, the solution rests with the house-keeper*

By Maude Petitt Hill

**MARCH 1928** **W**HY DOESN'T THE CANADIAN or American girl take to housework as an occupation? The houseworker is not indigenous to us. She is with us only as an importation from the British Isles, Finland, Norway or some other distance. Indeed, often when she comes to us from the British Isles she comes because some charitable organization has brought her out, and she hopes in this land of opportunity to work her way to some other occupation.

But why throw housework in the discard? Is it that the girl hates housework itself? No, she will marry and be quite cheerful over it as an unending vocation. Is it that she thinks it is a job only for people not clever enough to do anything else? No, she has every respect for her married friend who shows herself a master hand at fluffy cakes and savory soups. Besides, universities are conferring degrees on women who are masters of household science.

Hard work? No a girl will leave it and glue her eyes all day to a power machine till her head aches, for less pay. "Dirty work," the girls used to say! But electric fairies, hardwood floors and interior decorators have made housework a dainty job.

What then? We are back to an old chord harped on often before—the lower social status of housework.

For several years various periodicals and organizations have advocated raising the social status of the houseworker. The trained and educated worker, they say, is the solution to this problem. The worker who has her hours, her

uniform, her mastery of her job—the worker who lives out and has her evenings free for her own social life. And as part of this solution, comes the apartment house, where there is no extra room for anyone helping with the housework. The apartment and the small home have made a distinct demand for the worker who comes in for a few hours a day. The "living-in maid" would be as much in the way here as the butler or coachman of other days.

But, while the go-out-by-the-hour worker may meet the needs of the apartment dweller, there is still the moderate sized house with the family of children. Their need of help is not, for many a year to come, going to be met in this way.

To begin with, the trained worker is going to be too expensive a proposition for the average family budget. If she is sent out by an organization, there are going to be overhead charges, hostel and office upkeep and so forth. In one city where such a method was tried, we found the actual cost of having a worker come in every day till five o'clock for a month of thirty days was $97.50, without laundry!

It rests with the individual employer to raise the status of the employee in her own house. But how? Shall she take her meals with her? Shall she ask her friends to fall upon her neck and embrace her when they enter the home? Why so? Her husband does not introduce his stenographer to those who enter his office. Neither does he take his meals with her. Yet, she does no fussing about her social status.

Here is one woman's solution of her problem. And when a woman can get a girl who is fairly well educated and speaks good English to do all her housework and cooking and baking, do the family laundry, wax the floors, and appear trim for an afternoon tea; when an employer gets all this for twenty-five dollars a month, and, what is more, can keep her help even if a neighbor offers her five dollars a month higher; when she can keep her a second year or even a third—

then perhaps her solution, however imperfect it may be, is worth hearing.

Mrs. B. attributes her ability to get help to having studied housework from a business-like angle—to having had, before her marriage, a professional career and a knowledge of the business world.

"It began about twelve years ago," she said, "when help was almost impossible to get. The children were all small. I advertised in vain. Then, I had to advertise for a housekeeper for a brother, a widower, outside the city. And lo, a hundred and three applicants! His house was in the country and had no conveniences. Why a host for his home and none for mine? Matrimony? That says a lot. But not all, as is proven by the fact that, a few years later, an invalid spinster friend advertised for companion help and got a hundred and one applicants—and a girl can't marry an invalid spinster.

"I determined, after the advertisement affair, to try doing my own housework under exactly the same conditions as if I were my own 'cook-general.' I did excuse myself from the washing, because I remembered that when the maid was doing the washing I was doing the morning's housework and looking after the children. Otherwise, I carried out her programme and wrote a few lines in my diary every night.

"Monday—Stayed in all day and all evening.

"Tuesday—Ironed. Weather was tempting. Would like to have gone for walk. Mrs. Grant phoned and reminded me that Mrs. Allison, the bride in our club, was receiving both afternoon and evening. Jean Gray would have stayed with the children, but I remembered that it wasn't my day out. I mustn't go.

"Wednesday—In all day and evening. House seemed still and terrible stuffy. Tomorrow—joy of joy—it's my afternoon off! Oh, I hope it doesn't rain! Our club had a shower for Mayme Lawrence to-night. I couldn't go, of course.

"Thursday—John came home late to lunch, unexpectedly. It was my day off, but by the time I got the late lunch out of the way and dressed and out, it was three o'clock. My, didn't the air feel good in my face again! If I were really a maid I'd have another maid to go out with, and I'd have a beau after five o'clock to take me to the show.

"Friday—It didn't seem so bad staying in all day after being out yesterday. There was a social in our church to-night. But, of course, I couldn't go. If I did go the young people would ask me to attend things in the church that I couldn't attend. And, perhaps, as a girl had once told me, 'when they find out you are doing housework, they don't pay any more attention to you.'

"Saturday—In all day again. Hubby wanted me to go to the theatre, to-night. But it wasn't my night out.

"Sunday—In all day and company for tea. I let myself out for the evening service and I had a little sleep in the afternoon. Next Sunday, I get the afternoon as well as the evening off. But by the time I get the dinner dishes done, it will be too late to accept the invitation of Miss Muir's Bible class for girls.

"Then," says Mrs. B., "as I studied my diary, I began to realize one reason why girls don't like housework. First the lack of outdoor air, sun and change. Secondly, the social status of the girl in housework.

"I began to see," said Mrs. B.—"it was up to me to raise the 'social status' of the girl doing my own housework. First of all I had to let her 'land in Jamaica,' with other young people of her age—with the girl from the candy factory and the parcel counter.

"I wrote an advertisement, offering five evenings free after 7.15.

"Be it remembered this was in war times, when household help was almost impossible to get, when I had hitherto advertised for weeks and got no response. But presto, thirteen applicants! We selected one who wanted to go to business college at night.

"The plan worked on both sides. She put her very best into her work because of the educational chance she was getting. She graduated eventually from business college and left us."

This, then, was the plan our long-headed young housewife had been following ever since. Sometimes, she had a girl going to night school, sometimes a girl going out with her John or Billy, sometimes a girl who spent a good deal of time at the various week-night functions in her church. But, in all the years since there had been but a few days all told in which she had had to do without help.

*Ultra-Modern Kitchen, circa '39*

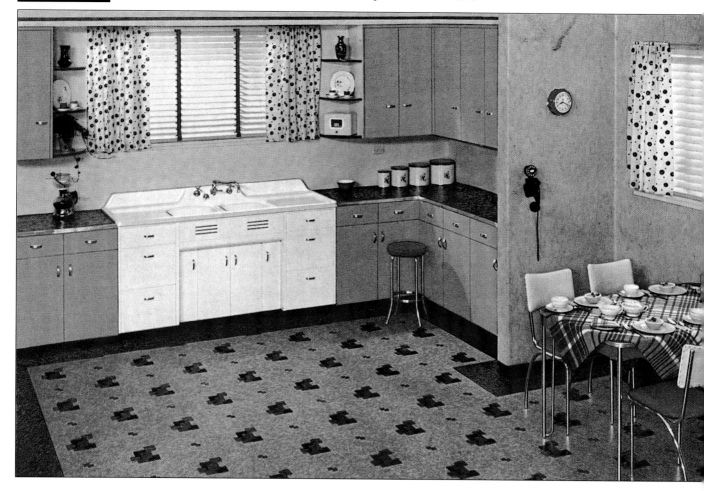

# Starter Apartment, circa '74

# The Household Budget

*A little earnest concentration now will mean purchases without pain three months from now, and money in the bank at the end of '43*

| WEEK'S WAGES | $15.00 | $18.00 | $20.00 | $25.00 |
|---|---|---|---|---|
| **Expenditure Budget:** | | | | |
| •Board | $7.00 | $7.50 | $7.50 | $8.50 |
| •Lunches | .50 | .50 | .50 | 1.25 |
| Streetcar or bus fares | 1.00 | 1.00 | 1.00 | 1.00 |
| Clothes, cleaning, repairing | 2.00 | 2.70 | 2.75 | 3.30 |
| Personal care, toilet articles, etc. | .59 | .65 | .75 | .73 |
| Recreation, candy, cigarettes, etc. | 1.00 | 1.14 | 1.20 | 1.25 |
| Holidays | .25 | .30 | .40 | .60 |
| Medical, dental care, medicines, etc. | .25 | .35 | .45 | .60 |
| Church, community welfare | .25 | .35 | .45 | .60 |
| Christmas and other gifts | .20 | .25 | .30 | .40 |
| **Income tax; compulsory savings:** | | | | |
| Deducted from salary | 1.07 | 1.97 | 2.57 | 3.80 |
| Balance payable Sept., 1943, (est.) | .15 | .30 | .33 | .60 |
| Unemployment insurance | .24 | .24 | .30 | .30 |
| Savings | .50 | .75 | 1.50 | 2.00 |
| | $15.00 | $18.00 | $20.00 | $25.00 |

• In budgets of $15, $18 and $20, it is assumed that lunches are brought from home. The small item under lunches covers cost of milk, tea, coffee or possibly a dessert bought each day. In $25 budget, board covers two meals only for five working days.

# Beating Inflation

*Alan and Grace: Until last September, they had got along without anything but makeshift living-room furniture. But they saved $1,500 over many years to do it really well. They have four children.*

| YEARLY | 1968 | 1973 |
|---|---|---|
| Standing expenses: | | |
| Mortgages | $1,620.00 | $1,650.00 |
| Interest | 265.00 | — |
| Taxes | 720.00 | — |
| Education bond | 590.00 | — |
| Pension | 504.00 | —* |
| Savings certificates | 910.00 | —* |
| Hospital | 78.00 | —* |
| Total | 4,687.00 | 1,650.00 |
| | | |
| | | |
| Monthly: | | |
| Food | 59.40 | 124.00 |
| Utilities | 32.20 | 44.68 |
| Medical | 12.30 | 30.92 |
| Household | 8.13 | 60.23 |
| Clothes | 19.45 | 37.11 |
| Gifts | 13.09 | 14.50 |
| Books, etc. | 13.54 | 21.75 |
| Car | 32.90 | 106.40 |
| Education | 2.26 | — |
| Insurance | 31.85 | + 97.30 |
| Offering | 36.90 | 106.21 |
| Entertainment | 58.15 | 93.06 |
| Manse | 1.52 | — |
| Personal | 4.81 | 41.33 |
| Allowances | — | 42.38 |
| Miscellaneous | 4.44 | 11.95 |
| Total | 330.94 | 831.82 |

*deducted at source.

+and savings.

# Chatelaine Designs a Modern House for Canada

## Architectural Advisory Board of the Chatelaine Studios

Eric Haldenby, b.a.sc., m.r.a.i.c., TORONTO

A. T. Galt Durnford, b.arch., a.r.i.b.a., MONTREAL

AUGUST **1934**

THE MODERN STYLE IN HOUSE designing—known as the International style, since every country is adopting its principles—believes in designing for use, first of all, and in the effective proportioning of mass rather than in ornament and decoration. Thus, rather than adapting the interior of a home to fit the exterior design of a house, modern thought plans the comfortable and practical arrangement of rooms and then encloses them in a compact, simple structure.

*Chatelaine* takes pride in presenting a modern home, designed for Canadian conditions of living and climate, with our Board of Consulting Architects. *Chatelaine*'s model house Number One adopts the new feeling for simple, horizontal lines. It is shown here in white stucco. The house turns its back upon the street to face a beautifully planned garden, for the designers feel that the Canadian homemakers are more concerned with a pleasant and private outlook than they are in the old-fashioned notion of having the important rooms overlooking the street. It is set on an average size lot. Sixty feet allows for a garden path between it and the next house, although fifty feet will carry the house comfortably.

While many modern homes are dispensing with the dining room and using only a square bay set off the living room, *Chatelaine* feels that the tradition of Canadian hospitality is so much a part of the nation's life that we have planned a dining room to seat eight comfortably at dinner.

On the second floor, two bathrooms strategically placed are shared by the four bedrooms, all of which have generous windows and roomy cupboard space. The bedrooms overlooking the garden have access to the circular verandah and the same beautiful window treatment of the rooms downstairs.

The basement contains the laundry and room space for the furnace, air conditioning plant, fruit storage and play room.

*Chatelaine*'s house is equipped with an air-conditioning system which cleans, humidifies and heats the air in winter cleans, cools and dehumidifies it in summer. Air is gently blown into the living room, the dining room, the halls and owner's bedroom. Concealed radiation is used in the other rooms.

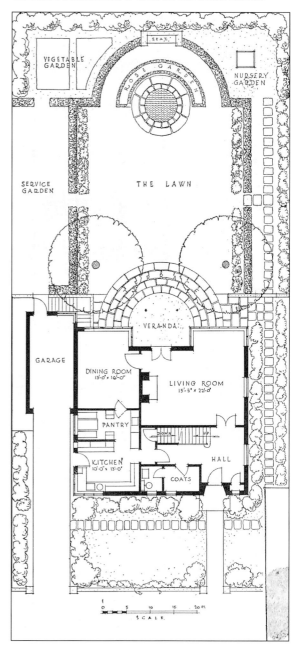

*Front or Street Elevation*

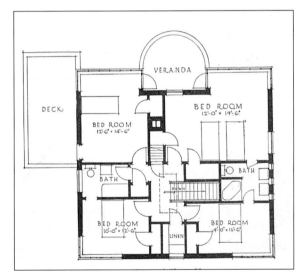

*Second Floor Plan*

The first floor plan shows the original treatment of the hall unit with its large cloak room and wash room, the beautifully placed living room and dining room with windowed embrasures overlooking the garden, and the compact kitchen group.

*Rear or Garden Elevation*

# Mrs. Majority's House . . .

*For the first time—a home to satisfy known needs of most Canadian families, reported by 2,000 Chatelaine Councilors*

**FEBRUARY 1952**

**H**ALF-A-MILLION NEW HOMES have pushed down foundations and pushed up roofs and chimneys in Canada since the war, in a furious program to try to satisfy the living needs of Canada's constantly growing population. Garish "dream houses" taken to nightmare extremes clash with superbly functional "ranch style" homes, and both are threatened by the spreading flood of monotonous box-style bungalows and story-and-a-halfs.

But in all this are Canadians getting the sort of homes they really want and need? Until recently no one had ever asked them—but now for the first time it is possible for an architect to design a home which satisfies the known living requirements of the broad majority of Canadian families. It is the house pictured on these pages.

We call it Mrs. Majority's House because it expresses the practical needs and desires of a majority of 2,000 representative Canadian women from coast to coast. To these members of Chatelaine's Consumer Council were mailed detailed questionnaires which they were asked to fill out after close study with their husbands.

The Toronto architects Gibson and Pokorny eagerly accepted Chatelaine's challenge to design a house to satisfy these majority needs of Canadian families.

Cost of building Mrs. Majority's House is difficult to estimate accurately because climatic conditions and available materials vary so widely in Canada. The architects say $15,000 would be about right, but variations of 20% more or less are to be expected.

## Here are the practical, livable features women asked us to put in the house

**PICTURE WINDOWS** that link outdoors with indoors, dress front and side of Mrs. Majority's House. Sixty per cent asked for big windows provided these do not interfere with effective furniture arrangements. For smaller windows, ordinary "up and down" variety won the favor of 74%, in preference to casement windows.

**SEPARATE DINING ROOM** was provided because a strong 43% asked to retain this traditional feature, remainder being divided about combining it with kitchen or living room. But in view of 60% desire for breakfast nook and a strong preference for entertaining at home (70%), architects devised a novel snack bar between kitchen and living room.

**SPACIOUS LIVING ROOM** is planned with conversational grouping of furniture around fireplace. Large open area permits easy circulation of guests. French doors give access to terrace.

**THREE BEDROOMS** are located at rear to form a "quiet zone" isolated from the active living and working portions of the house. More than half the families wanted three bedrooms, but said they'd like to have one bedroom double as a den.

**EFFICIENT KITCHEN** incorporates laundry, as preferred by 50% of Chatelaine housewives. With ample cupboards and work surfaces, footsteps, bending and stretching are reduced to a minimum.

**HOBBY ROOM** off basement rumpus room, was included because 60% have special leisure time interests that require work space.

**OUTDOOR FEATURES** which add to home enjoyment are drying yard, easily supervised built-in playpen, and a covered passageway to garage. An outside entrance to rumpus room was included so children don't have to track through the house.

**IDEAL LOT** would have 60 feet frontage. Average size preferred was 53 feet wide by 120 feet deep. Fifty-nine per cent of councilors interviewed want to live in towns or suburbs, only 16% in cities.

Mrs. Majority's house.

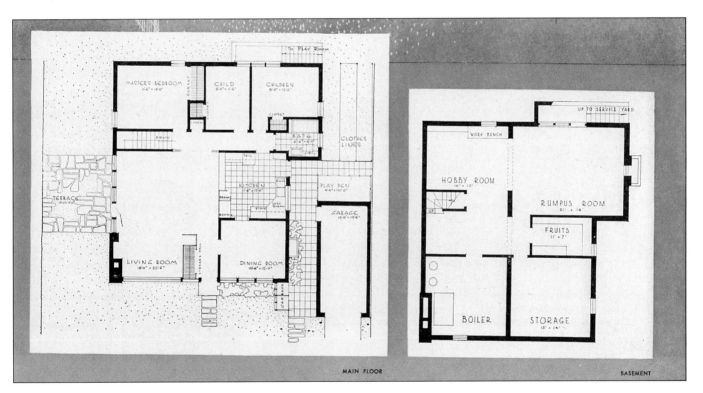

Mrs. Majority's plans.

*A Basement Looks to the Future*

# Modernism: The Beginning ...

## MARCH
### 1928

The group at left shows a marble-topped table with beautifully spaced drawn reinforcement rods, glass and metal sidelights by Simonet and a striking panel of decorative fabric—a combination of cotton and kapok.

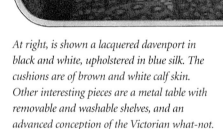

At right, is shown a lacquered davenport in black and white, upholstered in blue silk. The cushions are of brown and white calf skin. Other interesting pieces are a metal table with removable and washable shelves, and an advanced conception of the Victorian what-not.

## What Is This Modernist Movement?

### An explanation of the new and sometimes bewildering note in decoration

BY ANNE ELIZABETH WILSON

**MARCH 1928** WE HAVE BEEN privileged in the twentieth century to see the practical application of a new creative principle. Strange and often bizarre beyond our understanding, it has often often seemed, yet fascinating; and when we have learned to accustom our minds and eyes to the rhythm of cycles, the harmony of planes, the huge design and contrast, even the sharp punctuation of angles, we have been able to see interest, if not beauty in its form and color.

"I would not," says the standfast woman-with-tradition, referring to modern furniture, "give it house-room—" and yet, before she has said the words, she will be choosing a lamp for its unusual indirect lighting, or buying a cactus in its twisted little pottery bowl—and the new art is upon her!

It has affected almost everything. Fabrics are ablaze with its influence. The very choice of wood in furniture-making has been changed; glass and lighting are seen in weird and wonderful use— while even underfoot the lightning zig-zag (that typical new art line,) swirling curves and symbolic figures, proclaim the rug l'art nouveau. And it is not only in the expensive fabrics and in furniture which is of interest to the collector, or on the individual who has money to spend on whims, that the influence has laid its mark. It is to be seen, in one form or another, in almost every phase of interior decoration to-day.

Twentieth century furniture began to develop early in the nineteenth century. Gordon Russell was a craftsman who employed ebony and such woods as box and laburnum for punctuating the fine natural colorings of his pieces—an experiment which was later to form one of the outstanding characteristics of l'art moderne in England.

In France, Sweden, Germany and Austria, the twentieth century designer and maker of furniture developed his own bent. But one thing all had in common—the striving for sincerity of expression.

"The designer of to-day has shaken off the tyranny of curves, twists, twiddles and the confusing flow of ornamental line," writes John Cloag, the noted furniture historian, and he voices the basic characteristics of the new furniture age. In sculpture, painting, decorative design and architecture, this new spirit was coming into its own.

∾

We can no more stem the tide of this new century movement than turn our faces against the onmarch of time. Whether we like it or no, it is a thing that must be reckoned with and made place for, and if we are wise in our generation we shall learn to know its foibles early!

## FEBRUARY 1996  *Modernism: The End?*

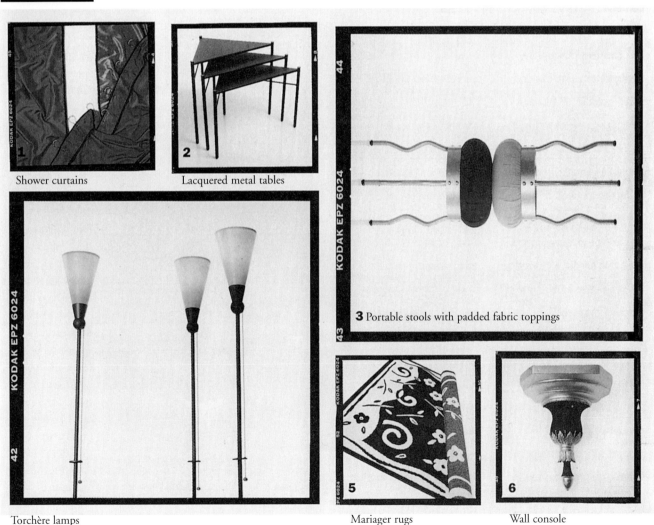

Shower curtains

Lacquered metal tables

**3** Portable stools with padded fabric toppings

Torchère lamps

Mariager rugs

Wall console

# The Chatelaine

## A Magazine for Canadian Women

Vol. 1, No. 7, Toronto, September, 1928

September
1 9 2 8

10¢

# CHAPTER FOUR

# Parenting

**B**Y THE LATE TWENTIES, CANADIANS were realizing that the number of women who died each year in childbirth had become a national scandal. In "Must 1,532 Women Die?" (July 1928), *Chatelaine* traced the cause to a shocking lack of prenatal care, especially in rural districts. For urban mothers-to-be, a vital decision was whether to have their babies at home or in the hospital, and increasingly they were opting for hospitals. "Making Ready for the New Arrival" (November 1928) instructed women on both choices, including the sterilization of rags and the cooking of newspapers for home births. As a proponent of the back-to-nature movement, a noted British doctor also warned flappers that the binders used to flatten their chests were inimical to breast-feeding.

In "Mail-Order Babies" (April 1932), a male social worker told poignant stories of Depression mothers forced by poverty to give up their children for adoption. During World War II, Canadian families also opened their homes to refugee children from Europe ("The Little Visitors," January 1941). Then, after the war, young couples were ordered to produce babies of their own to offset Canada's shrinking birth rate ("Don't Delay Parenthood," May 1946). That they did so is evidenced by our baby boom—greater than in any other Western society.

Throughout the fifties, childless couples began turning to fertility clinics—first step on the road to sophisticated reproductive technologies, eventually including fertility drugs and test-tube babies. This, along with a rise in illegitimacy during the sexual revolution of the sixties, caused Canadian authorities to worry about a glut of unwanted children. Reversing traditional wisdom, they began to ask: "Should Unwed Mothers Keep Their Babies?" (March 1966). Increasingly, they did. That, plus the pill and legalized abortion, produced the opposite effect: a dearth of adoptable children.

With more seventies women working outside the home, hands-on parenting acquired a new wave of enthusiastic recruits: fathers ("Letter to a Pregnant Father," December 1972). That was the bright side of male engagement; the dark side began to surface a decade later, as described in such articles as "Portrait of an Incestuous Father" (April 1985).

During the nineties, the courts were being called upon to unravel the legal and emotional toll of "brave-new-world" scientific and life-style choices affecting children: custody battles, biological versus adoptive rights, surrogate rights. In February 1993, a Canadian judge was asked the same question put to King Solomon a couple of millennia earlier, but now grown much harder to answer: "Whose Baby Is It Anyway?" As kids were quick to understand, when everybody is in charge, nobody is. More began demanding the right to decide their own futures, and increasingly the courts took their side against their parents ("Should Kids Take Parents to Court?" November 1993). In fact, as the nineties scrolled to a close, it began to look as if children's rights might prove to be one of its defining themes.

# Must 1,532 Mothers Die?

## We lose four mothers every day in the year

By Bertha E. Hall

**JULY 1928**

THE FINDINGS OF THE REPORT recently issued by the Division of Child Hygiene of the Federal Department of Health tell the story in detail of maternal deaths for the period beginning Dominion Day, 1925, to Dominion Day, 1926. That this twelvemonth should have witnessed the death of 1,532 Canadian mothers between the ages of fifteen and forty-eight—an increase by several hundred over the figures of six years ago—with an average of thirty-one years, is truly an appalling situation and one which justly raises the question, "Were these deaths preventable, and if so, what can be done about it?"

When it is also reported that, owing to the deaths of these mothers, 5,073 children were left motherless, we realize more completely the peculiarly tragic nature of deaths due to maternal causes. In this connection, it is well to note the close relationship existing between maternal and infant mortality. According to statistics given by the United States Children's Bureau of the children whose mothers die within a year after their birth, the infant mortality is 450 per 1,000 living births. If the mother dies within a month after the birth, infant mortality is 607 per 1,000. If we are to further reduce our infant mortality rate, we must give the mother better care—"We must make Canada safe for the mother and she will make Canada safe for the baby."

According to the Dominion Bureau of Statistics, Canada stands seventeenth in a list of countries reporting maternal mortality rates. In 1925, the rate for Canada was 5.6 per 1,000 living births while in England and Wales it was 4.5, and in Denmark 2.4. For the year beginning July 1st, 1925, to July 1st, 1926, Canada's rate was 6.4, or a loss of four mothers every day during the year. Had these mothers lived in Denmark instead of Canada, a thousand of them would not have died!

Why should Canada's rate be so high in comparison to other countries? Letters of advice accompanying the questionnaire sent out to the medical profession in making the study of the causes of these maternal deaths repeatedly state: "Maternal life is held in too light esteem!"

It is a significant fact that of the 1,532 mothers who lost their lives in childbirth, 1,302 did not receive prenatal care. "Prenatal care was given in 230 cases only, about fifteen per cent. In forty instances, the physician reports that the prenatal care did not avail because the mother did not follow instructions, or because she came to see the doctor only once or twice at the beginning of pregnancy and did not return."

The Victorian Order of Nurses in its visiting nursing service aims each year to increase the number of prenatal visits made to maternity patients. Last year (1927), 37,493 visits were paid to 13,199 prenatal patients, an average of 2.8 visits per patient. This small average is due mainly to the fact that many patients report their condition very late in pregnancy.

Of the 13,607 mothers to whom Victorian Order Nurses gave obstetrical care under medical supervision last year, only 34 mothers died from causes incidental to childbirth. This is a rate of 2.5 per 1,000 living births. Observation of these mothers was maintained in the greater number of cases for a period of one month only, after the baby's birth.

Undoubtedly, it is at the time of delivery or soon after, that most of the fatalities occur. It is a rather significant fact that in 1925 the Red Cross outpost hospitals cared for 427 maternity patients and did not lose a single case, while 75 per cent. of the mothers who died between July 1st, 1925, and July 1st, 1926, did not receive hospital care at the time of delivery.

∞

But what of the problem in Canada's Hinterland? The following quotation is descriptive of sections of our rural areas in Western Canada:

"There is no doctor living in this whole area. The nearest doctors available in cases of great need, live in the towns along the lines of railway to the south and west, a distance of thirty to seventy miles. The same applies to hospital provision. With an estimated population within the four municipal areas of 4,500, it is easy to imagine the amount of distress and suffering that exists through lack of medical attention. Owing to the costs of obtaining medical advice, in most cases running from $30 to $70 a visit, it is only in extreme cases that medical aid is brought in, and when these occur in the winter months, the suffering is increased tenfold. During the last five years there have been over 800 births in these four municipal areas, and out of these only 60, or approximately seven per cent. had medical attention. In many of our little cemeteries there is a mound that covers the remains of some pioneer mother who has paid a penalty that would have been avoided had medical aid been obtainable."

∽

Roughly, it is stated that the number of mothers who receive no medical care at childbirth varies from 10 per cent. to 50 per cent. throughout the provinces of Canada. But there is still another way in which we may help to save mothers' lives. It must be remembered that the mother is the centre of a home and we must help her solve the home problems which stand in the way of her receiving adequate care. Of the mothers who lost their lives in the 59th year of Confederation, predisposing causes are given as follows:

| | |
|---|---|
| Exhausted with care of children and home | |
| 67 | |
| Exhausted for want of sleep and rest | |
| 68 | |
| Poverty | |
| 27 | |

These figures tell a pathetic story of overworked, worn-out mothers, who needed assistance which even the lay person can give. In some of our cities, we are meeting this need with the aid of visiting housekeepers, who are competent to take charge of the home and family during the mother's illness. A further extension of this type of service is greatly needed to remove this dark blot from our national health record.

# Making Ready for the New Arrival

*There are many important preparations for the expectant mother to make*

BY STELLA E. PINES, R.N.

NOVEMBER 1928

THE PURPOSE OF THIS ARTICLE is to help parents to understand their personal responsibility in assisting the efforts of the doctor and nurse in keeping the mother and baby well, and ensuring a safe confinement and convalescence.

An expectant mother's mother can be one of her greatest comforts, provided she has a sensible outlook. On the other hand, grandparents can do a great deal of harm through failing to recognize that "things *are* different" from their young days, and that the so-called "new fangled ideas" which preach "Back to Nature" are the means whereby we have become more humane, and reduced maternal and infantile mortality and morbidity to such an extent.

∽

The mother, by the end of the second month, should be thinking about the necessities for her confinement and baby. Where is our precious baby to first see the light—in hospital or at home? First of all, has the mother had the much talked-of prenatal care, to know whether everything is as it should be? If there is any abnormality at all, the hospital is the proper place.

Inquire as to methods of feeding the baby. Be sure all babies go out naturally fed and not on the bottle. "Satisfied maternity is the happiest condition of woman," and it is only the mother who is a whole mother by giving her baby his birthright in natural feeding, who can experience satisfied maternity.

Inquire whether the babies get a night feed between ten p.m. and six a.m. so that the habit of turning day into night is not established. See that the babies do not receive foreign food as routine in the first few days. If nature meant babies to have more food she would have provided for them.

Place pads and bag to hold them in clean piece of cotton (prepared as above) in oven, and bake for one hour. Pin up in rag on which they were baked, or clean sheet, and lay away in clean box or drawer. Be careful that the pads do not burn.

It is also wise to put all newspapers or brown paper to be used in the oven for several days in succession, making sure they do not burn.

Newspapers are safe when clean. Such organizations as The Victorian Order of Nurses and other maternity services have proved their safety. When saving them to use, *keep them away from dust.* These may seem unimportant as they do not cost much and are going to be burned or thrown away, but they can do a great deal of damage and cost a great deal of money if not properly attended to. Consider this case, for instance.

A woman had engaged a nurse for her second confinement, but as the doctor and nurse were notified too late, the baby was born before either arrived. There had been no examination of the mother before or after the birth, and yet the woman developed puerperal infection. The doctor or nurse could not account for it in any way, but on enquiry it was found that the pads prepared by the patient had been made of "old cotton" which had been washed but not boiled by the patient in anticipation of her confinement. This old cotton had previously been used for dressing a septic wound on the husband's arm and the patient died of blood poisoning on the sixth day.

Another case recorded in Public Health in 1893, is that one man lost three wives from puerperal fever, and when the last case was investigated it was found that all three had been confined in the same bed which had not been disinfected in any way.

We will next think of the binder. In most countries it has been recognized that the old-fashioned binder for the mother is unnecessary except in special cases which are recognized by the doctor. Grandmothers held the idea that the binder helped the figure to regain its normal proportions. This is not so, as the binder allows the abdominal

*The mother, by the end of the second month, should be thinking about the necessities for her confinement and baby.*

There are cases, of course, where babies need this, but it is the exception, not the rule.

Again, in hospital, babies can be trained to sleep all night. Nearly all babies cry for the first five or six nights. It does them no harm unless in excess. In fact, the exercise helps to establish good lung capacity, but it is one which is very disagreeable to a busy household and often leads to a night feed being established, and the mother's rest broken.

If you are going to hospital, have your grip packed and ready at least six weeks before the expected time. Have ready: Six nightgowns, twelve handkerchiefs, tooth brush, brush and comb, wrapper, bedroom slippers, little piece of ribbon or tape if you have long hair, bed jacket, baby's clothes and shawl, if these are requested.

If the baby is to be born at home we need much more preparation. No good business man or woman goes into business without knowing something about it, and he is dealing with inanimate things. How much more important is it to know about that most precious and complicated of all possessions, the human baby.

The mother is often instructed to maintain a supply of rags euphoniously termed "old linen." Out of *clean* rags, perineal pads and bed pads are to be made. They must be properly boiled in soap muscles to rest, and we know that muscles not exercised become flabby and soft. Again, a badly adjusted binder does more harm than good, and it is only experienced hands that know its value for special cases.

What about baby's "binder"? It is really only a bandage to keep the dressing in place until the stump of the navel cord separates in a few days. This dressing is sterile and is on an open wound, so that it cannot be of flannel, as so often supposed. Would any doctor or nurse put a bandage which could not be boiled, on a wound? Decidedly no! The so-called binder should be of cotton, soft and adjustable, and as its use is only temporary, it needs changing often.

Often mothers will supply one of the heavy brassieres which have come into general vogue of late among girls and women. Sir Truby King says: "This has for its avowed object the flattening of the bust . . . There could be no more injurious device, from the point of view of maternity, future or actual. Pressure for two-thirds of the twenty-four hours flattens nipples and inverts them."

∾

Telephone the doctor and nurse as soon as pains begin.

Before you telephone your doctor, however, put on a few saucepans and a kettle of water. You will need cold boiled water as well as hot boiled water. Keep covered. Have floor of room dusted with damp mop; wash tables and cover. Choose a room that is bright and sunny, clean and simply furnished with no hangings or upholstered furniture, and preferably near a bathroom.

Co-operation of doctor, nurse and mother is pointed out very well in the following way by Sir Truby King:

"At and about the time of childbirth doctor and nurse are generally all in all. After a few weeks the mother is generally in sole charge and everything depends on her. Is she ignorant or has she been well prepared in body, mind and habits to do the best for her child? If not, is she at the eleventh hour sensible enough to seek sound, reliable guidance and advice from a competent doctor or nurse and to act on the advice offered?"

Does this not speak volumes?

# Mail-Order Babies

*An unforgettable picture of what it means for mothers to leave their babies—and for the babies to find new homes*

By L. E. Lowman

APRIL
1932

"MY HUSBAND AND I HAVE been married for several years but we have no children of our own. We would like to adopt a little girl about a year or eighteen months old. Will you please pick us one out with fair curly hair and blue eyes?"

The above is a very fair sample of scores of letters received every day by social service agencies dealing with children all over Canada. The peculiar thing is that while the great majority of people specify fair hair and blue eyes in their prospective children, they will readily and willingly take children of dark hair and brown eyes.

The adoption of children is a pleasing business to those engaged in it. It is a salvage business almost entirely, because most of the goods in the shape of little humans have been more or less damaged by the moral and economic fire and smoke of poverty, immorality and crime from which they were rescued. They have to be polished up a bit before they are ready to be shipped out to fill the orders received for them. The salvage firms, consisting of such groups as Children's Aid Societies and Infants' Homes, are reputable firms, and take pride in delivering goods in as near a perfect shape as possible. Not always able to fill the exact orders received they will make substitution at times, with the consent of the customer, and often the order for a little girl is filled by the dispatch of a little boy who is sent "on approval." But generally the goods remain sold and very few come back for re-sale. Some of the salvaged goods are not damaged at all. They were handed out of the window before the fire reached them, by the owners, who, having themselves been badly burned, desired that these very precious bundles of merchandise might escape a similar fate.

These particular goods mostly take the shape of

babies born of unmarried mothers. They are given up voluntarily—although that isn't the right word—by girls who walk into your office very bravely but without the baby, and tell you of the bitter struggle they have made trying to get along and keep the baby properly. But because of unemployment, sickness, or in most cases the failure of the child's father to help, they have to give up. They will fix a day on which they will bring the baby to you, leaving themselves a few days grace, and when that time comes they invariably keep the appointment, sign the necessary documents, and with one long last kiss for the child, they go out to face the world again with streaming eyes and an empty heart. They have sinned but their punishment is great.

Then there are the deserted wives who have done no wrong except to marry worthless men. Caught in a home rapidly being destroyed by the flames of poverty and want, they fight the fire until they are physically and mentally exhausted, and, on the point of collapse, they, too, hand their most precious belongings, their children, to the ready arms stretched out to receive them.

In my early days as a social worker, I was sent on a case of a destitute, deserted wife with children. I made a very painstaking investigation into the circumstances and found that the young couple—she was only twenty-eight—had lived happily together for six years. Then he had gone overseas to take his part in the war and came through without a scratch. But on his return he was "never the same," as his wife put it. He seemed strange in his ways and would sit at times in a moody silence for a couple of hours, and then suddenly become his normal self, play with his two little children, and be the perfect husband.

One day he got up and had his breakfast. He kissed his wife and children good-by, went to his work and was never seen again. The municipality concerned was very good. It cared for these unfortunates for some time. It paid for hospital and confinement expenses, and supplied food for a period after the baby was born, but eventually decided that it could do no more. I interviewed members of parliament, and worried the life out of Cabinet ministers. I saw the soldiers' pensions board and

worked my head off in an effort to keep these children with the mother, but was always met with the statement that if deserted wives were assisted, there would be hundreds of husbands deserting, knowing that their families would be taken care of. So this poor mother gave her children up for adoption, and as I saw her off at the station to go to a position secured for her, I vowed that never again would I have anything to do with taking children away from a deserted wife. The picture of her white drawn face, and the hopeless look in her eyes, remains with me to this day. It may work out all right according to our man-made economic laws but I am quite sure that God doesn't like it.

Letters like the one that commenced this article are not written in a hurry. They are the result of weeks, and often months, of careful deliberation between husband and wife. The idea of adopting a baby was probably very casually broached one day by one or the other. Allowed to sink in for awhile, it is again spoken of, this time with a casual mention of Mrs. Jones who has had great success with a baby she took. It's a delicate subject. The husband doesn't want to give his wife the idea that he is disappointed because he hasn't any children of his own. The wife, with every normal woman's longing for a child to mother, doesn't like to broach the subject. But after a time, in a manner very hard to explain, but perfectly well known to married people, they get around to it. The cost of a crib and other nursery furniture is examined. The medical expenses in connection with measles and whooping cough are thought of. It's a serious business with these people, as it should be, although seemingly ridiculous to those who have had several children by the natural way.

The matter of sex is soon disposed of. The man wants a little girl almost invariably. The woman, with visions of curly hair and the cute little dresses she can make, is quite satisfied. So, the letter of application goes forth, and if the postman only knew what a precious missive he was carrying, and what painstaking thought has gone into it, he would treat all other mail as second-class matter in comparison.

Then comes a period of anxious waiting, until one day a salesman or saleslady turns up to make discreet enquiries about the moral character of the applicants and their financial ability to support a child. This satisfactorily disposed of, there follows another period of waiting.

Then comes the day of all days. Delivery is made and hubby is phoned to come home from the office at once. The plain and serviceable clothes the little girl or boy wore are immediately discarded, to be used for playtimes later on. The family doctor is called in, who, with a very serious face but laughter in his heart, pronounces the child quite fit. He is consulted very seriously about feeding, about sleeping, about how far the window should be open at night, about a score of things, all of which he takes in good part, and he goes away, knowing that for weeks to come his life is going to be made a misery over this particular child. No married couple with their first-born are more anxious over these things than these parents by choice with their first child.

And that night, when baby has been put to sleep, husband and wife will tiptoe into the bedroom and watch the quiet little stranger. A hand will go out and be met by another hand, and a firm clasp, more expressive than any words, will signify the intention of this couple to do their part toward giving one little waif at least a good chance to grow up with the love and care that every child should have.

Thank God for these people who number many thousands. They are willing to give up their bridge parties, shows and other social activities they have been used to. And they don't have to wait until they get to heaven for their reward: It comes to them gradually, and more and more all the time in the returned love and respect of the child they took to their hearts.

❧

Many children grow up to manhood or womanhood and never know that the people they call mother and father are not really their own relatives. Unfortunately there is still, even in this enlightened age, a stigma attaching to adopted children. One woman, I remember, announced to her friends that she was going to take a trip to Europe. She did and was gone some months. When she returned it was with a little baby supposedly born to her in England. The funny thing is that no baby was on the boat with them. It was picked up at a certain city in Canada by previous arrangement.

Another woman proudly told her friends that she was expecting to become a mother. She was, but not in the ordinary way. She lived in retirement for a few months and then went to the local hospital. Two weeks later she came out with a new-born baby boy.

❧

Damaged goods in the shape of crippled and sickly children also find good homes through this mail-order business. Some people are so made that they are not satisfied with taking ordinary normal children. They want something out of the ordinary. I have seen them take poor half-starved little mites, suffering badly from rickets, and looking as though they couldn't possibly live. They will spend hundreds of dollars on medical and surgical treatment for these unfortunate children, and, very often, go without things they have been used to in order to do it. And a few years later when they show you the result of their care, in the form of a healthy and often physically perfect child, in place of the bag of bones they took, you know from the pride that shines in their faces that they, too, are getting their reward.

Mentally defective children are about the only children who remain on the shelf and in whose department no business is done. They are booked to go to institutions as soon as there are enough institutions—if ever there are. They are mentally defective but able to propagate their kind, and so from year to year they grow up, and in wedlock or otherwise—generally otherwise—more little idiots are born, until today every institution of that kind in Canada is full to overflowing, and there is a waiting list that would fill three times the number. One of these days we shall see that we are cruel in letting this thing go on. And it is cruelty to allow thousands of little children to be born and grow up in a mental darkness for which there is no cure or hope. These are spoiled goods in this adoption business and the only sensible thing to do is to stop the manufacture. It is being done now in the Province of Alberta by the sterilization of mental defectives. It will be just as effective in the other provinces.

*Many children grow up to manhood or womanhood and never know that the people they call mother and father are not really their own relatives*

So this great business of adoption of children goes on from day to day, paying large dividends in the form of happy children saved from destruction and growing up to be a credit to themselves and their country.

# "The Little Visitors"

By Mary Agnes Pease

JANUARY 1941

THE INFLUX OF STURDY British boys and girls to this Dominion to stay with temporary foster-parents "for the duration" has called forth the sympathy of the Canadian people, and the desire to do everything possible for the well-being and happiness of these small and valiant visitors.

The privilege of taking care of over five hundred of these children in the few weeks' interim between their arrival and their placement in foster-homes was the happy experience of the members of the Imperial Order Daughters of the Empire in Toronto.

The Order's first association with the children began one morning when we had charge of the tables at breakfast in the beautiful dining hall of Hart House. It was an unusual sight to see hundreds of children of both sexes come trooping into this very exclusive hall with its high vaulted ceiling and panelled walls.

At the table at which I had the job of supervisor, the first lot were all boys. At my right was a little chap of about eight with tight, fair curls, and merry blue eyes. "I'm no wearin' ma kilt today," he offered by way of a conversational gambit. "I wear it only when the day's sunny." Then, after regarding me critically, he added: "Maybe you could tell though that I was Scottish?"

Another small boy at my table refused to be separated from one of the local schoolmasters who had brought the group to breakfast. In fact, the boy held tightly by one hand to the man's coat, and tried to manage his table implements with the other hand, until he was assured that "the nice, kind man who looks like Daddy," would have breakfast with him. Among the children

at the "second sitting" was a little girl, fair and ethereal-looking, but whose appetite belied this beatitude, as she ate everything put before her with neatness and dispatch, and asked for more. "But," I said, "you've already had fruit, porridge, an egg, bread and honey and milk." "I'd like another egg," she repeated, looking soulfully at me. She got it!

"My Mummy will be having lunch now," another little girl informed me. "I've just counted the hours difference in time." Tears were in her eyes as she added: "Mummy will be sad without me."

Few of these children belong to what is usually referred to as the "privileged class." For the most part they come from the middle classes, and a number of them from workingmen's homes.

These young guests were delighted with Canadian food, especially ice cream, which one child referred to as "dream food." Even dishes that they did not like at home, they accepted when told that these were "produced in Canada," but they drew the line at spaghetti which they dubbed "Mussolini's dish."

Some tall tales of the children are told by those who were in charge of the University guest houses. For example, Gordon, a Scottish lad, was found to be crying and, when interrogated, said that he wanted his pal. "But," he was told, "there's a boy in the room with you." "He's no ma pal, he's English," said Gordon heatedly. "I'm a Scotsman, and I'll no sleep wi' an Englishman. I prefer to sleep alone."

A boy from Glasgow was hunting about for his sporran before going for a walk, and was told by the person in charge to come along and not bother about it. "Oh, but I must find it. I dinna want to be taken for a lassie."

Another Scottish boy said: "I'm fair tired of that song, 'There'll Always Be an England.' What about Scotland? She's no likely to fa' any more than England!"

Insistence on the use of

a toothbrush irked one of the English lads, and in answer to the usual query as to whether he had used it, said: "It's absolutely unnecessary, sir."

These children are all now in their wartime homes, and are reported as well and happy. The intensification of submarine warfare and of stormy winter weather has hampered the exodus of further large numbers of young guests to this country for some time to come. When conditions of travel improve, Canadians hope that the thousands expected will arrive to be their guests for an indefinite period.

# A Note to Brides: Don't Delay Parenthood

BY RUTH MACLACHLAN FRANKS, M.D.
PSYCHIATRIST

**MAY 1946**

IT IS RATHER AMAZING, WHEN one stops to consider it, how many young couples are intent on the acquisition of a house, a garden, a car, furniture and other inanimate objects, which they plan for and discuss freely, yet when it comes to their greatest opportunity of investment in happiness for the future—a baby—the matter is quickly dismissed. It is all very simple: "We can't afford it."

This attitude is playing havoc with Canada's population. It is also storing up marriage disharmony for many of our best young people. Surely our magnificent young brides of today who have grown up during a tragic period will get together with their husbands and help the country out of this dilemma, and help themselves at the same time.

Canada has not been maintaining her population. Three children per married couple should be a minimum goal, but usually they say, "If we could have a boy and a girl, or one child, or none—how happy we would be!" Yet happiness is not an isolated factor. The happiness of the home is dependent on the happiness of the country, and likewise the happiness of the country is dependent on the happiness of the home.

Marjorie and her husband were fine, attractive, intelligent young people in their early twenties. He was earning $1,400 a year in an insurance company but he wanted to be an actuary. It meant study at home in addition to doing a good job during the day. Their parents did not want them to marry until financial security was assured. The families could have helped but they felt that that might make the young people dependent. Finally, they gave their consent provided there would be no children for five years.

It was a beautiful wedding. No expense was spared and finally they were settled in a flat of their own. All went well for three or four months. John was occupied with his study and work, but they celebrated on week ends. The fear of having a family was interfering a little, and sometimes Marjorie was restless when John was busy with his books in the evening. Often she thought it would be fun preparing for a baby. It would keep her busy too. Then she wondered about getting a job, although she was sure John would disapprove. Finally she approached the subject, and John certainly did disapprove! Why could she not be contented with her flat and household tasks? Disharmony, bickering and petty grievances sprang up, but John eventually made the grade and graduated in actuarial science. Just then Marjorie developed flu which ended in pneumonia. Her recovery was slow and it was a long time before she was strong enough to have a baby.

The five years were long since up. John was established, but somehow Marjorie just did not get pregnant. She took vitamins, had her thyroid gland tested, had her Fallopian tubes dilated and finally underwent a curettage—but still no family. Even the grandparents were concerned now. Marjorie was tired all the time and John did not look forward to his return home in the evenings. Eventually she did become pregnant, but she lost her first two babies. She was no longer young and fresh but ever so weary and always so anxious. When their son arrived, he brought great joy and happiness but he remained their only child. In their forties this couple had their boy and all the material things to make them happy, but they lived in constant fear that something would happen to their only child. Everything centred around the boy, interfering with his full enjoyment of life and

*She took vitamins, had her thyroid gland tested, had her Fallopian tubes dilated and finally underwent a curettage—but still no family*

providing a fertile background for a neurotic make-up. These three people were not really happy. Their contribution to each other and to their country was not the full happy one it could have been, and when they realized the situation, which they came to do, it was too late.

I must say once again to the brides of this year or last: You, our youth today—strong, intelligent, fine—are needed for the fathers and mothers of tomorrow, for a great race of happy sturdy Canadian peoples. By taking the first step toward family life, assure your own continued happiness.

# Should Unwed Mothers Keep Their Babies?

*Canada is running short of adoptive homes for its 26,500 annual crop of illegitimate babies*

BY KAY STEEN

**MARCH 1966**

LAST OCTOBER, IN WINDSOR, Ont., a five-pound baby girl was found abandoned in the back seat of a parked car. Doctors said she was less than six hours old when found. After the child was taken to the hospital, a woman called the switchboard and said: "Please take care of my baby." She hung up without identifying herself. Shocking? Before the establishment of child-care agencies, unwanted infants were frequently disposed of in this manner—or by infanticide.

In 1964 in Canada, the most recent year for which we have figures, 26,556 babies were born to unmarried mothers. We can safely assume that practically all of them were not wanted. Roughly seventy percent of the mothers placed their children for adoption.

Are there enough adoptive homes to receive all these children? The answer is not any more. Medical advances in the field of fertility research now enable many formerly childless couples to have children of their own. Babies survive who would once have been doomed.

S. H. Pinkerton, executive director of the Children's Aid Society of Vancouver, calls the situation truly alarming and says that for the first time in years his agency had to place healthy, normal infants in temporary foster homes while adoption homes were sought for them. D. H. Johnson, director of child welfare for the province of Nova Scotia, reports: "From the many enquiries we made we feel that in another year or two the number of infants available for adoption will surpass the adoptive applicants." Where at one time child-welfare agencies had as many as ten applications for each infant, the average ratio now is one and a half applications per child and, says Lloyd S. Richardson, executive director of the Children's Aid Society of Metropolitan Toronto, "The gap is narrowing very quickly."

*There are certain rules to the game, though, and the primary one is not to get caught*

An ancient law in Britain required an unmarried woman who had borne a child to be publicly whipped and turned out to be derided by the people. Nowadays we punish in more subtle ways those who violate the mores of society. What mores? A look at our communications media will convince the gullible that what makes the world go round is "fun"—anything that is fun is acceptable, and sex, of course, is fun. There are certain rules to the game, though, and the primary one is not to get caught. If a girl gets caught, all the fun suddenly ceases, and she is back in a Victorian setting, a "fallen woman."

An Anglican minister in Ontario stated not long ago that over fifty percent of the brides at whose weddings he was asked to officiate were pregnant at the time they got married.

Unmarried mothers come from all walks of life. The records of the Children's Aid Society of Metropolitan Toronto show that eighteen percent of the unmarried mothers in 1964 were high-school and university students; 40 percent were white-collar workers, such as secretaries, 9.2 percent were factory workers, waitresses and domestics. The rest came from a variety of occupational backgrounds, with a sprinkling of professional women.

Joan is one of the young unmarried mothers, under twenty-one, who account for over half of illegitimate births in Canada. She lives in a pleasant

Toronto suburb with her parents (the father is personnel manager for a large company), surrounded by pleasant, middle-income people. Joan is considered a nice, well-brought-up girl by all who know her, seventeen years old and a good student. She had a steady boyfriend for a year, a year older than Joan.

Last February Joan told her mother that she was pregnant. The mother couldn't have been more shocked if Joan had told her she had leprosy. Her first reaction was: "How could you! What will the neighbors say!" There was little solicitude for the mental state of her daughter who had been desperately trying to conceal her pregnancy for four months. Joan's father found the whole situation embarrassing and left it to his wife to handle.

Joan was packed off to an aunt in Ottawa until she could enter one of Canada's thirty-eight shelters for unmarried mothers to await the birth of her baby. She was fortunate. All the shelters have long waiting lists. Joan had a little boy who was placed with a child-welfare agency for adoption as soon as Joan was able to leave the hospital. Joan is back home but has not returned to school as yet. Her boyfriend is no longer in the picture. His parents thought it wise to move to a different part of the city when they found out about his involvement.

"Yes, I know, we shouldn't have," Joan says. "We went too far. I guess you can only neck so long and you are bound to lose control. Birth control? Yes, I have heard of birth control, but we didn't plan this to happen. It's kind of cold-blooded if you use birth control and all that."

Incredible as it may sound, there are parents who turn their daughter out of the home when they learn she is in trouble. These are the girls who flock to the big cities in search of anonymity, straining child-care facilities to bursting point in the urban centres. Of course, a good many unmarried women have been living on their own when they become pregnant. Some have had no family to turn to in their predicament, and others, like Anne, an attractive twenty-year-old secretary in Ottawa, are too proud to. "I would rather die before telling my parents," she says. "The father of the baby worked in my office. He was married, but he told me his wife didn't understand him. I was lonely. When I told him I was pregnant, I thought he might get a

divorce and marry me. Instead he accused me of being a tramp and said he would fight me every inch of the way if I named him as the father."

Anne worked until three weeks before her baby was born, trying to minimize her bulging waistline with tight girdles and suits three sizes larger than her trim size twelve. She had managed to save $150 to tide her over her confinement. She never got a cent from the father and found it too humiliating to ask him for help. "When I first saw Cathy, my baby," she says, "I felt so sorry for the child that I cried all day. I sure hadn't wanted her, but now I found it impossible to part with her. I thought I would go back to work and keep her and have a baby-sitter look after her during the day."

Between September 1964 and March 1965, little Cathy and her mother changed residence three times. "The baby cried at night and the landlady would give me notice," Anne says. "I couldn't afford a self-contained apartment, at around $100 a month; I clear $220. The baby-sitter cost me $10 a week and I was lucky if I could get one for that. Cathy had five different baby-sitters in seven months." When Cathy was eight months old and the fourth landlady was threatening to turn them out, Anne asked the Children's Aid Society to take

her baby as a permanent ward and place her for adoption. In her own words, she had "lost all hope of ever being able to provide a home for Cathy."

∾

As might be expected, Scandinavian countries lead in providing reasonable facilities for mother and child staying together.

In Sweden, approximately ninety-five percent of unmarried mothers keep their babies. (Out-of-wedlock births are about nine percent of total births, a decline from fifteen percent in the 1940s and 1950s. In Canada the 1964 rate was 5.9, up from 3.9 in 1950.) There is little social stigma attached to illegitimacy. Every mother gets a maternity benefit of 900 Swedish kronor ($174) at confinement. A mother who was working is entitled to sickness benefits, in proportion to her annual income, for a maximum of 180 days. If the mother chooses to await her baby in a maternity home, she pays a daily rate of $1.14. The mother usually stays in the maternity home for two to three months. If she is destitute, the daily rate is paid by Social Assistance.

*Both* parents of the child are liable for the child's support. Support by the father is adjusted to his earning capacity. If he fails to pay, his wages may be garnisheed and his property distrained. If the father fails to pay, the maintenance allowance can be paid out of public funds, and the authorities will collect from him. The amount of maintenance varies. It is at present roughly $250 a year. When the mother returns to work, she may place her child in one of Sweden's government-subsidized day nurseries, where fees are adjusted to the mother's income, varying from nothing to $2.85 a day.

In Canada, besides reassessing our near-fatal lack of community aids, we should also take a hard look at our inadequate system of enforcing maintenance payments. One Canadian social worker, who has been dealing with unmarried fathers for twenty years, says: "Unless you can get him to pay a lump sum, which is usually modest enough, you haven't a chance to keep collecting until the child is sixteen."

An 18-month survey in 1963-64 of sixty-eight girls admitted to the Church Home For Girls, a home for unwed mothers in Winnipeg, reveals how lack of parental supervision plays its part. As the locale for intercourse, a car was named by thirty-six

of the girls, their own home by twenty-three, the boys' home by thirty-eight. "It shows a lack of maturity in the girls and boys," the report admits. *"But,"* it asks pointedly, *"are they ready to be left all alone in these situations by parents?"*

# Letter to a Pregnant Father

BY ROBERT FULFORD

Dear Sam:

**DECEMBER 1972**

I CAN ANSWER YOUR LAST question—what was the best part?—without any trouble at all. The best part, undeniably, was the actual moment of birth and maybe two minutes on each side of it. When it happened I was so excited I could hardly stand on my feet. Geraldine was talking continually, mostly about hoping the

*Robert Fulford, here with his wife, Geraldine, and his seven-month-old daughter, Rachel.*

baby would be all right—there had been a lot of forceps work, and Geraldine was half certain the baby would be damaged. The doctor was working confidently, happily, almost exuberantly, and she was talking like a play-by-play sports announcer on TV: "Now the head's out . . . a beautiful head . . . I have a shoulder, the shoulders are out . . . and now, yes, and it's a beautiful baby . . . uh . . . GIRL." Really. It happened just like that.

Standing there behind Geraldine's head, next to the anesthetist, dressed in my doctor's suit with my face masked, I watched the baby emerge in the mirror above the doctor's head. I had my palms pressed on Geraldine's cheeks because I couldn't reach her hands. When the doctor said "GIRL," with a sort of triumph, I gasped "It's Rachel" and sobbed. I felt Geraldine's tears on my hand. We'd chosen names for either a boy or a girl, but both of us had secretly, passionately wanted a girl and now we had her. And in a way I'd only vaguely dreamt possible, we had received her together, we had been a couple at that earthshaking moment when she started to live on this earth.

I watched Rachel wriggling in the nurse's hands, then heard her scream—nobody had to hit her on the bottom to encourage her, she's got a mouth like her mother's. The doctor said "You can touch her now, you can touch your baby." I touched what looked like the safest part, her stomach. I reached out tentatively, not quite sure she was real. Then I looked up at the people around me.

Over their masks their eyes were bright, almost a little wild. The room was charged with energy and purpose. I realized that the atmosphere in this particular delivery room—we had the baby at Women's College Hospital in Toronto—had heightened and intensified the whole experience. The doctors and nurses—particularly the chief obstetrical nurse, a powerful West Indian woman who exuded intelligence and confidence—were clearly as happy as I was. They were high on obstetrics, as if they had taken drugs. As for me, I've never been so exhilarated. If we ever have another baby one of my secret reasons will be knowing I can go through this again.

So if you don't learn anything else from my letter, get this much: *be there when it happens*. During the two deliveries of my previous marriage I did that awful business of pacing up and down the corridors

imagining God knows what, accepting that as the way it had to be. Since the new baby was born I've developed a deep resentment of all doctors, nurses and hospitals who high-handedly ban fathers the delivery rooms and deny them this experience.

Rachel had been in the wrong position to emerge and Dr. R had to use the forceps to twist her around. For this she kept me out of the delivery room, possibly because she felt I couldn't stand it. God knows, even Geraldine was alarmed at the pressure the doctor had to use. She looked, Geraldine said, like a dentist pulling a reluctant tooth. Geraldine had the appalling notion that Dr. R was about to pull the baby's head off. Of course nothing of the kind happened. Rachel was born a perfect baby, without so much as a temporary forceps scar. Dr. R, clearly, was a superb craftsman.

I sat in the waiting room, wearing my gown and hat and special paper shoes, while all this went on. It crossed my mind, once or twice, that despite all I'd said I wasn't *desperately* anxious to get into the delivery room. But then Dr. R—who had said she *might* let me into the delivery room for the end—finally sent for me. My wife said "Hello, darling," I reached over to her, the doctor said "Look in the mirror, Mr. Fulford," I looked up and fifteen minutes later it was all over.

*Yours,* Bob.

# Portrait of an Incestuous Father

### *This is a true story—only the names and the father's occupation have been changed*

BY RONA MAYNARD

KEITH ALEXANDER OFTEN embraced his 10-year-old stepdaughter, Jennifer. Insecure and eager for affection, she loved to visit his basement darkroom. There they would chat, hip to hip, about everything from schoolyard tiffs to dinosaur bones.

On weekday mornings, they shared a private ritual before Jennifer dressed for school. While her harried mother dashed to an office job, Jennifer would carry a steaming mug of coffee to her stepfather's print-strewn worktable. The 30-year-old freelance photographer, still wearing his bathrobe, always asked the girl which shots she liked best. And he always welcomed his favorite critic with a kiss.

One morning in 1978—no one recalls quite when—Alexander overstepped an invisible boundary. Aware that his wife had just left for work, he drew his stepdaughter close and fondled her thighs and chest through the thin cloth of her nightgown. Jennifer's frightened silence did not daunt the man she had depended upon since babyhood. In mornings to come, Alexander would molest her again and again. "Love played no part in what I did to Jenny," he recalls. "I was simply exercising dominance over her. And I always knew it was wrong."

∾

Such scenes unfold in nearly every neighborhood. One in four girls and one in 10 boys are sexually molested by the age of 19. As few as 20 percent of these youngsters fall prey to the grizzled park-bench stranger parents warn them against. The remainder are abused by an adult they know—a baby sitter, teacher, relative or family friend. Their molester is a man in 90 percent of cases. In roughly half, he's the man they know best of all: their natural or substitute father.

Stepfathers pose special risks. A 1982 study by Diana Russell, a California sociologist, found these men six times more likely than biological fathers to molest their daughters. And stepparent abuse proved much more likely to include the rare extreme of intercourse.

Some of these stepdads may be pedophiles who marry the mothers to prey on their daughters. Others may take false comfort in the absence of blood ties, as if their advances aren't "real" incest. But researchers increasingly agree that covert fondling by a stepfather poses the same psychological threats as abuse by a natural parent—depression, promiscuity and suicide attempts, to mention a few. What counts is not a broken incest taboo. It is broken trust—the price of misused parental power.

Incestuous fathers know they are wrong. But they usually continue the abuse until the youngster protests, leaves home or suffers a telltale accident (pregnancy, injury, venereal disease). Sadly, most will never be known to police or children's aid societies, even though rising public awareness has recently doubled or even tripled exposure rates in many Canadian communities.

Once reported, few fathers are brought to justice. Their crime leaves no witnesses and little evidence. What's more, parental authority lends credence to their heated denials of abuse. A 1982 Toronto study prepared for the Metropolitan Chairman's Special Committee on Child Abuse suggests that charges are laid in 45 percent of all sexual offences against children—but in only 33 percent of incest cases. The man who evades the law may well harm other children. In a recent study of incest offenders at New York State Psychiatric Institute, Dr. Gene Abel found that 44 percent of subjects admitted to molesting youngsters outside their families.

∾

Keith Alexander, now 36, is a soft-voiced family man who would rather go fishing with his kids than drinking with cronies. His spirited brood includes a 20-year-old stepson, 16-year-old stepdaughter and natural sons ages 13 and 9—not to mention two dogs, a cat and a parrot. Last summer, he celebrated his 15th anniversary with his common-law wife, Christine, 39, whom he calls "an absolute gem."

Alexander believes in old-fashioned values learned on his parents' Ontario farm: hard work, orderly homes and a man's duty to support his wife and children. His past sounds as wholesome as fresh-picked apples. Not so. Like approximately 80 percent of all child molesters, Alexander was himself a victim of childhood abuse.

The oldest child of staunch Roman Catholics, Alexander grew up facing stern punishments and high expectations. "There was never any play time," he recalls. "By the time I was 6, I was spending the best part of a summer weekend weeding the garden." Keith's beloved but emotionally distant father spent most of his time working in the barn, and the youngster sought every opportunity to join him there. "I'd do anything to be with Dad." His mother, domineering and status-conscious, actively obstructed Keith's desires. He recalls running to the barn with a 5-year-old's passionate eagerness, only to be spanked by his mother for forgetting his socks.

The two parents bickered constantly. Worse, they showed no physical affection toward each other or their five children. Keith was 5 when he found another source for the cuddling he lacked: older female cousins who began to fondle him. "I didn't think of what they did as abuse," he says. "To me, it seemed normal." The boy became an abuser at the age of 13, when he molested his 8-year-old sister.

This time, he sensed that he mustn't be caught. But when his usually punitive mother once found them together, her reaction was curiously offhand: "You shouldn't play like that. The more you do it, the more you'll like it, and then you won't be able to stop." Indeed, Keith didn't stop for 14 years, until his sister became pregnant and had an abortion.

Alexander had also molested a second sister and one of his brothers by the time he met his common-law wife, Christine. He met her through a casual buddy—her first husband, Tom. When Tom was arrested and subsequently jailed for theft, Alexander stopped by to comfort the anxious young woman and help out with the kids (Christine's son, Michael, was 5, and Jennifer less than 2). He never left; and Tom did not write, phone or visit his children for the next eight years. At 20, Alexander had acquired a ready-made family.

Then 23, Christine had been sexually victimized in the foster home where she had lived between the ages of 5 and 16. But she didn't tell Alexander until he was already molesting her own daughter. Neither partner knew of the eerily acute emotional radar that joins exploiters and exploited. In Toronto, the Special Committee on Child Abuse reports that between 50 and 80 percent of mothers it counsels disclose memories of childhood abuse.

How did history come to repeat itself?

Abusive fathers are often described as rigid patriarchs—"without question, the heads of their households." So says Dr. Judith Herman, a Harvard psychiatrist, in an influential 1981 study tracing incest to sexual politics. But the flip side of macho dominance is the profound insecurity noted by other researchers. Certainly, Alexander showed both traits.

The fledgling father brought his parents' values to Christine's home. But Alexander couldn't become the patriarch his father had been. Because all of the children are hers while only two are biologically his, she had an edge in their 15-year power struggle. Observes Alexander: "I've never really felt I belonged in this family."

Equally painful, money problems dogged the household from the start. Their house, he says, was "the shabbiest on the street." Finally, after 10 years as a homemaker, Christine announced one Friday evening that she would be starting an office job the following Monday. "I said nothing and I did nothing," Alexander remembers, "but inside, I was angry and hostile. I felt like a total failure."

The incident highlights one of the family's greatest problems: pent-up emotion. Incest tends to spare open supportive families. "We never knew what would come of disclosing our feelings, so we tended to hide them out of fear." Physical warmth was also in short supply. The undemonstrative Christine shows her love by keeping the family properly fed and dressed.

Obsessed with paying the bills, Alexander neglected the family's emotional needs—especially Christine's. "Sex was still there," he remembers, "but I wouldn't call it making love. She never seemed interested, and that hurt." He sought refuge in fleeting affairs that gave him not only affection but a long-sought feeling of power.

Since every incestuous father fears detection, his crime requires an absent mother. The absence is sometimes emotional—illness, alcoholism or sheer browbeaten helplessness in the face of old-fashioned male authority. In Alexander's case, it was physical—Christine's job.

Responsible Jennifer quickly took over many of her mother's former duties. "When I came home," Alexander remembers, "she was at the door with a kiss, where I wanted Christine to be."

Incestuous fathers often silence their daughters with a stern, "Don't tell your mother." Alexander

*Jennifer missed her stepfather and blamed herself for sending him away. Desperate to restore the family peace, she recanted her story. The molester got a reprieve, and his victim was in disgrace for her "lies"*

needed no warnings. "An adult male dominance is what allowed me to get close to her without being rebuffed, and that same power said, 'Keep our secret.'"

In the spring of 1980, after two years of fondling, Jennifer confided her distress to a family friend, who promptly told Christine. Alexander came home to find his belongings on the porch and his normally placid wife in a frenzy of pained indignation. Her parting words: "Get some help for your sex drive!"

Alexander heatedly denied Jennifer's story. Although he did consult a psychiatrist, he dodged the real issue ("Sure, I hold my daughter. Doesn't every man?"). When the questions grew more probing, he ended therapy. Christine vacillated between conflicting loyalties to her daughter and her husband. Michael resented his sister for stirring up trouble.

Jennifer missed her stepfather and blamed herself for sending him away. Desperate to restore the family peace, she recanted her story. The molester got a reprieve, and his victim was in disgrace for her "lies." Alexander returned just two months after the disclosure.

Four months passed before Alexander dared approach Jennifer. Then, his demands escalated. "She was growing up fast," he says, "wearing her mother's clothes and working in the kitchen." One autumn weekday, when Jennifer stayed home with a cold, the two had sexual intercourse on the couch outside Alexander's darkroom. He was 33 and his stepdaughter 13. "I told her I loved her, that I couldn't help my compulsion. Some excuse!"

Love was the last thing on Jennifer's mind. "During the act, she cleaned her nails. That's how ambivalent she felt. She seemed to be thinking, 'I want my dad's attention and affection, *but not like this.*'"

Alexander never molested Jennifer again. Fearful of pregnancy and mindful of his close call in the spring, he vowed the abuse must stop. But it clearly would not while he remained at home. Early in 1982, he packed his bags and called the family doctor, who referred him to a psychiatrist. Then came the real challenge: explaining his departure to Christine.

Faced with the certainty of incest, many wives end their marriages. Some women confront not only their daughters' lacerating pain but their husbands' lies and stratagems.

Christine was no exception but she also took heart from her husband's obvious remorse. She would share in his therapy, along with the children. And on a new incest-free basis, she would eventually welcome him home. "That really moved me," recalls Alexander, who still marvels at his wife's generous spirit. "But I knew that if Christine was big enough to have me back, I'd have to earn her trust."

Men like Alexander cannot be cured. Increasingly, authorities compare their behavior to an alcoholic's drinking—both require lifelong vigilance. With a full course of expert therapy of up to two years, as many as 90 percent of child molesters can be helped. But without a court order enforcing treatment, 99 percent drop out.

Like all incestuous fathers, Alexander began by deflecting some of his own guilt onto Jennifer ("It shouldn't have happened, but she was running around in her nightgown"). He had to confront his subtle manipulation of a girl too young to give informed consent.

Like many young incest victims, Jennifer became sexually active soon after her loss of virginity. "Boyfriends come and go," Alexander says, "and I blame myself for Jenny's feeling that she has to prove herself sexually." Last winter, more than two years after the abuse finally ended, she had an abortion.

In the psychiatrist's office, Alexander told Jennifer that he alone was responsible for the abuse. The apology proved critical to the teenager's well-being. For the first time, Jennifer knew that neither her own "provocativeness" nor her mother's "neglect" had victimized her.

After an absence of nearly 18 months, Alexander came home last June to the same familiar problems: a hunger for power, a longing for tenderness and the frequent presence of Jennifer. Asked to describe her, he is pensive. "She's warm, considerate, beautiful—her spirit, not just her looks. She has goals too; she wants to work with animals someday. I think she trusts me, because she comes up and hugs me more than her mother does. If I pull away, she'll feel rejected. There's a delicate balance, because I'll probably always desire her. The first time I saw Jenny with a boy her own age, it really hurt."

Will the family survive? No one is sure. Alexander knows that unity depends on his own behavior. He is combating child sex abuse as a volunteer resource person to the Special Committee. "I tell other guys, accept your problem and deal with it. Give your wife and daughter a new life . . . with or without you."

# Whose Baby Is It, Anyway?

*Teenager Maureen Steenhill gave up her baby for adoption. Then, the estranged young father claimed custody. Whose rights should prevail—and what about the rights of baby Alexander?*

By Don Gillmor

**FEBRUARY 1993** THREE-MONTH-OLD Alexander, the odd prize in an expensive and bitter feud, squeals happily as he reclines in his Montreal Canadiens sleeper on the dining-room table. Surrounding him is the most recent version of his family: his student mother, Maureen Steenhill, 19, and maternal grandparents, Cathy and Claude Paquet, respectively a homemaker and a schoolteacher.

Before he was six weeks old, the child had been claimed by three separate households. Call him a living wriggling sign of the times: what with single-parenting, open adoptions, donor inseminations and surrogate motherhood, the definition of a parent is constantly being reevaluated as we move away from traditional ideas of family. The nuclear family still exists, but more and more as a reference, a legal template of what nature intended. The case of baby Alexander offers one more disturbing variation.

∾

The story began in the spring of 1991, when Maureen and Peter, both first-year students at nearby Champlain Regional College, dated briefly.

"I didn't really like Peter," Maureen says. "We didn't, like, hit it off." She is bright-faced, headed for university, hoping for a career in commercial design. She and Peter had sex once. Neither of them had considered using a contraceptive. And by the time Maureen found out she was pregnant, she and Peter had drifted apart. Maureen opted initially for an abortion, a decision Peter supported. He said he'd go to the clinic with her; she said, don't bother. "We hardly ever spoke to each other at school."

Maureen became increasingly uncomfortable with the idea of abortion and decided against it. She would have the child and put it up for adoption. She told Peter of this decision, and again, he endorsed it and offered support.

All the same, in October '91, a couple of months before the baby was due, Peter met with Maureen's mother, at her request, to discuss the situation. Cathy Paquet felt Peter should be more involved in the decision-making. "I wish I could hang onto the baby myself," he said vaguely but also agreed that adoption was the most logical answer.

Alexander Richard Benjamin Steenhill was born on December 20, 1991, in the Riverside Hospital of Ottawa. Maureen had gone to Ottawa to give birth in order to take advantage of Ontario's adoption laws, which allow the natural parents to choose the adoptive parents. In the Quebec system, the state makes all the decisions. She had found a suitable couple, Jim and Susan Johnson, through a mutual friend at Greenfield Park Baptist. In their late 30s, the Johnsons had been waiting eight years to adopt. They lived outside Toronto, where they were both in the grocery business, and met with Maureen in Ottawa in November. They had agreed that this would be an open adoption, allowing the biological parents to play a role in the child's life too. They tried to meet Peter as well, but he said he was too busy. The baby arrived at the Johnson home on December 24. "He was the best Christmas present we ever had," Susan Johnson says.

A few days later, Maureen phoned a reluctant Peter to come sign the birth certificate and adoption release papers. "He said he was going skiing," Maureen recalls. Peter did sign before leaving on December 30, and the matter seemed concluded.

At this point, Peter's parents—his mother,

Lorraine, a part-time bookkeeper, and his father, Marcel, a fire fighter—were still unaware of the baby's existence. They found out a few days later and raised the issue of fatherhood.

**With birth control, abortion and single motherhood, adoptive babies are scarce**

Ontario law allows both biological parents a 21-day change-of-mind period to reconsider their consent to adoption. After discussing the matter with his parents, Peter withdrew his consent in early January. With his parents now in the picture, it not only seemed possible to keep the baby, but the older Brassards felt strongly he should do so.

A few days after Peter withdrew his consent, there was a meeting between the two families which presented these intractable philosophies on child-rearing: the Brassards feel that children should be raised by a blood relative, whenever possible; the Paquets and Maureen, who had herself been fatherless between the ages of 2 and 7, before her mother remarried, feel the baby would be better off raised by two parents. The meeting lasted several hours and simply reinforced the impasse. During the meeting, the Brassards offered a possible solution: they had a cousin who was married, childless and waiting to adopt. "They would have adopted Alex in five minutes," says Lorraine Brassard. "And we were willing to have the baby adopted by someone within the family."

Maureen and her family discussed the idea but rejected it. They had chosen the Johnsons as the adoptive parents and felt they couldn't renege. Cathy Paquet says: "We thought it would be immoral." By this time, there was a Hatfield-McCoy quality to the debate; the families' positions had become entrenched and antagonistic. "If Peter's cousin adopted Alex, I would be shut out," says Maureen, who truly wanted some role in raising her child. But her family never really considered this as an option. "What you have," says Claude Paquet from the head of the table, "is two families who don't have much use for one another."

With no settlement in sight, Peter sued for custody. The Johnsons were out of the picture: as the acknowledged biological father, Peter had the absolute right to withdraw his consent to the adoption. With the adoption annulled, Maureen decided that, if she couldn't choose the adoptive

parents, she would keep Alexander herself. "I gave him away so he would be in a stable two-parent home," Maureen says. "It didn't make sense to give him up to a single parent [Peter]." The judge awarded custody to Maureen and "reasonable access" to Peter.

On February 6, Maureen, her mother and Pauline Richard, the Christian counselor, drove to Toronto and stayed overnight with the Johnsons, commiserating on their mutual unhappiness. They discussed the practical matters of Alexander's feeding and sleeping habits. After prayers in the morning, the three of them picked up Alexander from the hospital and drove back to Montreal. "I guess this is what God intended," Maureen says.

∾

In the Toronto-area home of Susan and Jim Johnson, there is the residue of their brief family life. A rocking horse and teddy bear sit in a corner of the living room. "Do you want to see pictures?" Susan asks, opening a photo album that shows Alexander in a series of family groupings. There is something ghoulish about observing this brief record. "We are emotionally and financially drained," Jim says of their five-week parenthood and the legal expenses—about $10,000—that they incurred.

Their adult lives have been geared toward the idea of family. In 1986, they were 104th on the Children's Aid Society adoption list; they have since moved to 33rd. With birth control, abortion and single motherhood, adoptive babies are scarce.

"We did everything by the book," Jim says. They are shaken by the experience, the awful proximity of their dream. They feel Alexander was their baby. "Maureen carried that baby for nine months," Susan says, "but not for Peter."

In this case, Dr. Maria Kapuscinska, a child psychiatrist in Montreal, gives her professional opinion that the best interests of Alexander took a backseat. "It was an unwanted pregnancy," she says, "and reasonable plans were made by the mother to put the child in a situation that was carefully chosen. We know from psychiatric studies that adoption is definitely superior to a single family household, particularly one led by a teenager."

"Peter just wanted an opportunity to love his son," Lorraine Brassard rejoins. "He didn't want to ruin Maureen's life. People are shouting for fathers to take some responsibility and then, when a father does, they criticize him"

In November, both parties were back in court squabbling over child support and visitation rights.

# Should Kids Take Parents to Court?

## *Increasing numbers of kids are claiming the right to sue parents for abuse or to choose which divorced parent they wish to live with*

By Barbara Wade Rose

*Names and some details of the family have been changed.*

**NOVEMBER 1993**

FOURTEEN-YEAR-OLD CHELISA Simpson twists her permed brown hair between nervous fingers as she sits silently beside her lawyer in a Toronto courthouse waiting room. It's an August morning in 1991, and the room is populated by a dozen similar groups in hushed conversation. A few meters away, two other lawyers are conferring separately with Chelisa's parents, both in their 40s: Fran, a school bus driver with cropped brown hair and big glasses, and her ex-husband, Alan, an unemployed construction worker whose heavyset frame is confined by an unaccustomed tie and jacket. Finally, the three lawyers enter the judge's chambers and shut the door. While Alan sits with Chelisa at the back of the waiting room, Fran walks out into the hallway to avoid her daughter. The tension between them is palpable.

The lawyers reemerge after 20 minutes, and tell their clients that Chelisa has won her case. The judge has granted her the right to rewrite her parents' divorce decree, taking custody from her mother and giving it to her father—thought to be the first time in Canada a child has been made party to a divorce proceeding. Fran is stunned; the judge's decision means she has no right to see her daughter or have any say in her life. Alan nods quietly as he listens to the verdict. He supported Chelisa's wish to live with him; since his divorce, he feels, he's missed too much of his kids' growing up. But he did not pursue the case himself for fear of jeopardizing his right to see her younger brother, Sid.

Chelisa's lawyer, Cheryl Milne, sits Chelisa down in a corner of the waiting room and explains the result of their two-month legal fight. Milne tells her that the judge, like most family court judges nowadays, regarded Chelisa as old enough to decide where she wanted to live, regardless of her mother's wishes. What's important, Milne tells her, is that by rewriting the divorce decree, Chelisa has forced the law formally to recognize her choice of a guardian. In so doing, she's shut the door on Fran's having any future control over her life.

Chelisa's smile shows her elation. Leaving the courthouse with Alan, she lowers her head as they pass Fran in the corridor. For her part, Fran keeps her emotions under control as she drives back to Oshawa, 50 kilometers east of Toronto. Once home, she breaks down in sobs. For the next three weeks, she'll be off the job, unable to do much more than sit around the house and cry.

Canadian courtrooms are seeing increasing numbers of children who, like Chelisa, demand the right to choose how they are raised and cared for. These cases are part of an international trend, highlighted by two recent court decisions in Florida: in August, 14-year-old Kimberly Mays won the right to bar her biological parents from any role in her life, after it was discovered she'd been switched at birth with another child; and last year, 12-year-old Gregory Kingsley "divorced" his parents so he could be adopted by his foster family. For all the headlines around these two cases, they didn't surprise Canadian children's rights activists; Cheryl Milne's Toronto office receives one or two queries a month from children like Gregory who want to break relations with their families.

Kids are claiming their rights for all kinds of reasons: to fight back against abuse, to demand stable homes, even to curb irresponsible behavior—drug-taking, for example—by their parents. One 15-year-old Ontario girl sued the Children's Aid Society to take her in as a foster child after the society said her allegations of abuse at home were unfounded; the court ordered the society to take her in. A group of teen wards in Winnipeg foster homes organized to demand a say in where they were placed and for how long; they presented their case at a meeting of the local social services agency. A dyslexic boy in Toronto sued for private-school funding from the Ontario government so he could get the help he needed without burdening his parents; he got it. Many teens, unhappy at home, have sued their parents and won monthly support payments to let them live on their own.

*Many teens, unhappy at home, have sued their parents and won monthly support payments to let them live on their own*

It's a far cry from the days when we assumed parents knew best. The first foster children in Canada, for example, were sent over from England in the mid-1800s as servants—some by their impoverished parents. Until thinking began to change in the 1960s, legal decisions regarding children were based on "the best interests of the child," a doctrine that assumed parents always had their children's best interests at heart. Now, control is shifting to the children themselves.

∽

Chelisa, now 16, is a pretty girl with a soft voice and a habit of hiding behind her hair. She remembers lying awake in bed as a small child, listening to her parents argue downstairs. Fran and Alan divorced in 1983 when Chelisa was 5. After a bitter fight Fran won custody of the two children. But the family soon settled into a routine, with Chelisa and her brother, Sid, spending every other weekend at their father's house in Cobourg, 60 kilometers from Oshawa. Fran Simpson describes her relationship with her children as "the same as with every other parent and kid: ups and downs."

As Chelisa grew older, the downs predominated. She and Fran fought more—over how much time she could spend at the mall with her friends, how late she could stay out. Chelisa would frequently say she wanted to go and live with her father. As Fran talks about those fights, her voice is brisk and matter-of-fact, but an occasional falter betrays the pain the memories hold.

On the weekend visits, Chelisa got along well with Alan and his new wife, Andrea. When Chelisa complained about how often Fran punished her, Alan suspected she was exaggerating or lying. He would have intervened if he'd seen marks or bruises, he says, explaining his position in a slightly defensive manner. Alan told Chelisa she couldn't stay with him permanently: under civil law, a parent can be charged with contempt of court if a child under 16 disregards a custody order by moving in with that parent.

But Chelisa was determined to act. At school and on billboards, she'd seen posters urging her to take charge of her situation if she didn't like it—ads for services that offered support, counseling and legal help. In June 1991, from her mother's spare bedroom, she secretly phoned one of the services, a children's legal aid clinic in Toronto called Justice for Children and Youth.

The clinic was founded in 1977 by an articling law student, Jeffery Wilson, concerned with children's rights. Now a family lawyer in Toronto, Wilson says he wanted to help kids in the child welfare system protect themselves from bureaucratic abuses such as unnecessary delays in resolving their cases, or shuffling from one foster home to another. In the clinic's 16 years, the client list has diversified to include youngsters accused in criminal cases as well as kids like Chelisa, seeking help to change their home situations.

Justice for Children and Youth is the only legal aid clinic exclusively for children in Canada.

Justice for Children and Youth's Cheryl Milne says that before pursuing Chelisa's case, she urged her young client to think carefully about what she really wanted; Milne has seen too many angry parents who no longer wish to have anything to do with their children after a court case. The lawyer also told Chelisa that she could move anytime she wanted to; despite the laws governing custody, children over the age of 12 are unlikely to be forced to return home unless they're in immediate danger.

On July 19, 1991, when Alan came to pick up the children for the weekend, Chelisa and Sid emerged from the side door of the house bearing garbage bags filled with Chelisa's belongings. She'd packed secretly and persuaded Sid to help her hide the bags, which they now hoisted onto the back of Alan's pickup truck. "I said hoo, whoa, here we go," Alan recalls. Chelisa urged him to drive away fast, assuring him that she knew what she was doing. But Fran, looking out the window, guessed what was happening and promptly telephoned her lawyer, Trevor Spurr. Before Alan could drive away, she ran out and called Chelisa inside to talk to the lawyer. Reluctantly, the girl listened as Spurr urged her not to take matters into her own hands. "Then, I told him: 'I've already talked to someone, and she said I could do it,'" Chelisa says.

The three drove away, and Spurr began legal proceedings to enforce the custody order. When the papers arrived at Alan's house, Chelisa called Cheryl Milne, who reassured her that it was unlikely a judge would send her back to her mother's house. Nonetheless, Milne said, they could avoid any doubts by applying to make her a party to her parents' divorce and to grant custody to her father. Chelisa agreed.

The fall of 1991 passed uneventfully at Alan and Andrea's house; Chelisa had responsibilities such as keeping her room clean, emptying the dishwasher and coming home promptly after school. Sid still visited every other weekend. Fran sent Christmas and birthday presents to her daughter, but their only contact was a few tense phone conversations about Chelisa's possessions.

After about six months, however, Chelisa began breaking the rules. "She was staying out too late, not doing her bit," Alan says. Once, Chelisa left a note saying she was going to baby-sit and didn't come home until 5 A.M., dropped off by a girlfriend. Alan and Andrea paced the floors that night waiting for her to return.

Chelisa admits she got into some trouble, but says part of the problem was that she resented how often Alan and Andrea went out and left her alone. After the 5 A.M. incident, Alan and Andrea went with her to see a counselor at the Cobourg children's aid society. But the session was a failure, Alan says, because Chelisa wouldn't talk. The social worker told Alan he was no different from many other parents—he had an uncontrollable teenager. A few days later, Chelisa went to visit Alan's 23-year-old niece and her husband in Newmarket for a week. First, she phoned Alan to tell him she was staying an extra week, then she called to say she wouldn't be coming back at all.

Chelisa spent a year living with her cousin and attended the local school. "A lot of people's parents are split up now," she said matter-of-factly last win-

ter. "Their kids are with one or the other. I'm just with neither." Her father described his daughter at the time as "out of reach." Despite their difficulties, however, Chelisa chose to return to Alan, who had relocated to another Ontario town, last June. She started grade 11 at her fourth high school this fall, and hopes to become a social worker.

Fran has seen her daughter infrequently in the past two years. For a time, Sid refused to speak to his sister—an unexpected fallout of her exodus from Alan's house. Through Fran, Sid declined to be interviewed for this story; although he and his sister are close again, he figures it's just one more way Chelisa is getting attention.

For some critics of the litigious direction the kids' rights movement has taken, ruptured families are an all-too-frequent result when the courts get involved in everyday parent-child disputes. Such a critic is Helen Jones, president of The Association of Parent Support Groups in Ontario, which offers advice to parents coping with difficult teenagers. "We support 100 percent that children have to have rights," Jones says. "But the rights they've been given are the rights of adults." She says it's a fact—one many adults don't want to admit—that children may not be as innocent or maligned as they seem. "There's an incredible imbalance," she says. "Children are seen to be victims always, regardless of whether or not they lied. Sometimes, it's the children who are abusing the parents." In the seven years her association has been in existence, Jones says, meetings of its member groups have attracted an estimated 5,000 parents in desperation over children who are acting out against them.

Cheryl Milne defends the court route as an effective option for kids like Chelisa, who simply want to control their own lives. By letting Chelisa decide where to live, the courts may have saved her from running away and ending up on the streets. "I've felt in talking to her that she's happy where she is," Milne says firmly, cautioning against any starry-eyed view of the sanctity of families.

Chelisa's mother, however, believes that greater rights for her daughter have prevented Chelisa from living up to her responsibilities. "What's going to happen to families if this keeps up?" Fran asks. "I'll tell you. There won't be any families."

# CHAPTER FIVE

# Food & Entertaining

OR A WIFE OF THE TWENTIES and thirties, a primary duty was the preparation of three meals a day—even if one went out the door in a lunch bucket. Unlike her own mother, she might be aided by a regiment of new "electrical servants:" coffee percolator, waffle iron, blender, hot plate, toaster. Though aluminum and glass ovenware were replacing iron, wood stoves still predominated over electric except in the cities, and ice boxes over the wonderful "mechanical refrigerators."

During the twenties, junk food had made its debut with Wise potato chips, Hostess Twinkies, Baby Ruth chocolate bars and Fleer's Double Bubble gum. The modern cook also enjoyed the convenience of prepared foods: canned fruit, vegetables, salmon, tuna and soup (tomato became available in 1897, cream of mushroom in 1934); canned milk (used by affluent mothers since 1853 but not generally available until the twenties); sliced bread, packaged cereals, Bisquick biscuit mix, processed cheese, Peter Pan and Skippy peanut butter, Gerber's baby foods and Nescafé. Though tinned goods were frowned upon as lazy substitutes for fresh produce lovingly prepared, they were welcomed as shortcuts in recipes.

Chatelaine Institute, with its test kitchen, assumed Canadian housewives were interested in the scientific approach to nutrition and meal-planning. Vitamins C and D had been isolated during the twenties and yeast was a health-food fad. Fish appeared frequently on menus, along with liver, kidneys, heart, tripe, tongue and sweetbreads—even for breakfast. Nevertheless, by today's standards, the Institute's Meals of the Month were glutinous with the kind of paste that kept wallpaper in good standing for twenty years.

From 1942 to 1947, war-time rationing of sugar, butter, meat, coffee and tea presented a challenge for Canadian cooks. Especially that butter. After a twenty-year battle with Canadian dairy farmers, the Women's Institute succeeded in persuading the government to lift the ban on margarine. To distinguish it from butter (and to discourage table use), manufacturers were required to bleach it white, but were allowed to package it with a color bud that, when kneaded in, turned it a hideous yellow—a typical Canadian compromise.

Since gasoline was also rationed, milk and bread continued to be delivered door-to-door in horse-wagons. Surplus produce from victory gardens promoted the rental of frozen-food lockers and the postwar purchase of home freezers. By then, frozen vegetables and orange juice were also commercially available. Though housewives still gained status from fussy cakes and cookies served at trousseau teas, the first cake mixes provided an alternative.

At the top of every fifties' bride's "must-have" list was an electric fry pan. She could also expect to receive an electric kettle (perhaps three) and an electric can-opener. To menus featuring overcooked British roasts, French pea soup, Italian spaghetti and German sauerkraut, innovative Canadian chefs were adding Veal Scaloppini, Quiche Lorraine, Weinerschnitzel and pizza. With the move to the suburbs, the outdoor barbecue became the center of summer entertaining, often featuring the man-of-the-house sizzling ever-rarer steaks. In a trend assailed by nutritionists, the family could also be found in the living room balancing TV dinners as they watched *Front Page Challenge*. Though Kentucky fried chicken and soft ice-cream products had galvanized the fast-food market, calorie-conscious Canadians were opting for skim milk, sugar substitutes like sucaryl and saccharine, no-cal soft drinks and rice (now instant) instead of potatoes.

Though the blender had been around since the twenties, the deluxe model was the "in" purchase of the sixties: Canadians, it seemed, would never have to chew again! With more wives working, the words "jiffy" and "instant" escalated in appeal. The exploding list of prepared foods now included muffin mixes, salad dressings and Sara Lee frozen cakes. At the same time, the proliferation of ethnic restaurants, along with increased travel, inspired Canadians to re-create international fare in their own kitchens: Hawaiian luaus, Swiss fondues and Indian curries—that last traceable to Western fascination with transcendental meditation and the Beatles' Indian visit to Maharishi Mahesh Yogi. In between splurges, everyone seemed to be counting calories: enter Weight-Watchers.

The inflationary food prices of the seventies made "cheap" an attention-grabber and led to the launch of generic products. Speed-cookery took a quantum leap with the introduction of the microwave, all but rendering the stove obsolete in some households.

The eighties elevated food and its preparation to the status of a sacrament. Nouvelle cuisine, with its emphasis on fresh, lightly cooked, colorful foods creatively displayed, allowed restaurants to charge more and more for less and less, served on ballroom-sized plates dribbled with raspberry purée and spiked with mint. The addition of calamari, clam and gorgonzola upgraded spaghetti to pasta, with subdivisions of fettucine, linguine, fusilli and penne. When transformed by sundried tomatoes and goat cheese, pizza also went gourmet. The wok took the humble vegetable to main-course status, and everyone had a secret salad dressing for which only virgin olive oil need apply. With irradiation and year-round air-shipment, shoppers discovered kiwi was a fruit as well as a bird; hosts no longer had to show their guests how to strip and dip an artichoke; and everyone knew the difference between arugula and cilantro—or pretended to. Ingredients like yogurt, zucchini and oat bran acquired cult status, as if adding them to a dish loaded with sugar and butter converted it into a health food. Muffins, coffee and breads went designer, while specialty shops sprouted up along neighborhood streets like shiitake on a log. Middle Eastern, Japanese, Thai, Caribbean and California-mesquite cookery all enjoyed a star turn. Every urban newspaper had a critic whose job it was to describe food in ever-more-orgasmic terms till it seemed chocolate cake had displaced sex as the thing Canadians felt most guilty about. As always, the call to redemption was just around the corner: diet, diet, diet.

By the nineties, health-conscious food-lovers were ricocheting between low-cal, no-cal, low-cholesterol, fat-free, lite cookery and indulgences in junk food, chased down with scoops of extra-rich, super-decadent ice cream. As the decade progressed, labels promising lactose-free, wheat-free, no-salt and nutrient-enriched increasingly caught the eye of aging baby boomers, even if they had to put on their bifocals to read them.

*From Lunch Bucket*

# Dinner's Changing Face

Fillets of sole with devilled lobster.

Tongue in aspic, jellied in a spectacular manner.

DECEMBER
**1928**

MAY
**1952**

# *Old-Style Home Cookin'*

# Zucchini Power
By Monda Rosenberg

# Electrical Servants and Others

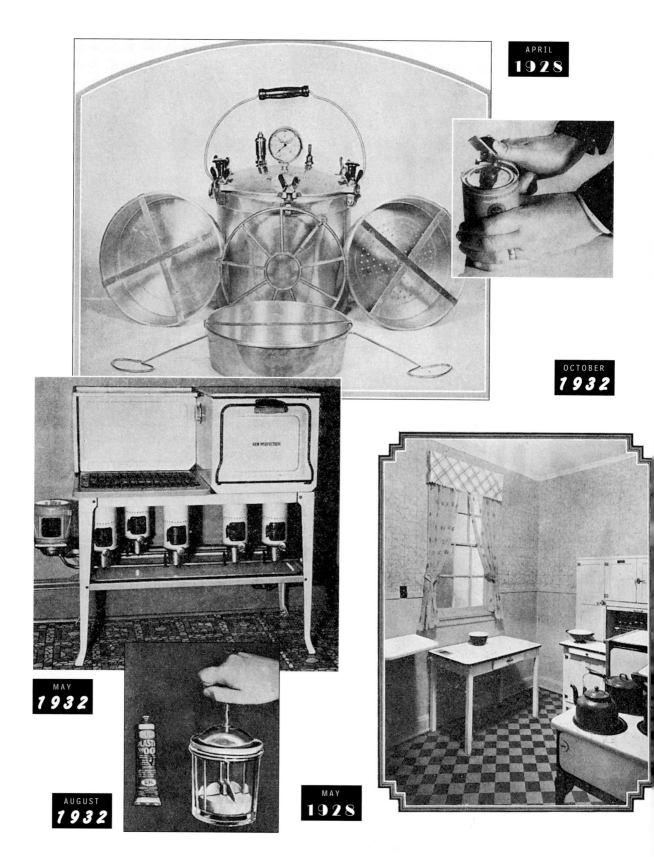

APRIL
**1928**

OCTOBER
*1932*

MAY
*1932*

AUGUST
*1932*

MAY
**1928**

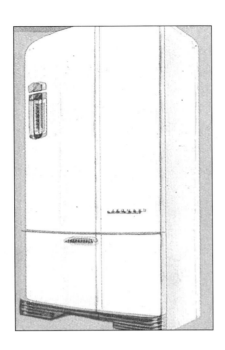

*From the 40s Trousseau Tea*

# Are These Some of Your Problems?

*These questions, typical of those which come into the Institute every day, are of such interest that they form part of a regular series of new articles*

By HELEN G. CAMPBELL

*Director of the Chatelaine Institute*

**FEBRUARY 1932** As EVERY WOMAN KNOWS, this business of housekeeping is no trivial matter. It demands a keen and alert mind to keep things running smoothly, and to cope with the problems that arise in even the best regulated households.

From our correspondence files I have chosen a number of letters with queries on a wide range of subjects, thinking that these problems may also be yours and hoping you will find in our answers a satisfactory solution.

## TO REMOVE STAINS

- *In an earlier issue of Chatelaine you have an article dealing with the removal of stains. I should like to have the recipe for Javelle water which is recommended for taking spots from certain materials.*

Answer: The recipe which you request is given below. You will find this bleach very useful for removing spots and stains from white linen and cotton.

### JAVELLE WATER

| | |
|---|---|
| 2 Cupfuls of washing soda | 1 Cupful of chloride of lime |
| 1 Quart of boiling water | 2 Quarts of cold water |

Put the washing soda in a granite pan and add the boiling water. Mix the lime with the cold water. Pour the lime solution into the soda solution, mix and allow to set until clear. Pour the clear liquid into dark bottles or keep in a dark place. The white residue may be poured down the sink and serves to clear the drain.

## HOW TO SERVE COCKTAILS

- *I have recently been given a set of glassware, which includes cocktail glasses. On looking up your recipes for cocktails, I notice that some of them have considerable solids, such as fruit or fish. How, and with what accompaniments, should these be served?*
- *Would a fruit juice mixture be suitable as the first course at dinner?*
- *May cocktails be served from a tray before the meal starts, providing they are the "drinkable" kind?*
- *Are special forks or spoons required for a cocktail containing solids eaten at the table?*

Answer: It is quite correct to serve a "drinkable" cocktail as your first course at luncheon or dinner. This may be either mixed fruit juices, sauerkraut or tomato juice. Such appetizers are often served in the drawing-room or living room, preceding the meal. They may be unaccompanied or tiny canapés may be passed on a tray at the same time. If they are served at the table, the canapés may be arranged on the plate at the base of the cocktail glass. These tidbits are very small pieces of bread cut in fancy shapes, toasted on one side and spread with some highly seasoned fish paste, cheese, relish or vegetable combination and garnished with pimento, olives, pearl onions, and other such foods. Small crackers also make a very fine base for a canapé.

Cocktails containing fruit or fish are eaten at the table with a teaspoon or a small fork designed for the purpose. It is not customary to use any accompaniment in this case. Fruit cups, which are really cocktails containing cubes or slices of fruit, are eaten with a small teaspoon.

## POURING TEA

- *Will you kindly give me any pointers to help me in pouring at a large afternoon tea? I am only recently married and have not acted in this capacity before.*

Answer: In pouring at an afternoon tea, the cups should not be lifted from the table while being filled. Sugar may be placed on the saucer, but it is usually passed with cream and lemon by those who are assisting in serving the guests. When refilling a cup, first empty any remaining tea into a bowl provided for the purpose. The spoon should be placed on the saucer, parallel to the handle.

Be at ease and unhurried and you will find this social honor a very pleasant one.

# Say "We Want Margarine"

*Our Consumer Councilors reveal the thinking of Canadian women on a bitterly debated issue of importance to everyone*

**APRIL 1948**

FROM COAST TO COAST, IN the cities and in the country, four fifths of Canadian housewives say, "We want margarine."

The attitude of many was summed up by one woman who said, "We have a prairie family near us with six young children who never see butter because of its price. Everyone should be able to have it or a substitute, because of its nutritional value."

A very high percentage of the rural women—more than three fifths—many of them wives of dairy farmers selling cream in the dairy market, were fair-minded enough to say that large families in moderate circumstances could not afford butter at its present prices and should therefore have the opportunity of buying a cheap substitute.

A few Councilors who were in favor of margarine "on principle," were not sure whether they would use it because they had never tasted it. One Councilor asked, "What is margarine—do you use it in your tea?"

Margarine went under a ban in Canada 25 years ago. It has been hushed so much that a whole generation has grown up without ever having seen it. On the other hand many housewives know that margarine is a good, nourishing, cheap food, and that Canada is the only country in the world in which it is banned. As for price, margarine sells in the United States today as low as 39c a pound, compared to butter which has gone as high as $1 a pound.

The Canadian Medical Journal last August stated quite bluntly that "from economic and nutritional aspects, good margarine is superior to butter."

Both margarine and butter contain 80% fat.

Margarine is made from vegetable oils—cottonseed, soybean, corn and peanut. These fats are usually churned with pure skim milk to give them the dairy taste. Units of vitamin A are added, bringing the product up to, and frequently beyond, the vitamin standard for butter.

In its natural form, margarine has a yellowish color, not unlike butter. Manufacturers in the United States, however, are compelled by law to remove this natural color by bleaching, so that it will not be mistaken for butter, and to enclose with each pound a small envelope of yellow coloring matter for the housewife to knead into the margarine. The paradox is, that during the winter season, when herds of cattle are not feeding in green pastures, coloring must be added to butter to give it the desired shade of yellow.

Last year a bill favoring the lifting of the ban on margarine in Canada was defeated in the Senate. Two more bills will be brought up during the present session, one in the Senate and one in the House of Commons.

## CONSUMER COUNCIL BALLOT BOX

This is the way Chatelaine Consumer Councilors voted. They were asked: Do you think that the sale of margarine should be permitted in Canada?

| They answered: | 80 Yes | 16 No | 4 No answer |
|---|---|---|---|

And for the second question: If margarine were made available, would you use it in your home?

| They answered: | 70 Yes | 24 No | 6 No answer |
|---|---|---|---|

# The Beatles and the "Indian Thing"

# News in Food...

IT COMES IN CANS!
*And the Label Tells the Story*
By J. B. SPENCER

JULY **1932**

# Packing a Box for a Soldier?

## This is what they'd like to get

**JANUARY 1941** CHRISTMAS IS OVER FOR another year, but there are long months ahead when your boy in camp will be looking for some remembrance from you. Birthdays—or special occasions and anniversaries are all first class excuses for a special parcel!

If you have a little over a dollar to spend you can make a hit with a four- to five-pound, home-cooked roast chicken. Or a two-pound chicken, canned. Or three pounds of spiced ham, canned. Or four pounds of home-cooked stuffed spareribs.

Another dollar or so will add some trimmings. These will weigh about four pounds unwrapped.

- 1 glass of currant or cranberry jelly—from your own shelves or your grocer's. Screw-top jars are the best for packing, so if the tops are the sit-on kind, seal the edge well, with a good coat of paraffin.
- 1 package of savory biscuits.
- 1 jar of pickles.
- 2 pounds of homemade fruit cake.

For another dollar you can add, three more pounds of popular "eats."

- 1 tin or jar of sandwich spread.
- 2 pounds of homemade candy.
- 2 dozen apples sauce cookies. Or if you know of a better 'ole!

To bring your parcel up to four dollars and a total weight of twelve to fourteen pounds, how about these?

- 1 package of graham crackers.
- 1 package of plain or flavored cheese.
- A pound or half pound of date and nut bread—use your favorite recipe or buy it in sealed tins.
- 1 tin of salted peanuts.

Aw, come on—bring it up to a Five Spot; it will cost you only another dollar and three pounds extra postage to send these to any lad with a sweet tooth. And who hasn't?

- 1 package of dates or figs or 2 cans of fruit juice.
- 2 packages of hard candy.
- H pound of maple sugar.
- 2 dozen homemade shortbreads, or your cookie specialty.
- 1 package of toffee.
- 4 chocolate bars.

# Your Family Rations

**SEPTEMBER 1946** RATION BOOK NO. 6 WILL BE distributed across Canada during the a week of September 9 to 13. As in the past, distribution will be handled by volunteer workers in co-operation with more than 600 Local Ration Boards serving every town and hamlet in Canada. It will be your responsibility to call for the books to which your family is entitled; they will not be sent through the mails. Late-comers who do not pick up their books by the final day will not receive a book before September 30. This will mean that those who do not get their books during distribution week will lose two weeks' supply of ration coupons.

The need for rationing is the result of world-wide food shortages, which will not be relieved sufficiently by this year's harvests. The world hungers for meat, and Canada is one of the few countries with meat to spare. Canada, through rationing, is providing millions of pounds of meat for Britain and the rest of Europe where hunger and unrest are a constant menace to permanent peace.

Sugar rationing is necessary because Canada does not produce enough sugar for her own needs, and must depend on other countries sharing the supply. Rationing assures a fair distribution of our allotment from the World Sugar Pool.

There is still a serious shortage of butter in Canada and, in order that everyone may have an equal amount, it is necessary to keep butter on the list of rationed foods. The shortage of butter is due partly to the increased consumption of fluid milk, and also to the large quantities of cheese and evaporated milk which the Government has pledged for shipment to Great Britain. In that country, where the meat ration is very meagre, cheese is a necessary item in the everyday diet of the nation.

Rationing is the fairest means of distributing available supplies on an equal basis. Every citizen in Canada is entitled to one ration book, and every citizen, regardless of financial means, is entitled to the same amount of rationed food. This is the only way to meet our obligations to the people in near-famine areas and, at the same time, ensure a fair distribution of basic foods to Canadians.

## SEPTEMBER 1974 — Sample Family Food List for a Week

**Number of adults: 2    Number of children: 3    Weekly food budget: $21**

| FOOD | AMOUNTS REQUIRED | AMOUNTS TO BUY LBS | PRICE PER LB | COST |
|---|---|---|---|---|
| Grains | 4.0 lb/100 lb | 18.0 | * | 5.66 |
| Legumes | .5 lb/100 lb | 2.2 | * | 1.37 |
| Skim milk powder | .7 lb/100 lb | 3.2 | | |
| | .7 lb/child | 2.1 | | |
| | Total SMP | 5.3 | .60 | 3.18 |
| Eggs | 7 medium/person | 35 eggs | .07 | 2.45 |
| **Vegetables** | | | | |
| Cabbage | .6 lb/person | 3.0 | .12 | .36 |
| Carrots | .6 lb/person | 3.0 | .13 | .39 |
| Potatoes | 1.0 lb/person | 5.0 | .08 | .40 |
| Rutabagas (turnip) | .6 lb/person | 3.0 | .12 | .36 |
| **Fats** | | | | |
| Total fats | .8 lb/100 lb | 3.6 | | |
| Fortified margarine or butter | .3 lb/child | .9 | | |
| | .5 lb/adult | 1.0 | | |
| | | 1.9 | .39 | .74 |
| Other fats | | 1.7 | * | .48 |
| **Sugars** | .8 lb/100 lb | 3.6 | * | 1.54 |
| Total cost of basics | | | | $16.93 |
| Miscellaneous | | | | 4.07 |
| Weekly Food Budget | | | | $21.00 |

*Hors d'Oeuvres for Over-Achievers*

# Sweet Dreams

**FEBRUARY 1996**

**C**ANADIANS ARE PASSIONATE about candy, according to a recent survey of 1,401 residents from coast to coast. In fact, many of us apparently find sweets, particularly chocolate, gum, mints and candy, a great morale booster: 22% of Canadians said they eat candy to increase energy; 21% to compensate for a stressful day; and 19% to "lift their spirits."

■ *If chocolate released the same pleasure stimulants in the brain as sex, would you indulge more often?*

Newfoundlanders are most likely to indulge more—53% said yes, compared with only 29% of Prince Edward Islanders, who rounded out the bottom of the rankings.

■ *Which would you prefer: more chocolate or more sex?*

• 73% of Quebecers prefer chocolate—15% think it's "pure ecstasy." It makes 19% "feel good all over."
• The sexiest province in Canada? Nova Scotia, where 80% said they prefer the bedroom to a chocolate bar.

■ *Who is most likely to throw nutrition concerns to the wind when indulging in a sweet treat?*

• University graduates
• Clerical workers
• Homemakers

# Chatelaine Charts Your 17 Best Meat Buys

**JANUARY 1963**

## PRICE PER POUND

| MEAT | (NATIONAL LOW AVERAGE) |
| --- | --- |
| Oxtails | 29 cents |
| Short ribs | 39 cents |
| Beef kidney | 39 cents |
| Hamburg | 45 cents |
| Beef liver | 49 cents |
| Chuck beef | 59 cents |
| Pork hocks | 29 cents |
| Pork liver | 29 cents |
| Pork shoulder | 45 cents |
| Pork, minced | 59 cents |
| Lamb flank | 19 cents |
| Lamb riblets | 19 cents |
| Lamb in a basket | 23 cents |
| Lamb neck | 29 cents |
| Meat-loaf mixture, lamb, beef, veal or pork | 59 cents |
| Chicken wings | 39 cents |

# Meals of the Month

| BREAKFAST | LUNCHEON OR SUPPER | DINNER |
|---|---|---|
| Figs in Syrup<br>Cream of Wheat<br>Toast Omelet<br>Tea Coffee Cocoa | Scalloped Cabbage with Tomato<br>Sauce<br>Nut Bread Jam<br>Tea or Cocoa | Fried Pickerel<br>Broiled Potatoes, Creamed Onions<br>Cranberry Tarts<br>Coffee |
| Baked Apples<br>Fish Cakes<br>Muffins Marmalade<br>Tea Coffee Cocoa | Bean Soup<br>Cabbage Salad<br>Ginger Drop Cakes<br>Tea or Cocoa | Broiled Pig's Feet<br>Creamed Potatoes, Buttered Beets<br>Apricot Cream<br>Coffee |
| Tangerines<br>Bacon<br>Rolls Honey<br>Tea Coffee Cocoa | Baked Potatoes on the Half Shell<br>Celery Stuffed with Cheese<br>Macaroon Cup Custard<br>with Whipped Cream<br>Tea or Cocoa | Roast Turkey<br>Mashed Potatoes Spinach<br>Angel Food Cake, Chocolate Sauce<br>Coffee |
| Sliced Canned Pineapple<br>Rolled Oats<br>Toast Jam<br>Tea Coffee Cocoa | Scalloped Salmon and Rice<br>Apple Sauce, Nut Cookies<br>Tea or Cocoa | Turkey a la King<br>Duchess Potatoes, Diced Turnips<br>Orange Souffle<br>Coffee |
| Cinnamon Prunes<br>Cornmeal Porridge<br>Bran Gems Jelly<br>Tea Coffee Cocoa | Shirred Eggs with Pimentoes<br>and Bacon<br>Canned Pears, Ginger Snaps<br>Tea or Cocoa | Cannelon of Beef<br>Franconia Potatoes<br>Creamed Carrots<br>Apple Dumplings<br>Coffee |
| Whole Oranges<br>Poached Eggs on Toast<br>Tea Coffee Cocoa | Corn Chowder<br>Dressed Lettuce<br>Jam Muffins<br>Tea or Cocoa | Sirloin Steak<br>French Fried Potatoes, Mushrooms<br>Glorified Rice, Maple Syrup<br>Coffee |
| Bananas<br>Broiled Ham<br>Toast Marmalade<br>Tea Coffee Cocoa | Creamed Eggs with Shrimps<br>on Toast<br>Gelatine with Whipped Cream<br>Tea or Cocoa | Shepherds' Pie<br>Buttered Cabbage<br>Jellied Tomato Salad<br>Upside Down Cake<br>Coffee |
| Grapefruit<br>Sunerva Cereal<br>Scrambled Eggs Toast<br>Tea Coffee Cocoa | Carrots and Peas in Pastry Shells<br>with Cheese Sauce<br>Preserved Figs with Cream<br>Tea or Cocoa<br>Fish Cakes | Baked Trout, Lemon Points<br>Au Gratin Potatoes<br>Creamed Parsnips<br>Chocolate Eclairs<br>Coffee |

# Fat in a Thin Society

*Let's face it: for most of us, thin equals sexy, self-disciplined and well-adjusted. Fat, on the other hand, spells out of control, sloppy and self-indulgent.*

BY SUANNE KELMAN

**SEPTEMBER 1993**

A FEW YEARS AGO, I THOUGHT I'd finally kicked my life-long obsession with weight. I gave up the diets that made me so savagely cranky and fixated on food. I found that, if I didn't diet, I didn't binge. My weight stabilized for the first time in years. I started going to exercise classes and discovered, to my amazement, that I loved them. I thought I'd achieved self-acceptance.

This January, a man I hadn't seen for years phoned out of the blue, newly divorced and flatteringly keen to see me again. He asked what I looked like now. The first words that popped out of my mouth were, "Well, I weigh too much." Somehow, self-loathing was back.

At five feet and 125 pounds, I'm about 12 pounds heavier than I'd like to be. A lot of the time, it feels like 50. I have "fat days," when I look in the mirror and see a blimp with arms and legs. That image fills me with panic and kills my interest in clothes, exercise and men. At the same time, it fuels a frantic rebellious desire to overeat. And I still fantasize that my life would be magically transformed if I were thin.

I may be crazy, but I'm certainly not alone. I can safely say that at least half of the women I know are obsessed with a real or imaginary 10 to 15 pounds of fat.

We used to talk about this obsession all the time. Today, nobody talks about diets; it's bad form. We claim that we accept ourselves as we are. But a lot of us are lying. We know now that body weight has as much to do with heredity as willpower, that permanent weight loss is far more complicated than we once believed. We know that the starvation diets of the past are counterproductive and potentially dangerous. But for a lot of us, the message hasn't sunk in.

In 1991, a report for Health and Welfare Canada determined that about 27 percent of Canadians are overweight, around 20 percent of women and 32 percent of men. That's too many, but it's far lower than the number of people who believe they're fat. The report quotes a 1985 survey showing over half of all adult Canadians wanted to lose weight: 65 percent of women, 43 percent of men.

It's easy to see why. Most of the people you see in movies, on television and in advertisements are very, very thin. Overweight is a joke (see how the entertainment industry trashes Roseanne Arnold) or a sorry waste of potential (witness the tabloid coverage of Elizabeth Taylor).

Believe it or not, our preference for almost flesh-less bodies is rare in historical and cultural terms. When I was in my teens, prom queens had breasts like melons and flaring hips that were padded with flesh. They'd be wallflowers now. In 1954, the reigning Miss America was 5'8" and weighed 132 pounds. Today, the average weight of a contestant of that height is 117 pounds.

Even today, our obsession with weight is incomprehensible in many cultures. Thinness in women has little value where food is in short supply and men get the first shot at it. In Sierra Leone, a West African country where I taught for a year in the mid-1970s, plump women were prized, and chunky matrons carried themselves with a jaunty confidence in their own worth and desirability.

We, on the other hand, regard fat with the horror that the Victorians reserved for sex and the Middle Ages for leprosy. At a time when we're increasingly sensitive about insulting other minorities, fat people are still fair game. American studies have found that fat people earn less money than others, that they're less likely to be hired or pro-

**JACQUELINE HOPE**

The 37-year-old president of Big, Bold & Beautiful never accepted the way our society sees fat: "I knew I was overweight at 220 pounds but I really liked my body."

moted, that they routinely face ridicule even from their doctors. The Canadian experience is n o better. In 1992, a Saskatchewan human rights board ruled that overweight was a legitimate reason to deny someone a job, even if it didn't affect performance. Dandra Davidson, 31, initially won a case against a nursing home thAt refused to hire her because of her weight; 300 pounds on a 5'5" body. But the board later reversed its decision and ruled that because her weight wasn't a disability caused by an illness, she had no grounds for a case.

When researchers at the University of Florida surveyed people who had lost large amounts of weight through gastric bypass surgery, they found most would prefer losing their sight, hearing or a leg to being fat again.

∾

We've invested weight with so many meaning that numbers on the scale have become a shorthand for self-worth. Slenderness is not just beautiful; it proclaims that you are feminine, self-disciplined, well-adjusted, sexy. Fat, on the other hand reveals that you're sloppy and self-indulgent, out of control and out of the running as a sexual being.

Feelings of shame and self-hatred are something most women would recognize. But there's another value we attach to overweight that may be even more powerful than a sense of sin. We see fat as low-class. It's no accident that most of the socialites seen in *Vanity Fair* and *Vogue* are so skinny their hipbones protrude through their sable coats.

Above all, our culture equates slenderness with sexiness. Weight gain—the woman's, not the man's—is a leading reason men lose sexual interest in their partners.

It sometimes feels as if we've confused thinness and sexuality so thoroughly that we've transferred our hang-ups about sex to food. Women often use sexual language to talk about eating. If we're "naughty" and have a dessert, we moan as if ice cream was orgasmic, trying to forget how much we'll hate ourselves in the morning. When I told my two sisters I'd be writing about "F-A-T"— spelling it out like a dirty word—one of them wailed: "Couldn't you write about something less personal—like your sex life?"

In her 1990 best-seller, *The Beauty Myth*, U.S. author Naomi Wolf notes that dieting first became a popular concern around 1920, at the time when Western women were receiving the vote. The pressure to be thin eased in the 1950s, when a postwar generation of women retired to their suburban homes to raise children and bake cookies. Wolf, a former anorexic, honestly believes that our cult of thinness is a plot to keep women politically and professional passive, their energy sapped by starvation.

Jackqueline Hope is one of Canada's leading missionaries for the right of large people—that's her term—to enjoy life and to be treated with respect. She's the 37-year-old president and CEO of Big, Bold & Beatiful, a Toronto modeling agency and boutique for large sizes.

Slender as a teenager, Hope ballooned to 220 pounds, after having son at age 18, on her 5'7" frame. Her husband dragged her to a diet clinic and monitored her eating so closely, she says, "that he counted the tomatoes in my salad. I lost 220 pounds—that was my husband—and I never gained him back. I knew I was overweight but I really liked my body and couldn't understand why other people didn't like this nice round belly, these curves. It was a pretty Rubenesque body and it was mine, and I couldn't understand the hatred I would feel for it once I started to diet."

My mind still can't silence the inner voice that tells me fat is repulsive. I have a long, long way to go. How about you?

# CHATELAINE

## FEBRUARY 1941

**10 CENTS**

CANADA

# CHAPTER SIX

# Mating Rituals

Even among flaming youth of the twenties, marriage remained the goal of all but a radical few. What this generation did seem to be rejecting was their parents' right to choose their partners, leading to a vogue for elopement. As young women found their prospects for employment dwindling during the "dirty thirties," marriage still seemed a necessity. In "Can She Manage Alone?" (April 1932), *Chatelaine* urged mothers to update their matchmaking skills. Also spurred on by the tough economic times, the mother of a young bachelor castigated Canada's debs for failing to appreciate that the swain at the ball might have reverted, like Cinderella, to impoverished clerk come morning ("The Stag Line Pays the Piper," October 1932).

As the Depression deepened, young people increasingly debated the pros and cons of delaying marriage till love became more affordable ("Marry Now? No! . . . Yes!" February 1934). Always on the side of romance, *Chatelaine* asked young women, "Are You a Good Date?" (September 1938), then offered suggestions for improvement: take him by surprise ("Curl your eyelashes, wear your sweater backward"); make him feel chivalrous ("Be a little petrified of fast driving"); gain his attention through specific questions ("Do you really enjoy cutting up frogs?").

Shortages also hampered romance during World War II—not of money but of men. An exception occurred in Canadian towns located near training camps, suddenly overrun by soldiers and their female camp-followers. Despite scandalous rumors, *Chatelaine* found no upsurge in illegitimacy, rape or venereal disease, and was reassured by the wholesomeness of the canteens and Host Houses set up by the locals ("The Soldier and His Spare Time Problems," March 1941).

In its preoccupation with marriage, the fifties were the heyday of the infamous do's and don'ts of dating, usually listing nine ways for a girl to efface herself, then ending with a jaunty "Always be yourself." Males were enshrined by *Chatelaine* as critics-at-large, and the new sport was comparing Canadian women unfavorably with the European ones they'd dated during the war ("Why Aren't Canadian *Femmes* More *Fatales?*" September 1957). Even during the sixties, magazines routinely polled men as to what they wanted women to be, with the implication that wannabe wives had best tailor themselves to fit these expectations ("What Is Sex Appeal?" August 1963).

In "Dr. Marion Hilliard Talks to Single Women" (February 1956), a noted Canadian doctor offered cautionary advice to unmarried women for dealing with loneliness and their sex drive. At a time when "old maids" were the objects of scorn, the bleak, second-best life she described was many a woman's reality. However, after a decade in which both men and women pursued careers and openly binged on sex, unpartnered women had emerged as an upbeat, self-sufficient group, as cheerfully described in "On Being Successfully Single" (April 1977). Unfortunately, not only did many men resent an even playing field, but they were openly bitter over the new definitions of sexual harassment ("Fear of Flirting," April 1993).

# Can She Manage Alone?

*Matchmaking mothers went out of fashion long ago—but is the modern girl going to need them again, if jobs remain hard to get—and the "surplus" women increase?*

By Isabel Turnbull Dingman

**APRIL 1932**

THERE WAS A WEDDING IN A certain Canadian city this winter which the papers described as "one of the season's loveliest." They failed to add that it was one of the season's most unique, in that the bride was the youngest of eight sisters, every one of whom had been married in the same church.

Friends, kind and otherwise, made due note of the fact, however, and I heard numerous comments in the club lounge one afternoon.

"Well, at last Mrs. Armstrong can come downstairs, sit in her own living room, and listen to the radio when she wants to," said some.

"Poor woman, she can sleep nights now without worrying about getting any more daughters off her hands," said others.

"Well, it wouldn't do a lot of mothers any harm to interview Mrs. Armstrong and find out her methods," declared one woman. "She has certainly made a success of bringing up those girls; every one of them is a credit to her and every one has married happily, yet nobody ever called her a matchmaking mother or accused the family of man-chasing. Think of it—eight daughters—eight married daughters—when many people have only one, or two, or three, yet find them slipping into spinsterhood."

Careful matchmaking in past generations was due to the fact that daughters were an economic burden. But now it begins to look as though careers for women are not so assured, and marriage may again become their most certain means of livelihood.

Experts say that the depression is by no means the whole cause, and that the trend started some three years ago, women beginning then to lose ground in the business world. Those already established are not yet badly off, though some women are finding salaries and prestige reduced, but the young girls just starting out present very discouraging reports. Every province has its hundreds of unemployed teachers. Every city has its committee dealing with office girls out of work. Clever young women who left university a year or two ago, confident of conquering the world, are to be found staying home with mother because there is nothing else to do. If girls cannot find jobs, the economic advantages of marrying them off again become apparent.

There is also the fact that nearly all parents want their daughters to marry because they think it means the greatest happiness for them. Any normal parent will cheerfully see a girl give up a dazzling career for a mere man. However, Canada being such a young country, with men outnumbering women, the great majority of girls have had no difficulty getting married without much help from anybody until the last few years. But since the war there has been a gradual change in conditions, until today, in every Canadian city, there is a growing number of girls who have little or nothing to do with men in a social way, and whose chances of marriage are correspondingly poor. They belong to girls' bridge clubs and badminton clubs, girls' study clubs, girls' recreation clubs; they have their jobs, and their lives are far from empty or aimless. But they grow restless as they see the years slipping by with no enlargement of social contacts to include men friends and possible husbands. And every year, another crop of girls, who were formerly "just kids," is growing up and joining the ranks of marriageable women—formidable rivals.

Are there lots more men in Canada than women? When statistics are considered, it would appear at first glance that there ought to be a Jack for every Jill in the Dominion. The 1921 census showed thirty more men per 1,000 than women, and it is expected that the present census will show the proportions still in favor of the men, though materially reduced. According to the *Canada Year Book*, the greatest excess of males over females in recent history was in 1911, when there were sixty more per 1,000. The Great War, however, both checked immigration and took some 60,000 young male lives as its toll, reducing the surplus by half in 1921.

Canada obviously is still far from having the "surplus woman" problem of European countries, but she has also gone far from the pioneer days when women were greatly outnumbered by men, and any girl who was at all passable could marry if she wished. In rural districts, especially in the West, there are still considerably more women than men, and the chief worry of parents in the country is that girls will marry too young. But when it is considered that the highly trained and highly paid business and professional women are concentrated in the cities, while city men include many laborers and low-paid industrial workers, it is easily seen that though there might theoretically be a man for every woman, there cannot be enough "eligible" men to go around.

What can be done about it?

❧

Social sets are formed naturally from among the children of the neighborhood, school and college associates, and young people who spend their summers together. For this reason, careful parents live in the best districts they can afford and encourage their daughters to have friends around the house from their sandpile days. Some parents spoil things by being too effusive. They gush and twitter and show such excitement at the novel situation of Mary Anne having some attention that the young men shy off. Other fathers and mothers adopt a cold, suspicious attitude, catechizing Mary Anne minutely about every boy she mentions, and being present whenever a young man comes in, to ask searching questions about his family, business, and views on life. Few boys so treated ever come back a second time, unless they are very hard hit. But the most common error of parents is to get in the way without meaning to. They like the young folks and are interested in them, and can't understand why it isn't perfectly all right for them to join the party and lead conversation for hours on end.

The Armstrongs did things very differently. When strange young men came to the house, they were there to meet them, greeting them with easy cordiality. But after a few minutes of pleasant conversation they slipped away, murmuring something about going to the movies, or being tired, and left the cosy living room to the girls and their friends.

With eight girls in the family there was hardly a night for twenty years that one or more young men weren't crossing that hospitable threshold, and the atmosphere within was so comfortable and natural that the boys liked it and kept on coming.

However, the Armstrong attitude did not at all mean that mother and dad were indifferent. Far from it. Within a few days after a new man had appeared, Father Armstrong made it his business to find out quietly all he could about his social and financial position and his desirability as friend or relation. If the report was favorable, the welcome sign remained on the doormat. If not, a few words to the girl concerned were usually enough. Another notable point in the Armstrong technique was that young men coming to the city as strangers were often taken up. It is much easier to impress a boy who is lonely and unattached than one who has his own circle of friends and interests.

❧

In England, marriage settlements among the well-to-do are the rule. But in Canada, due to the preponderance of men over women, these customs died out. The first question asked by father when interviewing a prospective son-in-law has been, "Can you support her in the style to which she is accustomed?" If the answer is "No," the deal is off. Father may have made a will leaving several thousand dollars to his daughter, but that she might get more value from the money by having it now never seems to enter a great many heads. Yet no greater happiness returns can be secured than by using money to help a young couple get started in the first ardor of romance and enthusiasm. Many young men, university graduates, start in to work at salaries of $75 and $100 a month. If they join big corporations it is impossible to make any meteoric rise, though they may steadily advance at the rate of $100 or so a year. But they will be twenty-six or twenty-seven before they are earning $150 a month, and though at that age they may have fallen in love and want to establish a home, they find the sum inadequate.

As a result, plenty of young men who would like to marry get the habit of taking out a lot of girls instead of one, for fear of becoming entangled, and girls who would fall in love with them, if given any encouragement, remain puzzled and resentful.

Any way you look at it, though, getting married is no longer for girls the simple affair of yesteryear. There will have to be patient and skilful co-operation between parents and daughters if the "surplus" woman problem is not to become acute in this young country.

# The Stag Line Pays the Piper

***When young men are crippled financially, paying for entertainments during the debutante season their vitality drained by all night revels—how can they get the best out of their day's work?***

By Ellen E. Mackie

"**W**ANTED—FORTY EXTRA men in the stag line." That is what my friend, Jack, tells me the modern debutante demands at her coming-out ball. It is part of the game of this debutante business—which, from the girl's standpoint, is her big scene.

It has always seemed to me rather sporting of those forty-odd men! What girl would go to the trouble of dressing for a ball, where the programme called for forty wallflowers and she was slated for one of them?

But these forty men . . . and their contemporaries in the stag line! What of them? Who are they? Where do come from? These youths who flutter like black moths around the galaxy of glamorous buds—who so gallantly act as their foil!—it is on them this entire debutante business hinges. They are the actual machinery of society's merry-go-round.

To watch these care-free lads with their nonchalant air, you would never guess the fight some of them are putting up to play the social game.

It takes the mother of sons to get below the surface. She alone of all women has the angle of the stag line. A slant that many a debutante might give much to know.

∾

Men become blasé with too much society stuff. Before the depression, parties crowded upon each other and overlapped. The men got very fed up; girls telephoning constantly—asking them to their homes, to supper-dances, house-parties and what not. The boys got to the point where they had to be coaxed. All kinds of inducements were offered. Now that this deluge of entertaining has stopped, they are getting keener on social affairs. But there are plenty of youths flitting about in the smart set, whose pay cheques are not equal to the strain. He will be on hand, however, when the moment arrives. How he does the trick is nobody's business. He will pay up cheerfully for taxis, table, drinks, tips . . . and when it's over, he takes her to a downtown restaurant for bacon and eggs in the wee sma' hours.

*When young men are crippled financially— paying for entertainments during the debutante season, their vitality drained by all- night revels— how can they get the best out of their day's work?*

How does he do it? His wits, my dears!

The boys help out each other. Perhaps the above lad has a friend with a car who is taking a girl to the same supper-dance. The four will motor there together—as one boy said—"We bum a ride and save taxi fare."

Or if this youth happened to buy a car when times were good, he may rent it out to other boys on his off nights. One chap tells of selling an insurance policy to his girl's mother—then using the money to take daughter to a night club.

Another lad gets into a game of cards. If, with luck, he makes a killing, you will see him the next night swanking it with a girl at a smart hotel supper-dance. And there is a bright boy, of my acquaintance, who coaches the sons of the newly rich in social etiquette. Does he "soak" them? Yes—and he's quite frank about it.

But it is a hand-to-mouth existence. Even worse, some are away in debt—and still the game goes on.

And so we come to the other side of the picture. Vision that other stag line; that line of lads, who with tired, drawn faces, trudge down to work on the cold, grey morning after; their nerves shaken, heads aching, money spent—and the grind and strain of the day staring them in the face.

Perhaps they are oblivious to all this—maybe dreaming of some deb, who at that very moment is curled up in her warm, comfortable bed—sipping her hot coffee from a dainty breakfast tray, or leisurely stepping into her scented bath.

Has she a thought this morning for the lad who paid for last night's revels? Perhaps he is the man she expects to marry. He is straining every nerve to make good, struggling to keep up the pace she sets and yet hold down a job that is to provide for her future.

Jack, my friend, who goes about with a set of young moderns, tells me that many a boy is found "sound asleep" at his desk, the day after an all-night revel. He confessed one day that he, himself, got into real trouble with his manager. "I had a head that morning," he confided later. "As luck would have it, the chief called me into his office, about a big deal he had on. I stared, cockeyed—everything went flooey. Not two ideas to rub against each other."

∾

Is it any wonder our boys don't get on in business?

I know of more than one lad, now in a sanitarium, after a futile battle to hold his job and follow his fiancee through her first season.

Are we not rather over-doing this debutante business? Aren't we giving the girls themselves, false standards of life? They sky-rocket through a season with head in the clouds. They are feted, photographed, flattered, fill society columns—and are over-rated out of all proportion.

Is it fair? Instead of splashing all this on the debutante—why should not the boys come in for their share? Let them, too, have a coming-out—but one with a purpose. Why shouldn't father give a dinner for son, introducing him to prominent business men? Think what it would mean to them when they start out to make their way—having met these powers of the business world under such favorable conditions?

∾

What would some of these hot-house society buds think, I wonder, if they overheard the comments of the "stags?" Why girls do, or do not click! Let no deb in the ballroom think she escapes criticism. Every mother's daughter is up before a mighty astute jury. Her personality, her gown, dancing, her prospects—are all under the male searchlight. Odd quirks in her nature will even provide a bit of amusement.

But in a way, my dears, you have asked for it. In your mother's day, a belle was a belle through sheer beauty, wit, and charm—not because dad paid forty extra men to cut in on her dances—to make her seem popular. At those olden day balls, the sexes were equal in numbers. Hence the young bucks were kept too busy prancing about in waltz and schottische, to drape the walls criticising the girls.

What sort of girls are popular? I heard one lad say, "Watch the gang flock around Peggy. She's throwing a dance next week."

Another girl sprang into popularity when her father bought a sort of country lodge for winter sports.

Popularity more or less hangs by a thread. A certain girl may vamp them all, at a dance. But watch her at a week-end party! At the country house, she becomes a strain; too stimulating. After a day or so, the men grow bored and weary.

For instance, a certain hostess invited a young

Apollo to bring a girl down to her country home for a few days. Imagine then, their pique when he chose as his week-end partner a quiet, self-effacing young woman, with whom he seldom danced! Even his mother was curious. "Why Jane—?" she queried, "I should think Patty would be your choice!"

The young bachelor threw his mother a wise smile.

"True, mater," he agreed, "Pat's the berries for an evening's fun. But for three whole days—ye gods! Jane isn't pretty, or peppy, but she never gets on a fellow's nerves."

Like the man who ate chicken's wings at banquets—and ordered roast-beef-medium, three hundred and sixty-five days in the year. So, flaming youth may hit the high spots with the scintillating Circe, but for steady diet, he will choose some mousie little wallflower to sit opposite him at the table three times a day.

# Marry Now? No!

—By a Young Man

**FEBRUARY 1934**

"I SEE BY THE PAPERS," SAID A politician friend the other day, "that the marriage rate is declining. We're having fewer marriages and fewer births. If this goes on, what is going to happen to the State? A young fellow like you should go out and take a wife."

My politician friend is the sort of patriot who would have you die—or marry—for his country. So, with the verbosity of his tribe, he went on to tell me that more young people should be responding to the "cosmic urge."

He would probably be talking yet had I not stopped him in his verbal tracks with a question. "You say," I said, "that I should marry for the sake of the State. Will you tell me what the State will do for the sake of my marriage?"

There being no answer, I went back to my bachelor apartment and thought the problem over. And the thinking wasn't pleasant.

I happen to be engaged to a girl, have been engaged to her for two years. Being a perfectly natural, normal girl, she thinks we should get married. Biologically, and from the standpoint of happiness, I suppose she is right. Unfortunately, my present salary is small, my prospects uncertain. In fact, unless we soon reach that corner round which prosperity is said to be lurking, I'll be exceedingly lucky to hold my job. True, the girl to whom I am engaged is working, but they won't let her go on working once they find out that she's married. The public likes to pretend that it is all for matrimony, that it encourages it. Yet let two young people go and get married and one of the first consequences is that the girl, if she happens to have a job, will be asked to quit. It is one way of subsidizing old maids.

I have some degree of self-respect and dignity, and, I hope, some small semblance of chivalry; and because I have, then I don't exactly relish the prospect of marrying a girl to put her on relief. The young lady to whom I am engaged has a home, and money to buy clothes and a few luxuries. She can afford to take an occasional vacation, can go to a theatre, to a hockey game or a movie. Why should I ask her to go without comforts, to slave for me in a kitchen, to do without a maid?

Personally, I don't think a marriage of that kind can make any man happy. And I know that many men agree with me. Perhaps it's because some of them have seen friends facing the tragedy of going to a relief station for food and clothing for their young wives, and sometimes suffering humiliation from the scorn of "in-laws" who thought they should have jobs.

This is a far different thing from reconciled bachelorhood. It is not a case of the man who is selfishly satisfied with his club and his golf, or who regards matrimony as a tyranny. Such fellows exist. But there are thousands of others who, like myself, don't want to be bachelors. They believe in marriage as an adventure, but as an adventure in which the principals have at least the ghost of a chance.

I know what some other critics will say. They will say that "the Lord always provides." He does. But the trouble is that the Lord leaves distribution to others, and they have managed to make a mess of it.

Preachers moralists, statesmen and psychologists, all unite to extol matrimony, yet nearly all of them, and the State as well, conspire to make matrimony difficult.

The proof? Well, let's see, for example, what happens to a man, so far as the State is concerned, when he makes his first marriage gesture. That first gesture is the purchase of an engagement ring, and the State's response to it, its encouragement, is a tax of forty-five per cent on the ring. Later on, if there's a wedding ring and a few old-fashioned girls still like a wedding ring—there's a tax of thirty-five per cent on that. Then, greatest irony of all, there's another tax for a marriage license; there's a tax on everything the bride puts into her trousseau; and, God forgive them, there's a tax on even the marriage bed itself!

Over in Europe, the State tries to promote marriage. There's Mussolini, for example. When, some weeks ago, 800 Roman couples, conforming with Il Duce's wish that more Italians should wed—Mussolini believes more in babies than in immigrants—went and got married in a sort of group, the Italian Dictator presented each couple with a cheque and an insurance policy to boot.

Over here they would have been presented with a tax bill. Our parliaments and our statesmen, for ever talking about the need of population, are ever ready to vote money for immigrants. Yet let a Canadian boy and girl decide to get married and present Canada with some good, lusty young Canadians and the only reward they can look forward to is a considerably higher tax bill. So don't talk to me about marrying for the State.

# Marry Now? Yes

## *The $5-prize-winning letter*

**APRIL 1934** **O**H, YES! TAKE THE CHANCE. We did it. Before we married, my husband and I both occupied good positions. We had planned marriage for two years but along came the panic and we were both let out, so my "to be" husband said: "We may as well 'swim' as sink"; and disregarding advice from world-wise mothers and reluctant dads—we took the plunge into the matrimonial sea.

After futile attempts to secure employment through the medium of the press, the primal urge which brought our forebears over the rolling ocean to seek their destiny in a new world, asserted itself and we decided to go to the wide spaces and secure a homestead.

We traded our small car for a truck, and packing the necessities of life we headed into a fertile part of the state, where we pitched our tent on the verdant slopes of a mighty inland lake.

Tragic and comic effects were often set to the tune of the wide waves ere we had located our homestead, fenced it and built the rustic, three-roomed bungalow, then tilled and planted a garden, our first agricultural attempt. However, the yields were prolific. Through the summer we continued work on the interior of our home, gathered and preserved the abundant wild fruits, accumulated some hens, planted a hedge, cut wood and prepared for the advance of winter's legions.

Space will not permit details, but today as I sit in front of my own glowing fireplace I am proud of what we have accomplished. We are now a happy healthy family of three; our little Daisy is the cutest, sweetest darling you ever saw. She daily gladdens our hearts with her sweet childish wiles.

We have twenty acres of good soil under cultivation, a team of horses, two Jersey cows and twenty thoroughbred hens, and our basement well stored with vegetables, while fuel, fish and game are abundant for the taking.

We have had hours of fatigue but few of loneliness, as nature supplants the amusements and lure of the old life, with trips through the forest, bathing at the glorious sand beach, or working among the pansies in the garden. In winter we have a small table radio, and dinners and dances while away the long winter evenings.

Living close to nature we have buoyant health, and look forward in mutual trust to an interesting future.—"Eureka"

# Are You a Good Date?

*When you see your closest friends being asked everywhere, while you sit at home, it's time to ask—What's the trouble?*

BY LORNA SLOCOMBE

**SEPTEMBER 1938** NO GIRL HAS EVER REALLY suffered until she has undergone the devastating experience of being a perfect flop. You know that feeling: somehow, somewhere, the date has gone wrong. You can't think of a word to say. You know the man is dying to get rid of you. And pretty soon you find yourself being said goodnight to, and the-only-man-you-ever-really-loved is fading out of your life with a casual, "See you some time!"

Well, what's the trouble? You feel disillusioned, and decide that in order to be popular, a girl has to be beautiful, or Bad, or have a convertible coupe. However, there are plenty of girls who are homely, unobtrusively virtuous, pedestrians perforce—and still popular.

If your dates are infrequent and unsuccessful, there must be a reason. Let's assume that you've done right by your face, and taken due heed of the warnings in the magazine ads. Maybe the whole trouble is just some little flaw in your technique. It may be nothing more fatal than a loud and persistent giggle. Or perhaps your whole attitude is wrong. How about it; are you a good date?

∽

Among the girls who wonder why their dates aren't

successful, you'll find a large group who start out on an evening's so-called fun, with the most amazingly cold-blooded attitude. The girl of this type thinks it's a good idea to go out with any man, however awful, because she may meet other men.

Now while you, yourself, may not be quite so practical as all this, you may verge on the type and give your date the wrong impression. For instance, do you pay attention to him, while you're dancing? Or do you devote your energy to staring with great interest over his shoulder to see who's at the dance, and who's likely to cut in next? When you get broken in on, do you remember to smile at your last partner as if you'd enjoyed the dance tremendously, or are you so relieved that you fall hastily into the new partner's arms, without a backward glance, a smile, or a parting word?

Of course, at a dance or a party, no date wants to have you hung around his neck like an albatross. He wants to dance and talk with other girls besides you. But it certainly is only civilized for you to be especially devoted to your own date. Don't be afraid to ask questions.

To get most men talking, your questions have got to be specific. "Do you like Greta Garbo?" "Don't you think the short skirts are prettier?" "Were you ever in an automobile accident?" "What do you do with your spare time?" "Do you really enjoy cutting up frogs?" "Tell me, what are you planning to do after you graduate?"

Perhaps, in your quiet way, you just expect to be taken to the movies and fed a lemonade afterward. But that all tots up to a dollar or so—which may be four times as much as the young man has in pocket after he's finished paying for his cigarettes, cleaner's bill and haircut. It really helps the cause along tremendously for a girl to say, "Let's not go to the Ritz-Platter. Let's all go up to my house and scramble some eggs." Incidentally, it's a grand opportunity for you to radiate domesticity and charm, as you raid your own icebox, with a becoming apron tied on over your evening dress—that Myrna Loy combination of glamor and comradeship.

Are you always the same sweet girl saying the same old things? Or do you drag out a startling opinion now and then, have some new ideas about what to do, or burst out in red fingernails, just for a change?

Don't invariably wear powder blue, just because it's your best color. Dazzle your beau some night by bursting forth in cherry red, or yellow, or chartreuse. Change your coiffure frequently, and ask his opinion on each change. Just for fun, go sophisticated some night in black, with a veil. Every date have something new as a surprise for him, even if it's just a bracelet he hasn't seen before, or a tricky compact. Curl your eyelashes, wear your sweater backward—anything.

Show a little originality some evening, and try something completely different. Go roller-skating. Call up some friends to come in and play charades. Take an evening off to learn the tango. Make fudge. Read poetry aloud. Hire a horse and carriage and go for a buggy ride. Have a rousing game of tiddly-winks.

Let your personality vary with the mood of the moment. Gay for parties, and sentimental on moonlit nights. Be practically pals for informal occasions—but when it's a real dress-up affair, put on a little glamor with your long skirts. Never let him be sure of exactly what's going to happen.

Men really enjoy being chivalrous, and will do themselves proud if you give them half a chance. So don't hop too ably in and out of rumble seats. Let your date open doors. Take his arm over rough spots and across streets. Be a little petrified of fast driving, thunderstorms, and roller-coasters. And get yourself generally looked after and cherished.

If you let a man be late for dates, ignore you at the dances he takes you to, go always where he wants to, and do what he wants to do, and then come home when it suits his fancy—then you're bringing out the beast in him. And he won't particularly enjoy it. In fact, he'll probably soon be dating some girl who keeps him up to scratch. Yes, men do love to put their girl on a pedestal. So if you want to have lots of dates, climb up on that pedestal and pose!

When he phones and asks you if you'd like to go to the show, don't pick that time to be blasé. Be pleased, definitely. Say, "Oh, I'd just *love* to!" And during your date, manage to give the impression that you are perfectly delighted to be going out that night, feel *just* like going to the movies, and would rather be going with him than anybody in the world.

And when it comes time to say goodnight, tell him what a grand time you've had. If you've fol-

lowed all of our suggestions, your evening has been a success, so—many happy returns of the date!

*If you want your beau to enjoy his date with you, let him know you are having a wonderful time.*

# The Soldier and His Spare Time Problems

*There are canteens both inside and outside the military camps. Here's one of the Red Triangle Clubs for men of the forces on leave.*

BY FREDERICK EDWARDS

MARCH 1941

AS GOOD A PLACE AS ANY TO begin this article is with the obvious premise that war, an abnormal condition, compels all sorts of unnatural things to happen. Because of war, husbands are separated from wives, brothers from sisters, sons from parents, parents from children, and sweethearts one from another. A state of war concentrates tens of thousands of men in huge encampments amid strange surroundings, often thousands of miles from home. To some small towns and to other big cities, war may bring a temporary prosperity, but that prosperity may be accompanied by a feverish unrest, sometimes leading to lawlessness. Upon social agencies and welfare organizations war thrusts an entirely new and unfamiliar accumulation of complicated problems.

And war is a great breeder of rumors. Ever since Canada began to enlist and train men there have been rumors of drunkenness, of assaults upon women, of robbery with violence, of deserted families left destitute, of prostitutes gathering at camp barriers, and of venereal disease being widespread.

Some weeks ago the editor of *Chatelaine* sent this reporter out upon an attempt to trace some of these disturbing hearsays to their sources, and to discover just how much of their content is true, and how much false. And this is what we found.

There have been in the past year and a half some instances of violence on the part of individual soldiers, and of small groups of men in uniform. One or two of them have been pretty nasty, exactly as such similar outbreaks are nasty in civil life. The toll of such incidents is now steadily decreasing, the military authorities say, because undesirables are being weeded out, and the passage of time is bringing the enlisted man into an understanding and acceptance of discipline.

Criminal offenses by men in uniform are rare, and when they do occur, the guilty man is severely punished. First he is turned over to the civil police for trial. When he has completed his prison sentence, a court martial has the power to try him and convict him again for the same offense, and his military punishment is followed by a dishonorable discharge. Knowledge of the severity of the double penalty seems likely to restrain even the most reckless.

⁓

Recently we spent a rather chilly week-end in a small city located near a large camp, the origin of many tall tales concerning soldierly saturnalias. It was about as dull a time as we can remember ever having experienced. There were at least four men in uniform for every civilian male on the streets that Saturday night. The hotel beverage rooms were jammed with soldiers and airmen. So were the picture houses; but there was absolutely no serious disorder, and we saw only three mild arguments. Hotelkeepers close their beverage rooms early when such action is indicated by their own judgment, or upon request from the military authorities. Military Police and Air Force were out in numbers, making the rounds at regular intervals. Beery individuals inclined to boisterousness were either taken care of by their companions, refused service by the waiters and eventually eased off the premises, or started on their way back to camp by M.P.'s.

On the streets, soldiers and their girls strolled arm in arm along the sidewalks, looking in shop windows, and almost every man in uniform who went to a movie had a lady friend by his side; but there was no more legitimate reason to spy out evil in those companionships than there would have been had the men worn civvies. Merchants, hotelmen and municipal officials are practically unanimous in their opinion that "generally speaking, the boys behave themselves splendidly, and we're glad to have them around."

Women "camp followers" of the most degraded type are a problem. They have gathered in considerable numbers in the vicinity of the big encampments, and in cities where servicemen are assembled. Control or elimination of this evil is a job for the civil police, since the naval or military authority does not extend beyond the men in uniform. Therefore, the extent of their depredations often depends upon the efficiency, or otherwise, of

the municipal police force immediately concerned. Military authorities and the civilian police say the sinister activities of these harpies are being held in check increasingly as time goes on and their occupation is noted and reported. Once they are identified, it is comparatively a simple matter to arrange for their removal to a less dangerous and more austere environment; in other words, to place them in reformatories. The association of organizations grouped under the various Local Councils of Women are now urging upon the proper authorities the appointment of policewomen to provincial police forces. They reason, and with sound logic, that a feminine officer is likely to be much more efficient than a man when it comes to tracking down undesirable members of her own sex.

A more perverse situation is created by girls and women whose chief characteristics are a low sense of moral responsibility coupled with a high hankering after excitement. All our large cities, and most of the smaller communities where camps are located, have among their populations a percentage of weak sisters of this type. They are not after the serviceman's bankroll, but they are out for a good time. Usually they are employed, and, like the servicemen, they are usually far away from their homes. They may have no relatives or close friends within hundreds of miles. What could be more natural than that the lonely working girl should make a date with the lonely soldier on weekend leave in a strange town?

The fact that, so far, there is no noteworthy increase in the number of children born without benefit of the marriage ceremony has a special significance. The Infants' Home at Toronto, caring for unwanted and neglected babies and children from all parts of the province, reports a total of cases handled during 1940, of 1,105 infants, an increase of only thirty-one cases over the 1939 figure. Of these, 832 involved unmarried mothers, but of the 832, only fifty-one fathers were servicemen, or about one in sixteen, a remarkably low figure considering the tens of thousands of enlisted men stationed in Ontario camps from September, 1939, on.

At the same time clinical records show a surprisingly small percentage of venereal infection among the men in uniform. Men in the service forces are better protected against the malignant menace of venereal infection than are civilians. Reports of exposure to possible infection are demanded by regulations, and prophylactic treatment is a matter of routine. Punishment for failure to report is severe. Medical officers talk over the subject frankly with the men. Also, recent discoveries have introduced new and highly efficacious drugs to their treatment. It may come to be counted the greatest triumph of science over disease since the conquest of smallpox.

Among all the women's organizations busy with war work directly in contact with the service forces, the Young Women's Christian Association seems to occupy a key position. The Y. W., through a system of Hostess Houses conveniently located near many military and naval camps—but *outside* the camp area—is providing clearing stations for all the troubles the enlisted man's flesh is heir to. Especially the Hostess Houses are appreciated by the servicemen's womenfolk; mothers, wives and sweethearts.

Hostess Houses plan parties, arrange dances complete with nice girl partners, run a light lunch counter that they call a "tuck shop," although just why an English schoolboy's name for a snack bar should have been transposed to fit a dry canteen is a mystery, arrange cozy corners for confidential chats, libraries for the literary. They arrange weddings, even whip up a wedding cake, and hand out rice to the guests. They send telephone messages to men in camp, advising them that their visitors have arrived safely. They find rooms for relatives and sometimes for soldiers and sailors on more or less permanent duty in Canada; they locate family apartments and see to it that the rent is what it ought to be. Hitchhiking wives and mothers are rested and comforted. There is a case on record of a seventy-year-old hitchhiker who travelled hundreds of miles to one camp so that she could see her son before he was sent overseas. She hadn't seen him for twelve years. The Hostess House located not only the son, but a grandson to boot, in service at the same camp.

In one camp at least, there is a boarded-off corner where the soldier who is going out on a heavy date can press his uniform before he starts.

Pay no attention to sensational stories of evil conditions in and around the camps. In most cases they are not true.

# Dr. Marion Hilliard Talks to Single Women

*How can a woman live a happy, useful life without a husband and without children? Here is what a noted Canadian doctor tells unmarried women who come to her with this great problem*

By Dr. Marion Hilliard

*Chief of the Service of Obstetrics and Gynecology, Women's College Hospital, Toronto.*

**FEBRUARY 1956**

A SUNDAY-SCHOOL TEACHER, unmarried and sedate of appearance, came into my office one afternoon with some symptoms of headaches and sleeplessness. She began telling me about a man she had been seeing lately. My attention wandered; it was spring, Gieseking had given a Beethoven concert at Massey Hall the night before and the fishing season was about to open.

Suddenly I became aware that my patient had stopped talking. I was dismayed because I hadn't heard a word for some time. I decided to try to bluff. "Well, then he asked you to his apartment. What did you say to him?"

The woman's jaw dropped open. "How did you know? I was just going to tell you that!"

I couldn't tell her that I've heard a myriad variations of the same tale in the more than twenty years I've been an obstetrician and gynecologist. No matter who tells it, from an adolescent to a matron, plain or pretty, virgin or wanton, there comes the moment when some man asks them to his apartment, or a hotel room. I am no longer as amazed as I used to be that each of these women appears to believe the man's invitation was an extraordinary and astonishing development.

They are victims of what I believe is a woman's greatest mistake: underestimating what I shall term her biology. Creation has gone to considerable

trouble to make her female, to grant her certain glands and desires and an aura to enhance her in the eyes of males, and then she is full of innocent surprise and wonderment when these attributes demonstrate that they are in working order.

"I'm not *that* kind of girl," they explain to me. This is outrageous nonsense. Except for a statistical handful who have abnormally low metabolisms, everybody is *that* kind of girl.

From the day she is born until she dies, a woman must live with her gender. Some women have the impression that being female is a bundle of tricks, such as squealing at mice, being poor at arithmetic, tears, perfume behind the ears and an attitude of fragile wonder in the face of an abstract like international justice.

Femaleness, as any doctor will tell you, is savage. Woman is equipped with a reproductive system which, even if she never uses it, dominates her fibre. It has vicious power that can leap out of control without the slightest warning, while a man and a woman share a companionable chuckle or happen to touch hands. In the time it takes to blink, they have reached a point of no return. The mechanism of woman can also be triggered unexpectedly by the low moan of a crooner, by a summer sky full of stars, by the sight of a man's hands working with metal, or even by fog collecting around a street light. Any pretense that this force does not exist is as bizarre and illogical as pretending there is no atom bomb.

When I was a younger doctor, caring for unmarried women who were about to have babies, I used to ask the more intelligent and sensible of them, "How could this have happened to you?" The girl would answer simply, "I couldn't help myself," and I used to turn away sceptically. I believed then, as almost all women do, that a woman controlled the quality of her relationship with a man. If it became intimate, I reasoned, it was because she deliberately chose to let it happen.

This just isn't true. I'm wiser now and I realize that an easy companionship traveling at about ten miles an hour can shift to a blinding passion going a hundred miles an hour without any warning, soundlessly.

A woman's first protection against this betrayal is to appreciate that the speed-up of her emotions is not only possible but natural and normal. Her best defense is to have no confidence at all in her ability to say nay at the appropriate moment.

For this reason women have to safeguard themselves with a standard of conduct that may seem quaint and archaic. I cannot be so unrealistic as to suggest that teen-agers, for example, should never kiss. But not enough mothers warn their daughters that kissing is intended by nature to be an appetizer, not an entire meal.

The same rules still hold for a college girl or one beginning to work in an office, factory or store. Some new situations, however, have been added. Visiting the man's hotel room or apartment alone is like playing with loaded dice—you lose every time.

My most important piece of advice for any woman is to play in her own league. A young girl shouldn't go with a man, a secretary with her boss, a naïve woman with a sophisticate, a sheltered youngster with a hoodlum in a windbreaker. Those who do are sure to be hurt.

Much of my practice has been with women who have been labeled career women. Most of them are highly intelligent, charming and attractive; most of them are also unmarried.

A hundred or more of them have whispered to me, "Doctor, I'm not married and it doesn't look as though I'm going to be married. What do I do with my sex?"

To me it is as ridiculous as asking what to do with lungs. She uses her lungs for breathing and her sex drive, properly channeled, for enriching her life.

A woman who feels unwanted is bound to get into trouble; she's looking for it. The unmarried woman has to face up to herself and her life. She's got to stop expecting life to be fair. Life doesn't owe her a handsome adoring husband and two beautiful children full of bright sayings.

This is the bitter, desperate adjustment that the single woman has to make. Nothing will again be as painful as the moment she realizes that she will live all her life alone; no moment will ever hurt so much. Once this is past she can begin to sort out her existence on the sound and sane basis of "This is how it is going to be" rather than the treacherous, doomed "This is what might happen tomorrow."

It's curious how many unmarried women have

the impression that a marriage license automatically assures an idyllic existence. I sometimes suspect that the myth is kept alive by married women who regard the Paris-copy clothes of their unmarried sisters, examine the unscratched coffee tables, listen to the tales of bus trips to Mexico and opening night at the theatre and then remark blandly: "Isn't it a shame you aren't married. You poor dear!"

The unmarried girl is wise to stay away from any activities that involve her married friends with their husbands. As her friends marry, her relationship with them must continue in the area that is unchanged by the marriage—luncheons, shopping trips, women's club activities. Otherwise the married woman and unmarried woman's lives are too different; they can only, unwittingly, hurt one another.

If the unmarried girl is fortunate enough to find another girl her own age with whom she can share her interest in art galleries or books, they are wise to consider sharing an apartment. Both girls, through their mutual respect and affection, can help one another through the lonely patches of their lives. The essential of such a relationship is that neither girl tries to dominate the other and that both are free to go on about their work unchanged. I was once asked for my definition of living in sin. It's this: any two people living together while one dominates and tyrannizes the other are, to me, living in sin.

This takes care of the surface details of the single woman's existence. We come now to the difficult and complex area of her biology. Some women have met this problem with the ingenious hallucination that it doesn't exist. They keep a tidy brain. They withdraw and become grey shadows, living grey shadow lives that are utter wastes.

The sex drive of the normal woman is capable of giving her great radiance. It's the force within her that makes her gentle with children; it's a power that can knock the cover off a golf ball or take her straight down an almost perpendicular ski trail; it's part of the passion she feels when an animal is mistreated; it's in the understanding she can give another human being who is desperately lonely.

It can also make her the most miserable of women. I recommend a policy of prevention in

*New Orleans jazz has a primitive tom-tom rhythm that does a single woman's peace of mind no good. Tchaikovsky wrote some mood music for two—and despair music for one.*

order to lessen the shattering effect of desire. If walking in the darkness makes a woman ache inside, then she should stick to daylight for her strolls. New Orleans jazz has a primitive tom-tom rhythm that does a single woman's peace of mind no good. Tchaikovsky wrote some mood music for two—and despair music for one. It's masochistic to listen to music that is disturbing.

The single woman must also avoid involvement in casual dates. "Sleeping around," as casual love-making is known in the vernacular, is destructive for a woman. A woman gets no real fulfillment in such flippant attachments; she is degraded and her spirit suffers terrible damage.

The human needs that a woman cannot do without don't include passion at all. They are affection, a sense of achievement, status and security. These four are the permanent necessities; the need for sex is a transient longing.

I've discovered, over an adult lifetime of looking at this problem, that each age group of the unmarried girl has its own distinguishing characteristics and must be dealt with separately. With girls in their twenties, the most common disaster is that an older man exploits the girl's admiration of him. Too often in offices, young secretaries come to adore worldly, urbane, middle-aged bosses. For a man of experience it is a simple matter to charm the girl into a hotel suite.

A woman in her thirties has a dwindling chance of marrying. She is calling herself a bachelor girl, but she knows the synonym is old maid. At this point in her life, passion is going to sear her to the bone. She is bound to fall in love and her love is almost sure to be married.

"I'm thinking of having an affair—with a married man," a patient of mine once told me bluntly.

"Are you truly in love," I asked her, "or is this a physical need?"

"I love him desperately," she cried.

I told her what it means in a community to have an affair with a man. She would have to give up all her friends and clubs and go into a social and moral retreat; she would have to lie to her relatives in an attempt, usually unsuccessful, to keep the knowledge from them; she would have to be strong enough to accept that she was a part-time, illicit wife. She would have to face the knowledge that a real wife, bearing children and welcomed by society, existed elsewhere. My patient had thought her way through all these separate agonies and she was prepared for them all.

"Come back to me in three years when it is over," I told her. "I'll try to help you put your life back together again."

She came back, quieter, drained and passive, almost exactly three years later. The affair had ended and she was paying a bleak price. She had been standing still, treading water, for those years and her friends had passed her and become strangers. She would be a long time catching up.

An affair is a relationship that doesn't fit into any pattern that our society accepts. I cannot in any sincerity condemn the relationship. If tarnish can be avoided, and disillusionment and doubt, she will have a brief love to cherish and remember all her life. Such a love must be held gently and relinquished, when the time comes, without tears.

Most women in their thirties are preoccupied with a search for status. They feel disgraced if they have to arrive at a party with another girl, exit from movies alone, play cards only with women. They are willing to barter anything in order to have a male escort. Because of this, she's a party girl, available without dignity or grace, or else she dates younger, immature men who are looking for a mother.

"But what do I do when I am in real distress because of desire?" I have been asked.

Read a mystery story, I answer. Visit a friend with five children under ten years of age. Take a very hot bath and plan your next vacation.

As the single woman grows older she comes to a time when she wants the affection and admiration of younger people. Teachers seek the approval of their students, social workers involve themselves deeply in the problems of young people, office managers fondly direct the training of stenographers fresh from high school. The difficulty is often that the older woman is vicariously having her youth again; she is deeply wounded when the younger person becomes self-sufficient. This kind of domination, all too common, is bound to damage both women.

The forty-year-old woman can make an extremely happy marriage—but it's not likely to happen. The great turmoils that spring from passion are almost finished and that terrible struggle is over. Life comes back into focus again and her job and friends look new and fresh. If she has been wise enough to join a group or lucky enough to be part of a close-knit community, this mass affection will keep her steady through her menopause. She will discover, when she looks at married women of her own age, that their adolescent children are keeping them in a continual state of apprehension and dismay. She may have a few pangs left over, but singleness no longer makes her so wretched.

Once the fifties have been reached and the menopause is passed, life can be clear and zestful. The unmarried woman finds that many of her married friends are now alone too, their marriages broken by divorce or death. Both women are in the same boat again, as they were thirty years before, and the only things that are really important are financial security and the necessity of being needed.

# Why Aren't Canadian Femmes More Fatales?

*Señoritas simmer, mesdemoiselles sizzle, but Canadian girls just fizzle . . . Could it be the climate?*

By Eric Nicol

**SEPTEMBER 1957** SAY "A CANADIAN GIRL"— and what picture comes to mind?

Probably a tousled towhead wearing an Indian sweater, being hit with a snowball. Or possibly a crisp figure in a business suit, her eyes sparkling with thoughts of a balanced ledger.

Does anybody think of a sexy siren, of sultry glamour, lounging in black velvet and bonbons, the full red mouth parting for something that's not maple syrup?

I doubt it.

For better or for wife, the Canadian girl has the connotation of clean living, of outdoor activity. We don't associate her with any pursuit that can't be made on skis. Any suggestion of sex appeal is buried under a snowdrift of wholesomeness.

When we say "a French girl" or "an Italian girl" or "a Swedish girl" we get a mental picture of something quite different. Certain womanly attributes are superimposed. The snow melts. We feel the unmistakable urge to move indoors, with the lecherous lope of Groucho Marx, eyebrows semaphoring a revised program of recreation.

Why is this? Why do we never expect to see Miss Canada chosen as Miss Universe? Because Miss Canada has patently less on the ball than Miss Israel, Miss Ceylon or Miss Bongo-on-the-Congo?

Miss Canada shines in the talent division, yes. Standing there in her Mountie costume she can play a bugle call like you never heard before. But when it comes to the department that makes beauty judges snap the points on their pencils, Miss Canada just hasn't got it. She looks like everybody's choice for his favorite sister. But oh, brother, get a load of Miss Finland.

Even English girls, whom Continental men have traditionally associated with paralysis of the libido, have more of the old voom-voom-voom than the Canadian variety. Princess Margaret is the sterling example of the current English lady, undeniably fetching in her low-cut voice. Something about the postwar Elizabethan Age Mark II has given Englishwomen a fillip of femininity they previously kept wrapped in tweed. The well-known peaches-and-cream is laced with a jigger of kirsch.

No such improvement is discernible in Canadian women.

On the contrary they continue to win the admiration of Englishmen whenever they visit the Old Country. This is the most damning piece of evidence that can be cited against their sex appeal, because the average Englishman is unnerved by a display of femininity, much prefers a girl he can talk to man to man.

He likes the Canadian girl because he can feel comfortable with her. But the whole crux of conjugation

of the species lies in the female's natural ability to make the male feel uncomfortable. The Canadian girl is an argument for the reproductive method of the amoeba, making a case for binary fission when her effect should be strictly nuclear.

Why? When Canadian men travel abroad and meet the flashing *señorita* of Spain, the Indian girl in her graceful sari with its exciting glimpse of dark midriff, the demure and delicate Mademoiselle Butterfly in Tokyo—why are they apt to do a double somersault off the deep end and marry the girl?

I suggest that the reason is that the lasses of other lands know how to make a man feel masculine. They have learned how to make passivity potent.

The Canadian girl, reared in the mistaken belief that equality of the sexes means loss of distinctiveness of the sexes, waits stolidly to be wooed as though this was her right by federal statute.

She is so inhibited in her capacity to be seductive that she has to have several drinks to let herself go, whereupon as likely as not she becomes playful in the manner of a large Springer spaniel.

The more highly evolved the Canadian girl is— the university graduate with every assurance that she can look any man in the eye, mindwise—the more difficult it is for her to assume the role of temptress. Many of these girls have to get married and have several children before the Delilah in them begins to assert herself, so that she alarms both her own husband and other stray males by leaning out of pantherish cocktail gowns and looking desperately accessible.

Assuming that this trend is undesirable—which is only one man's opinion, of course, supported by an intense faith that fifty million Frenchmen can't be altogether wrong—what can be done to make Canadian women more womanish?

Well, they have one strike against them from the start: this country's cruel climate. The Canadian girl can't loll about in a sarong, or invite attention by standing with her skirt pulled up in a field of bitter No. 1 hard wheat. She'd freeze to death.

The charms of *les Canadiennes* of Montreal manage to overcome some of the ursine bulk of their winter garments, but nobody's yet found a becoming outfit for the drizzle-struck Vancouver girl.

With their power to galvanize the male ogle badly dampened by weather, Canadian girls are justified, I think, in taking advantage of the general prevalence of central heating indoors. A girl doesn't have to run around the house dressed in a bubble, but she can modify her mania for practical (sic) clothes. One filmy peignoir can do more for nuptial union than a carload of marriage counselors.

Moreover, Canadian girls have the physical wherewithal to match the foreign charmer and can usually outclass her. But equipment is useless without the desire to devastate. A girl may be dynamite, but it won't explode until she sets her cap.

As one who is proud of Canada's natural resources, I'm distressed to see this great potential of Canadian femininity going to waste. I hope to see in my time (any later would be disastrous) a general realization by Canadian women that it is silly to don the trappings of sex equality when they can make men their slaves by slipping into something much more comfortable.

Despite advances in most other kinds of industry, there has been very little improvement of the method of making time with a man.

Paddling your own canoe may seem more upright and independent, but if it's furs you're after, *voyageuse*, why not choose the more effective method of transport? It's yours in a wink.

# Letters to Chatelaine

## *Take back your sirens, Mr. Nicol*

**NOVEMBER 1957**

SAY "A CANADIAN MAN"—and what picture comes to mind, why your own description of an Englishman, plus a few more muscles and a large lack of self-confidence. The *mesdemoiselles* sizzle for their French lovers, the *señoritas* simmer for their dashing *señors*. We fizzle for our Canadian men.

—"TWO WOULD-BE SIRENS," HAMILTON.

"SOPHISTICATED"

"KIND"

"CHILDLIKE"

"DETERMINED"

"PERT"

"GLAMOROUS"

"GAY"

"POETIC"

"PROVOCATIVE"

"OUTDOORS"

"GAMIN"

"INNOCENT"

"GIRL-NEXT-DOOR"

"ALOOF"

# What Is Sex Appeal?

### *One hundred men were asked to pick out their favorite from among these faces*

By Catherine Sinclair

**AUGUST 1963**

THESE FOUR POLLED MOST votes, had the greatest appeal

1. "GAMIN" came in first and was mentioned by seventeen of the one hundred men polled for their favorite. Men liked her quiet charm, warmth, innocence. "She's an outdoor type who's fun to be with." One thought she would have serious tastes and liked her "because she's intelligent and would like good music and literature." "She's home-loving." Another saw her as being "capable, but dependent, too."

2. "KIND," a close runner-up, was mentioned thirteen times, mainly for her soft loving appearance.

She was seen as a woman "who could and would expect a lot from a man," as a "responsible, highly strung woman who needs someone to care for her." Some liked her for "the combined intellect and beauty of her face." Many described her as "compassionate, thoughtful, wistful, understanding."

3. "GIRL-NEXT-DOOR" received twelve votes and placed third in the poll. Her appearance inspired happiness and a sense of well-being in many men, who described her as "enthusiastic," "happy-looking," "a casual, natural, fun-type." Her "lovely smile" prompted many comments. "She is fun to be with, even-tempered, easy to get along with."

4. "OUTDOORS" was mentioned ten times, inspiring the most votes for her "sexiness," and for "the look of devilment in her eyes." "She loves life and there is a knowingness about her," said one, and another liked her air of self-confidence. Men saw her as an intriguing pixie, "a blend of wife and the other woman."

# On Being Successfully Single

*Sometimes it's lonely, sometimes it's sad. But then, so is marriage, as women who are living fully, courageously—and singly—have found out*

BY BEVERLEY SLOPEN

**APRIL 1977**

**M**Y MOTHER CALLS ME EVERY Sunday, long distance from Windsor. She phones before noon and we exchange accounts of the week's events. Our conversations only rarely include intimacies. Those nuggets of girlish fears and fantasies I used to deposit freely in her lap, I now hoard. Instead, revelations are transmitted in a kind of code. I, single and past 30, a state she views with apprehension and confusion, offer subtle reassurances, usually by presenting a catalogue of the latest divorces and nervous breakdowns of former school chums. (*See, Ma, you didn't do such a bad job.*) I turn the conversation to recent marital sepa-

rations and other scandals in our large, extended family. (*You wept with romantic hope at their weddings and despaired for me.*) When my mother tells me that my cousin Cynthia has rushed into a second marriage, "because she couldn't make it on her own" (*Is your attitude changing?*), I don't let the subject drop. I remark with great pity in my voice that poor Cynthia is squandering an important opportunity for "personal growth." Our Sunday morning, Windsor to Toronto, mother-daughter ritual.

On another level, our conversations are not merely a personal code but a reflection of a major social shift. Despite the social decree that a woman can only find happiness in a good marriage, many women are frankly enjoying single life.

Television, especially, mirrors the change. Instead of "I Love Lucy," "Father Knows Best," and cozy family shows, we have "Mary Tyler Moore," the sweet single woman heading alone toward middle age with a good job, good friends, and yes, a sex life. In a similar mode, "Police Woman," "Bionic Woman" and "Charlie's Angels" reign over the ratings, all sleek, sexy and self-reliant. Amazingly, and almost imperceptibly, we have entered the age of the single woman as heroine.

There are approximately 30 million women in the U.S. living more or less apart from men—never-married, divorced, widowed—and an estimated three million in Canada. Among women in the U.S. between the ages of 20 and 24—when many of them marry—the proportion of those remaining single rose from 28 percent in 1960 to 40 percent in 1974.

As with any social change, the old order is mourned out of nostalgia for past comforts (real and imagined), while the new order is feared. Several commentators, witnessing the disintegration of stable family life, and noting the rise of cults, therapies, and the emphasis on personal satisfaction, have described this as the age of narcissism. Or, as Tom Wolfe has written, we are in the "me" decade. They tell us we are living in a time when friendship and family ties are fragile, the sense of historical continuity is disrupted, and, as a result, there is a great dread of old age and death. They see self-reliance, which they acknowledge as necessary for protection and survival (especially in an age where the individual is celebrated), as the beginning of the path toward self-absorption and eventual alienation.

The emergence of the mature single woman as "star" might be interpreted as part of the cycle of narcissism. Even so, after being the deprived spinster, bereft widow, or shameful divorcée, it is exhilarating suddenly to be wrapped by the media in a nimbus of glamour and potential. I and my friends were too young to identify with the romance of domesticity we were offered in the 1950s, and later we were too old or too cynical to join the silly flower children. We were the "nice" girls—diligent at school or work, respectful of authority and mindful of the rules. We rarely granted "sexual favors," and seldom "did it" with awkward boys in cars. Virginity was part of our value system, but it increasingly had less value. If we suffered from the rules, we did so in silence. Now that we are in our thirties and forties, at last, at long last, for better or for worse, we are being accepted in our time, in the age of "Mary Tyler Moore," the Cosmo Girl and Wonder Woman revisited.

We pick our way through the minefield, attempting to sort out the difference between self-fulfillment and selfishness; between loneliness on one side and meaningless associations on the other; between solid principles and deathly rigidity; between a generous, affirming sexuality and demeaning promiscuity.

If firm answers exist, neither I nor my friends have established them. Yet, somehow we cope reasonably well. We struggle to adapt to those wide swings of mood that range from depressed-dissatisfied to joyous-euphoric, and average out at content-to-happy. The important thing is that most of us have enough job skills to function in the marketplace. We range in age from 27 to 55, pay taxes, and are very fond of men. A few of us own houses, have children, and visit a psychiatrist once a week. Some of us are journalists, some work in offices, two are teachers, one is a social worker, one has aspirations for a television career, one sells light bulbs, and one denies she is a secretary. None of us is rich. As a group, we are not much interested in transcendental meditation, choir singing, or singles bars. But one of us has tried nude therapy. We go

to hairdressers, are interested in politics, and want love. We have all been under the surgeon's knife, some of us drink too much, and one of us died recently. On the whole, we are probably no more and no less neurotic than any other small group of happily married middle-class women.

What we appear to give and receive from each other is counsel. On jobs. On children. On men. On love.

The transparent webbing linking the pebbles of gossip, reassurance and advice is the stuff of intimacy woven into a diaphanous but tough support system. In a time of crisis it translates into midnight vigils at hospital emergency rooms, a quiet presence in a tense courtroom, hot soup and attention when you're home ill, companionship during mourning, diversion at the miserable end of a love affair. Some of us have helped each other get jobs, signed a bank note, or introduced another woman to a deserving man.

*We were the "nice" girls—diligent at school or work, respectful of authority and mindful of the rules*

They are right, those gloomy social philosophers who suggest that life is too burdensome, too unspeakably bleak without family and friendship ties. But the need for them is so strong and the rewards are so great that ultimately the prophets of doom are wrong. They don't seem to see the less formal, less structured systems of support that the more resilient are able to construct in the wake of the collapse of old forms.

For the single woman, behavior within the society of women is becoming translated into a rigid etiquette. You don't cancel a dinner date or a vacation with a woman friend simply because a man has called. If a woman friend is in desperate need, you cancel the man: friendship comes first. You might date a man who is no longer seeing your friend, but there are few secrets about the relationship. You'd also be very careful about dating a friend's ex-husband or ex-lover if raw feelings exist. It is expected that the two women would discuss it and take care not to jeopardize the friendship—especially for a mere male. You see, it is assumed that men come and go, but it is friendships with women that provide solid substance in the life of a woman on her own.

Men needle and tease each other, play tennis, bowl, shoot pool, and talk about business, but I know very few who share intimacies with other men the way women do among themselves. They tend to seek out women for that. It reminds me of Mordecai Richler's advice to a male friend who was chafing within his marriage. "Never leave your wife on spec," he warned, not knowing that the friend had a mistress and had absolutely no intention into going out into the cold cruel world by himself without advance arrangements for a soft nest. However, more women seem to be able to part from their husbands "speculatively," as it were, without a lover in the wings, provided there are no major financial hurdles.

If, just a few years ago, single women of a certain age were deprived of a community, a place in society, they were also denied an open sexuality. The change was signaled around 1962 with the publication of *Sex and the Single Girl* by Helen Gurley Brown, the widespread use of the Pill, and the rise of co-ed college dorms. Now the closet has been unlocked, releasing tales of amazing candor.

A married woman who swims regularly at an exclusive women's club, 21 McGill in Toronto, admits that she is frequently shocked by what she overhears in the locker room. "These are detailed accounts of technique, size, duration, performance, and sometimes the status of the man—how rich or successful he is. I heard one woman describe a married man she had slept with and then go on about his poor wife—what inferior lovemaking the poor woman has endured for 20 years. I confess I was shocked. I don't think married women disclose so much so casually about their sex lives."

There is no doubt that great tension exists between men and women and the sexual area is the chief war zone. Men, inventors of the Pill, the nude centrefold and 1,001 arguments to lure women into bed, frequently resent the expression of female sexuality, especially when they aren't controlling it. The language men use when they talk about women is fascinating and revealing. On the one hand, they damn women who "don't." Few women have refused a man without being called "frigid," "tease," "lesbian," and worse. On the other hand, the most vitriolic language is reserved for women who "do."

A Toronto mortgage broker works out at the posh Cambridge Club, an athletic club atop a downtown hotel where the movers and shakers of Bay Street puff their way around jogging tracks and squash courts, with the aim of slimming middle-aged paunches and fatty blood vessels. "The talk in the locker room is mostly about money but often it's about sex," he reports. "The guys who have split from their wives sound like managers of pro-athletes when they talk about women. There are some girls they say they've got on 'lock-up'— that means they've got exclusive rights for the duration of the contract. Some girls are on 'waiver'—the chick might screw other guys from time to time. The broads on 'sick list' haven't had their contracts terminated but they've been sidelined for a while. Then there's the 'taxi squad'—the chicks they use to fill in when they only want sex."

As far as I can tell, women are annoyed but not threatened by such responses from men. I haven't encountered anyone who advocated a curtailment of sexual activity, or a return to secretive, hypocritical behavior, merely to cater to male ambivalence. "Why?" I was asked by an incredulous woman. "Our financial security, our self-esteem, depend less and less on whether men approve of our sex lives. I don't give a damn about their resentment."

Instead, women's cruelty finds its target in specific men. A woman coolly and laconically refused a dinner invitation from a man she disliked, saying, "No thank you, I'd rather stay home and clean my oven." Explaining why she left her husband, another woman concluded, "Hard come, easy go."

Indeed, if anything elicits female contempt it is male impotence. Not the impotence born of nervousness. Not a loving clumsiness that is overcome with time. But the chronic impotence that indicates a fundamental lack of generosity or disguises hostility with weakness.

A friend had been seeing a man for several months. If she called him, he never sounded happy to hear from her. When she was reserved, he became ardent. But if she behaved warmly, he cooled. She described their lovemaking as "uncertain and never satisfactory. He couldn't maintain an erection, but it wasn't a question of 'performance.' I always felt it was his way of shutting me out, of controlling the relationship. I don't need a withholding man and I'm *not* sympathetic," she declared.

"I find impotence an attractive idea," a man at

a party tells me. "I'm not impotent but I often say that I am, especially if I'm attracted to a woman. I'm living with someone and I don't want to get involved with anyone else right now, and impotence is a convenient excuse. Like a woman can always say that she has her period."

Before I could ask him why he didn't tell women he was happily attached—an explanation any woman would gratefully accept and respect—he was off to flirt over the cheese tray with a svelte brunette.

# Fear of Flirting

## *Is gamesmanship dead?*

John Colapinto

APRIL
1993

USED TO BE WOMEN BATTED their eyelashes, and men made passes. Now, women are ready to blow the whistle on unwanted male moves, while men are disoriented and running scared. John Colapinto reports from the front lines.

∾

The other day, when I went down to check the mail, my letter carrier stopped to watch a woman pass on the sidewalk. "I love 'em," he sighed, "but I can't do anything about it." "Yeah," I commiserated, switching into Male Bonding Mode, "I'm married too." That's when he threw me a curve. "I'm not married," he said, "I'm just scared. I don't want some woman accusing me of messing with her. These days, I don't even whistle." Although not in the habit of whistling at women, I knew what the guy meant. Lately, the stakes have definitely been raised in the battle between the sexes.

This comes as a surprise to men like me who have rejected our rather casual 1950s chauvinism, know how to cook and clean, attend birthing classes and are present in the delivery room. By the late '80s, we dared to think women had achieved most of their goals and that intergender peace was at last at hand.

But in the past few years, as more and more cases of sexual harassment and date rape hit the courts and the headlines, women have become angrier, and men more defensive. Relations between the sexes have seldom been edgier.

So, as my letter carrier has noticed, these days, a man can't be too careful. I had a meeting with an editorial assistant at a magazine where I free-lance. Afterward, I commented on her shirt: a plaid button-down typical of the "grunge" trend popular with the 20something crowd. My comment was: "Cool shirt. Where d'yuh get it?" Her smile disappeared. A few heads actually popped up in the surrounding cubicles. I felt glad that I work at home.

But perhaps, we men, experiencing unaccustomed fear in the workplace, are simply getting a taste of our own medicine. My friend Betty, a 36-year-old stock trader, one of six women in a 23-person department of a major bank, says that even today, she routinely puts up with wisecracks about menstrual cycles, PMS, pregnancy—as well as being the object of more than a few unwanted sexual come-ons from colleagues. "If ever I complained," she says, "I wouldn't be working here." Last winter, when her firm circulated a memo defining sexual harassment, her male coworkers read it aloud to each other and laughed.

"These days, men really do have to be cautious about what they say and how they say it," says Oscar, a 45-year-old married man, who works at an advertising agency where women outnumber men. "Some women get a kick out of it when you say, 'Hoo, are you lookin' sexy today!' Others don't. It's like advertising. You have to tailor your message to your target."

Most of the men I spoke with mouthed well-worn axioms about men needing to change, needing to be more sensitive, needing to listen. But being a man myself I was not deaf to the unregenerate 18-year-old boy, who so often lurks beneath the New Man veneer. Jake, an easygoing 29-year-old market consultant, believes he is in tune with women's needs. "Women really have gotten a raw deal," he says. "I'm sensitive to what the feminists are saying." Although single and active in Toronto's dating scene, Jake wants me to know he's not some sexist pickup artist. "I've always accepted it when a woman turns me down." But then, Jake admits, he increases his odds by doing his cruising in singles' bars, "where," he explains with a knowing look, "you can find the type of girl who is out for a good time." Sometimes, he adds, a woman will "chew my head off for approaching her," but Jake dismisses such women as "radical feminists." He recounts a joke he recently heard, "No means give her another beer." "I find that funny," he says, with a note of challenge in his voice. "These feminists take the fun out of things."

*Far from requiring men to obtain written permission for sex, the law simply gives women legal recourse when sex is not consensual.*

Neil, a single 42-year-old ad salesman in Chicago, who earns a six-figure salary, at first sees my questions as an invitation to boast about his sexual prowess. To Neil, a smoothly handsome self-described "party animal" in an expensive suit, all talk of date rape, harassment and sexism is just so much bunk. Asked whether he has noticed a change in women's attitudes in the past year, he delivers one of the comments that pass for wit in many locker rooms: "Yeah, things have changed. These days, when I'm raping chicks, they scream. They never used to mind."

"But seriously," Neil continues, "it's getting bad out there." He describes women he has slept with who have the gall to accuse him of insensitivity, or worse. It all goes to prove how unreasonable women are. He recalls one instance in which he "banged" a business client in the trophy room at a party at a posh club. After using what he calls his "Andrew Dice Clay post-orgasmic etiquette" (he left and didn't call for days), Neil started to worry that his actions might be bad for business. So, he wrote the woman a short thank-you note. "She wrote back a bit snidely," Neil says, sounding injured. "She said I was kind of abusive!"

This was not the first such accusation for Neil. Even he was a little shaken to learn, recently, that one of his short-lived conquests was saying that he'd "forced sex on her." Neil got together with her and spent several hours "repositioning" her thinking. As far as Neil is concerned, the hardest thing about being a single male in these days of date rape and harassment charges is having "to cover my ass with these people." Meaning his sex partners.

Some men seem to be making an attempt to adjust. Ted, a 36-year-old site manager for a reforestation company, supervises college-age tree planters of both sexes each summer in the northern Ontario bush. "Last summer," he recalls, "one of our foremen was ribbing this young woman for having slept with a guy who had a girlfriend back home. The foreman was calling her 'Home-wrecker' and 'Ho' (a rap music abbreviation for whore). At first everyone laughed. But it went on for days. I could see what it was doing to this woman. I took the guy aside and said, 'Cut that out.' He said, 'I thought I was being funny.' I said, 'You're not. You're sexually harassing her.'"

Ted admits that, in the past, he dated women on his planting crew. But no more. "Today, when you're a woman's boss and have a certain level of power over her, it feels wrong and it's too risky."

But even Ted shares the disquiet most of the men I spoke to feel about Canada's "No Means No" law passed in August 1992. Bill C-49 requires the woman to have given actual consent to sexual relations. Without this, a man may face criminal charges. Ted, while agreeing with the law on principle, admits to "unease" about a government incursion into the most intimate area of his life. Jake, the self-described "sensitive" market consultant, describes the law as "Orwellian" and speaks fearfully of the day when men will be issued cards for a woman to sign before they have sex. Neil, the type of man presumably most threatened by such a law, says, "Sounds fine. A woman should have that protection due to her lesser physical strength." But then, Neil lives in Chicago; he can afford to be magnanimous about a law that has no effect on him.

Canadian men are afraid that the law seeks to make black and white what is actually a gray area: that point at which mutual attraction shades into sexual activity. Far from requiring men to obtain written permission for sex, the law simply gives women legal recourse when sex is *not* consensual. That we men should so consistently misinterpret, or distort, the law's aim points to a deep male fear that our role as "initiators" of sex is being eroded.

Challenging men's role as Boss of the Bedroom cuts deep into their machismo. This sexual insecurity is demonstrated by opponents of the No Means No law. Robert Wakefield, director of the Criminal Lawyers' Association, told the *Globe and Mail* that the No Means No law is dangerous because it tries to change society's traditional belief in the role of men as sexual initiators. Wakefield argues, "This has gone on for centuries. There's a biological imperative behind it. The new law is contrary to centuries of accepted behavior."

The men I talked to conceded that some men do force themselves on women but they saw it as the other guy's problem. As for themselves, they can always tell what "no" means. "I'm very intuitive," Jake tells me. "Ohhh, you can tell," Neil says.

But can even the "responsible" male who heeds a woman's "no" be sure she really means it? "The problem is," Ted says, "you sometimes wonder whether the girl isn't kind of disappointed and thinking, 'What a wimp. Doesn't he know I was just playing the game?'"

A few women concede that there is some game-playing on both sides. "When you first go on a date," Mary grants, "sometimes 'No' will mean, 'Not right now.' You're still making up your mind about him but you don't want to turn the guy off completely, so you sort of water down your signals because you're afraid he will disappear altogether." Mary sighs. "Basically, we do send mixed signals to men.' That's no good."

In the heat and smoke that followed the famous sex-harassment and date-rape cases in 1991, it was easy to lose sight of this fact of life: signals can be mixed and/or missed. The most frightening aspect of the Thomas/Kennedy/Tyson hearings wasn't that either the man or the woman might be lying but rather that both might be telling the truth: that the men truly believed their actions to be unobjectionable, and that the women lacked the language to communicate their displeasure.

Can men change? I don't know. You'll have to speak up, if you expect us to hear you. Men aren't going to get it on their own.

# Chatelaine

## Career Girl

### NUMBER

**TEN CENTS**       **FEBRUARY, 1943**

# CHAPTER SEVEN

# On the Job

URING THE TWENTIES, CAREERS for bright young things were in vogue; however, for every debutante who amused herself in the workplace, a thousand other women toiled at dead-end jobs for minimum wages. In "Do Women Want Protection?" (August 1928), feminists hotly debated the pros and cons of special legislation to protect women—just as they do today. In "Shall Women Preach?" (September 1934), Nellie McClung recounted how women had allowed themselves to be outmaneuvered in their struggle for ordination in the United Church.

According to a government bluebook of 1935, more women were employed as domestics than in any other line of work—133,966, more than twice the number of stenographers, their second most likely occupation (64,986). An almost equal number were schoolteachers (64,695), and an additional 25,885 were housekeepers ("Women at Work," November 1935). Telephone operators accounted for another 14,368, and in "City Order" (November 1932) *Chatelaine* tracked these "hello girls" through a humdrum day taking phone orders for a department store.

The labor shortages of World War II flung open the door to male strongholds like manufacturing and the military. Though women were urged to serve their country as a patriotic duty, hostility toward their "masculinization" simmered just under the surface ("Women in Uniform," April 1941). Despite such prejudice, a few exceptional women achieved exceptional success. Even rank-and-file women proved better at some jobs than men—usually the grindingly boring ones, "perhaps because of generations of house tending" ("What They Found Out about Us," September 1943).

After the war, the door was again flung wide for women—out of the work force and into the ranch house. Since "girls" were now supposed to work only until rescued by marriage, *Chatelaine's* career advice tended to center on good grooming, accompanied by lists of do's and don'ts that came perilously close to the ones for dating. What the business world wanted was a comely face and good-girl conformity with just a dash of spunkiness. In other words: don't rock the boat.

By the sixties, housewives were drifting back to work through necessity and boredom; by the seventies, they'd returned in sufficient numbers to warrant government and private pre-employment courses. Once again, these were essentially confidence-builders about filling in applications and dressing the part. For women who'd never left the work force, a clearer day was dawning: since they'd invested as much as men, why didn't they receive the same pay and opportunities? In "How to Turn 'Just a Job' into a Career" (February 1977), *Chatelaine's* revised list of do's and don'ts urged women to stand up for what they deserved: make waves.

By the eighties, "career woman" was no longer a pejorative—in fact, it had *cachet*. Even women who refused to call themselves feminists were demanding equity on the grounds of simple justice. A few—through luck, inheritance, marriage, tokenism or breakaway ability—had even busted through the glass ceiling into the boardrooms of the nation. However, while celebrating these breakthroughs, it was well to remember that economic freedom might also come driving a pink Cadillac ("Liberation the Mary Kay Way," July 1981).

# Do Women Want Protection?—No!

By E. M. Murray

**AUGUST 1928**

"Industry is to be made safe for men and women, not for women only; and industries can be regulated for the benefit of the workers, not for the purpose of discriminating against women, as is done at present."

Special legislation connotes privilege somewhere, and wherever there is privilege there is also injustice. For centuries women quietly accepted privilege in lieu of the degree of freedom men had won. It was during this period that laws were made and public opinion formed which prevented women from owning their own bodies, their own children, their own property, their own wages, their own clothes, and denied to them the right to education.

Often "welfare" workers are honestly mistaken as to the effect of sex discrimination laws. Experience, however, shows that they always work for the detriment of the sex they are intended to "protect." Among the strongest advocates of such laws are the great majority of well-meaning, non-wage-earning women, and some labor leaders and organizations. These latter fear the competition of women, and would shut them out from employment. The former group is merely a tool in the cunning hands of the latter group.

Such labor men have no real regard for the welfare of women. The condition of the women in their own homes proves that. Who seeks "protective" laws for the mothers of large families who toil and moil for sixteen and eighteen hours a day in the home, without holidays or rest days, or even change of shift? Certainly not the labor men who seek to "protect" women out of their best-paying jobs. Indeed, they are usually the very ones, who, with many other "welfare" workers, would deny to such women even the relief from suffering that a knowledge of birth control would give.

In New York when the law was passed making it illegal to employ waitresses in a restaurant at night, many restaurants soon replaced women with men for all time, because men could work when they pleased. What became of the women thus thrown out of a job, and of their dependents?

One big chain system of restaurants retained women for day work, which is of course the hardest work, because from 11.30 a.m. to 2.30 p.m. is peak time in that business. Night trade is far easier and much better paid.

The International Woman Suffrage Alliance Congress in 1920 went on record as opposing discriminatory legislation based on sex. Following that lead, the Republican party in New York State inserted a plank, prepared by a woman, in its party platform as follows: "We believe that legislation regarding hours and time of work should be based on a comparison of industrial strain, rather than put on the flat hour or sex basis. We are opposed to laws which discriminate against the right of women who seek to earn their living in competition with men."

That is the real secret of the difficulty. Women are competing against men, so they must be handicapped. Men have enormously improved their industrial position of recent years. How? By minimum wage laws and protective legislation? Not at all. Instead, men organize, and when they have settled among themselves what they think is a right wage, they bring pressure to bear upon employers until they get that rate.

When government says that a woman can live decently, almost comfortably on a given sum, generally just over the starvation line, why should employers bother to pay more? They do not. So what was intended to be the lowest wage anybody should offer, becomes the highest that employers do offer.

As *Equal Rights*, published in New York to maintain the fight for woman's freedom, well says: "Industry is to be made safe for men and women, not for women only; and industries can be regulated for the benefit of the workers, not for the purpose of discriminating against women, as is done at present."

Mrs. Sidney Webb, internationally known economist, and a member of the British Government Committee on Women in Industry, says: "I see no justification for classifying all the workers of one sex and subjecting them all to a differential rate. It is admitted that some women are, in nearly all occupations, found to be superior in efficiency to the common run of men; and I can discover no ground for penalizing those exceptional women because of the industrial inferiority of the mass of their colleagues."

∾

No one gave any study to the question of why wages were low in Canada for both men and women. Most of our people were of old country stock, where wages have always been on the low side. They were accustomed to have labor receive but a small share of the wealth it created. Girls were employed in Canada at starvation wages because that rate would have been good pay in the old land. Unconsciously, we were all going on the principle voiced by the acting-premier of an eastern province. When the woman suffrage movement was at its height in Canada, a delegation of women approached him suggesting a government bill giving the women of the province the franchise.

After hearing all the arguments quite patiently, he delivered himself thus: "I sympathize with your interest in this live question, but you will notice that Great Britain has not yet granted suffrage to women, and I think it would be very unbecoming for us to act before she does."

That was that. There was no more to be said, and be it noted, Great Britain did grant limited woman's suffrage before that province enfranchised its women. And that, in a less exaggerated form, has been Canada's attitude to things in general.

∾

The actual conditions in Canada, according to Government returns, are as follows: Seven out of nine Provinces have Minimum Wage Laws for women, Nova Scotia, Quebec, Ontario, Manitoba, Saskatchewan, Alberta and British Columbia. In Ontario, the minimum wage for experienced women workers is $12.50 per week; Alberta, $10 for inexperienced, $15 for experienced; British Columbia, $12.75 to $15 for women, with 40 cents an hour, or practically $20 a week, for men. What is the matter with the women of British Columbia that they have not protested as the New Zealand women have? Sex discrimination as usual, under the guise of "protection" for women!

∾

No effort is made to protect women in any indus-try where they do not compete with men, from the over-worked household drudge to the woman who scrubs office buildings after midnight. No man wants either job, so he does not suggest or support legislation to "protect" these women workers.

Let no woman be deceived as to the real purpose of all such legislation. Women must be free to work as they see fit. They have dependents as well as men, and nothing in the way of restrictive laws should prevent them earning as much as men earn to support such dependents.

# Do Women Want Protection? Yes!

By Maude Petitt Hill

AUGUST 1928
"Anna bella's fourteen on Monday. She's goin' to quit school an' go to work in Brant's Box factory. That will help us on at home a bit." Those few lines in a nutshell contained the early story of thousands of girls in cities like Toronto and Montreal not more than fifteen years ago.

Fifteen years ago, our readers could have visited one of the big industrial concerns of Toronto where little girls of fourteen worked from half-past seven in the morning until six at night, sitting at the same spot at the work table, making the same monotonous movement all day, for four and a half dollars a week. Most factories were closing by five at that time, or at least 5.30. But others were working even longer, from 7 a.m. until 6 p.m.

It was about this time that a good deal of agitation for reformed conditions for girl and women workers was started. Thanks in a large measure to the pressure brought to bear on provincial parliaments by our National Council of Women, we have now, according to the report of Professor H. Michel, political economy expert of McMaster University, Toronto, minimum wage laws in all of our provinces, except New Brunswick and Prince Edward Island.

Anna Bella no longer works for $4.50 a week. To be sure, economic conditions following the Great

War would, in any case, have changed that figure, but the Minimum Wage Laws have guaranteed her a living wage. In fact, according to Professor Michel's report on this subject for the years 1921-25, the average wage paid men went down, while the average wage of women increased.

*It was in the days when women wore long skirts. I noticed they came in every day in the winter with their skirts wet from the slush and snow.*

Of course there are the devotees of the Woman's Party in the United States, ultra feminists who say we want no protective legislation for women whatsoever. Out with the Minimum Wage Laws, the Mothers' Pensions! Let women stand and work on the same footing as men. This party has its enthusiasts in Canada as well. Let woman be free to work as long as she pleases, they say. Why should the government tell her when to quit?

This question affects 133,683 women employed in various industrial concerns in Canada—about 55,000 of them in Ontario alone, and 48,977 in Quebec.

Should their hours be protected by legislation?

YES. We write it with capitals.

Why so? Men are organized, and they who have less need of protection have their hours protected by their organizations. But with the exception of two or three industries, such as cloak makers and needle workers, the working women of Canada are without organization.

Did you ever stop to think some cold winter morning when you wake, turn comfortably on your pillow, and hear the whistles blowing at 7 a.m., that thousands of women in Canada between Halifax and Port Arthur are taking their places on their work stools at that hour? A great number of them have no doubt not only got their own breakfasts, but prepared breakfast for the family before they left home. This is not sentimentality; it is simply cold hard statistics from the reports of the Department of Labor.

This factory work, too, means in most cases intense concentration on one automaton-like movement. It is perhaps a ziz up endless seams, on a power machine all day long, with the exception of an hour at noon. Ziz-Ziz-Z-Z-Z! Or it is filling biscuits—dab of jam between two biscuits, dab of jam, dab of jam, dab, dab, dab, from the dark rim of dawn to the dark rim of night.

The most important consideration for the women of any land is not their economic position (important as that undoubtedly is) but their position as mothers. We have in Canada no special protective laws in industry for the expectant mother. In certain European countries and in certain parts of the United States, we find laws in the statute books forbidding a woman to work for a certain number of weeks before and after confinement. In some cases, she is given a maternity benefit.

❧

And just what protective measures as to hours have we in our different provinces? In the eastern part of Canada, from Nova Scotia to Port Arthur, there is still on our Statute books the old British law by which women and girls may be employed a ten hour day. The employer in each of these provinces may also, with the inspector's permission, lengthen the hours for the purpose of shortening some one day in the week, such as Saturday. In Ontario, he may also, if the exigencies of trade require, employ women workers twelve-and-a-half hours a day for a total of thirty-six days in the year. In Quebec he may employ them for twelve hours in the day for six weeks of the year; in New Brunswick for thirteen-and-a-half hours a day for thirty-six days of the year, and in Nova Scotia for twelve-and-a-half hours a day during rush period.

Fortunately, and it speaks well for our Canadian manufacturers, by far the larger per cent. of our factories do not take advantage of the ten-hour-day law. In Ontario about two-thirds of the women workers have an eight-hour day. Here is the story of the shorter day for women as it began in Ontario, very much as we heard it from the lips of the man who introduced it:

"When I took over the business," he said, "I found a good percentage of the women were being laid off because of colds all the time. This meant a steady loss to us. I began to study the prevention of these colds. It was in the days when women wore long skirts. I noticed they came in every day in the winter with their skirts wet from the slush and snow. I sat down and figured out that if they started work at 8.15 in the morning instead of 7.00, the sidewalks would be cleaned by that time and there would be no danger of wet ankles. We tried it and found at the end of the year that the output of the same number of workers was greater than it had been on the ten hour day. We mend our factory roof when it leaks. We repair the office furniture. Yet these things produce nothing. Why not look also to keep the help who produce our wealth, physically and mentally fit?"

❧

In western Canada we find a distinct forward step in legislation. Every province from the Great Lakes to the Pacific has a Mothers' Pension Law. East of Port Arthur, Ontario is the only one that has passed such legislation.

British Columbia has an eight-hour day for women, thanks largely to the good work of Mrs. Ralph Smith, M.P.P. In Alberta the Factory Act gives women forty-eight hours a week and, incidentally, Alberta has the oldest law on our Statute books in this regard, one passed in 1917. Saskatchewan in 1919, through its Minimum Wage Board, prescribed forty-eight to fifty hours a week. Manitoba put a nine-hour day on its Statute books, but took it off again. After this it prescribed through its Minimum Wage board a week of forty-eight hours.

With the passing of an Eight-Hour Act, the owner of the eight-hour factory would not then have to compete with the man running his factory ten hours. But in speaking to a member of the Manufacturers' Association on this subject, he shook his head dubiously, as he asked, "What about competing with Germany where they may work fourteen hours a day?"

To come down to hard facts, Canada has really ratified the eight-hour day for everyone, at the League of Nations. We wonder if the provincial legislatures have not so far, treated the ratification as only "a scrap of paper."

❧

But would the women workers themselves like their hours shortened by legislation? We asked Mr. Kirscher, head of the Cloak Workers' Union.

"Yes, surely," he said, looking with a smile at our ignorance.

"If the hours were shortened the work would stretch over a longer period. They work like mad during rush season, until nine or ten at night—then they are laid off. If hours were shortened, the manufacturer would have to begin earlier in the season to prepare for the rush."

Another great stride in protective legislation in the last decade, both for boys and for girls, has been the increasing of the age up to which children must be kept in school.

Little Anna Bella with whom we started, if she lives in Ontario, may no longer go to the box factory at fourteen. She stays at school until she is sixteen, unless her family can prove themselves too destitute to keep her.

# Shall Women Preach?

BY NELLIE McCLUNG

SEPTEMBER **1934** ONCE UPON A TIME, THIS question of the ordination of women to preach the gospel came very near to settlement in the largest church in Canada. There was a tide in the affairs of women flowing strongly toward complete equality.

That was in 1928.

It is easy to remember 1928, though to most of us it seems a lifetime ago. Everyone had money and the markets were rising. Great oil and mining activities, great flurries in stocks and bonds had come in bewildering excitement, and even the elevator boys and little cash girls were seeing visions of wealth. Farmers were deserting their ploughshares for oil shares, and ministers were resigning their pulpits to promote new companies and not the New Jerusalem.

The Home and Foreign Mission Departments of the churches were alarmed. In the United Church of Canada fifty-five places where churches had been built had no minister. Fifty-five districts, all in the Western Provinces, where there were no Sunday schools, no one to baptize the young or bury the dead. Sorrowing letters had come to the Home Mission Department, saying, "Our church is locked, spiders are spinning webs across the altar and dust lies thick on the pulpit Bible. Can't you send us someone? We would be glad to have even a woman."

Now the great United Church in the years preceding 1928, when pressed by some restless souls—and I was privileged to be one of them—to know when they were going to let down the bars of the ministry, had always discreetly said: "Wait until some woman asks for ordination and then we will deal with the case on its merits."

In the eventful year of 1928, there came a case before the General Council of the Church which met in Winnipeg. A young woman was asking for ordination. She had completed her theological course some years before at Saint Andrews in Saskatoon, taking the gold medal in a class of nineteen. She had already served on two fields with marked success. She could speak French as well as English, play the organ, lead the singing, drive a car, keep house, hold her tongue and get along with people. She had established Sunday schools on her fields, organized literary societies, reading classes and ladies' aid societies. She was an able speaker, a clever student and a good pastor. And she was asking to be ordained. The case had arrived.

The Executive Committee of the church determined to send out a questionnaire to the churches, asking them how they felt about the ordination of women. Replies were received, ranging all the way from enthusiastic support to flat denials. The church at large seemed to be either favorable or indifferent, but we knew that there was some stiff opposition from some of the executives of the church. However, what we hoped for was that Miss Lydia Gruchy would be given a Special License to preach, which would open the door to other applicants by establishing a precedent.

Now I hate to have to join the chorus of those who blame women for everything that happens. But I have to admit that the ordination of Miss Gruchy was killed at the 1928 General Council by the indifference of some of the women. I happened to be on the Committee appointed to deal with the question, and even before we met, members of the Committee declared the matter of no importance. A handsome young minister from Ottawa, with the assurance of youth, began by telling us the women in his church had told him they didn't want a woman preacher. Now, of course, the question of a woman preacher for the Church in Ottawa was not on the order paper. The only woman who was asking for ordination was far away in Northern Saskatchewan. The ladies in Ottawa would never have to listen to her (though they would not find that a hard thing to do). They would still have their handsome young pastor, with his bright brown eyes and engaging cowlick.

I knew what had happened. Women are such flatterers! They had paid the young man a subtle compliment when they said they did not want a woman to preach to them. The flattery of women is a subtle poison that has hampered and deceived many an able young man and made him think he was growing when he was merely swelling.

We got the same report from a western man; the women of his church did not want a woman preacher. I asked him if this was an official opinion from a representative body of women, and he admitted he had "gleaned it from conversations." I can hear the conversation!

∾

The Woman's Missionary Society has always seemed to me to be the spear-head of the church, with their hospitals and boarding schools at home, and their workers in the foreign field. The official report was being read, a good report of earnest work well done. Suddenly the reader stopped in her reading and said: "You have not asked us what we think of the ordination of women—and it is just as well. You will find us very conservative."

That was all, but it was enough!

When I spoke to the lady afterward, she was surprised and pained to find I resented her words with their implication that the whole society was indifferent or opposed. She said she was only expressing her own opinion and did not presume to speak for the society. Indeed, she said, she had given but little thought to the subject. But she had given the opposition the stick to beat us with. And how the men who had opposed ordination loved her for her few words! The man who reported that day's proceedings for the *New Outlook* spoke glowingly of her—how feminine and attractive she was, and how becomingly dressed. That is how it happened that the psychological moment for the United Church in Canada passed. The ordination of women has probably been delayed ten years, and occupies the shadowy place in the courts of the church once filled in British politics by the Deceased Wife's Sister Bill.

# Only a Super-Woman Can Juggle Both a Family and a Career

By Virginia Coyne Knight

JULY 1928

WE WERE TOLD NOT LONG ago in these pages that every woman should have a hobby.

I once knew a woman who had a five-roomed apartment, a husband and a dog. The dog was there all the time, the husband was on the road all week except Fridays, Saturdays and Sundays. She had a woman come in two days a week, one day to clean, one day to wash and iron. And yet that woman told me she had so much to do she couldn't keep up her music. But then she had a hobby—she played golf!

What would a woman like that think of the life of a woman who has small children and no help? She has no time for hobbies, that dear young soul. And if she had, say, one little tiny hour a day for her own diversion, can you blame her if she does nothing with it? For when a baby-carriage comes in the door, a hobby is extremely apt to take the bit in his teeth and gallop through the window. "Whoa!" you call after him. "I'll have time for you one of these days!" But he shakes his head with a knowing "*Neigh!*" and there is an end of him.

Then how much harder is it for the ambitious woman who swore she would keep up her profession after she married! For while a hobby may return when the children are older and be received with all the more zest for his absence, it is not so easy to recapture a profession.

Yet we sometimes look askance when some young woman whose work once showed promise sinks quietly beneath the waves of matrimony. "Spineless," we think secretly, and we feel perhaps a bit superior that we are single and splendidly carving out our lives. Little do we guess the struggle that has gone on under our eyes before she went down for the last time. She has not advertised it. When she found her strength unequal to two jobs, she gave up the least important and died from the professional world with no one to blow Last Post over her but her family and a few close friends. And for the rest of her life she will probably hear this or that complacent male with half her brains chortle out the list of men's achievements with the time-worn comment, "What have you women done that can equal this?"

Nothing very spectacular! What we have done has been only to populate the world, and we have done it so quietly that no one thinks very much about it. It is usually attributed to Nature and let go at that. And some of us have become famous, and are complimented by being told that we have "masculine mentalities." But the majority of us that have dreamed of becoming famous, end as Martha Brown did.

Martha had no reason to think herself a genius—yet, do we not all think in our most inmost hearts, that there is a vein of genius deep down inside us, and if we only keep on toiling and digging, some day we shall cut through this commonplace clay that hides it from us and the world? So she wrote and wrote for five years, and managed in the end to sell most of her stuff, though probably not a critic in Canada had ever mentioned her name. She told herself that she would stick at it ten

years more, and if she had not arrived then, she would give it up.

Well, she got married, and, this being the Woman's Age she kept on writing. Try as she would, she could never get the work done before ten in the morning, and then it seemed that she had scarcely reached her desk before it was time to get lunch for Charley. Having reached a spot in her story that she could scarcely bear to leave, she would fling some vegetables upon the stove and return for another half-hour's work, to be brought back to earth once more by the disconcerting smell of carrots burnt black in the saucepan.

> **Her head would get very heavy at her desk, until she would find it resting upon her manuscript**

However, in a few months she had things running smoothly, though, of course, she was not doing as much writing as she had done before she was married. And now her head would get very heavy at her desk, until she would find it resting upon her manuscript, and she would barely reach the chesterfield before she would go off into a sleep that would often last for hours. Charley Junior was on his way and wanted all his young mamma's attention.

After he came, she went at it again, but now it was real labor. For a baby, it used to be said, takes all one person's time, and even a modern baby, when perfectly healthy, takes a good four hours a day, not including his terrific laundry. And the preparation of even simple meals takes at least another three hours. And that leaves only fifteen hours, of which she must sleep eight. And the house has to be kept decent, and dishes will not wash themselves.

"One thing at a time, my dear," her mother would say. "Raise Bobby first, then write if you like."

"If I can, you mean," she would think. "I won't wait! I'll write now! Now!" And she would go in and hug her baby, feeling like a fierce little eagle penned in a cage.

Her husband helped her all he could. And even then, she never managed more than half an hour's consecutive work at her desk, unless she went there in the evening. She learned to leave in the middle of a word, and return, and go on without a pause. Great practice for the mind!—but she had not yet sighted the judges' stand.

They decided to advertise for one of those tools of Providence known as a Mother's Help. They secured a girl who was as slow as a snail. Martha told her to hurry up so often during the day, that she began to say it mechanically at intervals, like a parrot. And yet she was a help of sorts, as they discovered when she had to go home for six weeks to nurse a sick mother, for then the struggle really began.

Since Baby Esther was six months old and by necessity on the bottle, Martha was trying to write again. It is easy to say, "Wait until your children are older." But suppose you are teeming with characters that *must* crawl into stories? Suppose unspoken words roar continually in your ears like mountains of water pounding on a beach? Suppose it never leaves you night or day, this craving to create beauty and truth? And—you—can't!

Why is an eagle not content to be a robin? And it never will be content to be a robin, though it spend the rest of its life in the apple-tree.

The end of the struggle is here, for after Annie came back Martha had a nervous collapse, after which the waves of matrimony engulfed her. And now people say, "Oh, well, I don't suppose there was much in her, or she wouldn't have stopped."

# Women at Work

### *In which the demon statistician proves that women's work is never done . . .*

By John Duke

**NOVEMBER 1935**

GOT YOUR PENCIL READY? Take down these figures.

There are 133,966 women in domestic service in Canada; 64,986 women stenographers; 64,695 women schoolteachers; 20,441 graduate nurses and 11,462 more in training; 18,669 women running boarding houses and 14,368 "hello girls."

It is to be expected that women would dominate in these professions and occupations. The figures are thrown at you at the start just to get rid of them so that we can turn quickly to some other figures that are smaller but not so dull.

Yes, they come out of a bluebook. If we did not have the helpful census how would we discover, for instance, the arresting fact that there is one male millinery apprentice in Canada? Or that there are three women butchers, and one woman harness-maker, six running garages, two auctioneers and six female newsboys—a contradiction in terms at which the unimaginative experts in demography at Ottawa never blink a bespectacled eyelash?

Ottawa lists 367 separate occupations, apart from the hundred that must be included under that unsatisfactory and unrevealing word "other." In two-thirds of them, or 244, women are at work.

∞

Nowhere in Canada were the census-takers able to find a woman brewer, although they found 165 bottlers and cellarmen. There were no tanners although many women were dexterously working in leather goods. There were no millers but plenty of bakers. There were no taxi-drivers, captains or engineers of steam vessels (Tug-Boat Annie being an American); no furnacemen, no boilermakers, no machinists, no carpenters, no masons, no electricians, no painters, no plumbers, no veterinaries, no surveyors, no mining engineers, no aviators (a pilot's license does not make one an aviator); no radio technicians, no longshoremen, no soldiers.

Stranger yet was the fact that no woman put down her occupation as window cleaner. The 713 men had that field all to themselves. Apparently men get paid for cleaning windows but women do not.

Women do not run steam locomotives nor act as railway conductors, yardmen, firemen or baggagemen. But they sell tickets and collect them at the gate.

We have just about exhausted the list of the important occupations that women do not fill. The 490,150 women who were at work in 1931 were doing nearly everything else that needs to be done in this workaday economic world.

∞

Here are some of the chief occupations, other than those with which we began this article, that women have found to keep themselves off the relief rolls:

- Farming, stockraising, beekeeping, fruit-raising, etc.
- Proof reading
- Mail carrying
- Window dressing
- Peddling
- Teaching music, dancing and gymnastics
- Photography
- Art
- Acting
- Ushering
- Hairdressing
- Fishing
- Dressmaking
- Religious work
- Travelling and selling
- Insurance, stocks, bonds and real estate
- Electrotyping, lithographing and engraving
- Architecture, drafting and designing
- The professions

It would take two or three of these columns to list the different operations that girls and women perform in factories, such as polishing, canning, labelling, wrapping, intricate handwork on metal goods.

Women have invaded the professions and near professions in increasing numbers. There are 72 commercial travellers among them, 12 officials of banks and other financial institutions, 36 stock and bond brokers, 351 insurance agents, 151 real estate agents—but no pawnbrokers; two architects, 78 policewomen and detectives—but no firemen; 60 lawyers, five justices or magistrates, 208 doctors, 32 dentists, 16 opticians, 90 osteopaths or chiropractors, 207 actresses, 17 undertakers, 90 bellboys—but no bootblacks; 16 "clergymen."

∞

Girls start to work at a very early age. There are 540 girls between 10 and 13 years of age "gainfully employed" in Canada, some tending machines in factories. There are 1,975 aged 14; 6,101 aged 15; and 43,648 aged 16 or 17.

Over three-fifths of those girls under 14 who work, live and labor in Quebec province. What do these girls of 17 and under do for a living? One is overseer in a tobacco plant; two are butchers; one makes harness; two are proof readers; one is a mail carrier; four own or manage stores; three are pedlars; 22,290 are domestic servants. And there is a fair supply of schoolteachers and stenographers among them.

And if the girls start in at a very tender age to contribute to the family income, many of them continue work till they have passed the allotted three-score years and ten.

There are 7,897 women of 70 years of age and more who work in Canada. At least a third of them are farmers which means that they are carrying on after father has died. There are quite a few dressmakers and salefrom ladies and religious workers, nurses and schoolteachers. But several are listed as trappers and guides, 12 as telephone operators, four as doctors, 11 as fishermen, and, of course, there are factory workers.

There are some professions in which women have completely forestalled the intrusion of the male sex.

There is no male dressmaker in Canada, although there are 35 male milliners; no men are listed as nurses, though many of them classify as hospital orderlies. And against the 65,000 women stenographers we set down 3 male stenographers; against the 19,000 women boarding house keepers, we set the 1,750 men in the same work; against the 14,000 hello girls we set down nearly a thousand "hello boys."

In the very job of collecting the statistics, the women played a major rôle. But the statistics stop at an interesting point. They don't tell us whether or not the woman who does a similar job gets paid the same wages per hour or per week as a man gets.

# "City Order"

### *A vivid glimpse behind the scenes of a department store, anywhere in Canada, with the girls who take your telephone order*

By Helen Norsworthy Sangster

**NOVEMBER 1932** "**C**ITY OR-DER!" DO YOU EVER wonder about that voice? It answers when you call any of the big department stores to order safety-pins or electric light bulbs, toothpaste, or the meat for tomorrow's dinner. Always it says "City Or-der;" its owner is taught the very inflection to give the words.

Perhaps you have never thought of it as belonging to a person at all, but to a vast automaton which delivers your order with amazing promptness. It does belong to a person—to a girl drilled like a soldier until she reaches the maximum of efficiency in her particular part of the great machine's labors.

First, you are given a locker in which to leave your coat and hat—your purse you cling to like grim death—and a card bearing your number, which you punch at the time-clock. Woe to you if the gate goes down ere you reach it for three mornings! Jobs are hard to find now, and you are very likely to be looking for one.

In the order room, rows of girls sit at switchboards ready to begin work when the lights are flashed on at eight-thirty. The room is light and airy, since one whole wall is glass—frosted glass, which affords no distracting glimpses of the outer world.

The supervisor leads you to a "position" and consigns you to the tender mercies of one of her best operators. Before you is an upright board studded with tiny lights, each with a hole like a hungry mouth directly beneath it. The board is flanked by marked copies of the advertisements as they appeared in the two evening papers; above it are bulky price books; above that, the belt which carries the bills to be sorted.

A set is thrust into your hand—a complicated tangle of insulated wires, a plug, an earphone and a hornlike mouthpiece. You fumble with it awkwardly until the operator takes it and, with a few deft movements, untwists the wires, clamps the single earphone over one ear by means of a band that grips your head, fastens the mouthpiece around your neck with a piece of dingy tape, and shoves a plug into a socket. "Just listen in on me for a while," she says, reaching for a stack of bill books as eight-thirty strikes and the boards blaze with lights.

She thrusts a plug like a snake's head into one of the yawning holes beneath the lights. Out of a confused roar which sounds like static on the radio during a thunderstorm, her voice finally emerges, also mumbling sounds apparently made by the customer.

"—the dollar-fifty? Sorry, madam, there are no telephone orders on those . . . I beg your par-don, madam, but I have the paper right in front of me . . .

Yes, on page eight. We have a nice regular line at one-fifty, though . . . Yes, in a real dark shade . . . Well, I'd say size ten . . . What color's martinique? Just a moment, madam."

She flicks a button which temporarily disconnects the customer and shoves another plug into the bottom row of lights which are green instead of white. "Hello, operator. Gimme Ladies' Hose . . . That you, Grace? Say, what color's martinique, for cryin' out loud? . . . Kind of a brownish beige, eh?

"Hello, madam. Martinique's a kind of a brownish beige color . . . Hello! Hel-lo!" Disgustedly she flicks out the plug. "Wouldn't that tie you? Central's cut us off. I bet she's mad as hops."

She takes several orders at dizzying speed. At your bewildered look she grins. "Never mind. It takes a good month to get both ears trained in."

In spite of the supervisor's efforts to keep down noise, there is a constant clackety-clack of typewriters, whir of the belt, rip of bills being torn off, rattle of newspaper and price-book pages, sound of girls' voices. And if you cover your other ear with your hand, how can you make out bills? "Try the receiver on your right ear when your left gets tired," your operator advises. You comply. Nothing comes through but noise. You're practically deaf. Try it at home some time and see if it's not true. Then imagine having to do it in a roomful of noise.

You can't make many mistakes, either. A slip in the address or phone number or the order itself and the bill is returned to you. If this happens often, your presence is no longer required on the City Order board.

❧

By the end of the first day you will be filled with admiration for the girls who scribble orders, flip plugs and reel off information so expertly. There are so many things to remember—the letter or combination of letters which designates a department, since the big price books are indexed that way; the set phrases to be used in addressing customers; the different bills to be used for charge or C.O.D. orders, for fruit and groceries and general merchandise. You must learn to finish off bills while taking another order; speed is second only to accuracy. Your number is on every bill you fling on the belt, and every few days a count is taken. If your average

*Perhaps you have thought of that voice as belonging to a vast automaton which delivers your order with amazing promptness; but it belongs to a girl who has been drilled like a soldier until she reaches the maximum of efficiency.*

tally is low, some day a leaving slip will be tucked in with the bills in your pay envelope.

You must never "talk back" to a customer, nor waste time on personal calls. The supervisor listens in on the lines at unexpected moments from her monitor's board.

It's a wearing grind. Your ears ache from the pressure of the receiver, and the steel clamp binds your head cruelly. The smell of disinfectant solution on the mouthpiece is sickening, and if any of it gets on your skin it smarts and burns. The board glares like a Hydra-headed monster; each light means a voice waiting to clamor for something, and no sooner is it satisfied than another takes its place. The supervisor paces up and down incessantly, goading on aching fingers and tired voice. A weary back, cramped muscles, eyes that won't work quickly—ten minutes off in the morning, twenty in the afternoon and an hour for lunch are little enough relief in a day that stretches from eight-twenty to five-thirty.

∞

The girls themselves? Girls living at home; married women glad of a half-time to help out while their husbands are laid off or hunting for work; young widows with tiny children to support. Pretty girls in cheap bright dresses and flashy bargain-basement shoes; drab girls in tired-looking dark clothes; alert girls headed for one of the departments. There's Mabel, who takes orders with a speed which must intimidate the boldest customer. Her long nails, varnished a glittering pink, flash expertly among the plugs. She chews a large wad of gum; even when taking an order her jaws continue their rhythmic movement, ceasing only when the supervisor walks by. And Gladys, a dumpy little girl who has been in the department for six years. She has a string of charge customers; one is her particular pet. "Oh, Mrs. Crawferd," she purrs into the mouthpiece. "And how are you this morning?" Whereupon she murmurs sympathetic "Yes's" and "Noes" in the course of a recital of the ills which have befallen Mrs. Crawford and her numerous offspring, and is entrusted with the choosing of everything from a bonnet for the youngest Crawford to Sunday's roast of beef. "You'll be sure

to pick it out yourself, won't you, dearie?" Mrs. Crawford asks. "I don't want anybody else to do my shopping but you."

Then there's Mrs. Martin, next to Gladys. A thin little woman with a face always drawn with anxiety. A year ago her husband fell and hurt his back. His company still pays him part-time wages, but he wasn't hurt while at work and they are under no obligation to continue indefinitely. If the money should stop coming, or if he doesn't get any better . . . Mrs. Martin refuses to think about it. She got back her switchboard job, and her husband and little son live at her mother's. She phones home in the afternoons when the board is quiet. "Hello, is that you, sonny? . . . Yes, it's mother . . . Have you been out to play today? Tell grandma to put on your muffler; it's cold. How's daddy? Better, he says? That's good. Mother can't talk any longer now, dear. No, don't start to meet me yet; it's too early. Good-by."

And Mary Gray. Mary was a telephone operator before she came to the store, and she is the fastest operator on the board. Her tongue is as sharp as her thin, shrewd features, but underneath she's the kindest-hearted of the lot. Her position is next to Mrs. Martin's, and on days when Mrs. Martin is heavy-eyed from sitting up half the night with her sick husband, Mary's quota is much lower than usual, but Mrs. Martin's is, surprisingly, a little better. Mrs. Martin mustn't lose her job. Mary can always get back on the big switchboard. Or so she says.

Maisie wears expensive clothes. She has a seal coat with a kolinsky collar and a beautiful diamond which she wears on her right hand. Her husband is a young mechanic. When she leaves the building at night a long red car with nickelled fittings is waiting. Sometimes a shabby young chap watches it pull away from the curb with resentful, hungry eyes—Maisie's husband. He couldn't afford a car like that. He's lucky to be holding a job at all these days. So Maisie lives at home and enjoys herself, and he boards in a cheap rooming-house and goes to movies alone. Maisie is one of the best girls on the board. There's nobody like her for smoothing down annoyed customers, the supervisor says.

All sorts of girls; girls whose business it is, for

less than twenty dollars a week, to be patient, courteous, quick, helpful, industrious and untiring.

They grouse about working hard, yet they like it. Ask them whether they prefer a quiet day when the board is "dead" or one when the board is a continual flare of lights. Every one will tell you the same thing—the busy days are the shortest. There's a thrill in plunging ahead at top speed, in company with others. The speed itself is intoxicating, and there is an *esprit de corps* that is truly remarkable.

# Women in Uniform

BY NORMA GIBB

APRIL 1941

"IF THERE IS ANYTHING THAT I dislike, it is to see a woman strutting about in a uniform." You have heard this remark, and others like it, thousands of times in the last year. Criticism of the uniform takes first place. Criticism of the drill comes next. Occasionally, doubt is expressed as to the ability of these women to make a worth-while contribution to the war effort— and in rare cases, people have questioned their motives!

First, there is the uniform.

The uniform levels social barriers. This is important in a group embracing all types of racial, religious and economic backgrounds. The uniform is practical. The uniform sets the standard of grooming. The uniform is the visible reminder of the wearer's responsibility to her God, and her King.

∾

Let us say then, that the uniform is desirable from many angles, and take up the next question of the drill. Criticism in this regard is more vehement from men than women. Unnatural, exaggerated, aping the men, are only a few of the unfavorable epithets used by critics.

The benefits derived from the rediscovered art of walking would fill a book. Reviewing a few of the most important, we find—freedom from constipation, with consequent improvement in complexion and disposition.

Improved appetites with consequent toning up of vitality.

Straighter backs and better posture, due in no small measure to the comfort and support of the low-heeled shoes required to be worn.

More zest for work.

More power to you, Miss Canada! I am looking into my crystal, and I see vital, youthful-looking mothers, caring for beautiful, straight children—calm, cheerful nurses, unwearying in their devotion to their patients—quiet, understanding schoolteachers, beloved by their pupils—keen, vital professional and business women, respected by their associates.

∾

What service do these women expect to render? Assuming their qualifications in the offices as clerks, stenographers and secretaries, and acknowledging the special military training they are being given, where else can women replace men?

We offer you as examples of what women in uniform are learning:

The Land Army—the Farmerettes of 1941. There can be no question of women's ability to serve in this capacity.

Ambulance Drivers. Even the men admit that the girls in this group are first-class drivers. They are also able to look after the upkeep of their vehicles, thanks to the generosity and farsightedness of the General Motors and Ford companies. All members must have First Aid Certificates.

The Nursing Divisions of the St. John Ambulance Brigade. These members are trained in First Aid, Home Nursing, Air Raid Precautions, Massage, and a fortunate few are being given hospital training. The Queen is the commandant-in-chief of the Nursing Divisions, and the Duchess of Gloucester is her deputy.

# The Kitten and the Fighter

By Jack Mosher

AUGUST 1941

**F**OR DAYS THE YOUNG SCAMP had been hanging around that end of the aircraft plant where final assembly took place, and the men had grown quite fond of him. But they were pretty mad just the same when he hopped over a machine-gun mount and hid in one end of a wing—just out of reach.

"Better send for Elsie," one suggested. "She'll know what to do."

The "Elsie" they meant is Elizabeth Gregory MacGill, who has a string of degrees after her name as long as a fully grown cat's tail, and she not only knows how to get kittens out of wings—managed, in this case, by pushing in a bowl of milk, with string attached so she could pull it and the young stowaway out again.

Elsie also knows how to install deicing equipment in such wings, or handle any of the million other details that crop up while making fighter planes to strengthen Britain's air arm. For she is the Elsie MacGill who recently received the Gzowski Award, an honor rarely bestowed on any man and never before on any woman, for performing one of the biggest chores in engineering history.

That was when she took 3,600 blueprints, delivered from the Hawker plant over in England, and drew off the designs for the jigs required to manufacture the 25,000 parts of a Hurricane Fighter—planes now being turned out at Canadian Car and Foundry's Fort William plant, where she is chief engineer.

The little incident which opens our story might be called "The Kitten and the Fighter"—and that's Elsie all over. To meet her in her home, where she serves the best steaks west of Montreal, you'd never dream she is the human pivot around which turns one of the most vital operations of the Canadian war effort. Especially if you didn't know Elsie and you saw her reach for the cane alongside her chair and limp into the living room.

You have to dig pretty hard to get stuff out of Elsie. So it's quite some time before you learn that

# CHATELAINE'S
## Personality of the Month

she was a victim of the infantile paralysis epidemic which swept this continent just about the time a man called Hitler was beginning to put together a war machine which has since swept Europe.

Elsie also thinks it rather silly that anyone should think it strange for her to be designing planes. "People don't change so much," she observes. "They thought the same about grandmother just because she stumped for women's suffrage."

# What They've Found Out about Us

*Production managers, medical experts, recruiting officers are pretty well in agreement; they say women make magnificent workers, but you have to understand 'em!*

By Lotta Dempsey

SEPTEMBER 1943

**O**NE OUT OF EVERY THREE Canadian women between 15 and 65 are in the armed forces, munitions, or civilian services, according to the Dominion Bureau of Statistics.

How do we rate with the men on the job—or the ones we replaced?

*Chatelaine* wanted facts, figures, surveys, findings, opinions and data. The married ones and single, in and out of uniform, on long hours and short, working for men and women bosses.

We got them.

First and foremost, we got the key factor in the employment of women, as every close observer, from top executives to Shorty, saw it. Shorty is the janitor (with feminine assistants) in one plant which has swung from a pre-war woman ban to an 80% feminine payroll. "Sure, women are just as hep to the job," he said, magnanimously. And then, with a warning finger, "But you gotta realize one thing, for keeps. *Dames is different.*"

∾

Women will produce more at a higher speed than men in many fields; but they can't be forced or shouted at. They need understanding, appreciation, and a sense of the value and importance of their work. Some managers learned this the hard way—and it isn't for completely altruistic reasons that there are now trained personnel workers in practically all the Canadian plants where the 255,000 women in war production are employed.

Nor are the armed forces fussing with frills when they install, as an important part of their setup, skilled psychologists. "Get the right girl in the right job, show her why it's a real war-winning job, and you've solved half your problems," one of the chief psychologists in the CWAC told me. And a successful personnel worker who has thousands of girls and women under her direction put it this way, "Women haven't evolved water-tight compartments in their minds yet to take care of the different phases of their new kind of living. They bring their personal problems to work and take their jobs home."

∾

We're just as smart (or smarter?). Remember how there were always more girls in the top half of the class at grade school? Here are some of the jobs at which they've been proved superior to men: miscellaneous bench assemblies, sorting and handling rivets, punch press work, burring and reaming, spot welding, drill press operations, sewing machine work and hand sewing.

Checkup by a Chamber of Commerce in a large war-centre-city recently disclosed that the output of women and girls was exceeding that of men and boys on the same job in 25% of the plants. A survey in U. S. metal industries found 65% of production managers reporting that the output of women was better than that of men.

*How a woman looks is a matter of concern because it affects her efficiency.*

Canadian plant managers back up the U. S. findings that, in general, women are better producers on monotonous jobs (perhaps because of generations of house tending). For instance, they are found to be 50% to 100% faster workers than men in the wiring of airplane instrument panels. Women are also tops in work which requires quickness or delicacy of hand motion.

∾

But here's the kick-back. We're not so cool or ingenious in a crisis. There were a lot of women automobile drivers pre-war; but only one in a thousand knew what really made the wheels go round. A chief instructor of an RCAF Wireless School has had special success in training girls in wireless and in the new Radio Telephone Operations, but he learned to stop trying to teach women just what causes it all.

"Either they haven't the ability to understand involved mechanical or scientific stuff—or they're not interested," he says. "But that doesn't mean that they don't make cracking good operators. We teach them how to operate and what to do in every possible emergency. And for ground work, at least, they can do just as well."

Same goes for munitions plants. You'll often hear girls discussing their output or their skill, but in visits to dozens of plants and talks with hundreds of women I've yet to hear one able to explain to me just why her particular machine does exactly what it does. (Besides, I'm not interested, either.)

In many classes for wireless, motor mechanics, etc., women take top marks. But they need as high or a higher percentage in the classroom to come up to men when they're out on their own, according to instructors. It's that old story of working better under direction and not having such a quick and decisive co-ordination when quick action is necessary.

∽

We lack confidence. One of the joys of psychologists in the armed forces has been to "bring out" hundreds of girls—particularly from the hardest-hit depression areas of the West—when they get into uniform. At the RCAF wireless school, the O.C. found that girls were particularly nervous about starting in so new a field as wireless. So he starts them fooling around with electric cord and household equipment. In no time at all they can splice wires and do simple repairs on toasters, irons and so on.

∽

We're more erratic. Already wise men have learned to distinguish between the two brands of that old black magic—the use of tears. Several bosses said they had been fooled at first by the girl who could "turn 'em on!" But no more. It's the one who can't

*Farmers report that girls pick fruit more carefully, with more skill, than men.*

hold 'em back who causes them worry. Usually the personnel worker can get to the source of the trouble. In any event, there are fewer tears as more women become old hands.

Absenteeism has been definitely higher among women than men. Women can't always stand up to the job as men can. Absenteeism is associated, too, with the fact that a great many women workers today are doing two jobs—one at home and one at the office. As soon as they know that their shopping can be coped with and their children are in good hands, they're back on the job, full time.

An all-woman plant in Detroit, making machine-gun, airplane and tank parts, was suffering from a high rate of absenteeism and a dropping production rate. Music was installed—everything from soft and sweet to swing and hot—and production was stepped up nearly 40%. The musical treatment hasn't had such a stimulating effect on men.

∽

Most women overestimate their strength and their health, according to medical staffs in the armed forces and munition plants. The average woman's strength is 570-1000ths of a man's, and her resistance 679-1000ths, according to the National Safety Council. She should not lift more than 35% of her body weight.

Many women will pooh-pooh this, but they usually suffer if they do.

Women work better on shorter shifts. When one Canadian plant cut its nine-hour shift to one of eight and a half hours, production increased. Also, women need more frequent rest periods and longer lunch periods (at least 30 minutes). And here's an interesting point: tests have shown that women are at their best early in the day, while men take time to get going.

One of the big problems facing dietitians in plants and camps is to teach women to eat for health, rather than with an eye to shadowy figure proportions. However, well-prepared food at low cost is meeting this need, and it's the mother at home, *the worst fed member of the family* by recent surveys, who will be learning from her sister or daughter at work.

∽

We're eternally feminine. Ninety-nine-point-nine-nine-nine women out of a hundred want to look attractive. In a recent survey through all branches of the women's armed services, the uniform took on tremendous importance; you'd be amazed at the number of girls who had joined one particular branch because they liked the uniform; or who found their life less pleasant than they had hoped because they didn't like some feature of the outfit. So big is this point, in fact, that the armed forces have finally given permission to women to wear civvies on leave, and have spent long hours with designers fixing the line of a skirt here and the slant of a hat there.

The same applies in munition plants. Overalls and coveralls are a must for women on this job. Today the biggest plants have designed very slick uniforms that are figure-flattering.

∽

Will the women workers go back home when it's over?

Production heads are agreed that at least 85% of them want to. But they say it's up to You, the Public.

If you accept them as a normal, natural part of your town or city or neighborhood, if you consider them simply as women who happen to be away from their homes while working to help win the war—if you help to see that they get decent living places, decent food, a chance to have their children cared for—they'll slip back easily into home life.

But if you isolate them and set them apart as "those women," they may not.

As Mrs. Rex Eaton, Director of Women's Division, National Selective Service, said recently: "The contribution women have made in this war calls for a rehabilitation program of no less foresight and magnitude than that given to men. Women who are standing side by side with men in war should stand side by side with men in peace."

# Women's-Eye View of Professional Women

**JANUARY 1948** CHATELAINE ASKED ITS coast-to-coast Councillors this question: "If you had a choice between a man or a woman of equal capabilities, which would you tend to consult for the following services?"

## DOCTOR
Women in the rural districts would consult a woman doctor to a greater extent than those in large cities. Those in the lower-income groups like them better than those in the higher brackets. And women over 45 years of age show the greatest trust of all.

| The vote: | Man 48 | Woman 43 | No choice 9 |
|---|---|---|---|

## LAWYER
We tend to take our legal troubles to men. Only one in four women would go to a woman. The percentages for this question run about the same for all communities, age and income groups. A number of the women made it clear that there had been so little opportunity to consult a woman lawyer that they had had no chance to estimate female abilities in this field.

| The vote: | Man 64 | Woman 25 | No choice 11 |
|---|---|---|---|

## ARCHITECT
Women would like to consult women as architects, and gave them a slight edge in their voting in most of the provinces. One woman summed up: "After living in houses designed by men, we'd like to have women's experience and ideas on cupboards and space for the baby carriage!"

| The vote: | Man 44 | Woman 46 | No choice 10 |
|---|---|---|---|

## INTERIOR DECORATOR
An overwhelming vote in this field went to women, throughout the provinces and in all age and income groups.

| The vote: | Man 5 | Woman 88 | No choice 10 |
|---|---|---|---|

## PSYCHOLOGIST
Again women prefer women, even though only a few of the Councillors have had the opportunity or the need to consult one. This preference is remarkably high in British Columbia, the Prairies and Ontario; in the highest income group and among women over 45.

| The vote: | Man 30 | Woman 53 | No choice 17 |
|---|---|---|---|

# How to Turn "Just a Job" into a Career

*You have to plan for success, make the right moves at the right times— just as men do*

BY JOANNA MORGAN

**FEBRUARY 1977** IT'S NOT EVERY DAY THAT A former filing clerk finds herself promoted to senior management and her salary in the rarefied heights of $30,000+. So it was understandable that Janice Bernard was justifiably jubilant when we met. She'd been told earlier that day she'd been boosted to Bell Canada's fourth-level management (now the second woman in the company at that level) and her new job means she'll be coordinating budgets and monitoring productivity from several departments for a vice-president in the Ottawa office. Janice is 31 and she began with the company fresh out of grade 13. She's living proof that you can work your way up the company ladder, *if you know how*.

## GET YOURSELF A REPUTATION AS A HARD WORKER

"The average woman in a job is only interested in going out to business and working from nine to five and having her coffee breaks." Male chauvinist piggery? No—that's the rueful assessment of Margaret Leigh who went back to work at 32 as a cost clerk when her youngest child was four, and now 23 years later, is the cost manager of Toronto's Southam Murray Printing.

"I'm saying this because many times I've had people on our staff tell me they wouldn't take my job for all the money there was. It's very disheartening."

## ASK FOR MORE RESPONSIBILITY

Women tend to think, rather naïvely, that if they work hard, some beneficent body above them will take note and reward them with promotion. That's not always true. If you're quiet, it's assumed you're content. Ambitious men, on the other hand, *seek out* responsibility and recognition for what they've done.

"Women tend to think more about what they can lose rather than what they can gain, when the time comes to apply for a new position," Janice reported. Subconsciously, women assume they must be perfect; in effect, able to do the next job, *before* they even apply for it.

## ASK FOR THE MONEY TO GO WITH IT

"I think women tend to put themselves down, unconsciously or consciously," says Ruth Hammond, in business for 25 years, and now running her own public relations firm in Toronto. "Go in and say in a very calm and rational way, 'I've been here this length of time, I believe you're satisfied with my work. I would like to know why I can't have more money. I think I'm worth it.'

"If you have any absolute facts, not rumors, that somebody is being better paid for a similar job, you should bring them forth."

## EQUAL PAY FOR EQUAL WORK

Andrea's story, unfortunately, is still typical of the kind of abuse of female workers ongoing in large companies. A friend in payroll tipped her off that her co-worker, Bob, doing the same job, was making more than her $11,000. Bob, "a great guy and terribly supportive" according to Andrea, readily admitted earning $14,000 a year and was appalled at the salary difference. It was doubly unfair actually: Bob's single, and Andrea's the divorced mother of three kids.

At Christmas, the annual raises and some carping from Andrea to her boss narrowed the gap to $1,900. But when Andrea asked for catch-up pay in the New Year, her boss was not sympathetic.

Andrea mentioned her plight to two female friends a little more familiar with current legislation than her boss. They did some research on her behalf. Which is how she came to walk into her boss's office last summer with a scrupulously typed three-page memo with photocopied documentation attached.

She gave the company a chance to save face by diplomatically prefacing her memo with "perhaps the equal-pay section of the Employment Standards Act and the AIB regulations regarding catchup increases were not known within the company before . . ."

The outcome of Andrea's memo was a raise. With another promotion, that made her salary $15,300 a year. Bob's, though, is still more, $15,900. It seems, according to Andrea's boss, that Bob deserves that extra $12 a week because he's got "a little extra something." Since "that little extra something" seems to be what Andrea was born without, she's now out hunting for a more modern-thinking company to use her talent.

## ACT THE PART

If you're a young woman on the corporate make, you *don't* lunch with "les girls" in the steno pool. Your spare time at work is best spent fraternizing with those people who can help you—your peers or if you can swing it, your superiors—learning just what the XYZ contract means to the company or why the annual report is such a stinker.

My friend, Susan, was promoted to the higher echelons of an investment firm. Suddenly she found herself in a milieu where a brown-bag lunch munched at her desk was a faux pas. Susan was saving for a trip to Europe, had a trim figure to look after, and reckoned quite rightly that not much was accomplished being pressured into a second and third martini. So she compromised. Half the week she goes along to lunch with the men. The rest of the time she pleads a diet and works right through lunch.

A York University prof found some of his female MBA graduates had trouble handling social situations on the job. Ruth Hammond thinks these problems are easily overcome. "Say to yourself, 'What would a business*man* in my position do?'

"If I'm out with men and talking business, I have said frequently, 'I would like to take you out to dinner because I think we have many things still to discuss. Do you feel it would be appropriate for your wife to come along?' Let the man have his choice.

After a couple of decades in business, Hammond remarks: "When you're dining out with a man, the waiter always used to put the bill in front of the man. Now you find that he'll put the bill in the middle, just the same as he would with two men. Then you just reach over very firmly and take the plate and the bill and put it in front of you and *that's it.*"

## KNOW WHEN IT'S TIME TO MOVE ON

If you do consider changing jobs, make sure it's either going to give you skills you need, or considerably better pay. Jacqui Tirman heads up the female section of Career Path, a Toronto personnel firm staffing clerical and accounting jobs, and she finds "most women change jobs for a difference of $10 a week which is $520 a year. Most men will not change their jobs for under $2,000 to $3,000 a year."

And before grimly stating "I quit!," make sure you explore every opportunity *within your own company.* "If you're trying to change fields, it's easier in your own company," says O. J. Reynolds, especially for women.

## DEVELOP YOUR CONTACTS

Find out if there are professional associations in your field you can join.

Men, unlike women, traditionally play in groups as children—so they know the necessity of team work early. (Little Tommy down the street may have been a bully at football, but the other boys tolerated him at playtime because they needed a certain number of players.) Women more commonly played one-to-one as children and quite easily rejected a friend who disappointed them. So Tommy, when he grows up to be the staff accountant in your company, is still a creep. But his *work skills* make him invaluable at the office.

# What Will Unions Do for Women in the '80s?

## By Charlotte Gray

MAY 1981

WHENEVER YOU SEE NEWS pictures of strikers these days, chances are those strikers are women. Angry, determined, persistent, they wave placards and link arms as though accustomed to starring roles in labor dramas. It's hard to remember that until recently women unionists were regarded as bit players—the weak sisters of the labor movement. In the major labor disputes of the last five years, picket duties have consistently been filled by women prepared to hang in and hang tough for their rights.

At the Fleck auto parts factory in Ontario, 75 militant female members of the United Auto Workers (UAW) stayed out for five and a half months in 1978 as they battled, literally, for union security—not just recognition but the right to negotiate. They won. It took six months the following year for a predominantly female group, who were members of the United Steelworkers of America and hitherto regarded as the docile "housewife shift," to wrest their first union contract from Radio Shack. And in the fall of 1980, the picket lines of 40,000 federal clerks—77 percent of whom are women and none of whom had ever walked off the job before—brought the federal government and airports across Canada to a grinding halt for two weeks. They didn't get the cost-of-living allowances they'd asked for—but they did win a resounding wage hike plus a "family-leave

*The smaller the workplace, the less likely it is to be unionized—and women are more likely to work in small establishments*

package" including child-rearing leave for either spouse. As one member of the union, the Public Service Alliance of Canada (PSAC), said afterward with grim satisfaction: "We were real innocents. We didn't know the songs to sing or the slogans to chant. But we soon learned."

The percentage of women in the labor movement has more than doubled in the last decade. By 1978 (the latest year for which figures are available), 27 percent of paid women workers belonged to one or another of Canada's 178 unions and women made up 28.7 percent of all union members. We make up 39.3 percent of the work force. And we are heavily outnumbered by men within the unions: 43 percent of the considerably larger male work force is unionized. But back in 1962, a mere 16.4 percent of union members were women. So we are coming in on the fast track.

Women have been organizing at a faster speed than the rate they've infiltrated the job market and at a smarter pace than men. While the number of union brothers rose by 40 percent between 1966 and 1976, sisterhood strength shot up by 160 percent. By 1978, 835,263 Canadian women had joined unions.

∾

Yet, women are actually slipping behind in the labor market, losing ground in the fight for economic equality—the first step toward *real* liberation. Consider:

- The wage gap between men and women is growing—although a woman working full-time earned 57.8 percent of a man's earnings in 1977, compared to 54.6 percent in 1972, the actual dollar difference in earnings between women and men increased by $2,385—or 55.6 percent.
- Female unemployment was 8.8 percent in 1979, compared to 6.6 percent for men.
- Men and women don't do the same kind of work, and the kind that women do, mainly in the service and clerical sectors, is characterized by lower wages, higher layoffs and fewer opportunities for promotion. And these "pink-collar ghettos" are becoming entrenched. In 1962, women held 62.7 percent of all clerical jobs; by 1979 they held 77.1 percent.
- In the current recession, even some of the mini-

mal inroads into nontraditional areas are being erased. Last year, McDonnell Douglas of Canada Ltd. announced it was laying off a total of 1,000 workers at its Malton, Ont., plant by August 1981. The move will eliminate, on the old "last hired, first fired" principle, the remaining 17 of a total of 30 women hired during 1979-80 for assemblers' jobs on the plant floor.

- There has been little progress on issues of particular interest to women, such as equal pay, protection against sexual harassment, better conditions for part-time workers or improved maternity-leave provisions. According to Shelley Acheson, human rights director of the Ontario Federation of Labor, 2,600 day-care spaces have been lost in the last two years.
- By and large, collective agreements between unions and managements are still phrased in sexist language. Joan McFarland, who teaches economics at St. Thomas University in Fredericton, studied 59 local contracts that covered 13,827 female union members. "Twenty-four used he/him throughout . . . three [of these] were actually contracts covering more female than male employees. Only five [contracts] were completely nonsexist."
- Within the labor movement itself, there aren't many women in positions of power. Of a total of 977 Canadians elected to union executive boards for 1978, only 171, or 17.5 percent, were women.

∾

Why is progress so agonizingly slow?

For a start, women are only just beginning to accept the new financial facts of life—that most of us, from the most ambitious career-minded high achiever to the humblest pot-walloper, are going to be wage earners for most of our working years. Right now, about 50 percent of women work outside the home, and a federal report last year predicted that figure could increase to 68 percent by the turn of the century.

Even though half of all Canadian women are wage earners today, most still have to cope with the dirty diapers and dishes at home too.

A union can gobble up free time. Linda McLaren, a 28-year-old policy analyst in the federal government and the president of PSAC Local 70041 and of the Ottawa-Hull area council, is a fiercely dedicated union member—but she recognizes the price she's paying. "I go to meetings two or three evenings a week. Tonight, for instance, I won't be home until midnight."

More fundamental than women's attitudes and expectations is the fragmentation of the labor market. The smaller the workplace, the less likely it is to be unionized—and women are more likely to work in small establishments like stores, laundries, hairdressing salons and restaurants, workplaces often with fewer than 200 workers.

A subtler reason for the slow progress of unions in small companies is the "turkey at Christmas" syndrome. When there are fewer employees, relationships between boss and employees are cozier: even if the pay is lousy, the employer is perhaps a self-styled parent figure who is affronted that his or her workers feel the *need* for union protection.

Even in large institutions, overt hostility from the employer effectively blocks attempts to unionize. The classic Canadian case of such opposition is that of banks, where 72 percent of employees are women. Despite vigorous attempts to organize the 154,141 bank employees in the 7,420 branches of federally chartered banks over the last four years, less than two percent has been organized.

Since the Union of Bank Employees was formed in 1978 to fight the David and Goliath battle, Singler says the single most effective deterrent to progress has been "fear of employer reprisal." During these years, the banks have had more complaints laid against them than any of the other sectors dealt with under the Canada Labor Relations Board: according to its annual report of 1977-78, one third of all complaints were against banks. Complaints include charges of firing staff for union activities, transferring workers involved in a union, and requiring workers at unionized branches to make up cash shortages at the end of the day from their own pay—something not required by nonunion branches.

Another hurdle in the way of organizing women has been attitudes within the labor movement itself. The last few years may have seen a cluster of female stars shoot to the top of union hierarchies. Women like Grace Hartman, the first woman to head a major union when she was elected president of CUPE in 1975. Or Shirley Carr, since 1974 the first woman vice-president of the CLC. But these are the exceptions. Union hierarchies reflect employment hierarchies, with women at the bottom.

Another hindrance to progress within the labor movement on women's issues is the rift in attitudes on quotas. The idea that employers should be required to have a specific minimum proportion of women on their payrolls clashes with two of the sacred cows of union philosophy: the merit and the seniority principles. Unions have always argued that the individual with the best qualifications should get the job, and the employee who has been on the job longest should have the most security.

∾

As the new wave of women activists works its way up union ladders, the old guard and its dinosaur attitudes should leach out. "I've noticed a difference in the six years I've been president of CUPE," Hartman reflects. "Today, women are given the same attention as men at our national conventions when they rise to speak. It's because so many more women are participating in *real* decision-making jobs: presidents and stewards in union locals, rather than in the traditional slot as secretary. In addition, among all the groups we've been recruiting most actively—library and social workers, graduate students, day-care centre staff—are women, and they are changing the balance in the union. Women will soon comprise over 50 percent of our members."

Male unionists are beginning to grasp that equal pay isn't just a women's issue, because if we got equal pay, there wouldn't be that vast reservoir of cheap labor to undercut their jobs.

The catalog of sad statistics about the deteriorating conditions for working women is weighed down by the nonunionized women in the private sector—waitresses, part-time shift workers, cleaners, employees of corner stores and large retail chains—the women who do the drudgery jobs. Grace Hartman sighs at the mention of these women. "The employers use all the old union-busting techniques from the 1930s and 1940s to stop them from organizing. And many of those women just don't know what unions are *for*."

The kinds of tactics that management may use

to prevent store workers from organizing were described in graphic detail in an Ontario Labor Relations Board decision last January. K-Mart Canada Ltd. was severely criticized for using intimidation, surveillance and harassment of employees in its Peterborough store in order to smash a union-organizing campaign by members of the SEIU: "Conduct so extreme," read the decision, "as to include an employee being escorted to the washroom by her supervisor, in the plain view of other employees, because of her wish to be represented by a union, constitutes an abuse of employees that will not be countenanced in this province." Two women had had a particularly rough time: a couple of management trainees dogged their footsteps wherever they went in the store, followed them to their table in coffee breaks and eavesdropped on their private conversations. K-Mart was ordered to pay them $500 each for the humiliation they had suffered and to refrain from any further actions that interfered with their employees' legal right to join a union.

In the last analysis, the main achievement of the last five years of union activity seems to be in attitudes. Grace Hartman recalls an ironic example of the gulf from the CLC's Banff conference last December. "The first night, an inspiring speech was made by Addie Wyatt, vice-president of the Washington-based United Food and Commercial Workers. She spoke about discrimination against women inside and outside the union movement; she's black, so she knew all kinds of prejudice. When she'd finished, one of the dozen men present stood up and asked if sometime over the weekend he could have an opportunity to rebut her statements. I went up to him afterward and said, 'Rebut? This is *our* rebuttal, after hundreds of years of discrimination!' He was flabbergasted; he just couldn't understand."

# Liberation the Mary Kay Way

*A startled male ventures into the world of Mary Kay, the entrepreneurial great-grandmother whose wholesale cosmetic sales in Canada this year are expected to be $35 million*

BY ALLAN M. GOULD

**JULY 1981**

ROCK MUSIC BLASTS OUT OF giant speakers. Fountains of water shoot up from both sides of the huge stage, as green strobe lights zap back and forth across them. Slides are now cast upon a mammoth screen. A Cadillac. A Buick. A full-length mink coat. Diamond pins. Two pink hands, shaking one another. Hundreds of pink hearts.

I look around, embarrassed, sinking lower in my auditorium chair. I, an infidel, a man whose wife doesn't wear makeup, who himself disapproves of it. When will it all end? I glance down at my watch. Heaven help me, it's only 8.07 in the morning!

Suddenly, 2,000 women are up on their feet, singing their hearts out and clapping their pink hands, like hysterical teenagers at a Beatles concert:

*I've got that Mary Kay enthusiasm/Up in my head/Up in my head/Up in my head*
*I've got that Mary Kay enthusiasm/Up in my head/Up in my head to stayyyyyyyyyy!*

These are women from across Canada, meeting at the First Canadian Seminar of Mary Kay Cosmetics at the Harbour Castle Hilton on the Toronto waterfront. Now there are audible gasps around me, as tears well up in a hundred mascaraed eyes. There's someone on the stage! Sinatra? Elton John? Phil Donahue? No. It's Mary Kay, founder and chairwoman of the board herself, walking into the centre of all the aural and visual chaos, acknowledging with a smile the wild applause and cheers. The liberator of 100,000 women from 500,000 soap operas is being received like the victorious René Lévesque on Nov. 15, 1976.

Bright shiny car keys are presented to winners of

53 pink Cadillacs and 49 Buick Regals. Immaculately dressed women squeal in ecstasy. Banners and streamers are waved endlessly.

"Mary Kay is one of the most wonderful people God has ever created. She is an angel in my eyes. I'm a better person since I became a Mary Kay consultant."

The speaker is Bette Whiteside, plumpish, childless, "between 50 and 55," from Winnipeg. Bette Whiteside's words start to grate—"It's an opportunity! It's a way of life!"—until her husband, Frederick, a Winnipeg transit worker, now on his way to a class for husbands to learn how to give his wife moral support in her business, leans over awkwardly to shake my hand. He looks tired, rundown, older than his half century or so. His wife looks at him with deep affection and proudly claims, "I hope that in a short period, I'll be a Sales Director of Mary Kay. That's my goal. Frederick will then be able to retire early."

I get up and move through the milling crowd in the lobby of the Hilton, and find myself face to face with a very beautiful woman, nearly six feet tall, wearing a green dress with a split skirt that falls sensually over her perfect figure. Her name is Kyli Cahoon-Cox and, at 29, she has already reached the goal to which breathless hero-worshipping Bette Whiteside aspires: she is a Senior Sales Director, in Calgary.

"I was a single parent, struggling to make ends meet," Cahoon-Cox declares. "I was working nine to five, even till nine, with another cosmetics firm. I had to have a baby-sitter for my son. I felt like someone *else* was raising him.

"Then I became a Beauty Consultant for Mary Kay. Seven months later, I went into training to become a Sales Director. In the following three months, the women I brought into the company and I shared the opportunity with 22 others. I was soon making $25 an hour and I'm earning far more than that now. I'm remarried now, to a teacher, and making nearly three times as much as my husband. He's going to teach one more year, and then quit his job and help me full time in the business."

I turn to the Mary Kay bible, *Your Guide to Your Mary Kay Business*. The pieces begin to come together.

A woman who wishes to become a Mary Kay Beauty Consultant (a euphemism—these "girls," as they call each other, do not call themselves salespeople) must send in a certified cheque or money order for $100 plus tax (cash on the barrelhead for Mary Kay) to receive her Beauty Showcase, containing all she needs to give facials and skin-care classes in the homes of friends or acquaintances. "The Basic," the complete skin care kit, sells for about $50. At up to 50 percent commission, an average evening yielding the sale of three or four Basics, plus the occasional order for shampoo, cologne or blusher, can make a good worker $75. Not bad for two hours' work.

"Sharing the opportunity" is another euphemism—for recruiting. When the leader has brought in three recruits, she may wear the Mary Kay jacket, an attractive red blazer; when she has brought in five, she receives brass buttons to wear on her blazer. Once she has gathered eight others under her Non-Aerosol Hair Sprayed wing, she becomes a Future Sales Director, and Mary Kay pays her 5 percent per month of her recruits' wholesale orders. Six underlings bring in 6 percent; seven, 7 percent; eight or more, 8 percent.

Meanwhile, the Future Sales Director is stroked like a cat at weekly meetings run by *her* Sales Director. Ribbons for $100, $200 and $500 in sales are given out like candy to well-behaved kids. Applause. Tears. Enthusiasm songs. To become Sales Director, like Kyli Cahoon-Cox, a future Sales Director must bring in at least 24 Beauty Consultants and fly down to the international office in Dallas, Texas, to take an intensive week of seminars and training sessions.

In the meantime there are the prizes, including: a bracelet for bringing in one recruit; a lambskin rug for two; a rattan rocking chair for four; a snakeskin handbag from Italy or satin sheets for six. Duvets! Diamond rings! The pink Cadillacs are far in the future, of course. But apparently hundreds across the U.S. and Canada receive them each year. The Caddies go to Sales Directors whose unit places $72,000 in wholesale orders within a six-month period.

∾

I may meet Mary Kay herself in her executive suite on the 34th floor of the Harbour Castle Hilton.

Mary Kay Ash is all Southern charm, hospitality and warmth. She's a great-grandmother in her 70s, but she looks more like a woman in her 50s. She's heavy-set, it's true; and how the magazine articles love to point this out, as if her full figure calls her success into question. Her dyed-blond hair is teased into an outdated bouffant, but she is immaculate, her eyes and face barely wrinkled, her light Texan accent recalling Nick Carraway's description of Daisy Buchanan in that other American tale of lavish success, *The Great Gatsby*: her voice sounds like money.

"You know," she proudly announces, "most of the things we do are really not like any other company. When our girls share the opportunity with three new consultants, they have to buy their own jackets."

"They buy their *own*?"

"Oh, yes. That way they respect it. And when they come to Dallas to train to become Sales Directors, they pay for their trip themselves as well."

It occurs to me that Mary Kay really does treat her "girls" like girls—children who need discipline, strictness and love. And her "girls" need punishment as well: if a Beauty Consultant falls *below* the three recruits she has, she may not wear the jacket ("It's an honor system, you see," Mary Kay says with a smile).

Mary Kay's rags-to-riches story has been told in countless magazine articles over the past 18 years, since she created her cosmetics firm in Dallas. At the age of seven, Mary Kay was forced to take care of her invalid father while her mother managed a restaurant, putting in 14-hour days. She did brilliantly in high school but, lacking the money for college, she ended up doing what most of her tens of thousands of followers have done—she got married. It was not a good match and the marriage ended in divorce. To provide for her three children, she started selling cleaning products for Stanley Home Products at home shows.

In classic gift-from-the-gods fashion, she realized how much she loved the quality of a locally made skin cream she had been using for years. With a $5,000 investment, she bought the rights to it and in the fall of 1963 started Mary Kay Cosmetics Inc.

Today Mary Kay Cosmetics Inc. has 150,000 freelance Beauty Consultants in the United States, Canada, Australia and Argentina, and more than $300 million in retail sales worldwide. In Canada, wholesale sales reached $10 million in 1979, $25 million in 1980 and they're expected to reach $35 million in 1981—an increase of more than 200 percent in 24 months.

"Canadians are *incredible*!" enthuses Mary Kay. "They are teaching *us* how to do it!" The statistics seem to bear her out. The firm moved north of the 49th parallel in December 1979, with a projection of $1 million in net sales for its first year and maybe 1,000 consultants. At the end of 12 months, it had hit $2 million in net sales and had about 1,700 Beauty Consultants and 18 Sales Directors in this country. As of this writing, there are about 350 Sales Directors and 14,000 Beauty Consultants.

According to Mary Kay and her myriad followers, hundreds of marriages all over the world have been saved by the wife bringing home much needed extra cash—or by her losing weight and dressing better in her desire to achieve the "Mary Kay Look." (No drinking at seminars or study sessions; no smoking allowed during facials.)

Yet it must be acknowledged that the company, in its promotion of cosmetics and traditional female roles, radiates an irritating "Total Woman," almost reactionary sensibility. It's as if Gloria Steinem had been grafted onto a Marabel Morgan tree. Mary

Dianne Hall, Nova subsidiaries

Claire Bertrand, Bank of Montreal

Betty Kennedy, Bank of Montreal

Agnes Benidi, National Trust

Helen Margison, Bell Canada

Gail Cook, Manufacturers Life

Kay's own deeply felt Baptist origins, which hark back to the biblical precepts of parenting, mothering and being a "good wife," help account for this. "God first, family second, business third" is a phrase that echoes through the halls of every Mary Kay meeting.

"I do not consider myself a feminist," insists the boss herself. "I want my women to have *everything*, to be successful as career women. But I don't want them to lose their happy families, children who love them, husbands who adore them. I want women to bake their cakes and eat them too."

Some of the women I interview confess to feeling embarrassed at having to sing the Mary Kay enthusiasm song at the beginning of each meeting, and many critics complain the name of God is invoked so often, that one might think He is the Chairman of the Board and Chief Executive Officer.

*Mary Kay:* I sincerely feel that we are not as smart as the balance sheets would show, that God has blessed this company beyond all belief . . . and He wants you to become the beautiful person He knows He created.

Mary Kay's continual references to God are dis-comfiting. Yet is remembering every birthday of every one of over 100,000 Beauty Consultants silly? Is mailing 2,000 hand-signed letters a week foolish? Is the image of a woman in her mid-70s baking cookies to feed her latest entourage of 200 new Sales Directors in her own home laughable?

Some Beauty Consultants do drop out. Some leave after a few months of sales, having made only a few hundred dollars. The average consultant earns about $2,000 a year, and the average Sales Director in Canada, even with those two dozen or more drones working under her, brings home around $20,000.

Still, one cannot deny the potential, nor take away the camaraderie and enthusiasm of the Mary Kay way. This country could use a shot of that.

I can see it all now: Pierre Trudeau shares the opportunity with all 10 of the provincial premiers and becomes the senior Sales Director. Joe Clark becomes King of Sales and finally wins the love and admiration of the entire Tory caucus. Peter Lougheed loses his oily skin, while Cleansing Cream Formula 2 solves acid rain problems. And Lloyd Axworthy learns to get along with women, at last.

**Boardroom Women**

APRIL
**1981**

Sonja Bata,
Alcan Aluminium

Margaret Hamilton,
Thomson Newspapers

Jean Pigott,
Morrison-Lamothe Inc.

Mona Campbell,
Toronto-Dominion Bank

rdson,
nce

Dr. Reva Gerstein,
Maritime Life Insurance

Dawn McKeag,
Royal Bank

Muriel Kovitz,
Imperial Oil

Beryl Plumptre,
Dominion Stores

Louise B. Vaillancourt,
F. W. Woolworth

*By the early 80s a few women had tip-toed into the sacred boardrooms of banks and corporations under the startled gaze of the all-male incumbents.*

# NO "NICE NELLY" WAS
# Nellie

# CHAPTER EIGHT

# Citizenship

A S THE FIRST FEMALE POLICE magistrate in the British Empire, Judge Emily Murphy of Edmonton found herself being addressed as everything from "Your Majesty" to "Sir." More seriously, her right to preside in court was being questioned because of her lack of "personhood." This motivated her to challenge Canada's Supreme Court as one of five female appellants in the landmark *Persons* Case. In December 1929, after the British Privy Council had ruled that women were indeed persons under the British North America Act, Judge Murphy felt it wise to take to the pages of *Chatelaine* to assure the country that if women were appointed to the Senate, as they now could be, no one need fear they would make the Upper House "less safe for man" ("Now that Women Are Persons, What's Ahead?").

Despite a few such hard-won victories, Agnes Macphail—elected Canada's first female MP in 1921—remained the Commons' only female for most of her nineteen-year term. Why were Canadian women so slow to use their franchise to empower others? That was a question *Chatelaine* posed in September 1928 ("Are Women Wanted in Public Life?") and many times thereafter.

In lieu of direct representation, women formed lobby groups. In "Women Begin to Speak their Minds" (June 1928), candidates reported enthusiastically on the First National Assembly of Liberal Women held in Ottawa; one amusing sidebar was the failure of convention leaders to invite Agnes Macphail—still, seven years later, the Commons' only female—to attend any events because they feared her forthright tongue. In September 1938, Controller Nora-Francis Henderson of Hamilton explored an auxiliary problem: the heightened expectations for the few elected women to be all things to all women ("When Women Enter Public Life").

It's hard not to compare the optimism and idealism of these feminine voices with the scorn heaped upon all Ottawa women in "Mrs. Grundy at Ottawa" (April 1932). With the witty patronization that seemed to epitomize thirties males, the author proved himself to be pure *Mr.* Grundy. By contrast, a male press-gallery veteran of 1946 lamented, with some gallantry, the defeat of all but one woman—yet again!—in the last federal election ("I Miss the Women," February 1946). That lone survivor was Gladys Strum of Saskatchewan—a member of the opposition.

As candidates prepared for another election in 1957, they nervously eyed Canada's 4,300,000 female voters, wondering if they might unite to produce a women's vote ("How the Candidates Will Woo You," May 1957). One encouraging result was the election of Canada's first female cabinet minister—Conservative Ellen Fairclough of Hamilton. Nevertheless, in October 1963, *Chatelaine* was still able to profile *all* of Ottawa's elected women in a single article. This time we had four, including Judy LaMarsh—Canada's second female cabinet minister.

In October 1971, *Chatelaine* went pro-active: it challenged politicians, who habitually

OPPOSITE: *Nellie McClung, c. 1914.*

blamed the lack of female MPs on the refusal of women to run, by publishing a list of 105 credible female candidates who'd already stated they'd accept a nomination. The accompanying article no longer asked why so few women were in Ottawa; it answered that question by exploring the anti-female bias within the political parties themselves. In May 1972, the magazine again took the offensive: two years after Pierre Trudeau's Liberal government had tabled the report of the Royal Commission on the Status of Women, *Chatelaine* interviewed, or polled by registered mail, Canada's 262 MPs with its own questionnaire, covering issues of vital importance to women ("Women's Status: How the MPs Rate You"). One of those interviewed was the NDP's Grace MacInnis—again, our single female MP.

In April 1974, *Chatelaine* was still counting female MPs. This time there were five. In January 1985, the tally was six . . . *cabinet ministers*, out of an unprecedented twenty-seven elected females. Going into the election of October 1993, forty of Canada's 295 MPs were women. When the ballots were counted, we had fifty-three: eighteen percent of the House of Commons.

But . . . the country had lost its first female prime minister ("Woman of the Year: Kim Campbell," January 1994).

### POLITICAL MILESTONES FOR CANADIAN WOMEN

| Year | Event | Year | Event |
|------|-------|------|-------|
| 1916 | Women granted provincial vote in Manitoba, Alberta, Saskatchewan<br>Emily Murphy appointed first female police magistrate in British Empire | 1953 | Coronation of Queen Elizabeth II |
| | | 1957 | Ellen Fairclough, first female cabinet minister |
| 1917 | Women granted provincial vote in B.C., Ontario | 1962 | Mme. Claire Kirkland-Casgrain, first female in Quebec cabinet |
| 1918 | Women granted federal vote<br>Women granted provincial vote in Nova Scotia | 1970 | The report of the Royal Commission on the Status of Women |
| 1919 | Women granted provincial vote in New Brunswick | 1972 | Muriel Ferguson, first female speaker of Senate |
| 1921 | Agnes Macphail, first woman MP, in Ontario<br>Nellie McClung elected to Alberta legislature | 1974 | Pauline McGibbon, first female Lieutenant-Governor, Ontario |
| 1922 | Women granted provincial vote in Prince Edward Island | 1980 | Jeanne Sauvé, first female Speaker of House |
| 1925 | Women granted provincial vote in Newfoundland | 1982 | Bertha Wilson, first female appointed to Supreme Court |
| 1928 | Supreme Court of Canada rules women are not persons | 1984 | Jeanne Sauvé, first female Governor General |
| 1929 | British Privy Council rules women are persons | 1989 | Audrey McLaughlin, first female federal leader, NDP |
| 1930 | Cairine Wilson, first female appointed to Senate | 1991 | Rita Johnston, first female provincial premier, B.C. |
| 1940 | Women granted provincial vote in Quebec | 1993 | Catherine Callbeck, first elected female premier, P.E.I.<br>Kim Campbell, first female prime minister |

# Are Women Wanted in Public Life?

## And the important question is, "Are they really needed?"

BY HELEN GREGORY MACGILL, M.A.

*Helen Gregory MacGill, a judge of the Juvenile Court, Vancouver, B.C., and a member of the British Columbia Minimum Wage Board.*

**SEPTEMBER 1928**

PROFESSIONS, TRADES, occupations in general are in the United States and Canada as open to women as to men, though not everywhere or everything. Some states and some provinces still refuse to call women to the Bar, and recently by a decision of the Supreme Court of Canada women were declared ineligible for seats in the Federal Senate as not being "persons" within the meaning of Canada's constitution—the British North America Act. The Act is signed "Victoria Rex."

Resolutions passed by national and international association of women indicate clearly the world over that there is as yet between men and women neither equality of pay or opportunity, nor are the honors equally divided.

Women are apparent in the audience; if the drama is big or important, they are onlookers, and a few occasionally play minor rôles. All this might not be serious were it merely a matter of getting more and better jobs, or even more money and more honors for women. But the important question is, are women really needed in public life? If so, why are they not there?

In spite of our demand for equality and our enthusiastic advertising of the abilities and attainments of women, we ourselves are not firmly convinced. We are suffering from the depression of an implied and accepted inferiority, and we get out of the difficulty by wrinkling our brows, wringing our hands, and regretting that for the particular position under consideration "we have no suitable women."

∽

Despite allegations to the contrary, it is not differences of opinion, petty animosities, likes or dislikes, that prevent more women from holding high place. Men suffer from these, too, sometimes differing in kind and variety, sometimes similar. But men have no ingrowing doubt as to their own ability. They are convinced that the Lord gave them dominion over all the animals, and the rest of the world, including women. They have held undisputed sway for so long that it requires education on both sides to make each realize that both are needed in national housekeeping, not because of any inherent superiority of one sex over the other, but because of their essential differences.

We know, whether we admit it or not, that men and women view life from different angles. The age-old division of life work makes for this diversity. While the aims are common the stresses are not alike.

Women are needed in municipal councils where questions arise concerning milk and water supply, housing, pure food, street cleaning, health, licensing baby and adult lodging houses, street lighting, supervision of parks, dance halls, market regulations. They are needed on factory commissions and inspections, minimum wage, hospital, school, pensions, workmen's compensation and other city and government boards. They are required on juries which deal with human difficulties of all sorts, including those arising between women, girls, boys and men. On the bench there is urgent call for their services as judges in juvenile courts, district county and supreme court judges in all courts where cases of rape, seduction and the wrongs done very young children are tried.

Departments of labor deal so much with human relationships that it seems an anomaly that sometimes the labor commissioner or deputy minister is not a woman; or that there should not be two commissioners, one of whom should be a woman.

By a singular coincidence in countries civilized and in countries sometimes described as uncivilized, women as reigning sovereigns in their own right have held supreme power by virtue of birth or accident, marriage and widowhood, while at the same time the women of their nation neither have been eligible to hold office or to vote, much less to become lawmakers or administrators. If women can make or help to make laws, can reign over nations as queens or empresses, they surely can interpret the laws they have helped to make. Nature has a well-established custom of starting out each member of the human family with two parents. Nations being but the larger families might well have been expected to follow nature's lead, and see that the viewpoint and ideals of both fathers and mothers were expressed in legislation, interpretation and administration.

Each and every nation calls frantically upon its women to help "win the war," but women are beginning to perceive that they are not earlier consulted to help prevent the war. Being asked to sacrifice their all, should not women sit at the peace table?

Even during the war when there was feverish effort to pretend that women were equal to men, there were still no titles, except unimportant ones, no ribbons—except in the shops—for women. We were expected to give, and did give—the women of all nations—the tremendous enthusiasm, the sustained ideals of patriotism, even though sometimes misplaced, of which we are peculiarly capable.

Yet "equal pay for equal work and equal opportunity" has yet only a few sincere advocates. It is as ornamental and necessary in a women's association platform and public speeches, as a National Anthem which may be poor music, bad poetry and indifferent sentiment, but which its nationals accept without criticism or analysis of meaning. It is just one of those pleasant things we say in the same way that we proclaim the child as our greatest asset, but refuse to vote for child labor laws.

In the same group of men and women taken at random, there are conceivably fewer women than men who can or should hold public office or enter public life at the moment. Some are the wives of invalids, or mothers of young children and have other vital duties to perform, but mothers whose children are grown up should have nearly twenty years of usefulness to devote to public service.

The salary, aye, there's the rub! Women must be paid salaries. The idea so casually voiced that as a certain office in an association brought no emolument or honor, it might as well be given to a woman, "went over well," as the advertising men say, and is still going strong in public life. We still prefer to base salaries on sex rather than on service, and to assume that men require larger salaries because they have dependents. The old "pin money" and because she "wants better clothes" or she is "only waiting till she gets married" arguments are running well. Yet investigation shows that most women work because they must and that a large percentage of them have dependents.

◌

All questions of world politics affect women and children, whether the problem involved be limiting the growth of the poppy and reduction of narcotics, abolition of slavery, better housing and town planning, or building railways to open country to new settlers. But women will never sit there until other women determine we shall. Women cannot run for office without money. That is a fact we have never yet faced. Economic independence is so little a real fact that women with salaries reckoned "good" have little surplus. In the days of the suffrage campaigns, women did raise funds usually through entertainments and small personal subscriptions. This meant sacrifice. Occasionally here and there wealthy women gave more largely, but the campaign supplies were hard won and usually given from hard-earned money.

*Equal pay for equal work and equal opportunity" has ye only a few sincere advocates*

It is obvious then that more women are not in public life for three reasons: First, the lack of confidence. Second, lack of funds. Third, lack of understanding that suffrage was a means and not an end. This attitude is perhaps the result of the fact that the political parties worked feverishly to offer women as many glittering generalities with small salaries, or positions of honor without salaries, as possible. It has taken a few years to learn once more that all that glitters is not gold.

# Now That Women Are Persons, What's Ahead?

*All the world knows now that women are "persons"; that the appeal launched by five Canadian women before the Judicial Committee of the Privy Council was officially won on October 18, 1929; that henceforth women may be members of the Senate. But what will this mean for women?*

BY EMILY MURPHY

*Judge Murphy was one of the appellants in the famous "Persons Case"*

**DECEMBER 1929**

WHEN QUEEN VICTORIA came to the Throne, some of the less loyal of the population in Upper Canada made forecasts of "Petticoat Government," and hazarded a guess that the Speech from the Throne would dwell chiefly upon "nurseries and soap."

Since then, we are led to believe that nurseries are vastly important things and, if we are to trust the advertisements, the same is equally true of soap.

For the consolation of all saddened souls who claim—unfairly we believe—that the Senate must be less dignified with women therein, we presume to make prophecy that it will at least be different. There can be no doubt that the presence of women will serve to popularize the Upper Chamber—the position of which is being increasingly challenged—in that senatorial deliberations will immediately become possessed of what is known as "news value." Indeed, among newspapermen there is an oft quoted axiom which declares that any piece of news is more interesting that has a woman in it.

I am not one who looks for radical, and far-reaching reforms from the appointment of women to the Senate, or that the Senate is to become less safe for man because, generally speaking, women are cautious and conservative where matters of business and politics are concerned.

Besides, we women are not especially cognizant of the provisions of the Constitution, and so, of necessity must proceed with deliberation. The same is true of men. There are millions of people who know nothing about the Canadian constitution other than the fact that the clear articulation of the phrase is recognized by the police to be a proof of sobriety. This does not matter much, however. What Senators of both sexes should know is that politics is a science, the object of which is the happiness of mankind and not an exciting "game" at which the unscrupulous gambler comes out ahead.

There are other saddened folk in Canada who predict that women will enter the Senate as a perverse and refractory body, with brickbats under their blouses and terrible chips on their shoulders—that they will be found lacking in the graces of comity and co-operation. These predictions have no more basis in fact than that all Senators—unless entirely senile—are uncompromising and arrogant fellows who are never happy except when vetoing bills that come up from the House of Commons. Something like this is also believed of the Upper House in England. "The House of Lords," said Mr. Augustine Birrell, "represent nobody but themselves and they have the full confidence of their constituents."

It is probably true that women will occasionally be desirous of decapitating or otherwise slaying one of the honorable gentlemen who seems wholly to deserve it, but, as a general thing, women are more likely to adopt the very excellent plan of Mr. Cecil Rhodes who acknowledged that he never quarrelled with governments, preferring to persuade them.

For the most part, if women can do nothing else in their new sphere, they can render service by interpreting the Senate to the public. Hitherto, it has only been reported.

There are editors and others who prophesy that the women applying for senatorial appointments will be few in number. We hope sincerely that they err.

# Women Begin to Speak Their Minds

By Anne Anderson Perry

**JUNE 1928**

Having regard to the revolution now going on in the minds of our Canadian women in connection with not only party politics, but the whole matter of political expression, it may be stated that two main features emerged very clearly from the first national convention of Liberal women which was held in Ottawa in the middle of April last, and that these two features are probably as applicable to Conservative as to Liberal women.

The first is, that it was made abundantly clear throughout all the proceedings that our women are, at last, attaining some measure of political consciousness, with a corresponding desire to use their political power as adequately as possible.

The second is that experience in practical politics has shown in the past ten years in all the provinces of Canada, as it has shown in all parts of the United States, that this political consciousness can best express itself and most effectively operate in separate organizations of women within the party folds, even though the ultimate ideal of women and men working side by side in the political arena be strongly held.

This conference was unique in several ways. It was the first political convention to be called by women for women. It was free almost entirely from the influence of the "hidden hand" of the male party organizers which has so grievously afflicted feminine voters since the granting of the franchise to women almost a decade ago. It heralds, indeed, the real coming of age of the woman voter, who has belatedly discovered that it is not through a Ladies' Aid to men's political organizations that she can best function, but in autonomous groups where she can use to the fullest advantage those highly successful methods of agitation, education and activity which have been found to work so effectively in other than political clubs of women in the past.

That interest was very general in all parts of Canada and among many classes of women was evidenced by both the quantity and the quality of the delegates, who travelled in such numbers to the capital that the management and billeting committees under the patient Miss Florence Edwards of Carleton Place were at their wits' end to find hotel or private roofs to cover them.

This was the more remarkable when it is understood that, except in a few cases of the far western women, whose expenses were very generously met by the eastern women, all persons attending the conference had to meet their own costs of transportation and their hotel bills. Yet from the province of Quebec, whose women, Premier Taschereau is reported to have said recently, were "not really interested in the vote," came over three hundred delegates. Seventy of these were from the City of Montreal alone. A good showing for a province which has recently been refused the franchise! From Nova Scotia, always a politically-minded province, there arrived over fifty; from New Brunswick and Prince Edward Island, thirty and thirteen respectively; from Saskatchewan and Manitoba, about twenty each; from Alberta and British Columbia, a half dozen each, while Ontario made up the rest of the thousand women who attended.

Among the rank and file of both French- and English-speaking delegates in attendance, large numbers, of course were drawn from the class known as "housewives" or heads of homes. But there were considerable numbers, too, of others who came from the business or professional world, there being present women from the legal, medical, journalistic, teaching and nursing professions, besides a large injection of officialdom in the persons of the wives of members of parliament and of cabinet ministers, with two women members of provincial parliaments.

Among those unrepresented were the wives of laboring men, factory and store workers, the armies of stenographers and other business women now in our midst, and the farm women.

Another class which might well be said to have received no recognition or representation at the convention was that of which Miss Agnes Macphail, the lone, lorn woman federal member of parliament, is representative. Apparently Miss Macphail's liberal

*The Hon. Mary Ellen Smith, M.L.A., of Vancouver, B.C., the first president of the National Federation of Liberal Women of Canada.*

The business of the convention met many difficulties. It was necessary that official proceedings should be in both French and English and this necessitated a chairman of each persuasion. Beginning, however, with the national anthem and "O Canada" sung in both French and English, there was apparent a spirit of good will between both sections of Canadian women.

Then the agenda was overcrowded, for it was found necessary to spend one whole session over the constitution, which contained a number of contentious clauses. Many women for the first time at any such gathering spoke their political minds, and spoke them just the more freely because they were untrammeled by the presence or prejudices of men, or by their own phobias in connection with the same.

But not from all parts of Canada did they speak equally freely. The degree of frankness varied, being most marked among the delegates from Quebec and the western provinces, and least noticeable in those from Ontario, with the Maritimes holding the happy medium.

A noticeable feature was the intensity of political feeling and conviction expressed by speakers from Quebec, where women still lack the provincial franchise, where they labor under what they consider to be many mediaeval restrictions on their economic freedom, where their legal status is thoroughly unsatisfactory, and where the age-long, ingrained prejudices of men, combined with the unenlightened condition of much of rural Quebec have, so far, precluded the extension of political or other rights to women.

❧

"So far we women have been pretty well chloroformed in politics," said the Hon. Mary Ellen Smith in accepting the presidency of the National Federation of Liberal Women which finally emerged from the convention, "but we ought now to refuse all anaesthetics. We want to raise the status and advance the political education of women; to aid in securing, as well as maintaining, good government. And, above all, we wish to encourage a sound, broad spirit of Canadian nationality within the British Empire."

views on many subjects, as well as her alignment with the Progressives, precluded her being invited either to address the assembly or to attend its social functions. A somewhat timorous and "fearsome" policy, for it was remarked that the only Liberal courageous enough to ask the able Miss Macphail to even a tea party was the Prime Minister, Mr. Mackenzie King. He bade her attendance at the memorable reception which he so graciously extended the delegates at Laurier House on the opening day of the convention. At this function, where a number of the wives of the Cabinet Ministers very happily assisted the bachelor Premier to withstand the surging crowds of Liberal women who wanted to shake his hand and to view the historic shrine of Sir Wilfrid and Lady Laurier, Miss Macphail was greeted by many delegates. They were glad to meet the one woman who, despite the handicaps of sex in the political game, and especially that of living in Ontario (the most conservatively-minded part of the Dominion save rural Quebec), has been able to reach the capital as the chosen representative of a constituency.

# What the Woman Citizen Should Know

## The woman's franchise in Quebec

**JANUARY 1929**

Quebec, as the only province in Canada still withholding the provincial franchise from women, is focussing the attention of the feminist movement. It is paradoxical that the exception to what is now the accepted rule throughout Canada should take place in the province of Quebec where, under the French régime, women exercised the functions of advocates in all the courts, and in the nineteenth century British rule permitted them to vote before their sisters in any country enjoyed electoral rights. Article XX in the Constitution Act of 1791, which divided Canada into Lower and Upper Canada, permitted that where the property was in the name of the wife, it was she, and not the husband, who had the right to vote. Women lost this prerogative at Confederation when the British North America Act delegated to each province jurisdiction over matters purely of provincial interest. There is no lack of male championship for the feminist cause in Quebec. In speaking before the Canadian Alliance of Women's Franchise in Quebec, Edouard Chauvin, managing editor of *Le Petit Journal*, Montreal, voiced this opinion: "The right to vote is given to the illiterate, to alcoholics, to the depraved and to ragamuffins but it is refused our sister, our wife and our mother, who are intelligent, upright and well educated. Seeing women vote according to the dictates of their conscience, would not men learn to vote with dignity?"

# Mrs. Grundy at Ottawa

## An onlooker with a sense of humor reports on the feminine ambitions and foibles—the tragedies and laughter behind the social splendor of the capital

By Leslie Scott

**APRIL 1932**

Some poet once described Parliament as "that playhouse that politicians have made on that glorious plateau in a Valley in Wonderland with a river of dreams rolling past to the sea." I thought of these lines when, on a cold, grey morning in February a stream of taxis brought scores of women to Parliament Hill, left them there to stand in line and shiver through hours of waiting for Parliament to open. For these women, obviously, were not concerned with politics or economics, nor drawn by interest in Mr. Bennett's panaceas for our national ills. They were not that sort of women. What beckoned them, quite clearly, was their feminine instinct for the dramatic, their tendency—so common in Ottawa—to regard Parliament as a great show.

Year after year, it is always the same. Nine-tenths of those who go to openings, who crowd the galleries of Commons and Senate on the first day of the session, are women. There are men in Ottawa, old residents, who have never seen the House in session—men who vote. But their wives and their sisters and their aunts are among Parliament's devotees, never missing an opening, eager for the annual invitation to the Drawing Room, proud holders of tickets for the galleries. Parliament is their theatre.

It is one of the strange things of Ottawa, strange and often amusing. For there is no rational explanation for any human desire to watch Parliament. Most often the actors are sitting indolently, hearing the clack of worn-out principals whose struts and grimaces and cadences are those of men whose cues should lead them to the dressing rooms. Yet day after day, through a succession of deadly sessions, women sit in the galleries, admiring and quietly applauding their heroes below, indulging in whispered controversies, repeating bits of political gossip, being violently partisan about the merits of the show.

Some are the wives of members, or of ministers or of senators, proudly believing that they are playing a part in a sort of "Petticoats and Power" drama, that they are of moment behind the scenes. Their stage is a triangle—Rideau Hall, the Château Laurier, the Parliamentary Café. Up in the Parliamentary Restaurant, at tea hour or at luncheon, one finds scores of these women, French and English, chattering about the great masquerade, which is Parliament, or retailing the latest bit of gossip about some Cabinet minister, or some Cabinet minister's wife, or speculating about the next ball or dinner at Rideau Hall, wondering whether So-and-so has been, or will be, invited.

❧

And they are all the same. Sometimes, after an election, a new type of woman comes to Ottawa, the plain wife of some farmer M. P., or of some small lawyer or doctor or tradesman elected from some small town. She is timid at first, a bit awed, and perhaps a bit cynical and critical; thinks that openings and Drawing Rooms and all the social froth of Ottawa are just fuss and feathers, a foolish waste of money. But she soon changes. Long before her husband has discarded his coon coat, and started to affect the little habits of statesmen, she is caught up by Ottawa's social-political swirl and discovers that she likes it.

The Ottawa papers, of course, play up to it all; give the actors and actresses generous notices. Year after year, after an opening, the *Journal* and *Citizen* give page after page telling how the wife or the daughter of So-and-so—it is frequently the wife or the daughter of somebody of whom nobody has ever heard—was "charmingly gowned" in some sort of a model, the name of which nobody understands but the chief buyer at some fashionable establishment.

Then there is the Drawing Room. Time does not wither nor custom stale its extraordinary fascination. There are women in Ottawa who go to Drawing Rooms year after year, just as there are men in Ottawa who wouldn't for a kingdom miss the Governor-General's new year's levee. It is, in the Hollywood jargon, their epic night. Weeks before a Drawing Room Rockcliffe and Sandy Hill dream about it, talk about it, shop for it. And if by chance there is a flowering young debutante in a family, then the excitement and preparations are prodigious. The presentation, the insouciance of that curtsey, may mean so much! Isn't there always the chance that the lovely young Chloe or Alice may catch the eye and fancy of one of those young aristocrats of Rideau Hall with real Bertha M. Clay consequences? Such things have happened before—happened more than once in recent years—and these are inexplicable times, anyway. So as the day approaches there are hectic preparations, endless shopping tours, rehearsals, temperamental outbursts, a strain on family budgets. Feathers and trains cost money.

Feathers! During the war they dropped them; and the Byngs, homely, democratic people, wouldn't revive them. But Lady Willingdon, who loved pomp and circumstance, and thought that social grandeur should be a part of government, brought them back, much to the joy of Ottawa. This year, the depression notwithstanding, they were everywhere; and—let it be shamelessly confessed—gave the show vast more of "it" than when without them.

Then there are the "trains." The regulations told that they must be two feet longer than the ground, if the reader knows what that means, but some seemed two yards longer.

Slowly, like a long, winding, gigantic piece of fluff, the parade went past Their Excellencies, the women flushed with excitement, looking frightfully happy; the men looking bored, or ashamed-like, or terribly unhappy.

As always, there were those devastating curtseys. Some, seasoned veterans, emerged with flying colors; others showed at least that badminton or skiing supples out the limbs; but not a few behaved as though they hadn't even knelt to say their prayers for years and years. And these things, of course, are important—in Ottawa.

And the men, or some of them, are so clumsy. One unfortunate, who shall remain anonymous, put his hoof, for that is what he must have thought about it afterwards, on his wife's train. There was a giving of delicate stitches, and the victim of the desolating *faux pas* saw her train and her world go crashing down together.

These little things, or tragedies, are among the legends of Ottawa, told and retold over tea cups, a part of the Capital's lore.

❧

And so flows the stream of society and feminine politics in Ottawa. The depression, of course, has made a difference; and that cut in the indemnities. Then, too, there's been a change at Rideau Hall. The Bessboroughs, gracious people and stately, have that austere, English country-house aloofness which has had a devastating effect upon the social hopes and yearnings of scores and scores in Ottawa. The Willingdons were so different. Their invitation list reached out everywhere, seemed almost at times to be taken from the telephone directory. It mattered not that many of those honored with invitations took too great a fancy to Lady Willingdon's Chinese jade, with which she used to decorate her tables, or left lighted cigarette butts on her costly Chinese rugs. If it happened—as it happened once—that the elastic of a well-known statesman's ready-made tuxedo tie snapped, splurging into his soup, the conversation went buzzing on in a blessed unconcern, and an aide, with almost sleight-of-hand deftness, provided another tie. Or if it should happen—and it actually did happen—that the wife of a Senator dropped a vital portion of her lingerie on the ballroom floor, then a gallant and chivalrous young aide was there to rescue it with but a minimum of embarrassment.

It is somewhat different this year. Lady Bessborough, shy and beautiful, and Lord Bessborough, looking always as though he wanted to be back in Lombard Street, send out few invitations, are sparing with dances and dinners. The glory of the place—its part in the Ottawa masquerade—has largely vanished.

# When Women Enter Public Life

*What happens to the feminine aspirations? Does disillusionment follow any actual governing experience?*

BY CONTROLLER NORA-FRANCIS HENDERSON

**SEPTEMBER 1938** WHEN WOMEN ENTER public life, the first lesson they learn is that the business of government is highly complex and that feminine aspirations, so enthusiastically voiced in the women's organizations for social betterment, are not nearly so easy of attainment as they appeared to be.

In public life they actually become sympathetic to men whom possibly they once severely criticized for their apparent unwillingness to bring about sweeping reforms in which women are especially interested. Sometimes the women they have "left behind them" are resentful of the fact that those whom they thought were to be their especial ambassadors have "gone over" to the men!

Perhaps they have. Let us say that they have become "persons," a state of being which the women of Canada, without perhaps realizing all the implications, had legally conferred upon them some years ago by the Privy Council. For there is neither male nor female in government!

Women in government find that women, just as much as men, are divided into economic and social groups whose ends and outlook clash, and that democratic administrations can do nothing better than to step as warily as possible in the fields of these conflicting interests.

Recently in Hamilton the city council received a petition for early closing from seventy-five per cent of the grocery stores. For two months the twenty-five per cent of the small grocers who did not want early closing literally besieged the city hall. Many of these shop owners on both sides were women. The women who wanted the early closing showed the humane considerations involved in regard to their employees. On the other hand women who kept small stores without help showed that they would be ruined, because it is in the evening that many people who cannot purchase during the day go to the small merchant when the big chain stores are closed.

Women's organizations on the whole took the broad social outlook—that early closing is a step in the right direction. But numerous housewives and women whose work during the day did not permit them to shop until evening, gave good reasons to show what an inconvenience this change would cause.

∾

A woman is elected to the city council largely on the enthusiastic votes of thousands of her sister women, with a special mission to "fight for more playgrounds, more public health clinics and other increased social services for the people."

When she gets down to business, inspects the lengthening lists of those who cannot pay their taxes, learns that when taxpayers default, other taxpayers must make up the deficit, begins to understand what the present high property taxation is doing to people who own their homes, what the decline in the home-owning ideal is doing to the building trades, and what the decline in the building trades is doing to the sixty per cent of breadwinners who normally are employed by them, she begins to get a headache. Perhaps it is a heartache. Perhaps it is both.

Is it conceivable that the average woman will ever be as free to enter public life as the average man? Can we anticipate a time when wives and mothers will leave their housekeeping and their new-born babies and their growing children to the care of others, and devote as much time outside the home as the average man?

The answer is that men have young businesses and professional careers to take care of, just as women have growing families. It is only when a man is in exceptional circumstances, or has brought his business to the place where he can leave it in the care of a partner or manager, that he can devote himself to public affairs. In this respect the limitations placed on men and women are pretty well evened up.

There will always be women whose circumstances will permit them to represent their sex in government, and it is my belief that there is also a great opportunity for women in middle years, who can

*A brilliant newspaperwoman, now a vitally interested member of the City Council of Hamilton, Ont., Controller Henderson is a unique figure in Canadian public life.*

bring to the management of society all the rich practical experience of life that they have gained. But they will not be fitted for this enlargement of their responsibilities unless they have taken a keen and intelligent interest in public affairs during the years they have been unable actively to participate in them.

# I Miss the Women

### By Austin Cross

**FEBRUARY 1946** WHAT CANADA'S PARLIAMENT needs most is more women. As a word-scarred veteran of five parliaments, and a case-hardened male in the Press Gallery, I feel that the girls could do things to our House of Commons. I have known all the women M.P.'s from Agnes Macphail to Gladys Strum, and I think every one has made a great contribution to our Government. I likewise feel that we are the poorer for their passing.

This Commons is more or less a bachelor hall,

and, as every woman knows, there is something wrong with all bachelors. Any man who has been married and who has lived alone while his wife is away knows how quickly a pleasant home becomes just a house. I think a few more women could do things to this House, too, and while not exactly making it a home, could yet contribute as only women can, to anything they touch. The present setup is inadequate, dull, and *wrong*.

Hard-boiled statisticians will tell you that the purchasing power of this continent—certainly of the English-speaking world north of the Rio Grande—is now more than 70% in the hands of women. It does seem anomalous that in Canada where the practical affairs of daily life are so largely in the hands of women, our top legislative body should be overwhelmingly composed of men.

I am not being original either when I say that if the women couldn't have made a better job of Parliament than the men have thus far, in this our Confederation's 79th year, then I am a poorer judge of women than I think I am.

∽

Let's look at the five women Canada has sent to Parliament to date. Agnes Macphail was the pioneer, who came to Ottawa away back in 1922. She was a schoolma'am with definite ideas of right and wrong. In her earliest years she was a high-minded but inexperienced gal, and her contributions were often more picturesque than valuable. (Such as her turn-down of some of her parliamentary indemnity, which she later found was little enough to support her as a hard-working M.P.) But she learned, and she became an effective representative in the Commons. She had a low-pitched voice, and she spoke deliberately. I liked her dash of sarcasm. There are those who thought she was a bit of a scold, but I for one would give her extra marks for that. A purely male discussion can do with the intervention of a woman's tongue, sometimes. Indeed, I have always said that the trouble with our Mr. King was that there was no Little Woman yelling "Will-yum" up the back stairs at him.

One of the best stories of the Macphail epoch concerns Mr. King, too. It seems that Miss Macphail had boarded a ship for Britain, holiday-bound, when a Sense of Duty called her back to Ottawa

where the Prime Minister's hold on Parliament (it was in 1926) had worn as thin as the seat of Mr. MacGregor's pants, which, as everybody knows, you could read the Word of God through. Bag and baggage she landed back at the Chelsea Club, then phoned for Mr. King. The P. M. lost no time getting down to that Ladies Only club. It was midnight, hardly an hour to go calling, and just as he arrived, the lights in the parlor went off. They sat in a Hydro blackout while they discussed the political situation, and only when they said good night did they come to sufficiently to realize the unconventionality of the situation and to laugh heartily. Very, very few ladies can write in their memoirs that they have been alone in the dark at midnight with Bachelor King.

Agnes Macphail, when she came to Ottawa, started off dressing to type. She was the Flesherton schoolma'am. With hair to match. But later on she wasn't above looking in on the French Room, and her coiffure changed and smartened to suit.

She made a notable contribution to Parliament, worked for Canada and for her sex. But catty women could not forgive her for being "an old maid," and never rallied behind her as they should. This first and only spinster in Parliament has been gone for six years now, but I can't help feeling that the House of Commons would have been a better place, all along, had we had Aggie Macphail there.

∽

Certainly one of the most charming women to enter the House was Mrs. Martha Louise Black, replacing her husband as Member for the Yukon. She was not young, even 10 years ago, because like the frank woman that she is, she gave her real age in the Parliamentary Guide, for all the world to see. She was born in 1866, and took her place in the Commons for the first time in 1936. It required courage to run an election and start a political career just when the biblical lifespan fell due, but Mrs. Black had never been one to scare off easily. Her capacity to run a career had been shown many years before. She had become an authority on the flora and fauna of the Yukon, and her garden in Dawson City was something to remember. She was on the Victorian Order of Nurses' Board, was a councillor and is a life member of the IODE. She has been a Fellow of the Royal Geographic Society for a good many years.

She was also a sensible wife and the mother of sons, and when she entered the House, at the age of 70, she had come to know men, of all ages, pretty well. She gave the M.P.'s motherly little talks, and they liked it. Most of them felt like eating their porridge and wearing their rubbers after Mrs. Black had told them what was what. She was liked and respected, and when her husband's health was restored she stepped aside and let the popular George have his seat once again. She had merely kept the place warm for him.

But we remember her for the picturesque figure she added to the House, with her bright colors, her white hair, her twinkling smile. In this her 80th year, Mrs. Black's mind is sharper than a lot of people's 40 years her junior. I conclude her case by saying that the lady from the Yukon, both as Member herself and Member's wife, has made an outstanding contribution.

༄

Surely the best orator of all our women parliamentarians was Dorise Nielsen from Saskatchewan. When she was on an unpopular subject, she had enough of the soapbox in her system to outshout her hecklers. Her first speech was an eloquent tearjerker—on the budget, as I recall it. When she told of balancing her meagre family budget while living on Saskatchewan relief, she had the House eating out of her hand.

Dorise Nielsen was a British-born schoolteacher who landed in remote Spiritwood, Sask., with a husband and, ultimately, three children. She struggled

through the depression somehow, and out of her bitter experience came political ambition. She joined with the Rev. Walter G. Brown, Saskatoon, in what he was calling a Unity Party, and with nothing more than her own skill and her persuasive personality on the platform, she won a dramatic victory over a longtime Liberal Member.

In Ottawa her arrival was something of a sensation. She was striking to look at, with gorgeous black hair, an attractive face and no sparing of the make-up. But she became a Fellow Traveller, was known as M.P. for Moscow more often than for her riding of North Battleford, and thus lost ground. Politically, as part of the Labor-Progressive movement, she seemed to have attached herself to the one group who could do the least for her. The gloomy pre-election prophecies were only too well borne out when the ballots were counted.

Dorise Nielsen was nevertheless important to Canada's 19th Parliament. Her smart brain, her lovely voice, her tall impressive figure are all of

*Dorise Nielsen struggled through the depression somehow, and out of her bitter experience came political ambition*

*Senator Iva Fallis (above) and Senator Cairine Wilson.*

*Agnes MacPhail, M.P. (above) and Mrs. George Black, M.P.*

them missed. Yet to this day I have not heard a woman's organization raise its voice to regret her passing. Sometimes it seems to me that women in this country get the legislative neglect they deserve.

∾

Cora Taylor Casselman has been the least colorful of all the women M.P.'s. Like Mrs. Black, she replaced her husband in the Commons. She reached Parliament Hill from Edmonton when she was 53—a widow, a club-woman, a housewife, a mother. She looked the part, quiet, unobtrusive, unglamorous, and more than any of the other women members, she was truly representative of our million or two Canadian housewives.

I can remember the night she made her bow. Mr. King himself went out with Hon. James MacKinnon, and, taking the black-clad Mrs. Casselman by the arms, they led her in. She bowed, and as she did, her silver hair reflected the lights above and took on a wonderful nimbus quality.

Mrs. Casselman was the spoiled darling of the Grits from the very start, and that, I think, was her trouble. First of all, the Liberals had never had a woman member before, and they were prepared to make the most of it. Again, they hoped that she could handle Dorise Nielsen. But not 10 Coras could handle one Dorise!

I was disappointed in the member for Edmonton East, at least till I began making allowances. After all, I said, this woman, for all her clubs, is the good typical wife who used to get her housework done early to get out of an afternoon. She wasn't a hard-bitten campaigner like Our Aggie; she couldn't hit a pile-driver blow like the gorgeous-headed Dorise. Nor was she as nimble-witted as Gladys, yet to come to Ottawa. Mrs. Casselman did represent the average housewife who, when asked for a statement on the world situation, would generally reply: "John says . . ."

Yet she was an important symbol just the same. Where she sat, sat a million Canadian women. East Edmonton, I believe, missed a good bet when they didn't send Cora Casselman back.

∾

Gladys Strum, our baby lady M.P., arrived in Ottawa, riding the crest of a Saskatchewan socialist wave, at the age of 39. Attractive, neat as a pin, skilfully combining the homebody with the politician, Mrs. Strum looks, from where I sit, like a parliamentary woman who is going places.

How she taught school on the prairies, was quickly snapped up in marriage by farmer Warner W. Strum, how she and her husband made the long trip to New Zealand to see if they'd like to live there, how she sideswiped a couple of candidates during the 1940 elections out on the Pacific coast, are all part of a record you can find elsewhere. Perhaps her most important achievement up till the time she got elected was the way she almost beat ex-Premier Patterson of Saskatchewan. She was shy a scant six votes. But destiny spared her from the banks of the Wascana for the banks of the Ottawa.

Gladys Strum hasn't hit her gait yet. She has a terrible sense of frustration, she has told me, and doubts if she will ever be able to accomplish much as an opposition member. She now finds, of course, what others before her have learned, that you can talk big on the prairie, but you find you become awfully unimportant among several hundred others in Parliament. I think this place has humbled Gladys Strum a little.

She doesn't want to be considered just as a woman. "The price of wheat is as much the wife's business as the husband's," she has often said. "If a binder costs more that it should, then it robs the children and it deprives the home of something. Fifty-two per cent of our voters are women, yet they stay submerged!"

The Lady Strum has a beautiful smile and exquisitely shined teeth. Her room is by far the most feminine of all the rooms used by the lady M.P.'s thus far. The draperies and furniture make it cosy and boudoir-like after the austere cells of the men.

I think, if she is given a chance to show her stuff, that she will come through.

# Do Women Want Women in Public Life?

## Chatelaine *Consumer Council reports*

**JANUARY 1948** **O**UT OF 245 FEDERAL SEATS, only one is held by a woman. Out of nine provinces, only three—all western—have elected women to their present legislatures: two in British Columbia, three in Alberta and one in Saskatchewan.

*Chatelaine* questioned its 2,000 Consumer Council members. Because Consumer Council is balanced as to age, income and locality, it is able to give an accurate reflection of the thinking of Canadian women as a whole.

## WHY 26% PREFER MEN IN PUBLIC LIFE

- **Men are more** experienced in public affairs than women as a result of their business life.
- **Men will argue** a principle and remain good friends afterward. Women take too personal an attitude, and resent a difference of opinion.
- **Woman's biggest job** is in the home.
- **Public office** should belong to men as they need a life job to support a family.
- **With such a** preponderance of men in public office now, a woman would encounter more obstacles in fulfilling her duties, due to man's prejudice against her.
- **Canadian women** are tiresome in voice and manner on a platform.
- **Women are too** domineering; too quick to jump to conclusions; too easily swayed by gossip and what their friends think.

## WHY 68% PREFER WOMEN IN PUBLIC LIFE

- **Women have a** different slant to men on many problems.
- **Over half** the population are women.
- **Women have a** greater interest in, and a deeper sympathy with problems which concern the home.
- **Women have** the same mental capacity as men.
- **Women are more** honest and trustworthy than men. They are less likely to be influenced by political pressure or monetary gain.
- **Women usually take** the time to investigate. Businessmen haven't time.
- **Let the women** take over! The men may wake up to the fact that they have not come up to the mark of their high calling.
- **It's time** women had a voice in making decisions. Our laws today are man-made for men.
- **A woman fights** harder for what she wants.
- **Women are laboring** against prejudices which will tend to disappear as more women appear in public life.

CONSUMER COUNCIL BALLOT BOX

## WILL WOMEN VOTE FOR WOMEN?

- *Have you ever voted for a woman in a political election?*
  They replied:    30% Yes     70% No
  *If "No" was it because:*
  (a) No woman up for election?  (58%)
  (b) You preferred a man candidate?  (5%)
  (c) You never voted?  (6%)   No answer  (1%)

- *Would you support a campaign to encourage more women to go into politics?*
  They replied:
  73% Yes     23% No     4% No Answer

- *Which of these factors would you say had the greatest influence on the way you vote in an election?*
  (a) What you read?  (31%)
  (b) What you hear on the radio?  (13%)
  (c) What you hear at group meetings or party rallies?  (7%)
  (d) Husband's advice?  (12%)
  (e) Or do you make up your own mind after careful thought and observation?  (73%)
  (Some columns add to more than 100% because of multiple answers.)

## WHY ONLY ONE WOMAN IN PARLIAMENT?

- *Councillors were asked: Out of 245 House of Commons members, only one is a woman. What do you think is the reason for this?*

- 22% say **other responsibilities**. Women are involved at home.
- 21% say **fears**. Women are too timid, modest, fearful of publicity and of being defeated.
- 18% say **indifference**. Women don't care enough.
- 17% say **education**. Because politics have always been considered a man's world, no one has any confidence in women.
- 15% say **prejudice**. Prejudice against women outside the home; against equality of the sexes.
- 6% say **too emotional**. Not enough stability.
- 5% say **men preferred**. They are better speakers; have more logic and stimulate more confidence.
- 4% say **dislike graft**. If there were less graft, more women would run for public office. Women will not lend themselves to misrepresentation, name-calling.
- 3% feel that women should be encouraged to serve in minor public offices to fit themselves for political service on a national level.

- *For what particular branch of public office do you feel women are best suited?*
  92% School Board
  54% Town or City Council
  41% Provincial Legislature
  35% Dominion House of Commons
  12% Mayoralty

## How the Candidates Will Woo You . . .

*Canadian women represent a mighty but untapped political power. Here's how the politicians, full of scalloped potatoes and pretty compliments, are planning an important part of the coming campaign*

BY GEORGE BAIN

MAY
*1957*

IN THE COMING GENERAL ELEC-tion there will be something like 4,300,000 women eligible to vote. When it's considered that it took only 2,800,000 votes to give the Liberal Party a landslide last time, 4,300,000 will be seen to be a powerful lot of votes—"powerful lot" in this case not being horse-opera talk but the simple truth.

Is there such a thing as a "women's vote"? That is, do these 4,300,000 women constitute a separate electoral group to be appealed to by different means and different issues?

If men voted on blue ballots and women on pink, a keen analyst might be able to draw some deductions about the main direction of political appeals. The ballots unfortunately are a sexless black-and-white, and one black-and-white ballot in a ballot box looks pretty much like another. And you can't prove it by the politicians themselves. Most of them, I know, profess the opinion that there is no such thing as a distinct women's vote, to be wooed and won as such. But most of them also seem to proceed on the prudent assumption that they are wrong.

How do they woo them? Politicians generally agree that the questions which most interest women voters are those related to social security—family allowances, hospital-care plans, pensions and the like. It is perhaps more than coincidence that most of our social-security programs have come into existence in the forty years since women first got the vote.

It was only forty years ago. The coming election will be just the eleventh since that frosty morning of December 17, 1917 when the first Canadian woman Xed her first ballot and dropped it into a ballot box in a Dominion election.

She and that other band of pioneers who voted with her in that wartime election were allowed to vote somewhat in the role of pinch hitters for absent men. The vote was given first to "every female person" who was the wife, widow, mother, sister or daughter of someone serving outside Canada in the armed services. With expressions of misgivings from a few, the legislators hurled caution to the winds the next year and gave the vote to all women on the same conditions as men.

Now, forty years later, in what also happens to be an election year, some eight hundred or so politicians, almost all of them male, will be out bright-eyed and smiling in pursuit of what they consider their fair share of those 4,300,000 votes.

The door-to-door canvass is a method of campaigning much favored by the present-day politician, and since a lot of door-knocking must be done in the daytime, it brings him in contact more often than not with what is known as "the lady of the house." He makes his little pitch, presses some of his campaign literature into her flour-coated hand and departs, hoping that in the evening she will tell her husband: "There was the nicest man at the door today. Now what was his name . . .? Wait, I've got a pamphlet right here."

I might mention that there are dangers in this sort of personal-contact campaigning. Once I covered the tour of a political leader through northern Ontario. When the genial leader bolted toward a house, hand outstretched to greet a woman who was taking the sun on her front veranda, the local officials blanched, no doubt envisioning pictures in the local newspaper of their man glad-handing this particular lady of the house, who happened to be the town bootlegger. Back from the lip of the political abyss, the leader took the news of his danger calmly. "Her vote," he said, "is as good as anyone else's."

Many politicians will have worked assiduously between elections to cultivate the women's vote by turning up whenever asked—and sometimes unasked—at home-and-school, club meetings, meetings of the Women's Institute, church suppers and the like.

In fairness, it should be pointed out that regularity of attendance at such social events isn't the last or best test of a member's interest in his constituency. In fact, the more he advances in his party, the fewer of these he likely will be able to attend.

How does the party leader establish himself as worthy of the women's vote? Unless I have been misreading the signs, one way is to establish himself first of all as—and I quote—"a family man." To this end it is desirable that he appear at not infrequent intervals in person or in pictures in the family group—preferably with a dog, dogs being very potent politically.

The wife of a politician in most cases has many small chores to perform in his behalf, ranging from actually speaking for him at political meetings, to being simply charmingly present at various teas and other feminine revels. Another chore which may fall to her, particularly if he reaches leadership or cabinet rank, is that of seeing that he gets away from one place in time to get to another.

Mrs. John Diefenbaker was much cast in this role at the Progressive-Conservative convention which chose her husband leader last December. Political conventions are loaded with handshakers and delegates who want to pledge their undying support to this or that candidate—sometimes to two or three of them at once. It is difficult for a candidate to walk away from a handshaker or a pledger-of-support. Like a car in heavy snow, though, a politician in a crowd of well-wishers usually is all right so long as he can keep moving forward. Mrs. Diefenbaker was frequently at her husband's elbow to assist his forward progress through the lobby of Ottawa's Château Laurier. She also posed for pictures with him, sat on the platform with him, stood with him in receiving lines shaking hands with hundreds, and between times attended any number of gatherings of women delegates or wives of delegates.

The wife of a leader may accompany him on a cross-country election tour, to be seen by the public and if possible to influence the women's vote. Mrs. George Drew traveled with her husband in the 1949 campaign, with results which are still occasionally debated by newspapermen who covered the tour.

Mrs. Drew makes an excellent speech in either English or French. She is an intelligent, attractive and charming woman who meets people well—and she met thousands of them on that trip. But it is an undeniable fact that the elegant Mrs. Drew doesn't look as if she'd be much of a hand at gutting a herring or wringing a chicken neck, and there was some feeling among the correspondents—all male, of course—that the women's vote in, say, the fishing villages and farming communities wasn't won over.

In the election of 1957 what are the candidates going to talk to women voters about? Certainly one of the things the Opposition will be talking about—and just as certainly Liberal candidates won't be—is the increase of three percent which occurred in a mere seven months in the cost of living. Family allowances go directly into the home, and it wasn't entirely for social reasons that when family allowances were enacted in 1944, it was decided they should go out marked "Mrs." And since women tend to live longer than men, and women who work generally retire earlier, old-age pensions and the age at which they are paid may be matters of relatively greater importance to women. Hospital-care plans have a special significance for women if for only one reason: hospital insurance may mean the difference to many mothers between being able to afford to have a baby in hospital or having to have it at home.

One reason why the so-called women's vote so much merits the special attention of politicians is that it is to so large an extent an unmined political resource. Those 4,300,000 votes are a power, but only if they actually are dropped in the ballot box.

*Meet the woman who broke a ninety-year taboo: Progressive Conservative Ellen Fairclough of Hamilton West, Canada's first woman cabinet minister (August 1957).*

# Why There Are So Few Women in Ottawa

BY BARBARA FRUM

OCTOBER
1971

THERE ARE FIFTY-SIX WHOOPing cranes in Canada, and one female federal parliamentarian. The odds on either species ever flourishing are rather long, but with firm political commitment to wildlife—as opposed to spongy political rhetoric for women—the better bet is on the cranes.

Not that there's a political party or a politician in the country that won't publicly lament that only eighteen women were ever elected to the House of Commons (an average of just over one per election), and won't insist that that meagre showing must be bettered this next time. Privately there isn't a political pro worthy of the designation who, at the same time, won't tell you why it'll never happen.

In a madrigal of cross-party consensus politicians harmonize that, though they personally wish it were otherwise, "run a woman and right off you're thousands of votes behind—men won't vote for them, and women trust them even less." Or, "Women aren't really interested anyway, either in running for office or in governing."

And so, even though it is wearying in this year fifty-one of women's suffrage, it is still necessary to make the case that women would represent their constituents at least as adequately as men and run departments as judiciously; that women should be in Parliament, not because they are warm and compassionate and intuitive and would end all wars, but because as citizens they have a right to be there.

The leadership of the national parties insist that nominations are strictly up to the local associations, hoping, one senses that the enquirer will be polite enough to leave out of the discussion how seats came to be found for men like Trudeau, Marchand, Pelletier, Sharp, Turner, Sidney Smith, Wallace McCutcheon, Tommy Douglas and Lester Pearson when they were needed.

It would seem that local autonomy is sacrosanct when women are looking for seats. It's not been inviolable however in the reverse, when the parties saw their interests served by keeping women out.

Judy LaMarsh learned after winning Niagara Falls for the Liberals in 1960 that the then national director of the party, Jim Scott, had personally come down to Niagara Falls before her nomination to try and convince the local brass they were jeopardizing a good Liberal seat by running a woman.

Both Ellen Fairclough and Margaret Aitken found their party actively engaged against them hustling up men to oppose their nominations. In the case of Miss Aitken to the point of twice delaying the nomination meeting until one could be found.

To their shame there is one set of circumstances when the parties feel no hesitation, in fact are downright desperate, to run a woman. That's when they have a deceased MP to replace and a freshly bereaved widow to garner the sentimental vote. Judy LaMarsh wryly notes that party executives seem to get to the widow almost as fast as the undertaker.

Running widows conforms to the political dictum that winning isn't just the only thing, it's everything. Anyway running a widow isn't so much running a woman as running the memory of a great man.

But even though some of the widows so elected (and a third of all the women who've ever been in the House of Commons got there first that way) have proved themselves just as able members and just as able vote getters as their dead husbands, the parties remain steadfast in their devotion to that second political "truth"—women are poison at the electoral box office.

Frankly, how do they know? Women haven't contested enough seats to prove anything. In the fifteen general elections since 1921 women have only had 300 out of a possible 12,262 nominations (2.4 percent), and most of those nominations were for contests where their failure was almost guaranteed; fulfilling one of the most venerable of political strategies, "When disaster confronts you, run a woman."

And so the Liberals boldly put up a woman against Diefenbaker in 1965 in Prince Albert, and the Tories nominated a woman to demonstrate women's political muscle against one P. E. Trudeau in '68.

Yet when women do get a crack at likely seats, as Judy LaMarsh did in Liberal Niagara Falls, or Ellen Fairclough in the Tory territory of Hamilton West,

they prove that women can win seats. And hold them. Fairclough held hers through four subsequent elections, LaMarsh through three, and proved to be the most publicly popular minister in the entire Pearson regime. Even those widows brought into Parliament on the black-crepe ticket were able to hold their own. Margaret Rideout of Moncton, now a Citizenship Court Judge in the Maritimes, was returned once after her by-election win with a bigger majority than her husband's. Jean Casselman, later Wadds, won three subsequent general elections and the respect of colleagues on both sides of the House for her political gamesmanship.

There's even good political science to explain why sex is no handicap at the polls. According to political scientist John Wilson of the University of Waterloo, if you're running for the party that's going to win anyway it doesn't matter who you are or what you look like. Most Canadians vote for the party not the man. If a voter wants Robert Stanfield to be the next Prime Minister say, and the local Conservatives have had the temerity to nominate a woman, if the voter's serious about Stanfield he's obliged to vote for her anyway, no matter what his opinion of women. In a closely fought, iffy seat the characteristics of the candidate could be decisive. In practice they rarely are.

Yet riding nomination committees still go on looking for the candidate that most closely resembles their ideal of a parliamentarian; successful, good looking, between thirty-five and fifty, and male, presumably because, for some reason, it makes them feel better to be around somebody like that.

It could be too that the parties tend to see in the electorate those prejudices that mirror and confirm their own. For example, party pros insist that women won't work or vote for other women, yet an analysis of Judy LaMarsh's first victory written by Dr. Pauline Jewett and published in the *Canadian Journal of Economics and Political Science*, showed that she was supported about equally by women and men. More recent polls, including one done by the Liberal Party itself, indicated that the electorate doesn't harbor many misgivings about women in public life any longer, and three quarters in fact would vote for a woman prime minister.

*Not only have women played a significant part in getting the few women who've been in politics elected but, once elected, women have crossed party lines to help each other.*

Not only have women played a significant part in getting the few women who've been in politics elected but, once elected, women have crossed party lines to help each other. Judy LaMarsh tells of refusing to go to Grenville-Dundas to help a Liberal colleague campaign against Conservative Jean Wadds. And Pauline Jewett in '68 turned down an excellent opportunity for a parliamentary seat because she refused to run against a woman (Jean Wadds again) until there were more of them in the House. "I just couldn't, I thought it was wrong, especially against a woman I think so highly of."

Even when a few women do manage to overcome all the hurdles, and do get themselves elected, they come smack up against the walls of real distrust and indifference, and clubbiness that anthropologist Lionel Tiger labeled male bonding.

Everyone by now has heard the story of how Judy LaMarsh had to post her cabinet colleague Bud Drury to guard duty while she used the men's washroom outside the Privy Council Chambers. The failure to provide women's washrooms, inconsequential in itself, is symptomatic of the unpreparedness for women in Parliament.

The plush and private Rideau Club across the street from Parliament Hill, long used by the Ottawa power structure as a political salon, still has rules against the presence of women, Members of Parliament, cabinet ministers or no. Ellen Fairclough had to decline a special luncheon invitation there when she was a minister in Diefenbaker's cabinet "for obvious reasons." Her hosts were deeply embarrassed. They simply hadn't thought.

On another occasion Margaret Konantz and Pauline Jewett, both Liberal MPs, were invited there by Paul Martin to a small lunch in honor of U Thant. "We hadn't gotten half way up the centre stairs," Dr. Jewett remembers, "when a horrified attendant, gesticulating wildly, came running out of the woodwork yelling, 'What are you ladies doing here?' He wouldn't even allow us to return the way we'd come but ushered us down a side stair, through the kitchen and out the back door. Poor Martin felt so badly."

Well, maybe not all that badly because sometime later, when Dr. Jewett wanted to join a Commons' study tour of Yugoslavia and the Soviet Union, she was told that Canada couldn't possibly impose a woman on its Russian hosts and thus oblige them to provide dual facilities.

There is a footnote to that story. About a year later the Russians sent a comparable study mission to Canada and apparently didn't mind inconveniencing their Canadian hosts by including several women in the Soviet delegation.

But not only is Ottawa unprepared for women, prejudices about them lead the parties to miscast and underuse the women who manage to get there.

When Judy LaMarsh was Opposition Justice critic Mrs. Davie Fulton, wife of the former Justice Minister, recalls that she was "brilliant, absolutely brilliant." Yet when the Liberals came to power she was given the totally unsuitable portfolio of Health and Welfare because of stupid notions about women's special talent for "the humanities."

That same kind of reasoning allowed the Tories to ignore Ellen Fairclough's background as an accountant and give her the more comfortable, womanish posts of Citizenship and Immigration and Secretary of State.

Trudeau has never been faced with Pearson's problem of two exceptionally able women in caucus and having to exclude one ("Oh, Mr. Pearson," Dr. Jewett chided him, "why don't we be really radical and have two women in the cabinet and settle this numbers game once and for all"), but Trudeau is hardly liberated on the subject of women. His speech last March in Toronto, remembered mostly now, I suspect, as a gallant salute to the fair sex on the eve of his still secret marriage, perpetuated the sentimental view that women never would have tolerated environmental damage and would have brought compassion to the treatment of criminal offenders.

The prejudice experienced by women doesn't end with their political colleagues. The press, too, underscores and entrenches the specialness of women in politics.

Claire Kirkland-Casgrain, a lawyer and now Minister of Tourism, Hunting and Fishing in the Bourassa government, complains that, when she first arrived in the Legislature, *Montreal-Matin* used to keep a daily box score on the color of her nail polish.

Profiles about women in politics aren't complete without a discussion of their hosiery, housekeeping schedule, taste in hats and makeup, even the size of their shoes. What's described as commitment in a man is considered one-track minded in a woman; conviction in a man is emotionalism in a woman; what makes a man a maverick and colorful makes a woman formidable.

The legions of women that Agnes Macphail said she heard behind her when she entered the House in 1921, the first woman to be elected after women won the right to vote and stand for office, have turned out to be seventeen in all, more a reconnoitering party than a legion. Ellen Fairclough thought the footsteps were getting louder when she was made a minister of the Crown in 1958, and exuberantly predicted that there'd be twice as many women politicians within a decade. Well, ten years have passed and the footsteps are receding.

We're still making political "firsts" for women. Economist Sylvia Ostry, first woman to hold a government job at the assistant deputy minister level (deputy ministerships still to go); Judge Réjane Laberge-Colas, first woman named to a Superior Court; journalist Anne Francis, first Canadian woman named to head a Royal Commission. Things are always supposed to be getting better for women, but somehow good times keep staying just around the corner.

# Women's Status— How the MPs Rate You

*How seriously does out male-dominated House of Commons regard women? To find out, Chatelaine sent a questionnaire to every one of our MPs (261 men, one woman)*

By Erna Paris

**Y**OUR LOCAL MEMBER OF Parliament may be a charmer. He may have a quick smile and a twinkle in his eye for the ladies. When speaking to a female audience, he might compliment the women on their collective beauty. Maybe he adores his mom, and makes a point of saying so. She might even be there, beaming love from the front row. Perhaps you never thought of him as condescending, or that this approach might indicate his belief that women can be conned into votes. You may be personally convinced Joe Blow MP is a kind man, but have you questioned him on the issues that will affect *you* when he is your representative in Ottawa?

What do the 261 men and one woman who govern this country really think of women? How able are they to represent the needs of women who make up over fifty percent of their constituents? How deeply are traditional male-female stereotypes entrenched in their psyches? A man who consciously or unconsciously thinks of women solely as "mothers and wives," or "charming" or "gentle" or "sexy," may be prejudiced when it comes to legislation concerning equal employment opportunities, educational grants, issues of day care and abortion.

In December 1970, the Royal Commission on the Status of Women made 167 recommendations on these subjects and others that affect women. For months, Prime Minister Trudeau neglected to assign responsibility for the women's report to a particular minister, saying that a document of such importance deserved the attention of not one, but all. What is everyone's business is no one's business. Finally, the job was given to Robert Andras, then minister of urban affairs, and subsequently switched to Bryce Mackasey, then minister of labor, and now minister of manpower and immigration.

In this election year, we thought women should know where they were placing their votes. We selected fourteen Members of Parliament representing all four parties, including Liberal cabinet ministers whose departments affect areas of particular concern to women, as well as Opposition critics of these departments. We asked questions about whether your pay cheque should be the same as the one the man working beside you on the same job gets, and whether you, as a housewife, should be entitled to a Canada Pension of your own. We questioned their views on day care and abortion reform. Finally, we checked attitudes by asking what human characteristics they considered most attractive or valuable in a woman.

We saw most of them personally, but those we could not interview, due to the pressure of time, have been quoted from Hansard and speeches they have made on the subjects we were interested in.

Only two MPs of the fourteen, Grace MacInnis and Stanley Knowles, supported the suggestion that women at home receive a salary.

Opinion was sharply divided on whether women need "special treatment" in the short-run in order to reach equal status. Those opposed to a special women's council, special Manpower offices and quotas, spoke of "counter-discrimination" and the fact that women must make it on merit alone.

Though many people felt that abortion should be a decision taken by the woman and her doctor, no one supported "abortion on demand," as women's liberation groups express it. Some of the men interviewed had conjured up fantasies of armies of pregnant women marching aggressively into doctors' offices "demanding" abortions.

In attitude, the most reactionary, when it came to legislating women's rights, claimed to "love women" best, in a special categorized way. Conservative Philip Rynard "puts women on a pedestal." Conservative John Lundrigan says he "likes to discriminate. I like women to be soft, gentle and feminine. You can't legislate roles."

Most of the women we spoke with in Ottawa (who were not government spokesmen) were far from jubilant or even optimistic about real reform. Florence Bird, chairman of the royal commission, said she's pleased the report has been taken seriously and respected—which is not saying much. Gordon Fairweather, one of the most enlightened Members of Parliament, was pessimistic. "While there's *machismo* in society, nothing much will happen in government."

The Royal Commission on the Status of Women documented a long history of subtle discrimination against women. Stanley Knowles pinpointed the dilemma. "We love women, so we have special places for them." If it is true that women's rights are not a political issue in Ottawa today, as people who live there suggested, it is because Canadian women don't care enough yet.

# BIG CHIEFS SPEAKING WITH FORKED TONGUE

## *What you hear isn't necessarily what you get*

### Pierre Elliott Trudeau
PRIME MINISTER

In March 1971, in Toronto, Trudeau made a major policy speech on women. "Canada is not so wealthy in human or in natural resources that we are able to ignore or misuse the talent in our midst," he said. Then he pledged the full support of his government to the removal of discrimination and the provision of opportunity to women.

But his funny-flippant attitude to women was apparent in the House of Commons the day he was asked which minister would be responsible for the Status of Women report. "Those who wish to make representations on labor matters [should address themselves to] the minister of national health and welfare," he laughed. In October 1971 he told a high-school class in Nova Scotia that women should be the ones to decide whether they should have the legal right to abortion. But one week later, when asked by Grace MacInnis whether he would be willing to put legislation before the House of Commons that would allow Parliament to decide whether to remove abortion from the Criminal Code, Trudeau answered, "No, that is not what we said in the Speech from the Throne."

### Robert Stanfield
LEADER OF THE OPPOSITION

Stanfield said he favors establishing "something special" for women until they reach parity, though he hasn't decided what exactly.

Playing it safe right down the middle, Stanfield said he doesn't like the idea of quotas in principle, but they *may* be necessary for the time being. "However, backlash problems could arise, so I wouldn't want to push for too big a quota." "The question of abortion is not entirely for the woman to decide. I would legislate it as a doctor-patient relationship, and do away with the therapeutic committee." It is a Stanfield policy that on the touchy question of abortion, every member must vote according to his own conscience.

## OUT OF TOUCH

### Woman's place is on a pedestal—out of the way

**Réal Caouette**

LEADER, SOCIAL CREDIT PARTY

Speaking on abortion in the House of Commons, Caouette had this to offer: "Nature was not created by psychiatrists, nor by the minister of justice, nor by the Prime Minister of Canada." Nature was created by "superior being . . . we must conform to that nature . . . mothers are not the only ones to die . . ."

## "YESTERDAY" MP

### Woman's place is in the home, but she can get out sometimes . . . if she's not too noisy

**David Lewis**

LEADER, NEW DEMOCRATIC PARTY

Though Lewis has championed the rights of minorities all his life, he is regarded by some to be the "male chauvinist" of the NDP. He admits that many of his attitudes remain basically those of his generation. Lewis thinks it would be difficult but possible to amend the Canada and Quebec pension plans, but he'd hate to have a law where wives received a salary. His own wife has not worked outside the home since they married, but has devoted herself to the NDP and particularly to Lewis's career.

"The stridency of women's lib has done a lot of damage," he said. "They effectively dramatized the cause in the beginning but now it's time to become more rational . . ."

## "TODAY" MP

**Grace MacInnis, NDP**

VANCOUVER-KINGSWAY

Grace MacInnis is adamant that women must get where they're going on ability. She is not in favor of quotas, but feels that until child care centres and part-time work are available women do need some special machinery for an extra push.

She thinks that women running as independents won't get to first base. The battle must be won with the support of favorably-minded men.

# Chatelaine's Women of the Year 1985: 6 Cabinet Women

By Charlotte Gray

**JANUARY 1985**

ONE OF THE MOST DRAMATIC events of 1984 was the break-through of women into federal politics. Twenty-seven women were elected to the House of Commons—almost double the number in the previous Parliament—and an unprecedented six women became Cabinet ministers. They shattered the myths of prejudice once and for all.

Jean Pigott, the former Tory MP largely responsible for opening up her party to her sex, comments with glee: "The psychological barriers that have kept women out of politics for too long are finally breaking down. You can feel the yeast bubbling and the dough rising throughout the system."

*Clockwise from the left: Monique Vézina, Minister of State for External Relations; Barbara McDougall, Minister of State for Finance; Pat Carney, Minister of Energy, Mines and Resources; Flora MacDonald, Minister of Employment and Immigration; Andrée Champagne, Minister of State for Youth; and Suzanne Blais-Grenier, Minister of the Environment*

The climax of the achievement was the Cabinet appointments—six women in the Cabinet, an unprecedented 15 percent. Two veteran parliamentarians—Flora MacDonald, Minister of Employment and Immigration, and Pat Carney, Minister of Energy, Mines and Resources—were joined by four newcomers to Parliament Hill: Barbara McDougall, Minister of State for Finance; Andrée Champagne, Minister of State for Youth; Monique Vézina, Minister for External Relations; and Suzanne Blais-Grenier, Minister of the Environment.

"What has changed in this election," says Flora MacDonald, 58, "is that there are six of us at the critical decision-making levels." For the first time in Canadian history, there is at least one woman on every Cabinet committee. MacDonald, Carney, McDougall, Champagne, Vézina and Blais-Grenier have shown more clearly than ever before that women who run can get elected, and if they are elected, they can get a top job in Cabinet. In the 1980s, politics is a game both sexes can win."

| QUESTIONNAIRE | % | NO. | LIB. | PC | NDP |
|---|---|---|---|---|---|
| TOTAL REPLIES | 100 | 87 | 45 | 18 | 18 |

**1. Have you read the report of the Royal Commission on the Status of Women?**

| | % | NO. | LIB. | PC | NDP |
|---|---|---|---|---|---|
| *Yes (or indicated partially)* | 83 | 72 | 37 | 16 | 15 |
| *No* | 17 | 15 | 8 | 2 | 3 |

**2. Do you think women are discriminated against in Canadian society?**

| | % | NO. | LIB. | PC | NDP |
|---|---|---|---|---|---|
| *Yes* | 78 | 68 | 34 | 14 | 16 |
| *No* | 20 | 17 | 10 | 3 | 2 |

**3. Should a federal council on the Status of Women, directly responsible to Parliament, for implementing reforms and research in women's rights be established?**

| | % | NO. | LIB. | PC | NDP |
|---|---|---|---|---|---|
| *Yes* | 38 | 33 | 14 | 6 | 10 |
| *No* | 25 | 22 | 14 | 4 | 2 |
| *Undecided* | 33 | 29 | 16 | 7 | 6 |

**4. Should special offices be established in Canada Manpower Centres to counsel women on non-sex-typed job opportunities and retraining?**

| | % | NO. | LIB. | PC | NDP |
|---|---|---|---|---|---|
| *Yes* | 48 | 42 | 18 | 9 | 13 |
| *No* | 34 | 30 | 19 | 5 | 4 |
| *Undecided* | 16 | 14 | 8 | 4 | 1 |

**5. Quotas for women in the Senate and in management-training programs in the public service (CAP) should be established.**

| | % | NO. | LIB. | PC | NDP |
|---|---|---|---|---|---|
| *Yes* | 17 | 15 | 6 | 5 | 2 |
| *No* | 78 | 68 | 38 | 12 | 15 |

**6. The Canada and Quebec Pension Plans should be amended to include housewives independently of their husbands.**

| | % | NO. | LIB. | PC | NDP |
|---|---|---|---|---|---|
| *Yes* | 66 | 57 | 26 | 10 | 17 |
| *No* | 25 | 22 | 13 | 7 | 1 |
| *Undecided or no reply* | 9 | 8 | 6 | 1 | — |

**7. Housewives should receive salaries from the government and/or their husbands' employer for household services.**

| | % | NO. | LIB. | PC | NDP |
|---|---|---|---|---|---|
| *Yes* | 16 | 14 | 5 | — | 7 |
| *No* | 66 | 57 | 33 | 16 | 5 |
| *Undecided* | 17 | 15 | 7 | 2 | 6 |

**8. My views on abortion are closest to the following:**

| | % | NO. | LIB. | PC | NDP |
|---|---|---|---|---|---|
| *a. I cannot sanction abortion except to save the life of the mother* | 15 | 13 | 4 | 6 | 1 |
| *b. The law should remain as it is now* | 36 | 31 | 23 | 5 | 1 |
| *c. Abortion should be a matter concerning the woman and her doctor and should be removed from the Criminal Code* | 39 | 34 | 14 | 5 | 14 |
| *d. Abortion should be granted on the sole request of the woman within the first 12 weeks of pregnancy* | 5 | 4 | 2 | — | 1 |

**9. Birth control information and devices should be available to everyone—free of charge to those unable to pay.**

| | % | NO. | LIB. | PC | NDP |
|---|---|---|---|---|---|
| *Yes* | 92 | 80 | 44 | 14 | 18 |
| *No* | 7 | 6 | 1 | 4 | — |

**10. The fed. gov't and the provinces should together adopt a national day care program.**

| | % | NO. | LIB. | PC | NDP |
|---|---|---|---|---|---|
| *Yes* | 87 | 76 | 39 | 16 | 17 |
| *No* | 11 | 10 | 6 | 2 | 1 |

**11. This day care should be available to all women seeking it.**

| | % | NO. | LIB. | PC | NDP |
|---|---|---|---|---|---|
| *Yes* | 59 | 51 | 24 | 8 | 16 |
| *No* | 36 | 31 | 18 | 9 | 2 |

**12. This day care should be available only to women who must work out of financial necessity.**

| | % | NO. | LIB. | PC | NDP |
|---|---|---|---|---|---|
| *Yes* | 39 | 34 | 18 | 12 | 5 |
| *No* | 54 | 47 | 24 | 6 | 12 |

**13. Do you think the women's liberation movement has helped the cause of women's rights?**

| | % | NO. | LIB. | PC | NDP |
|---|---|---|---|---|---|
| *Yes* | 45 | 39 | 18 | 6 | 11 |
| *No* | 37 | 32 | 19 | 7 | 5 |
| *Undecided* | 15 | 13 | 7 | 4 | 2 |

**14 Pick three qualities from the following list that you think are most appealing and/or valuable in a woman.**

| | % | NO. | LIB. | PC | NDP |
|---|---|---|---|---|---|
| *Understanding* | 71 | 62 | 33 | 14 | 12 |
| *Possesses initiative* | 57 | 50 | 23 | 11 | 13 |
| *Intellectual* | 34 | 30 | 12 | 8 | 7 |
| *Loves children* | 29 | 25 | 13 | 9 | 3 |
| *Independent* | 24 | 21 | 6 | 4 | 11 |
| *Soft and feminine* | 22 | 19 | 10 | 2 | 3 |
| *Beautiful* | 13 | 11 | 6 | 3 | 1 |
| *Dynamic* | 10 | 9 | 6 | 1 | 2 |
| *Ambitious* | 7 | 6 | 5 | 1 | — |
| *Good listener* | 6 | 5 | 1 | 2 | 1 |
| *Unaggressive* | — | — | — | — | — |

# Woman of the Year: Kim Campbell

*For 19 weeks, Canada had a woman as prime minister—and now, she's history. Was Kim Campbell's victory our victory? And if so, do we share in her defeat?*

By Charlotte Gray

**JANUARY 1994**

A NEW PHOTOGRAPH HANGS in the echoing Gothic splendor of Parliament's Centre Block. The somber image joins a gallery of 18 former prime ministers, from Sir John A. Macdonald to Brian Mulroney. Like the others, it speaks of ambition, courage and power. But this time, the camera has captured a new reality in Canadian politics, as well as reflecting old themes. This time, the subject is a woman.

The Tories' crushing election defeat in October cannot detract from Kim Campbell's achievement: as Canada's first woman prime minister, she made her mark in history. But her giddy rise and brutal fall say a lot about our political system.

How did Kim Campbell reach the top? There were two factors. First, her own determination, her willingness to take risks. Second, a huge change in Canadian political structure over the past quarter century. Kim Campbell did not create her moment in history—but when it came, she seized it.

Her star potential was recognized as soon as she plunged into federal politics in 1988. She made all the moves that any junior minister must make to succeed. In 1990, she became first woman minister of justice; in 1993, she became first woman defence minister. Her candidacy as a successor to Brian Mulroney was never in doubt. "Who needs a leadership race?" she grinned, after her defence appointment. "I'll just stage a military coup. Don't mess with me. I have tanks."

But when Brian Mulroney finally announced his resignation, everyone was stunned by how fast Kim Campbell's campaign took off. More experienced rivals (Perrin Beatty, Barbara McDougall and Michael Wilson among them) found their own ambitions burned to cinders in the firestorm of last spring's Campbellmania.

The early euphoria was largely the result of the second factor in Campbell's success: a fundamental shift in Canadians' political expectations. Senator Pat Carney, a senior minister in Mulroney's government between 1984 and 1988, argues that "the public is way ahead of politicians in terms of expectations about women. Canadians today are bothered if they *don't* see women in positions of power. Political parties are playing catch-up."

We are ahead of the U.S. on social benefits such as equal pay. In 1982, when Canadian women got an equal rights guarantee in our charter of rights, American women watched their Equal Rights Amendment go down to defeat. Hungry for votes, political parties have jumped on the equality band-wagon. In 1989, the New Democrats elected Audrey McLaughlin to their leadership; in 1991, Sheila Copps became the Liberal Party's deputy leader. Even the scarcity of women in the House of Commons was finally recognized as a problem (although Canada can boast a higher percentage of female legislators than either the U.S. or the U.K.). Conservatives, Liberals and New Democrats all trumpeted their intention to run more women in the 1993 election and gave them extra help with expenses. Partly thanks to these efforts, 53 women were elected on October 25, making them 18 percent of the House of Commons. This is hardly a breakthrough, but compared to the 1980 parliament where only 5 percent of MPs were women, it's progress.

The Conservative search for a new leader played out against this backdrop. To take them into the next election, Tory insiders wanted someone as distant as possible from the deeply unpopular Mulroney. "This was a party in the dumps, with lots of money but no public appeal," comments Sylvia Bashevkin, professor of political science at the University of Toronto. "They were primed for a candidate who was 'different'—which could have been a difference in ethnic background or gender or something else."

And then, in late 1992, the photo of a bare-shouldered Campbell flashed across international news services, earning her the sobriquet "the

Madonna of Canadian politics." At the time, notes *Toronto Star* columnist Richard Gwyn, Americans were poised to elect Bill Clinton, then viewed as new, dynamic and exciting. "The Clinton envy factor was important: Kim was our baby boomer."

❧

In March, "The fast-talking blonde from Lotusland," as the *Ottawa Citizen* described Campbell, appeared to be on a cakewalk to a coronation. But that changed soon after the leadership race got going, and Jean Charest came within an inch of beating her in June. Perhaps, in the light of what followed, she now wishes he had.

Some of Campbell's wounds in that leadership race were self-inflicted. She was slow to dispel assumptions that she had finished her doctorate and she claimed a fluency in German and Russian that proved unjustified. A whiff of sulfur hung in the air after she described those who didn't get involved in party politics as "condescending SOBs."

But as the leadership fight wore on, Campbell and her advisers discovered that the "difference" that so excited her party initially couldn't compensate for the uneasiness that, in the 1990s, a forceful woman still provokes. Specifically, Campbell contradicted four basic assumptions of what constitutes leadership material in Canada today.

Assumption One: The candidate should have a settled home life, preferably sporting a gorgeous wife, telegenic kids and parents bursting with pride at their offspring's achievements.

Such a family is the exception in Canada today; most adults and kids do not live in *Leave It to Beaver* households. There isn't a single female high-flyer in federal politics past or present who can boast such a comfortable image. Flora MacDonald, Pat Carney, Monique Bégin, Audrey McLaughlin, Sheila Copps, Mary Clancy—all never married or divorced. Politicians are intense ego-driven people who work horrendously long hours. Male politicians seem to be able to find partners who will tolerate the demands of political life; female politicians aren't so lucky. After three years in Ottawa, Campbell's second husband, Howard Eddy, walked out, leaving a note for Campbell. Critics whispered that her marital track record indicated "instability."

Assumption Two: The candidate's career should present a neat narrative—a steady climb from graduation to the top of his or her profession. Think of Brian Mulroney, the boy from Baie-Comeau, who became the wealthy head of the Iron Ore Company of Canada; Jean Chrétien, the *p'tit gars* from Shawinigan with 11 Cabinet posts under his belt. Before each man became his party's champion, each had made the smooth transition from "outsider" to "insider," with a network of important friends.

This is a typical pattern for middle-aged, middle-class Canadian men. It is not typical for women, however, whose careers are often interrupted by diversions such as marriage, child-rearing and divorce. New Democrat leader Audrey McLaughlin had several careers (a teacher in West Africa, a social worker in Toronto, a community worker in the Yukon) before she became an MP. Similarly, Kim Campbell's pre-Ottawa career path included university teaching, a seat on the Vancouver School Board, law school and private practice, and political backrooming in B.C. premier Bill Bennett's office. She surprised everyone in 1986, when she ran for the leadership of the Social Credit Party after Bennett's resignation. Two years later, she abruptly plunged into federal politics as a Progressive Conservative.

> **Male politicians seem to be able to find partners who will tolerate the demands of political life; female politicians aren't so lucky.**

A feminist reading of Campbell's story shows the progress of a smart individual who has made self-reliance her guiding theme. Campbell's more traditional critics see the erratic path of an opportunist who never finishes anything. In one biting *Maclean's* column, Alan Fotheringham cast her as a "sharp-tongued mini-Thatcher with an ability to leap wherever ambition leads her."

Yet, at a deeper level, the story reveals an inner ambivalence, a fundamental uneasiness in Kim Campbell's relationship with the central Canadian political and financial establishments. Some of this tension probably originates in the clashes between Campbell's father, an old-fashioned authoritarian lawyer, and her mother, described by Campbell as "a free spirit." After the Campbells' marriage breakdown, their youngest daughter announced that from then on, she would be known as "Kim" rather than the romantic names her mother had christened her: Avril Phaedra.

The decision to rename herself could be interpreted as a youngster's brave attempt to take hold of her own life. Instead, this evidence of self-affirmation unnerved those accustomed to campaign biographies celebrating pride in roots and a smooth journey toward the centre of power.

Assumption Three: A candidate for party leadership will have paid his or her dues during years of frontline service. Brian Mulroney was only 17 when he attended his first Tory leadership convention in 1956. Jean Chrétien has been in the House of Commons for 30 years. Preston Manning was born into a political family and first ran in a federal election in 1965, at the age of 23. All three have bursting Rolodexes.

*Simply by becoming the first woman prime minister, Kim Campbell has made a difference*

Few women, however, have had the opportunity to develop such a web of contacts. Campbell had spent only five years in Tory trenches, and her inexperience was a handicap.

Assumption Four: A woman who aims for the top won't rock the boat on behavior stereotypes. This means showing she's a kinder gentler kind of person, while proving that she will be a tough leader.

Of course, this puts women in a hopeless bind—given the competitive nature of politics, no one lacking an ample dose of aggression is likely to aim for the top. "I was aggressive," Sheila Copps remarked recently, "and I got called a bitch." Kim Campbell soon discovered that the media considered her aggression over the top. "The Burning Ambition of Kim Campbell" read a *Maclean's* cover last May, underlining society's lingering distaste for female ambition with a subtitle "brash and calculating."

But thanks to the early surge of support and a good organization, Kim Campbell won the leadership. In June, the Tory faithful roared with tribal enthusiasm when the stocky figure in a plain suit, adorned as always with the gold "K" brooch, waved exuberantly at her supporters, in their pink baseball hats. To her advisers' glee, she hit record levels of popularity last summer as she crisscrossed the country. At the Tokyo meeting of the seven largest industrial powers, when she was the only woman among the dark suits, she radiated the dignity and self-assurance shared by those at the pinnacle of power. She seemed to offer a new kind of politics: candid, straight-talking—and female.

Women shared Campbell's sense of arrival. Older women whose hopes had been thwarted by discrimination, women in their 40s who wanted to see someone like themselves at the top, young women making career decisions—Campbell's success resonated for them all. Everyone talked about what it meant for their daughters. And Campbell acknowledged this. When an early poll showed that voters saw her gender as a positive attribute, she said, "What really pleases them [is] . . . to see a woman whose competence and resolution and strength are beyond question."

Of course, she tried, over the summer, to prove that her "difference" was about more than gender. Tales of Campbell's frugality—she didn't splurge on new sheets and she made a point of buying her own berries and milk—were a welcome contrast to the Trump-size tastes of the Mulroneys. Cabinet shuffles showed that she would run a frugal government too.

But the memory of Brian Mulroney, the most unpopular Prime Minister in Canadian history, was too entrenched to eradicate. And Kim Campbell herself failed to live up to the expectations she had aroused.

Her talk of "the new politics" implied more honesty, more realism, more humanity. But as her election prospects sank, she started to look as arrogant, as out of touch and evasive as her "old politics" predecessors. By October 25, she had even lost her particular appeal to women voters: on election day, she lost her own riding. Even before the Conservatives limped into political ignominy with just two seats, the Tory ol'boys had begun to plot Campbell's political demise.

∿

How has Canada's first woman prime minister changed Canadian politics?

Some feminists and Campbell supporters argued last fall that it was old-fashioned sexism that defeated Campbell. Had there been any chance that the Tories would win the election, ran the argument, a man would have won the party leadership. Like so many female candidates who run in unwinnable ridings, they said, Campbell had been a "sacrificial lamb." In fact the reverse is true. Last March, it looked as if a woman leader was the Tories' only hope of election victory. By October, it was obvious that even gender couldn't save the party.

Nonetheless, simply by becoming the first woman prime minister, Kim Campbell has made a difference. Unlike Britain's Margaret Thatcher, she acknowledges her debt to the women's movement for opening doors and defines herself as a feminist. As justice minister, she worked hard to make the law reflect women's concerns. One of her lasting legacies is Canada's "No means no" rape law.

Campbell's Tory feminism is different, of course, from the left-leaning feminist orthodoxies of the past 25 years. She is committed to women advancing on their own merits and dismisses sug-

gestions that women are society's victims. During the election, her silence on issues such as child care and the needs of immigrant women exasperated activists such as Sunera Thobani, president of the National Action Committee on the Status of Women: "The significance of having a woman prime minister is soon lost if she doesn't do anything to help women."

What Campbell did do, however briefly, was to inject the reality of women's lives in the male world of politics. Speaking at a journalists' conference in 1992, Campbell articulated more clearly than any of her predecessors the challenge facing a woman in politics. Women, she argued, have only been accepted as ersatz men: "The frontal lobes have always been accepted . . . but the bodies and the lifestyles and the gender-specific aspects of our personality have not. And that is what I see now as the next frontier."

# CHAPTER NINE

# Gender Wars

**W**HILE WOMEN HAVE GROWN wary of fatalistic pronouncements like Freud's "Anatomy is destiny," most of us would acknowledge that biology remains a major shaping force in our lives. This is partly because of the real needs and desires of our bodies, and partly because of the prejudices, stereotyping, fables and forces that have exaggerated our differences from men.

In "The Problem of the Missing Girl" (March 1929), *Chatelaine* explored the loneliness and vulnerability of single women drifting like moths to the bright lights of the city, with dreams larger than their opportunities. Unlike male migrants, they lived in double jeopardy: as sexual and economic prey.

As noted in other chapters, the anxieties of the thirties seemed to play themselves out in an edgy battle of the sexes. Despite the cleverness of "I Wish I Were a Woman" (April 1932), *Chatelaine* readers were swift to spot that its author wouldn't give up one jot of male privilege for the so-called advantages of being female. Contrast this with the genuine bitterness and frustration of the young woman who wrote, "I Would Rather Have Beauty Than Brains" (February 1931). Metaphorically, she was a passenger in a beat-up compact while he was driving a limousine.

The article "Marriage Is My Career" (January 1941), plus the response of readers to it, reminds us that one of the most enduring rifts in the gender wars has been between women who define themselves as wives and mothers and those who don't. However, when women met on turf not staked out for them by men, as they did in offices and plants during World War II, they usually came to trust each other ("I Like Other Women," May 1943).

By the sixties, women were growing canny and confident enough to begin analyzing why, in targeting each other, they so often shot themselves in the foot. On closer examination, they found their real enemy to be the patriarchy that set women against each other in competition for men ("Why Are Women So Hard on Each Other?" February 1963). This insight paved the way for the female bonding that became such a gratifying feature of the seventies. It also freed women to turn a wry but sympathetic eye toward Macho Man, robbed of his potency by changing female expectations ("Are Men Obsolete?" April 1974).

For women who believed the attack on the patriarchy was overstated, "The Irene Murdoch Case" (November 1974) came as a wake-up call: if an Alberta ranch wife of twenty-five years, who'd worked side by side with her husband and invested her own money in their property, could end up divorced, destitute and with a broken jaw, how could any woman trust Canadian justice?

Behind such social, political and legal discrimination, feminists were uncovering centuries of misogyny in which the battleground was often women's own bodies ("Unmasking the Curse,"

---

OPPOSITE: *Although the role of the 1920s woman was restricted in many ways, savvy advertisers recognized the power of the female consumer.*

January 1974). This realization led directly to the gender conflict that dominated the eighties: the prevalence of male violence and society's refusal to confront it ("Are We Winning the War against Rape?" September 1981). Tragically, the eighties were punctuated by a burst of gunfire that, for many, confirmed their belief about male hatred of women: in December 1989, a deranged gunman massacred fourteen women at the Montreal École Polytechnique to protest their invasion of a traditionally male profession.

By the nineties, feminists who'd grown used to solidarity in their fight against social injustice were chagrined to discover that they were divided, sometimes irrevocably, on issues vital to women. One of the bitterest battles was detailed by *Chatelaine* in May 1996: "The Abortion Wars: Guns and Money."

# The Problem of the Missing Girl

## Chatelaine *goes over the path she may have to tread in Canada*

Anne Elizabeth Wilson

**MARCH 1929**

It is not with the girl who is spectacularly "missing" or for whom the countryside searches, that we are so greatly concerned. It is that vast army of restless, seeking and pathetically unprovided-for youth that looks to life for a little color, a little glamor, a little romance, and which, by reason of its very eagerness and freedom from worldly wisdom—normally the most lovable essences of youth—is the greater victim of calculation and the lure of the tawdry gaiety which cloaks vice.

Take the actual case of Dorothy and Grace in Toronto. They went to the movies. Their parents told them that if they ever went again they would thrash them. So Johnny K——, whom they met at a dance hall, suggested that they take a room downtown where they could go to the movies all they chose. He would gladly provide it for them. Johnny lived with them both, which he assured them was customary. Later on, when Johnny insisted that they bring men to the room, it was more or less in the nature of events, and they were afraid to go home.

When Grace was arrested one night, Dorothy was also taken into custody, but Johnny went free. He can supply many witnesses who will swear that he had nothing to do with the girls. Meanwhile, the only hope for them is to give them an indeterminate sentence until Johnny can be got out of the way. They are now completely in his power, and to send them home would mean only a repetition of the whole affair. Their indeterminate sentence at the reformatory is not a punitive but an almost purely expedient measure. The reformatory, dread, antisocial institution though it may be considered, is in reality their only refuge.

Here is the advantages of the indeterminate sentence: It gives no clue as to the girl's probable time of release. Reports of sentences in the papers still furnish information utilized by men in locating girls for immoral traffic. Choicer material is often found with much less effort. Consider this method, quashed within the past week by city detectives and a representative of a large Canadian metropolitan paper. An item was noticed in the classified advertising section for "chorus girls—previous experience unnecessary." An address in a poor part of the city was given, with instructions to call for a personal interview during some part of the evening. The possibilities of the case interested the city editor, who made arrangements with several detectives and a woman member of his staff to do a little investigating. Accordingly, at the appointed time the young woman entered the house whose number had been given. The detectives waited outside, instructing her in case of any trouble, to throw out an apple which she had secreted in her pocket. Within she found a very prepossessing mulatto who greeted her with great interest. In the room, already seated and beaming with enthusiasm, were three or four very pretty young girls, obviously green as the grass in the country districts from which they came.

Did they know how to dance? No? Well, that was immaterial; they would be trained. Could they sing? No? It really made very little difference. Had they any particular ties that would keep them at home? If so, this might prevent them from traveling through Canada, eventually to New York and finally to Europe. Round-eyed, the prospective chorus drank in this romantic potion. New York! Europe!

In this case, the incident ended more happily than might hundreds of others. The detectives entered the supposed booking-agency, where a number of girls were already "in training," and although the law could not technically charge these promoters with an offence warranting arrest, it succeeded in sending the girls home to their parents. In almost every case they were country or very small town girls.

The bogus advertisement is one of the most fruitful means of securing the "green" girl for immoral purposes. Promises of "pay while learning" have brought countless girls from farms and

> *The bogus advertisement is one of the most fruitful means of securing the "green" girl for immoral purposes.*

villages to mingle in the vice and crime which is the undercurrent of any sizable city, and women as well as men act as procurers for this type of prey. Though one may look upon it as a difficult task to hold a girl to a life of vice against her will, one may also look upon it as a difficult task for an ignorant, frightened and inexperienced young creature to do anything else once Nature's natural safeguards of honesty and modesty have been stripped from her. Her one impulse is to hide—a tendency which may greatly serve the unscrupulous person who wishes to exploit her further. Documents in the possession of the morality departments of this country prove that where will and personality have been so deadened as to place the victims of vice in another person's power, there can be no application of such a phrase as "against the will." There is no will.

> *He was common, familiar, and took everything too much for granted, but she couldn't stand the everlasting round of loneliness any longer*

❧

Yet one sometimes hears of marvellous examples of courage, such as the little country girl who had come to "learn the business" with a flourishing milliner. She had fortunately taken temporary lodging with a kindly landlady, who helped her dress with much interest for the "party" which her new employer was giving her "girls." It was evidently a grand affair, for she was called for in a limousine.

Her landlady went to bed dwelling on the improvement in the condition of working women since she was a girl. However, she was awakened at four o'clock in the morning by a feeble scratching on her window, and looking out beheld a bedraggled, barefoot little girl, evidently ready to collapse. The "party for the girls" had proved to be a stag party of six at which she had been the only member of the gentler sex present. Doped, maltreated and deprived of most of her clothing, she had still managed to escape and run halfway across a large Canadian city in wintertime, to reach safety. The doctor who examined her declared it a case for the police, but the girl's mother preferred to take her child home without the danger of newspaper publicity. It was a natural reticence, and one which shields many offenders of like character.

❧

But what greater courage is evinced by the woman who, steeped in the pernicious atmosphere of vice, pulls herself out of it? I have recently read a letter from May H—— written to the well-known woman police magistrate who sentenced her to two years in the reformatory—a sentence, by the way, which although it embittered her at the time, she admits was the breathing space which gave her the final strength to break with the life. She, like many girls in her city, had been the victim of a suave trafficker in drugs and women. He had forced her into prostitution through the power he exercised over her in withholding drugs. Yet while she was completely in his power physically, when he would hide her clothes to prevent her leaving him, and take her money to keep her utterly helpless, she actually broke herself of the drug habit. Still, in her delirium, she was forced to carry on his trade. In describing her state of mind, she says over and over again, "Remember, I am not weak-minded or 'soft', but you have no idea what power that man had over me." Her arrest freed her from him for a long enough time to regain her footing—and she is to-day leading a normal and useful life.

❧

When one goes back and back into the case histories of girls and women who have gone voluntarily into the gray world of vice, one usually ends in a great void—loneliness.

"I used to go to the stores and brush against women, hoping they'd speak to me," railed one girl, "but no woman would ever speak to me—only men."

Perhaps you can see her in this composite picture. She came from a small town, looked up a downtown lodging house—something that would be near her work and cheap. She used to get up at 6.30 and go out for a cup of coffee and a roll for breakfast at a cheap restaurant nearby. She came home at six in the evening and sometimes had sandwiches and a bottle of milk in her room. She used to wash out her few underthings, do a little sewing and try to read—but the light was very poor. Then she'd go out to the movies if she could afford it, or walk out to look in the windows of the little shops.

The men in the house used to be always on the

stoop, lolling and watching her. Doors used to open and shut in the house at night; she heard men and women in rooms together. The only other women in the house were taken up with men; they seemed to have a good time. When the man who always watched her when she went in and out one night spoke to her, she thought she might as well be friendly—and that night he came into her room to say good-night. One of them had to sit on the bed; there was only one chair. He was common, familiar, and took everything too much for granted, but she couldn't stand the everlasting round of loneliness any longer. His attentions seemed to be about the same as other men's to women in that house; it was such a natural and accepted thing.

The question of safe lodging for young women is a vital one, yet one which it seems very difficult to control. When one reads in a rooming house advertisement the word "privileges," it may mean the doing of laundry in the bathroom, the cooking of breakfast in the kitchen, or unrestricted use of a room for any purpose whatever; usually, according to investigation, the latter.

Of course, there are always the Y.W.C.A. and W.C.T.U. residences for the girl who consciously seeks reasonable lodging and safety. But usually a girl leaves when she has acquired a beau. Youth demands some privacy and privilege. It cannot do its courting on the street, in the park, on the street cars. Then where?

❧

According to the League of Nations' latest report on "Traffic in Women and Children," Canada has the finest laws for the protection of women against untoward exploitation in the world. Read, for instance, Section 216 of the Criminal Code: "(L) Where a male person is *proved* to live with or to be habitually in the company of a prostitute or prostitutes, and has no visible means of support, or to live in a house of prostitution, he shall, unless he can satisfy the court to the contrary, be deemed to be living on the earnings of prostitution."

It is, however, difficult to control the professional of this type.

What then, must be our solution? Dr. Margaret Patterson, Magistrate of the Women's Police Court,

Toronto, quoting Harold Begbie in his *Life of the Convict*, says: "We must accept the unchallengeable fact and act upon it, that there are men and women in the world who for their own sakes, as well as for the community's sake, should never have a moment's freedom. The minds of these incurables are definitely bad, bad, bad; don't let us be afraid to use the word. There is no greater danger to a nation than the modern tendency to find excuses for badness."

# I Would Rather Have Beauty Than Brains

By Nan Robins

FEBRUARY **1931** WHEN IT COMES TO leaping off the deep end, beauty has it over brains, yesterday, today and forever. Of course, I am talking about matrimony. Why not? Haven't I had it drummed into me that a husband is the prize packet in the lottery of life and that a family and a home is every normal girl's real job? The only choices left are abnormal and subnormal—take your pick. Haven't I been told by mother and all the relations on both sides of the family, from Great-Aunt Hoidge down to my kid brother, that I'm improving my chances every day of being pushed in behind the pickle jars on the shelf and bringing lasting disgrace on the family? Haven't I heard my aunt boast that none of the girls in our family ever reached the age of twenty without at least seven proposals (audible aside, that I must be nearly twenty-four now). I have, and that isn't a fraction of it.

It is just the same at the office. I do a man's job. But the Boss told me that the reason that they do not pay girls as much as men is because a girl will probably go off and get married just as soon as she is properly trained and getting useful. I ventured the remark that when a boy is well-trained some other firm grabs him, but he just shot me an uncomprehending stare and grunted caustically, "It's different with men."

In the meantime, if she happens to be plain, not

ugly, just ordinary and plain, she does twice the work for half the pay of an average man and then gets the following definition. "Oh, that's our Miss Brown. Been with the company twenty years. Faithful old sort, very competent and all that—but, you know how it is. She's set in her ways, and her methods are old-fashioned. One of the boys sent her a box of flowers once and she was so flustered that she could hardly work for a week."

Take a plain girl's girl friends. When Betty Beautiful wants a girl to make a fourth in any party does she call up her prettiest girl friend? Not she, she asks Polly Plain and then proceeds to enamour both the boy friends. She raves all the while about how clever, how wonderfully clever, how enormously, magnificently and splendiferously clever is Polly. In fact, Polly is much cleverer than most men, Betty tells them confidingly and says, "Aren't you flattered that I asked you to meet Polly?" By this time Polly hasn't a ghost of a chance if she ever did. Why? Because, while a man expects his wife to be wise enough to make a $200 salary do the work of $400, and boasts about her ability to make Paris models out of ginghams and prints, he avoids a girl who is supposed to have brains.

So coming or going the girl with brains loses. If she elects to stay single and run her own show, it's automatically decided that the entire male population passed her up. If she likes a man and offers to give him a square deal; if she refuses to deal in subterfuge and deceit, she is chasing him and he goes faster than a newly broken ten dollar bill.

I know because I am one of the unfortunate intelligent ones. I'm not conceited about my brains—why should I be? One isn't overjoyed by "pink tooth brush," pimples or a cantankerous mother-in-law. My brains never bring me anything but boring old men for dinner partners. I could gnash my teeth when my hostess says, "Oh, Colonel, I am putting you next to our dear Miss Brilliant; you will enjoy talking to her, she is so clever."

Give me a cute nose, and I won't need to know how to spell. Correct spelling will bring me in twenty-five dollars a week, perhaps, but a cute nose will give me a meal ticket to punch for the rest of my life.

∽

I live with a couple of girls. Mabel is slim with cute wide-set eyes, brown, curly hair, an adorable dimple, and a peaches and cream complexion. She can wear clothes, she can look unbelievably sweet, but she hasn't an idea in the world beyond. "He's the handsomest thing, girls, and you should have seen the look Margaret gave me when I took him away from her." But the way the male population trail into our suite after her—and the telephone!

Beth, the girl she chums with, makes a delightful background for her. She is so plain. She can cook, she is brainy and she admits quite frankly that she would rather be married and care for a home of her own than anything else in the world. Any boy lucky enough to get her would be getting one of the finest girls in the world. But they can't see her for Mabel. What chance has a star when the sun comes out? Beth skimps all year so that she may be able to take her young sister for a holiday during the summer. Mabel spends all her money for glad rags, and then accepts one of a dozen invitations to spend the holidays at a summer home.

Can you blame her? Certainly not. Her face is her capital and believe me it's a gilt-edge stock. She can cash in on it every day of the week and the dividends only get higher.

Then the other girl I live with—she is one of those deep mysterious girls. She has long languid eyes of a queer shade of blue that have been compared to "Ma's blue granite preservin' kettle" by her rural Romeo, to "Smoldering pools of blue fire" by a defunct poet.

When I introduce her and say, "This is my friend, Sonia Donaldson," the masculine part of the party look at her auburn hair, catch the "wanta learn" spark in the pools of blue fire and immediately enroll for instruction. The female section of the crowd hope that she may be cursed with halitosis, the only known cure for a pretty face.

Of course, there is the odd man who is attracted to a brainy girl, but "odd" is usually the word. The first is the man who is looking for a wife who can be depended upon to bring home the bread, butter and baloney when he quits, because the boss doesn't appreciate him. The curious thing is that while these girls have the goods under the dome on everything else, they invariably show no sense at all along this line. I feel the same way.

The other type that get them is the absent-minded, near-sighted, studious type, wracked with calculus, and stewed in learning. Whether it is instinct, or just blind groping for someone who will take care of his physical needs or not, I do not know, but somehow he manages to get a clever girl. She takes care of him and is usually so tender-hearted that she won't leave the poor boob even though he never really sees her well enough to tell whether her nose is straight or a pug.

Then take me as an instance. I don't get many breaks between my two room-mates. Dorothy Dix and some of these experts say—learn to cook—do something better than any other girl can. Men will admire and respect you and then a real man will come along and want to marry you. Well, how does it work out?

I learned to cook and can say that my pies will melt in your mouth. I ask over the charmer of my fancy. He sits up and eats the pie, gazes at Mabel and thinks it is her pretty face that gives him that glorified feeling of satisfaction. Next time he comes over it's Mabel's turn to cook. She says she can't and he says, "Never mind, girls, let's go down town and eat."

Be a sport. Yes, and when you get to be a decent golfer, some day you are going to slip up and beat him. This causes a disease known as inflated ego. If you lose it's just as bad. Being plain, you can't look up at him appealingly, let a roseleaf lip tremble and cause him to think, "Poor pretty little thing, what does golf matter anyway." Instead he thinks, "She's not only homely, but she can't even play a decent game of golf."

If I look the world straight in the face as is natural for me to do, I look like a rather plain, intellectual girl without any sex-appeal. Men only believe what they see, and a pretty face makes a showing no set of brains in the world can emulate. That's why I'm telling you, "give me beauty, just an ordinary amount, and I don't need any brains."

# "I Wish I Were a Woman"

*A mere man launches an explosive attack against the prevalent theory that men get all the breaks in this world*

By R. F. Faryon

**APRIL 1932**

EVERY MORNING, AS RAZOR in hand I face the bathroom mirror, I wish I were a woman.

For, if I were, I would have no wiry beard to shave, and a new day would bring no greater difficulties than the simple planning of three meals, the ordinary routine of a housewife, or the mechanical unimaginative work of a stenographer.

Women are supposed to be the suffering sex, the cross-bearers of trouble, the martyrs of the world. Personally I don't agree. For instance, supposing that by a reversal of circumstances, women were the unfortunate possessors of whiskers; would they be obliged to continue with the age-old custom of shaving? Of course they wouldn't. Some enterprising male would have long ago invented a painless permanent method to replace the daily tactics that are considered good enough for men.

If I were a woman, I wouldn't have to be content with the meagre beauty with which Nature endowed me. If we were to see the average woman in the privacy of her own boudoir, unadorned by make-up and other accessories of her stock-in-trade, we probably wouldn't recognize her. A woman can paint her face and dye her hair, cover physical defects by various devices, add to her height with heels and, by the clever use of style and color, completely camouflage her real appearance. But if I were as much as to pluck a few hairs from the beetling eyebrows that wander all over my forehead, I'd be scorned.

I wish I were a woman so that instead of wearing one suit for months at a time, I could get a dress for quarter of the cost and have four of them. I wish I could wear light comfortable things that wouldn't stifle my movements. If I were a woman, I could cover my ears with hair and snuggle down into a fur collar in winter, and go about in a yard of silk and a pair of earrings in the summer.

But I'm a man, and men are the Pollyannas of the world, who, because women expect it of them, uncomplainingly swelter in heavy suits on the hottest day, and brave the rigors of the coldest weather in Derby hats.

I wish I were a woman so that I could, by the use of a smile, leave my car under a "No Parking" sign; drive past a red light for a flirt of my eyes, and exceed speed limits with no other payment than a few coaxing words. I wish I were a woman so that I could take a long motor trip without having to change tires when punctures occur, or fiddle with a dirty motor when things go wrong.

Frankly, I am afraid of snakes and hate bugs and creepy things. If I were a woman, I could scream and be touchingly frightened at them, but as it is, I've got to swallow my feelings and be brave and manly. I've got to sit nonchalantly on a roller-coaster and be amused and protective as my partner squeals and hangs on, while, all the time, I feel worse than she does and would like to let out a few yells on my own

> **I wish I were a woman because I think it's the grandest racket in the world to which men pay exacting tribute from the day they are born.**

accord. But, of course, that wouldn't do. I'm a man.

Everyone likes praise. The average man accomplishes worthy things practically every day in his professional or business occupation. He is up against competition that drives him to the limit of creative or building achievement, but, unless he hits on something spectacular or is a master of publicity, it is all accepted as just so much work. But let a girl show the slightest signs of intelligence or the smallest ability to do anything that men are masters of, and, "She's so clever, my dear, I really don't know how she does it."

I wish I were a woman so that a wistful look and a gentle hint would produce tickets to a show; a subtle manner and a drop of perfume, chocolates and flowers. I wish I were a woman so that I could dine and dance at the smartest places and never have to worry about the bill.

Statistics show that women make about eighty per cent of all purchases in this country. I like to buy things and I wish I were a woman so I could get in on some of this spending.

Married women claim they haven't any freedom; that they are tied to their homes and that their working hours are long and tedious. Personally, I think they must be kidding, for the stores, downtown streets, theatres and parks are crowded with them every afternoon, and you've only to watch their leisurely progress to know that they are in no hurry.

I wish I were a woman so that I could do odd little things without being called eccentric; change my mind without being labelled unreliable; express my feelings without being accused of temperament; get a seat in a street car without being pierced by hostile glances; and go to bargain sales and push and pull, and not be rude.

I wish I were a woman because I think it's the grandest racket in the world to which men pay exacting tribute from the day they are born. I wish I were a woman so that I could make some big oaf, whose size and strength cows me as a man, tremble at my word and jump to do my bidding. I wish I were a woman so that I could order a fat and pompous banker to bring home a spool of number forty thread and tell my boss not to forget the spinach. I wish I were a woman so that I could get up enough nerve to touch things that have a "Wet Paint" sign on them, pinch fruit, poke vegetables

*If women had whiskers, would they be obliged to shave? Of course not—some man would have invented a permanent method to replace the daily tactics that are considered good enough for men.*

and handle articles plainly labelled "Do Not Touch," bawl out a grocer, cheat a butcher, and get my shoes shined without giving a tip.

I wish I were a woman so that I could have someone to chase tennis balls, pay for my badminton birds and honor the chits that I sign. I wish I were a woman so that I could play on short-holed golf courses, and that no matter how poorly I played or how ridiculous I looked at any sport, I'd be cute, cunning and—oh, so feminine!

I wish I were a woman so that I could inwardly chuckle at the weakness of some poor sap who takes his hat off in an elevator; so that I could walk up to bank cages and ticket offices and get served without waiting in line; go fishing without having to row the boat, and have magazines like the *Chatelaine* plan my work and do my thinking for me.

I wish I were a woman for many reasons . . . but mainly so that I wouldn't have to listen to women tell me how lucky I am to be a man.

### One of the spirited replies to Mr. Faryon's article says in effect "Is that so?"

I'D LIKE TO be a man—well, part of the time at least. If I were, I'd go stag to a dance if I wanted to, and not have to stand around fiddling with a programme string and wishing someone would take pity on me and ask me to dance. I'd like to be a man so I wouldn't have to mend runs in my hose at 8.30 in the morning and worry because I couldn't afford a new pair. I'd like to be a man so I would never have to worry about how my food was cooked so long as it tasted right; so I would always be sure of some adoring woman who would be only too glad to amuse me for an evening if I wanted to be amused; so I could make business my irrevocable alibi if I didn't want to spend a dull evening playing bridge; so I could distribute largesse to the poor at my office door with a patronizing pat on the back and a "Hope that will help, my man."

And lastly, I should like to be a man so I could write a smart article like Mr. Faryon's, with my tongue in my cheek and have ninety per cent of the women of Canada think that I really wanted to be a woman.

—MARGARET L. STEVEN.

# Marriage Is My Career

BY M. L. YOUNG

MARCH 1941
"SHALL I MARRY—OR TRAIN for a career?"

I've heard this question discussed many, many times. Recently I was with a group of young friends who were talking about it, and they looked at me in amazement, when I said suddenly, "Marriage *is* my career!"

Marriage is not a gamble; it is not a game of chance. It is like hockey or baseball, perhaps, for you must learn to play, and the zest and skill with which you play determines whether you win or lose.

When I was fifteen years old I decided that what I wanted to do more than anything else was to marry and have a large family! My mother told me that if that's what I wanted to do I must train myself for the work I wanted just as definitely as anyone who prepares for any profession. So I began to "learn the business." I helped mother with the younger children from the time they were babies. I learned to sew, cook, bake, plan meals for the family, and to can fruits and vegetables. I read every article I found on child training and took several courses in cooking. I cared for the children of friends, and "kept house" for friends and relatives at various times. I took a course in first aid also—and, believe me, I have had many occasions to use it too!

There was nothing spectacular about my romance. I married a lad who had been in the same class in collegiate at seventeen. Because we were interested in so many of the same things we became good friends. But if anyone had told me then that I would marry him, I would have told them in no uncertain terms that they were crazy! I left school the next year to help at home, and for a couple of months did not see him. When we met again, it seemed as

if we had been separated for years instead of months, so we built on our friendship and later were engaged. We were very much in love when we married at twenty-two.

We began our married life on the basis that we could not live without each other—so we must learn how to live together! To do this we developed certain rules of conduct which I have since found are much the same rules as those to be found in any successful business.

For example, we took pride in our marriage just as my husband takes pride in his firm's name. We did not carry tales about our quarrels and problems to either friends or relatives. During the first year we were married we lived entirely away from our people. Sometimes I would get lonely and fed-up and would catch the next train "home to mother." But my love for my husband and my sense of loyalty to him kept my mouth shut. I would stay for a week or so and enjoy the visit; but I found I could not be content to stay longer. I hit the trail back to home and husband—and believe me I was glad to see them and ready to make a fresh start! When we quarrelled I told no one, but when it had blown over I tried to make right my share in it.

As the years went by and we faced certain difficulties, we made a point of acknowledging them and discussing them from every angle, in order to find a way out. I believe most successful businesses are developed with frequent "conferences" of the key men and women concerned, and a definite plan of action is laid. In our home we frequently have conferences at which both my husband and myself and our children discuss what is happening.

I regard the children very definitely as shareholders in the success of our home. We speak to them constantly about our ideal of what our home should be. I look on them as members of the family to be trained just as I would train any new members who entered the firm. They must know what we are trying to build. They must contribute their share. The children started with the most simple little incidents which had

occurred in their life. Through the years as we have learned to talk naturally together, they are presenting points of view which are of vital importance in general to their way of thinking.

The duties of my job are laid out very definitely for me, and I try to work at them with the realization that I should very soon be fired from any important position if I did not fulfill them. The proper planning of meals, the right diet to build nerve strength as well as physical energy, the constant awareness of the development of my children—this all represents a very important phase in the successful handling of my own particular career.

Through the years there have been periods of depression. The financial strain of several children, the restrictions of a young family, my ill health, and the ordinary wear and tear of life, have all been a part of our lives.

After going through various stages, we are at the place where life is interesting and living is fun. We take time to read, talk, and play games with the children, and use constructive suggestions to correct their faults and wrong behavior. My career is paying me dividends in a richness of living that is a better return than I could find anywhere else for the investment of my life's work and interest. My husband and I are more in love than ever we were, and there is no monotony! We are finding marriage a thrilling adventure in co-operation between a man, a woman, and God.

### The prize-winning $5 response

**MARCH 1941** THIS WRITER'S SMUGNESS IS as irritating as a hair shirt. She is wearing a halo. She really should take it off, and buy a mirror.

We do not know how long she has been married, or the size of her family, but we *do* know she never had any business experience. Yet she glibly talks of running her "career" as a business is run. "Career," in her case, is a misnomer. A real career is a joyous, broadening daily adventure. The oil of experience makes the wheels turn smoothly, so that there is a time for work and a time for play. Her life is as narrow and monotonous as a treadmill. It is cluttered with "conferences" to which sleepy Junior

and tired Dad alike are dragged. Small children do not understand "conferences," and a businesslike mother, knowing this, attends to their troubles in the same manner as a competent secretary answers the phone—promptly and courteously—saving "The Boss" time whenever possible.

I was in business for a decade prior to my marriage twenty years ago, and sat in at many "conferences" in a secretarial capacity, but never remember the office boy "on the executive." As with office boys, so with children—those at the head do the directing, and if *that* is sound there are few complaints.

There is no place in a world so full of pain and sorrow, for such egotism as this woman's life shows. She should *really* cast her lot with the married women who are clever enough to run happy homes, and still find time to work for others, at Red Cross or other charitable organizations.

—MARY THOMSON, WINNIPEG, MAN.

# I Like Other Women

*"I'm going to keep my women friends when he comes back. Earning them has been my great good fortune out of the emotional bankruptcy of war."*

By Felicia

MAY 1943

I'M THE GIRL WHO USED TO SAY, "I don't get along with women. If I want a real friend, I go to a man." Always, of course, with a melting, I'm-the-cream-in-your-coffee look in the direction of the big strong male I was parked beside.

For some reason or other I never found myself giving tongue on the subject to rheumatic old uncles or hard-working, earnest fathers-of-six. Me, I wanted men for friends—but only the eight-cylinder, special-finish jobs.

I'm being honest about it now, the way you're honest about how you used to sneak two extra eggs and another half pound of butter into the bridge-club cake and pass its richness off as just a little trick of your clever fingers. Men being rationed where they exist at all, and right off the market in other areas, I can look back upon my attitude like a reformed drunkard.

I'm amazed at what war has taught me about women. I think I sensed it all along. I mean, that women make the best friends. But it took a war and a husbandless existence to bring it home to me.

The biggest surprise of all was to discover that, once I found I liked women, and wanted to tag along with the girls, I had to work darned hard to get their friendship. Once I took the trouble to investigate, I turned up evidence to prove that there is a snug and pleasant petticoat society; they have fun and games together; they hold to a kind of unwritten code about priority rights on spoken-for males, and they can be kinder and more understanding than any mere man within miles (one perfectly good husband being on loan to the Armed Forces, 3,000 miles away).

∽

After I was left to my own resources—in those first months of temporary husbandlessness—friends asked me as a singleton to parties and dinners. There would often be an extra man along, and I found myself right back in the teenage terrors, panting with eagerness and interest to hold the attention of the (usually) insipid escort, no matter how I felt. This didn't make sense after years of that happy contentment of jogging along with your one-and-only, talking nonsense or world politics or grocery bills or just not talking at all.

Then, I discovered that my married friends could be sorted into two groups, from my new point of focus. The not-so-nice ones, the wives who flirted discreetly from behind their marital status with my escort (which was unimportant but unflattering, since he usually basked in it and neglected me), and the corresponding husbands who tried to be flattering, or comforting (I don't know which) by flirting with me! This was even sillier, since for years we had talked families, houses and gardening.

The second group comprised the Kind People—the ones who tried to look after me so hard and so pityingly that they depressed me.

Besides all this, I was back working now, and didn't quite fit into my old niche of family groups. It was like trying to force the wrong piece into part of a jigsaw puzzle.

As for going out with men, alone, that resolved itself very simply into one conclusion. If it wasn't dull it was dangerous.

～

With our husbands overseas, thousands of us have gone back to the status of working women. We are again typing letters, balancing ledgers, hoisting trays or wrapping parcels. We snatch hurried hair-do's at the nearest beauty parlors and rush unescorted here and there. Or rather, I *did* rush unescorted until I realized that I could be having a lot more fun with women. Other women—the ones I had paid so little attention to in pre-Hitler days.

So I began to look longingly into the inner circles of the little feminine groups I saw everywhere. The girls who went in threesomes and foursomes to gay, laughing lunch dates in downtown rush hours. The ones who went together to war-work meetings at night or met for movies and a sundae. And I began to discover that they had something I wanted very much. An honest, candid friendship I hadn't had since I was a schoolgirl. But I had forgotten the password.

The first real meeting-ground I had with my neighborhood women came the day my small daughter got lost. Tearing home from work when Sheila's disappearance from the neighborhood play lot was discovered, I found every woman on the street out looking like mad. Precious gas was being used in scouring the neighborhood. One woman had started off on her son's bicycle. Another had called the police, and by the time I arrived the posse was dragnetting the district. When she was found in the alluring atmosphere of the closest ten-cent store, I looked around at the other women, and realized that they were as white and shaken as I was. At that moment I knew I had a kinship with other women, through our children, that no man could ever share.

In the office I began to make timid gestures to the girls I worked with. I asked one of them home to dinner. I offered to stay late one evening when I wasn't in a hurry, and finish some stencilling for

another. I happened to overhear that it was a third's birthday, so I brought back a rosebud at noon and slipped it on her desk. That was the straitlaced, old-maidish type I had always found fair game for jokes with the men I had known. She's one of my best friends now—and I've spent many happy hours in her charming little apartment, listening to her symphonic records. Every mother of young children who hasn't at least one unmarried "girl friend" whose apartment is a quiet sanctuary is losing a great bet.

Maybe I was wrong in being so sure that George wouldn't want me to bother with other women when he was around; that he would laugh at me for going to movies and concerts and a dinner downtown with other girls. I realize now why George clung so tenaciously to his men friends, some of them strange, dull creatures I couldn't see for sour apples. He got a kind of refreshment and kinship from them that I get from other women; enjoyed them as "people" in a clear uncolored atmosphere.

I'm going to keep my women friends when he comes back. Earning them has been my particular good fortune out of the emotional bankruptcy of war.

# Why Are Women So Hard on Each Other?

*By nature, we're tender, warm-hearted and loyal to our friends. But, says the author, let a woman become "too ambitious," aspire to public office, be too attractive to men—and in a flash we unite in acid-tongued attack*

BY EILEEN MORRIS

**FEBRUARY 1963**

MEN, GOD BLESS 'EM, can't understand it. After a few uncomfortable minutes spent listening to women taking verbal, tea-thin slices out of one another's hide, they flee in terror into For Men Only citadels.

Women *are* hard on women.

Even the many fine, gracious and kindly souls quick to help, to comfort or to rejoice with their many women friends will balk at working for a woman, or refuse to vote for a woman. Amiable matrons who work well with their sisters in ladies' auxiliaries become critical of the woman acquaintance who is appointed to the library board, or who is picked by the town paper as Mother of the Year.

Civilization, as Freud explained, is not natural. It involves constant and painful repressions of primitive natural urges. And man's age-old tendency during the mating season to wander from flower to flower, seeking the sweetest, sparks a sexual jealousy among women that bubbles away beneath our garden party effusions.

A girl who is husband-hunting sights every skirted competitor down her gun barrel, ready to pull the trigger if a rival comes in firing range. And after the wedding the bride plays it safe and snaps the transom on her old girl friends, including the four who furled themselves in nylon tulle and stood up with her at the altar.

This prickly heat breaks out inside the family circle, too. Vance Packard, author of *The Hidden Persuaders*, describes a home-permanent-wave ad picturing a mother and daughter with identical hairdos and captioned, "A Double Header Hit with Dad." When interviewed, wives said that they didn't object to the implied competition for the husband-father's admiration, but depth interviews revealed that women did indeed resent the hit-with-dad theme as too great a strain on mother love, and it was hastily dropped.

We women have been raised on a heady diet of female folklore, to wit, that the one thing holding Woman back from the heights is the perversity of men. But in his long lift up from the veldt, man has fought for his woman, protected her, and brought her the sweetest bits of Brontosaurus and boxed bonbons. Now, when occasionally men invite women to help run this battered planet, where are the girls? Peeking out from the cave, aiming pot shots at any woman rash enough to step ahead of her species.

With status in the community now largely determined by do-good groups, the society page, that quaint anachronism in the modern newspaper, provides a daily stock market report on how well such women are forwarding the careers of their husbands. Two University of Chicago professors, surveying over eight thousand U. S. VIPs, conclude that the wife's participation in community work can be a direct steppingstone to getting to know "the right people."

The one job a good many well-off women can take without breaking caste is that of community servicewoman. Possessing enough executive ability to boss the amalgamated transport systems for all of Canada, such a woman pours all her energies into committee work, inevitably gaining a reputation a sergeant-major might envy.

Sociologist Mhyra S. Minnis took her scientific microscope into New Haven, Connecticut, to find out why clubwomen aren't the power they should be. She reports women there divided into dozens of racial, religious and foreign-background groups and subgroups. She found members of each group disinclined to work with women of other social groups of their own race, religion, or ethnic stock. Concludes Dr. Minnis: "Not until women become more democratic among themselves can they exert their full force politically, for public welfare, and for their own advancement."

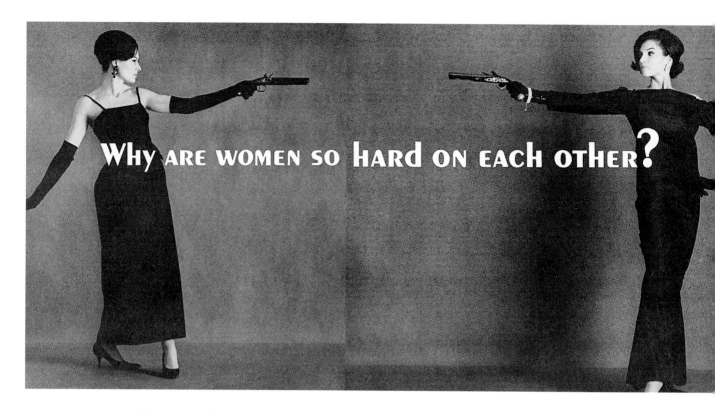

# WHY ARE WOMEN SO HARD ON EACH OTHER?

Psychiatrist William Menninger notes: "It seems more difficult for women than for men to live and mix indiscriminately—dullards with college grads, the poor with the rich, the gauche with the cultured."

The plain-Jane in sturdy shoes is permitted freedom of speech and action; as the girl of no man's dreams, women view her with forbearance. Criticism increases in direct ratio to a woman's sex appeal. Let an experienced woman—especially a pretty one—declare she's going to run for public office, and overnight the female electorate begin handing out those familiar swatches of Victorian crepe: "Women aren't as clear thinking as men." "A man is more practical minded." "No woman is stable enough for public life." It isn't a question of sex, they contend, but of capacity.

The woman candidate learns a painful fact: women are far more prejudiced against their sex than are men. Says Mrs. Jean Newman, of Toronto, "When I was defeated in the (Toronto) mayoralty race I had women tell me I should have been satisfied with remaining a controller for life because the mayor's chair was no place for a woman."

Let the son of a male councilor wrap the family car round a pole and women agree how distressing it must be for the father. But let the son of a woman alderman err, and she is viewed with all the sympathetic understanding of a hanging judge: "Of course what can you expect, the poor lad has *no mother*."

An ambitious woman intent on climbing the career ladder learns en-route that many female hands are raised against her. Pay as you go up is the rule. Employers agree the main hindrance to advancement of women is the problem faced by women supervisors of acceptance by other women employees. A Toronto job-placement agency report shows seventy percent of women job seekers don't want a woman boss.

We anticipate criticism, because we women are so very critical ourselves. A woman tends to see everything in terms of herself. Ask a man to explain his file system and he'll explain it. Ask a woman and she'll flare, "What's wrong with the way I do it?" Every remark is a wound, especially when it's dished out by that devil, the woman boss.

We are so personal in our approach because woman's life has been intensely personal, focused on her family. For centuries woman was a chattel, submissive, with no property but her man. Many a woman still sees herself and her sex through male eyes, judging all women by the valuation which men have traditionally set on them. Thus married women are elect and bound for glory, worthier than single women. The woman who holds fast to the male oak is more "virtuous" than the woman who steps out of its shade.

Many of our attributes, mental experts will tell you, are the sign of an inferiority complex.

Simone de Beauvoir in her book *The Second Sex* recognizes the handicaps of woman's subjection and those that have been imposed by cultural forces. She points out that women have no past, no history, no religion of their own. We live dispersed among the males, attached through residence, housework, economic condition and social standing to certain men—fathers or husbands—more firmly than we are to other women. If we belong to the middle class we feel solidarity with men of that class, not with lower-class women: if we are white, our allegiance is to white men, not to Negro women.

Women, a house divided, rush in to damn their own. Working wives twit single girls while declaring that wives who stay home are aimless time-wasters; wives at home pat their back hair and show single girls heavy sympathy while labeling working mothers inhuman monsters. We don't like the work women do. Domestic service is looked down upon as menial; the charwoman marks the cellar on the social scale.

Women lose a great deal because we are unkind to each other—so does the world. "The task will not be complete," says Lynn Whyte, Jr., in *Educating Our Daughters*, "until women respect women as much as they do men, until women by achieving respect for themselves, win the full respect of men and until women are as glad to be women as men are to be men."

# Unmasking "The Curse"

*Or, how did such a perfectly natural function get to be such a terrible shame?*

By Michele Landsberg

**JANUARY 1974**

THERE IS NO MALE PARALLEL to menstruation. There is no other normal bodily function that has cast half the adult population, in almost every society in every age, in the dark shadow of a stigma. If future historians were restricted to the study of just one phenomenon, menstruation, they would have a perfectly complete history of male chauvinism . . . and of how deeply women have accepted male evaluations of female functions.

Listen to a group of young women, most in their early twenties:

"I got my period when I was ten . . . My brothers used to tease me about it; they called it "riding the rag," and later, when I had a crush on the older boy next door, they'd tell him and he'd tease me, too. It was agony, really."

"It was a complete shock to me when I started. In my small town, no one ever breathed a word about these things; it was too horrifying. I thought I was bleeding to death. I never really got over my feeling of distaste."

"It was mysterious and thrilling and disgusting all at once . . . like joining a secret club."

"The worst terror was the thought of 'showing.' Every time you got up you would feel the back of your skirt to make sure . . . as though one harmless spot of blood was so shameful you could die of it."

"In my hometown we all heard about the thirteen-year-old girl who went to the store to buy pads. On the way home, a bunch of boys grabbed the bag from her and took the box out and started throwing it around the street. But I'll never forget that it was two of the toughest, roughest guys in town who made them stop."

"To this day, I can't say the words 'table napkin'

in front of people, because 'napkin' is such an embarrassing word."

"The worst part of all was wearing that bulky, chafing pad between your legs. It made you feel so strange. You couldn't wear jeans in case it showed. You couldn't use tampons . . . only bad girls used them, because it proved you had lost your virginity."

Tampons, of course, have been one of the greatest liberating factors in many women's physical lives, outside of the birth control pill. Revealingly, although crude forms of the tampon (rolls of wool or cotton) were commonly used in ancient civilizations, fifteen centuries B.C., and doctors had been using them therapeutically for the past century, nobody even thought of making them commercially available until just before the Second World War.

*If you eat fruit with pits, you'll get pockmarks; if you pour milk, it will turn sour; you can't go out in the rain, go barefoot, eat oranges, watermelon or coffee or anything cold*

When they did come on the market, they caused a storm of controversy: many doctors were outspoken in their conviction that tampons might cause all sorts of infections, cancer, immorality (due to excess stimulation of the vagina!) or even might be used illicitly as a contraceptive.

The most basic medical homework would have revealed that a) such tampons actually cause less irritation than pads; b) there are no medical side effects; c) there are no nerve endings within the vagina to be stimulated; and d) tampons would seem to be an efficient barrier to intercourse rather than to conception.

Even today, though it was medically proven as long ago as 1945 that tampons in no way interfered with the hymen, most young girls still are restricted to pads, for no other reason than their mothers' mistaken sense of sexual delicacy.

All ancient religions stigmatized the menstruating woman as unclean, and women internalized the disgust, dutifully isolating themselves or taking themselves off to the ritual bath.

Women who adhere to orthodox Judaism and Catholicism, which emphasize the traditional feminine role, are far more apt to suffer menstrual distress than the career-woman type, according to a detailed study reported in *Psychology Today*. Undoubtedly some cramps and anxiety are due to

hormonal influences, the researcher, concludes, but "the blues may be born of the pervasive, negative cultural attitudes about menstruation and menstrual blood." A Toronto health educator confirmed that many New Canadian girls from traditional backgrounds (Italian, Portuguese, Polish, Chinese, Indian) still refuse to swim during their period. "We had a whole class of girls, not so long ago, who were convinced that they mustn't touch their baby brothers or sisters during their period, or that if they touched any plant it would die," he commented. "Their teacher had to keep a plant on her desk and have them touch it every day, for a whole term, before they were convinced it wasn't true."

One high school class in an immigrant community yielded the following myths: if you preserve tomatoes during your period, you'll hemorrhage; if you eat fruit with pits, you'll get pockmarks; if you pour milk, it will turn sour; you can't go out in the rain, go barefoot, eat oranges, watermelon or coffee or anything cold; if you go out on a date, he'll know by your eyes that you're menstruating.

That menstruation has been viewed with horror in so many cultures has been attributed by some (including Freud) to the male's fear of blood, which he unconsciously equates with castration. And there may have been a fear of the unknown, since the cause and purpose of menstruation was not discovered until the late nineteenth century, when doctors linked lack of menstruation during pregnancy to ovulation, conception and birth.

Most women will have cramps (or dysmenorrhea) at some point in their menstrual life; some women always have. Half of all women have them severely enough to complain of them.

The gynecology textbooks, to this day, tend to brush off dysmenorrhea as "more frequent in a high-strung, nervous or neurotic female than in her more stable sister." One medical article goes so far as to state, "Pain is always secondary to an emotional problem."

The truth is that once again, women are the victims of male propaganda and faulty socialization.

Drs. Jean and John Lennane pointed out last year, in the *New England Journal of Medicine*, that an imbalance of hormones released during ovulation apparently causes uterine cramping. Despite the complex hormonal changes in your body during the menstrual cycle, experts are finally proving that a woman's actual performance is very little affected by the cycle, no matter how she may feel. Olympic athletes, according to a research report in the *British Journal of Physical Medicine*, are undeterred by their periods; a significant number even reported that their performance improved during menstruation, and they set world records to prove it.

## WHY WE NEED TO TALK ABOUT IT

### *A selection of recent quotes from 13- and 14-year-old girls in a Canadian high school.*

- Menstruation is the bad blood that needs to come out.
- It's when you have too much blood for your system and it's forced out through your virgina.
- The waste of food is formed into blood and you get rid of it. And it is also a time of month.
- Minenstration is when the stuff that should hold on to the egg is discharged.
- It happens when the ovaries loose an egg and it goes through the cyclopean tubes.
- An ovary is released from the two passages and comes down the virginia.
- It occurs because we need to bring in new blood in case of a baby so we let off the old blood.
- You get rid of the wasted blood and this cleanses the body.
- The lining of the fallopian tubes dissolves . . .
- The cells drop out . . . unless the woman has been intercoursed.

## WHAT HIGH SCHOOL GIRLS ARE CALLING IT

| | |
|---|---|
| Charlie Brown | The Vampire |
| Dracula's Coming | The blessing |
| "28" | The plug (*a tampon*) |
| Matilda | Vampire's tea bag (*tampon*) |
| Mattress (*sanitary pad*) | |
| Kwash (*a reference to the disease kwashiorkor*) | |
| Harpoon (*tampon with insertion stick*) | |
| Lollipop (*tampon with paper covering*) | |

## ANCIENT (MALE) HISTORY OF MENSTRUATION

Nearly all primitive tribes, from Eskimos to Australasians, had rigorous taboos about the menstruating woman . . . particularly about the girl experiencing her first period, who was universally believed to be in the grip of some awesome power. Some examples:

An Australian native, who discovered that his wife had lain on his blanket during her period, killed her and died of terror himself within two weeks. Women of this tribe were forbidden, on pain of death, to walk on the same paths as men, or touch their belongings.

Among some American Indians, a "polluted" woman had to live in an isolated hut, live on dried fish and water, wear a special bonnet that completely covered her head so her gaze might not fall on any living things, and must not touch anything belonging to a man.

In New Ireland, an island in the West Pacific, native girls from the age of eight to ten were secluded for four or five years in totally darkened grass cages, with room only to crouch. Meager provisions were set out daily in bowls; the girls were allowed to emerge from their darkness only once each day, to bathe in a tub near the cage. Several Canadian tribes sewed the pubescent girls into hammocks suspended from the hut roof for a week at a time. In other parts of the world, pubescent girls at their first period were buried to their necks in the earth and forced to starve until they were skeletal.

"Bees . . . will forsake their hive if touched by a menstruous woman; linen boiling in a cauldron will turn black . . . copper vessels will contract a fetid smell . . . A mare big with foal, if touched by a woman in this state, will be sure to miscarry. Indeed, so pernicious are its properties that . . . a pregnant woman, if touched with it, or indeed if she so much as steps over it, will be liable to miscarry . . ."

—THE NATURAL HISTORY OF PLINY

"If you had an investment in a bank, you wouldn't want the president of your bank making a loan under these raging hormonal influences at that particular period . . ."

—DR. EDGAR F. BERMAN, PHYSICIAN AND A
FRIEND OF HUBERT H. HUMPHREY, 1970

# Are Men Obsolete?

BY JUNE CALLWOOD

APRIL **1974** THE DAY BEFORE yesterday, when everyone knew what manliness was all about, Hollywood presented it best. Movie males had an immutable set of characteristics, all of them rooted to inner conviction. The screen was an ode to maleness.

"Don't go out there, Frank. They'll kill you!"

"Out of my way, woman. A man's gotta do his duty."

No one doubted it, certainly not the audiences, most certainly not Frank, and least of all the grateful woman. Only the day before yesterday Frank was neither a chauvinist nor a joke.

Women's lib, and related insights, have sent Frank to Boot Hill, that all-male preserve inhabited by knights and other wearers of armored codpieces. His ghost still haunts porno movies, board rooms, beer commercials and Parliament Hill, but the snap has gone out of his performance. He's a closet king who has to pick his audience very carefully. He doesn't say "Out of my way, woman" any more, not out loud.

Whatever he does say in a well-intentioned attempt to be contemporary has a bewildering tendency to turn against him.

"I've always let my wife work," explained a pleased and paunchy executive to a woman he judged to be a feminist.

"Did you say '*let* her'?" she enquired.

"Darling," said a husband proudly, "I've washed your kitchen floor."

"Darling," she responded, "it's your floor, too."

At a rally in Toronto's Town Hall of women interested in politics, a man in the audience rose to his feet when the discussion was growing heated and with a charming smile and both arms upraised declared, "Ladies, I love you all." He was resoundingly booed.

The New Woman is everywhere, dancing a jig, snapping her fingers, making up new steps, looking full of judo. The New Man is nowhere. He doesn't seem to have been invited to the celebration.

This clearly is a dicey time to be a male. The Tarzan-Jane syndrome, embedded in a society dominated by confident hunting males who kept females at the back of the cave, was full of creature comforts for both of them. Jane and Tarzan knew exactly what was expected of them, even to the personalities they were to assume.

When that insane sanity vanished in a welter of liberation slogans, fair employment practices, procreation control and atypical female spunkiness, the visible gains went entirely to Jane. She's now swinging in the treetops, mobile and frisky in the jungle for the first time in her life, and having a fine time.

It's less easy to be Tarzan. He's been requested not to obstruct progress, but no one has informed him what else he is supposed to do.

Jane attends a consciousness-raising session and returns briskly with a new design for keeping the cave clean. Tarzan figures very large in the scheme. How did that happen?

Sound, established marriages are creaking as conversion sets in. Last Christmas a grandmother rebelled at cooking the traditional dinner for four generations. "It's too much work," she told her husband. "Let's go away this year." He was shocked; he said he'd help her, and he did. As they finished the clean-up together at two in the morning, with him at the vacuum cleaner and her in the kitchen, he called out, "How about Acapulco next Christmas?"

Young marriages may look as though they have it all figured out—the baby in a pack on her father's back, the wife at her office in faded jeans—but they are not collision free. Many young men have it in their heads what equality is all about but, in a crunch, when the woman's springiness suddenly invades some unperceived male territorial space, their sense of injury comes from deep-rooted, gut-sensed, old-fashioned masculinity.

Women in their twenties speak of the wooden carefulness of the men around them, the watchfulness to submerge old habits and adopt new that underlies the open willingness to share the cooking, cleaning and marketing. They are the first men in a different space, and are full of caution, apprehension, faith, and nerve.

Their ears and eyes, however, were trained in another generation. They can't hear the small child calling for release from the bathtub or see the laundry piling up. "And I've yet to know of a man who doesn't leave cleaning the toilet bowl to women," groaned one young wife.

Few men older than three are prepared for women's liberation. Frank Movie Hero never touched a broom in his life and no one wanted him to. In his day, just a short time ago, boss and man were interchangeable words. Authority and mobility in women were considered hormonal aberrations, like a man weeping.

Archetypal manhood had certain natural attributes, beginning with superiority to women. *Noblesse oblige* demanded gallantry towards the less endowed, which resulted in patronizing laws, protective restrictions and door-holding. A suggestion of the brute beneath was an exciting asset. Rape, the ultimate demonstration of male authority, haunted fantasy lives. It solved the problem of males who fundamentally disliked women and had nothing to say to them and the double bind of sexually adult females who were constrained by the requirement that ladies be passive and prudish.

Male parents used to tell their male children, "When you grow up you'll be a *man*, my son."

"When you grow up you'll be a *person*, my son," is likely a larger challenge, but it doesn't have the same ring, not yet.

It is familiar wisdom to observe now that the outrageous expectations men and women put upon men could only be maintained by gerrymandering both sexes. Women pined only for those men who were taller, older, smarter and stronger than they were. The necessity for women to be dumber than men was more adjustable. Women cultivated incompetence, often brilliantly.

Some thirty years ago, wartime shortages in the labor market put women in skilled jobs for the first time since the previous war. They adjusted to the unfamiliar landscape in ways that were not threatening to the men around them: they flirted, they admired, they smiled a lot, and they made the coffee. When things went wrong they didn't curse or shout, they cried.

It was the era of the double message. A man inherently was the boss but he could be conned. Women employed by men ingratiated themselves into job security either by being motherly or faintly siren, whatever worked best; married women swapped fond condescending anecdotes about how they bought new living-room drapes and Harry didn't even notice.

During the late fifties and early sixties this very magazine was a paramedical journal that addressed itself to an inexplicable epidemic of housewife discontent. Its symptoms included such phenomena as housewife fatigue, housewife depression, the housewife shrew, frigid housewives, and a condition known as the nervous breakdown which, peculiarly, occurred almost exclusively in thirty-five-year-old women.

The cure for all ailments was the same: the housewife was instructed to get more bread out on the waters. Husbands were to be coddled and praised, homes were to be converted to welcoming bowers; women should fake orgasms. The intent was to bolster male self-esteem and instill guilt, which would produce for the woman a fallout of appreciation and improved foreplay.

The advice was so luminous with The Word that it wasn't noticed much at the time that it was also patronizing. If one sex was to disseminate noble sweetness and light and the other merely to receive and reflect it, it set women up as competent and crafty and men as simps.

Women raised their sons so that other women—wives, secretaries, whatever—could do that to them successfully. It begins in the cradle. Harvard psychologist Jerome Kagan notes that women fondle male infants less frequently than female infants. He suspects that on a subconscious level it is early training for independence. When all of the rest of society's reinforcement for male isolation falls upon him, the man is likely to have a flat emotional tone and not much ability to reach out and touch. He's a set-up for a warm, outgoing someone: woman.

A great many women cuddled naturally into

> *They flirted, they admired, they smiled a lot, and they made the coffee. When things went wrong they didn't curse or shout, they cried*

playing the game, but it was hard on perceptive men and harder still on brainy women. In the postwar era they shared a nightmare that their cerebral deformity would show, taking them off the marriage market. They hid their talents under their hairdos and worried that they wouldn't be able to find a man strong enough and smart enough so they could relax and let him steer. They said to one another, "I wouldn't want a man I couldn't look up to."

That was Frank's job, protecting women; their job was to applaud and reward. It was a zany arrangement from the point of view of human self-realization and full development, but it worked for a very long time as we are aware.

Movie heroes in the sixties began to reflect the change. Marlon Brando scratching fleas and bellowing for Stella lost its raunchy appeal. John Wayne's taciturn masculinity became so funny he noticed it himself. Paul Newman's best role, that of cool-eyed stud, was less and less anyone's ideal for a lifetime companion.

Dustin Hoffman arrived, sensitive, small and unsure; recognizably human. *Dustin Hoffman!* He was labeled a nonhero, which isn't accurate. He is a genuine hero of emerging alternatives for maleness. Robert Redford, a man of obsolete perfection, found himself a decade too late and was relegated to playing boyish caricatures.

There is no firm shape to the ideal mate any more. The tugs of erotic allure continue to be the capricious element, but the trend these days is for people to mate in order to find partners and friends. Yesterday's classic authoritarian-with-satellite model was not seen as healthy for either men or women.

The shift has been a pure pleasure for women, to whom the visible benefits accrue. However, it is difficult for men not to imagine that if women are getting more, men must be getting less. This would be true if the world were a cherry pie, but not if human development is an infinity. If the outcome is that both men and women expand their capacities to love and enjoy, no one loses.

The New Man, Frank Movie Star's successor, is around after all. He isn't obvious for a good reason: the New Woman's growth is outward but his is inner. When they are finished, they'll have a lot to talk about. And the children they raise will be people.

# The Irene Murdoch Case

*When they separated, the law said: Husband take all*

By Eve Rockett

WHEN THE SUPREME COURT of Canada's decision came down in October of 1973, denying Irene Murdoch any legal right to her share of the Alberta family ranch, thousands of concerned women realized, perhaps for the first time, how fragile their own property claims were under family law.

For over twenty-five years, Irene Murdoch was a rancher's wife. She didn't have to fight to work on an equal basis with her man. She was right in there—an equal partner—vaccinating, dehorning and branding cattle; haying, swathing, raking and mowing; driving trucks, tractors and teams of horses. When her husband, Alex, was away for five months of the year (he worked for a stock association) she ran the entire ranching operation.

In 1968 the Murdochs had an historic argument. It started when Alex announced that he wanted to sell out and start all over again, and feelings became so inflamed on the subject that there was a scuffle and her husband broke her jaw in three places. He then took her to the emergency ward at the Holy Cross Hospital. She had with her just the clothes she was wearing—blouse, slacks, ankle socks and slippers.

Unlike in the movies, there was no buoyant, instantaneous recovery. (In fact her shattered jaw has resulted in a partial paralysis of her mouth, and she can't afford any more dental bills.) Alex drove Irene to the hospital, but when she returned home, jaw wired up, she found the door locked and all her credit cut off at the local merchandisers.

She, of course, turned to the courts, assuming she would be granted a share of ownership rights in the ranch. Five years ago it was valued at $75,000 and has probably tripled since then. Apart from the considerable manual contributions she had made in twenty-five years, she was also instrumental in financing the property they acquired, and money from Irene's mother helped pay for three new properties, which were later sold to buy their present 480-acre ranch in Turner Valley. Irene produced the canceled cheques as evidence of this in court, but lost her case in the Supreme Court of Alberta.

The case was finally presented to the Supreme Court of Canada, where a panel of five judges (the exception, Mr. Justice—now Chief Justice—Bora Laskin) resoundingly ruled that Irene Murdoch had made "only the normal contribution to the farm that most farm or ranch wives make." After twenty-five years of laboriously building a business, she had no rights to the ranch. No rights at all.

Alex Murdoch has the land, the farm buildings, the machinery, the matrimonial home, the furniture, the car and all revenue from the farm and cattle. Irene receives a maintenance allowance—based on her husband's net income before today's inflation of land and wheat prices. She works as a cleaning woman to supplement the pitiful $70 left after the $130-a-month rent is paid on the house where she now lives. She still faces $2,000 in medical bills from her fractured jaw—1968 was pre-medicare—and was ordered to pay the entire court costs of about $3,500.

In the past, Irene has managed to thwart her husband's divorce proceedings, which upon divorce, would also rob her of inheritance and dower rights. But time has run out; the five years of noncohabitation since their separation have provided legal grounds for divorce.

If the case of Irene Murdoch has given a new flush of energy and meaning to the cause of women's rights, the woman herself is weary. She has presented her case to three major courts—and lost. There is only one chance left: divorce action in the Supreme Court of Alberta, or settlement of an as yet undesignated lump sum. If she loses that—at the age of forty-nine she has lost it all.

In the beginning, she answered questions and agreed to be interviewed by the media because she thought it would help other women. But the rudeness of familiarity finally got to her. She has no phone; if something important comes up, she is reached through a neighbor.

At the beginning of April, her husband entered the hospital for an operation, and until she knew if he would be all right, she refused to talk. Says Irene's lawyer Ernest Shymka, "No matter what happened, she doesn't want to hurt him. She *never* attempted to hurt him. There is no maliciousness in Irene Murdoch whatsoever."

A lot of women find it difficult to realize that the nature of our law courts is based on the "adversary" system of justice. After decades of sharing a man's bed and destiny, they can't seem to think of him as an "adversary," and that here in court it's a *fight*, and you just can't care about your opponent.

# Are We Winning the War Against Rape?

*In the last few years we have seen changes in the law and in the treatment of rape victims by police, doctors and courts. Does this mean women no longer suffer a bitter aftermath to sexual violence and that rapists are less likely to go free?*

BY MYRNA KOSTASH

SEPTEMBER 1981

LET THIS SINK IN. THE accused, 31, bodily carried his ex-fiancée from her parents' home to his car and drove her to his apartment. There, he said, he grabbed her pajama top and pulled it off. "She said, 'Boy, I hate you.' I said, 'I love you and I want to spend the rest of my life with you.'" He said she participated in sexual intercourse and there was no indication that she did not want to have sex with him. Verdict: acquittal.

*Let this sink in.* The complainant, 17 years old: a nice friendly man approached her at a bus stop and offered to drive her around as she looked for an apartment to rent; he then drove into the country, ordered her into the backseat of the car and raped her. The accused, 26 years old and married: she was hitchhiking, he drove her around, they then drove into the country where they drank and had sexual intercourse; no violence, threat or force was used. Verdict: acquittal.

According to the Canadian Advisory Council on the Status of Women, a woman is raped every 29 minutes in Canada. Somewhere, in this country, every six minutes, a woman is sexually assaulted. Since 1969 reported rapes have increased 125 percent. We all live in Rape City.

Rape. Legally, under the current law, the vaginal penetration of a woman against her will. Mythologically, the lust-crazed bogyman jumping on us from behind bushes. In real life, in a bar with friends, we meet a friend of a friend, we talk, we joke, he says he'll drive us home, we trust him, he drives us to a dead-end suburban street, slaps us around, he does this and that to our body, we are crying, we think we are going to die. It is finished. He helps us put our clothes back on.

Rape crisis workers say that two-thirds of reported rapes are between people who know each other, if only casually. Four-fifths are planned. A third takes place in the victim's home, and almost a fifth takes place in broad daylight. Half of reported rapes are gang rapes, the most vicious of all. Four-fifths of rapists either carry a weapon or threaten their victim with violence. If caught, they will report they were "amazed" at what they got away with, at her lack of "response," at her "nerve" for having reported what happened: she was hitchhiking, wasn't she?

The aftermath of rape has always been the same. Today, however, it's called "rape trauma syndrome." In the first phase, the victim feels physical pain from the attack and may suffer headache, edginess, stomach pain and nausea. She will also experience a gamut of emotions, anything from humiliation, self-hatred, anger, false calm to fear and disbelief. In the second phase, which may last years, she may experience life-style disorganization (changing her residence and telephone number, friends and habits, for instance); she may suffer

> *She may experience life-style disorganization (changing her residence and telephone number, friends and habits, for instance); she may suffer nightmares, sexual repulsion, fear of the indoors, fear of the outdoors, of being alone, of crowds, of being followed, of falling asleep*

nightmares, sexual repulsion, fear of the indoors, fear of the outdoors, of being alone, of crowds, of being followed, of falling asleep.

❧

Who is she, this ubiquitous victim of rape? In the Clark and Lewis study of reported rapes in the city of Toronto in 1970, 58 percent of the victims were 14 to 24 years old, slightly younger than the majority of their assailants. Fully one-third, however, was older than 30. The majority was single. Their occupations ranged from student to professional to housewife and included the unemployed. The rape victim is you and me and the woman next door.

The psychological profile of the rapist reveals just what you'd expect. *Child at Risk*, a report of the Standing Senate Committee on Health, Welfare and Science, 1980, says: "Most of the violence that develops in the lives of young people who become miscreants of one kind and another—thieves, bullies, even rapists and murderers—can be ascribed to the aggressive behavior these . . . individuals received as children."

Sex itself carries the prodigious baggage of the masculine identity—power, authority, dominance, aggressiveness—and if it is true that rapists are the "epitome of the insecure man" (according to Dr. Luke Glancy of the Abbotsford, B.C., Regional Psychiatric Centre), then, for such a man, sex and women are intertwined with feelings of frustration, humiliation, rage and revenge. Sex to a rapist is not about seeking pleasure, but about establishing masculinity, having *power* over women.

Now add to this a vivid fantasy life, the consumption of pornography and the subconscious flashbacks to childhood trauma, and you get men who, in the words of Johns Hopkins University sex researcher Dr. John Money, "instead of getting rid of sex, get rid of females." Are these, as the police would have it, sex perverts? Or are they the boys next door, the ones we grew up with, the ones we date and marry?

I give you the experts. Dr. Elliott Barker, a psychiatrist at the social therapy unit of the Penetanguishene Mental Health Centre in Ontario, says in *Why Men Rape* (edited by Sylvia Levine and Joseph Koenig, Macmillan, $7.95) that his rapist patients are convinced they are okay and that it is someone else's fault they are there; treatment is directed toward showing them they *are* sick. Dr. Herb Pascoe, a psychiatrist in the forensic department of Alberta Hospital in Edmonton, says the "control rapist" is far more common than the "butcher"—and the hardest to prosecute. "With the former, threats are used, but not beatings," he says. "Semen in the vagina tells you intercourse took place, but not how it was precipitated." The butcher is easier to prosecute because of the violence and mutilation that take place.

As Clark and Lewis state, the "discovery that the rapist is 'normal' has had a significant impact on general attitudes toward rape . . . Its main effect has been to undermine even further the status of rape as a serious offence. If most rape offenders do not fit the picture of the 'real rapist,' then it follows that their crime is not considered 'real rape,' but . . . a misdemeanor of the everyday variety." In other words, boys will be boys.

∾

The rape. The police. The hospital. Then, for a fraction of rapists and rape victims, the courtroom. A man who rapes in Canada stands a 94-percent chance of not being arrested.

According to Clark and Lewis, about 55 percent of prosecuted rapes in Canada in 1971 concluded in a conviction. (The general conviction rate for criminal offences is 86 percent.) But in Vancouver in 1975, 104 rapes were reported, 24 accused committed to trial, six dismissed and four convicted, a rate of 4 percent. And if it's true that only about 10 percent of rapes are reported, as is estimated by the Advisory Council on the Status of Women, the *real* rate of conviction was 0.4 percent.

The maximum sentence for rape is life imprisonment. For attempted rape, 10 years. For indecent assault on a male, 10 years. Indecent assault on a *female*, five years. A particularly violent rape, seven to 12 years. A "normal" rape, two years less a day to four to five years.

In 1976, amendments to the Criminal Code limited examination of the complainant's sexual history. The accused's lawyer must inform the prosecutor that he/she wants to conduct such an examination; and the judge must decide, after a closed hearing, whether the complainant's sexual history has any bearing on the case or on her "credibility" as a witness.

At first, feminists and antirape activists welcomed the amendment. Five years later, considerable disillusion has set in. Under the old system, a complainant under cross-examination could simply say she had never had intercourse with anybody other than the accused and that was the end of it. Now, if the judge has ruled she must answer a question about her sexual history and she denies sexual experience, the defence can bring in its own witnesses to try to contradict her. We're back to: "Isn't it a fact, Miss X, that you are not a virgin?"

To make matters worse, in 1978, a trial judge in Toronto refused to allow the lawyer for Gregory Forsythe, an accused rapist, to cross-examine the complainant; the lawyer challenged his ruling, arguing that he had an "absolute right to question an alleged rape victim about her sexual activities" and that his client had been denied justice as a result of the ruling. The Supreme Court of Canada heard the case and in 1980 came down with a ruling that worries many women. It interprets the 1976 amendments to mean that it is not the complainant's sexual conduct that is at issue, it is the sheer *believability* of her testimony that counts.

We are moving here into the phenomenon known as "blaming the victim." A "good" woman, says society, resists rape to the death; may we not conclude that the woman who *is* raped wanted it, sought it?

# Guns and Money: The New Abortion Wars

*On today's abortion battlefield, government funding is the weapon of choice, but the fear of violence rules*

BY DEBORAH JONES

**MAY 1996**

ON NOVEMBER 8, 1994, B.C. pro-choice activist Joy Thompson walked into her office at the British Columbia Coalition for Abortion Clinics and played her phone messages. One began: "You murderous slut, you killer of unborn innocent children, you bimbo bitch and slag heap." It ended with a threat on her life.

Earlier that day, a bullet from an assault rifle had smashed through sliding glass doors into the kitchen of Dr. Garson Romalis, sliced an artery in his thigh and nearly killed him. Thompson had vented her outrage in the media; the phone message was the result.

The shooting of Garson Romalis changed everything in the war over abortion rights in Canada. As in the United States, where there have been five murders of abortion doctors and clinic staff in the past three years, our war over abortion has rolled inexorably from the courts and registered, from rallies and demonstrations, onto a volatile landscape where the stakes are life and death.

The past 25 years have not exactly spelled progress for the pro-life movement in Canada. The number of officially recorded abortions has risen almost tenfold, from 11,200 in 1970 to 104,400 in 1993—nearly one abortion for every four newborn Canadians (albeit a drop in the worldwide ocean of 45 million abortions each year). The Supreme Court of Canada decriminalized abortion in 1988; two years later, the Senate defeated legislation aimed at imposing new controls. Today, aside from the sort of professional regulations that govern all medical procedures, no law governs abortion in Canada. Opinion polls suggest that about eight out of 10 Canadians believe abortion is a private issue to be decided by a woman and her doctor.

Given this record—and given that, for a pro-lifer, an abortion equals a murdered baby—it should come as no surprise when a fringe few take desperate action.

∾

Joy Thompson joined the abortion battle in the late 1980s. It was a fraught time. In Ottawa, on January 28, 1988, the Supreme Court of Canada agreed with abortion doctor Henry Morgentaler's view that the anti-abortion law infringed on the Canadian Charter of Rights and Freedoms. Across the land, Morgentaler led the charge against provincial governments and, in some cases, medical societies, to allow freestanding abortion clinics.

Thompson, a wiry energetic 39-year-old, had trained as an orthopedic nurse in Britain before emigrating to Canada. A month after the landmark Supreme Court ruling, she was working in a women's health collective when she answered a distress call from a 17-year-old from northern B.C. who desperately wanted an abortion. With abortion de-insured, the teen could not afford the $1,100 hospital fee. Thompson directed her to a group of women in the collective who had raised an emergency abortion fund for just such cases.

Thompson could relate: at 19, she had also been pregnant and single. She chose to have that child, a son, now 19—and a second son, now 10. She has suffered a miscarriage and an ectopic pregnancy—and had an abortion (she says her birth control failed and she could not support a third child). "I know what motherhood means," she says fiercely, "I know one can't make a decision to be a mother casually. It's a decision that profoundly, to the core of your existence, changes who you are in the world."

So, in 1988, Thompson joined other women volunteers to create Everywoman's Health Centre, a freestanding abortion and contraceptive clinic on Vancouver's east side. Today, she is the unpaid public spokeswoman for the British Columbia Coalition of Abortion Clinics, which lobbies for pro-choice issues in the province.

Wendy Barta's commitment, to the pro-life cause, is equally intense. Raised in a conservative New Brunswick town, Barta had discovered feminism in her women's studies courses as an education major at the University of Winnipeg. She simply accepted the prevailing feminist opinion that choice on abortion was a basic woman's right. As a student living in Winnipeg, near one of Morgentaler's abortion clinics, she saw "people marching up and down outside the clinic. I felt they were nuts. I did my part in snubbing them."

That winter, a friend mentioned the Supreme Court ruling, noting that in theory abortion was now legal *right up to nine months*. For Barta, this was going too far. Then, she had an epiphany. "In my mind I went back, from nine months, to three months, to the day after conception. It clicked. The person who is there at nine months is there the first day." Barta felt duped by the feminist orthodoxy. "I was upset, angry that I had followed the pro-choice dogma," says Barta, a teacher-turned-homemaker who now home-schools her daughter, 8, and son, 4. "I was very, very angry with myself."

Almost overnight, Barta turned into a fervent pro-life activist. But, a professed feminist, she was at odds with conservative right-wing pro-lifers who opposed equality for women. An agnostic, she took issue with religious fundamentalists who opposed sex education and, in the case of Catholics, contraception. And she disliked pro-lifers praying outside abortion clinics. Most pervasively, Barta felt that almost none of these pro-lifers "addressed the reasons why women have an abortion . . . the social and economic problems women face."

Then, a colleague told Barta about Feminists for Life, a pro-life group based in Washington committed to issues such as opposing poverty and violence. She was drawn to the group's pro-life but socially liberal agenda and, in 1990, helped found Canadian branches in Vancouver and Victoria.

∾

Winter 1996: year two of the new post-Romalis era of politics in Canada. It's unusually cold for Vancouver today, and Joy Thompson and I huddle over an antique wood table in her kitchen. Amid the domesticity of potted plants, a pile of children's coats and boots at the door, Thompson talks about the price of being a front-line pro-choice activist today.

After Romalis was shot, Thompson, speaking for the B.C. pro-choice community, criticized right-wing groups for inciting violence. The next month, a newspaper reporter warned her that her name was on a telephone message by a right-wing organization linked to skinheads and white-supremacist groups. The recorded message told callers to find Joy Thompson and "have fun, boys and girls." A few days later, someone broke into her house and stole, among other things, her files and computer records.

While no one has confessed to either shooting, a handful of activists have issued congratulations. "It was a nice piece of shooting because it sent a warning," said B.C. anti-abortion activist Gordon Watson of the Romalis shooting. "That bullet brought the message home to Dr. Romalis,"

Watson told CBC-TV's *the fifth estate*.

How many have heard the message? The Canadian Abortion Rights Action League (CARAL) estimates that of about 200 doctors who once performed abortions in Canada, 10 have quit recently in the face of violence or the fear of it.

The tension is evident when I visit Everywoman's one bright afternoon. Doctors and nurses perform abortions (2,200 a year) in a state of siege—steel bars, double doors, a security camera and an intercom system. Workers are trained to handle bomb threats. Like Thompson, some have had police risk assessments.

*Barta felt duped by the feminist orthodoxy. "I was upset, angry that I had followed the pro-choice dogma"*

Across the misty Strait of Georgia and on the other side of the abortion war, Wendy Barta is also alarmed by the effect of guns. Barta, who campaigned with people who now espouse violence, felt a paralyzing sense of betrayal when the violence broke out. "There's no single person to blame," she says, "so the whole pro-life movement is smeared with blood." The pro-life message, she says, is "that all life is precious and must be respected." Her logic is clear: what's true for babies is true for doctors. She also argues for social responsibility—everyone has a mandate, for example, to stop parents who abuse their children. "Stopping abortion is no different."

In the near future, medical developments could make ending a pregnancy easier than ever—and take abortions out of the range of guns. A non-profit health organization in New York has taken over the rights to market the European abortion-inducing drug known as RU486. If the drug is approved by U.S. regulators, its entry into Canada may soon follow.

Does the future offer pharmaceutical abortions, prescribed in the doctor's office with only the woman and the doctor ever the wiser? It's a pro-life nightmare; so far, pro-lifers have used consumer power and political clout to keep abortion drugs out. If that fails, violence could be the next step.

The shooters and bombers are still, thankfully, on the fringes, while the mainstream pro-life movement concentrates on funding issues.

*Diana Kilmury,* UNION ACTIVIST (MARCH 1993)

*Antonine Maillet,* AUTHOR (MARCH 1981)

*k.d. lang,* SINGER-SONGWRITER (JANUARY 1988)

*Kate Aitken,* RADIO PERSONALITY
(JULY 1957)

*Juliette,* SINGER (JANUARY 1966)

*Joyce Wieland,* ARTIST (OCTOBER 1976)

# CHAPTER TEN

# Role Models

**J**UST AS EVERY HOUSE AND STREET and township across Canada has produced its own role models, so each paragraph and page and issue of *Chatelaine* over the past seventy years is populated with women who have made a difference. Most of those profiled in this chapter have also achieved international acclaim. Since every story but that of Nellie McClung is a snapshot of a life in progress, it remains incomplete, catching its subject in mid-leap, or about to take off, or land, or fall. That's history . . . a continuing story.

Through the eyes of our subjects, and over their shoulders, we catch glimpses of Canada in evolution: the one-room log cabin, surrounded by howling wolves, where little Nellie spent her first prairie winter; the gabled Cavendish home where Lucy Maud Montgomery penned stories of the redoubtable Anne; the headless corpses and strange prehistoric creatures that roamed the fertile imagination of Ma Murray, chronicler of the Northwest; alienated memories of "the Soo" as recounted by Roberta Bondar, Canada's first woman in space.

We also discover a dark social theme sliding serpentine through many of these stories: the indifference with which we in Canada treat our shiniest talents until they have proven themselves internationally, and then the perversity with which we punish them for having done so. That, unfortunately, is the Canadian psyche, too.

*Margaret Atwood,* AUTHOR (JANUARY 1981)

*Marie Dressler,* ACTRESS (JANUARY 1932)

# No "Nice Nellie" Was Nellie

*In yesterday's Canada Nellie McClung fought for women's suffrage and "personhood," and against sweatshops and drunkenness and unwanted births. She was handsome, fiery, a best-selling author, devoted to her husband and children—and to her remarkable mother-in-law*

By Gwen Matheson & V.E. Lang

NOVEMBER
1974

They called her "Calamity Nell," "Mrs. Western Canada," or sometimes just "that woman." They burned her in effigy in Manitoba. They threatened her with lawsuits, and sometimes with violence. They caricatured her as a buzzing mosquito. Teacher, lecturer, reformer, suffragist, politician, novelist, wife and mother, the leading figure in the early Canadian feminist movement once wrote that if anyone wanted to hurt her feelings they would have to submit their case in writing. Her motto was "Get the thing done and let them howl."

Nellie was born in Chatsworth, Ont., in 1873. She was the sixth and youngest child of Irish John Mooney and Scottish Letitia McCurdy. The family farm was small and stony and Nellie's mother worried constantly over the future of her children, particularly her sons. What could they become but hired men or shop clerks? Finally, Will, the eldest boy, inspired by glowing reports of the northwest, set off to see for himself. Will was just twenty, but he was to choose a homestead for his middle-aged parents and his five younger brothers and sisters.

Almost a year later, the family set out by boat and train for St. Boniface. There, they packed two bulging ox wagons and began the trek to the new homestead near Wawanesa. Over the rough, swampy roads, ten miles was a good day's traveling and seven-year-old Nellie walked every muddy inch.

That first prairie winter almost broke their spirits. At night, they huddled together for warmth, stoking the wood stove in their one-room log cabin, while the snow fell heavily on the prairie grass roof. Little Nellie buried her head beneath a pillow and shuddered at the relentless howling of the wolves.

Spring did come at last. Soon a new log house, with a cozy kitchen and three bedrooms, was built. Neighbors, too, began to move in. But not until Nellie was ten years old were there enough children to start a school.

Though the prairie farm life was hard and demanding, it was suffused by a strong feeling of unity with the natural world. All the animals on the Mooney farm, in addition to the beloved dogs and a succession of cats, were regarded as distinct personalities and family friends—even the hens had names.

At the same time Mrs. Mooney was stern and conventional, with an "old-world reverence for men," and the growing Nellie began to chafe at the restrictions she imposed. The Mooney girls—Hannah, Lizzie and Nellie—were always urged to defer to men, to accept male opinion and not to "put themselves forward." None of them was allowed to go out unaccompanied by a brother or father. Nellie wasn't to race against the boys lest her legs be seen and, worst of all, she could not play on the "shinny" (hockey) team, in case her red bloomers drooped.

Once Hannah and Nellie created a minor sensation during a political discussion at a Christmas party in the Mooney parlor. They defended the condemned rebel, Louis Riel. Nellie, however, quickly learned that it didn't matter what she thought about that, or any political matter. Women couldn't vote.

Nellie threw herself into her studies. She had to get to the teachers' college to carry out her plans to help other women and to effect her own escape from a life of farm labor and "acid little economies." At last, having passed the Second-Class Teachers' Examination, Nellie set off for Winnipeg, just barely sixteen but fortified by a new green dress with military braid, a yellow and blue crocheted petticoat, kid gloves and goatskin buttoned boots.

The normal course was one year long and Nellie made the most of it. As her beloved principal, Mr. Goggin, bade farewell to his graduating class, his final exhortation was to be a shaping influence. "Demand decent salaries, and wear clean linen."

The young graduate secured her first teaching post near Manitou in 1890, earning the grand sum of $40 a month. As an old lady, Nellie was to say that her teaching years were the ones she would most like to relive. In Miss Mooney's school, teacher played football, too, and no one complained about red bloomers.

Nellie had always proclaimed her intention of copying Queen Elizabeth I by staying clear of emotional entanglements. Marriage she had once defined as the case of the "tied-up woman" and the "footloose man"; and she believed that too often society "taunted" women into marrying, refusing them respect or fulfillment outside the home.

However, a new Methodist minister arrived in Manitou and the young teacher was captivated by the progressive philosophy of his wife. "She is," Nellie said enthusiastically, "the only woman I have ever seen whom I should like to have for a mother-in-law." Fortunately, there was an appropriate son—Robert Wesley McClung, known as Wes.

"I made no pretence of being the Victorian maiden who sits on the shore waiting for a kindly tide to wash something up at her feet—not at all! Having seen something on the skyline rocking on the current—something that looked like a treasure, I plunged boldly in and swam out for it."

Nellie and Wes met at church meetings, sleigh rides, impromptu parties, debates and socials, and, when she went to Winnipeg to study for a higher teaching certificate, she and Wes wrote constantly. Wes encouraged Nellie in all her ambitions, particularly in her desire to write. He did not, Nellie exulted, think that "his wife should always be standing behind his chair, ready to spring to attention." They didn't, of course, agree on everything. But Nellie eventually decided that she would rather disagree with Wes than agree with anyone else. So they were married at the little church in Wawanesa at eight o'clock on a rainy morning in 1896.

Nellie's granddaughter, Marcia McClung (living in Toronto), has as one of her treasured mementos a book once given to Wes by Nellie. On the flyleaf is written "To R. W. who is 'more like a friend than a husband,' in that he really likes my stories, and although my keenest critic is also my greatest inspiration."

The newlyweds settled down in a four-bedroom apartment over the Manitou drugstore now owned by Wes. Although Nellie very much desired motherhood, she evidently did not regard the "waiting period" as a particularly glorified state. Suffering from what she called "this infernal nausea" during her first pregnancy, she reflected somewhat bitterly that if men had to endure it, medical science would soon have found a remedy.

Nellie gave birth to her first son, Jack, in June 1897, in her own bedroom, without anesthetic. The young mother described the moment that she first held her baby in her arms as the most exquisite of her life.

With Jack's birth, the twenty-three-year-old Nellie experienced a great upsurge of fierce, protective love, directed toward all the children of the world. Nellie's own immediate response to this feeling was to join the local branch of the Woman's Christian Temperance Union.

Her mother had always favored prohibition, and Nellie herself had been terrified as a child when an enraged ox, spurred on by a drunken rider, had nearly trampled her and the tiny baby in her charge. Alcohol was one of the few diversions available on the harsh frontier and women were always its victims. In Nellie's mind, religion, temperance and female emancipation were inextricably linked.

It was, she admitted, impossible for these early reformers to conceive of women themselves drinking. They were too horrified by figures like those which claimed that over 3,000 women had been murdered by drunken husbands during one year in the United States. The WCTU was also, however, one of the most progressive organizations of its time.

Yet, even when Nellie was in deadly earnest, she never lost her incomparable sense of comedy. At one of the schools she was visiting as a temperance speaker, she used the customary demonstration of showing the class two glasses—one filled with water and the other with whisky—into both of which a dew worm was dropped. After this slimy martyr to the cause had performed its "act" of surviving briskly in the water and then curling up and dying in the stronger stuff, Nellie proceeded to ask the children what "lesson" they had

*Marriage she had once defined as the case of the "tied-up woman" and the "footloose man"*

learned. One little boy replied, "We learn that if we drink lots of whisky we'll never have worms."

Jack was not yet two when Nellie's only daughter, Florence, was born, and less than two years after Florence, Paul joined the family circle. The McClungs moved from over the drugstore into a bigger, rented house.

Fortunately for Nellie, her in-laws were still living in Manitou. And her gentle but determined mother-in-law one day marched into her daughter-in-law's kitchen, took over the housework for the day, and disposing of Nellie's protests with the comment, "Life conspires to keep a woman tangled in trifles!" sent her off to write a short story for a competition in *Collier's* magazine.

The story didn't win, but it was later expanded into a romantic comic novel about earlier Canadian family life under the title *Sowing Seeds in Danny*. Published in 1908, with distribution in both Canada and the United States, the book sold over 100,000 copies and made its author close to $25,000. It was the first of nine best sellers and of her total output of seventeen volumes, including collections of short stories and essays as well as novels. Mrs. McClung senior then proceeded to arrange for the successful author to give readings from her novel.

For her first engagement Nellie bolstered herself by an excursion into what she called "applied beauty." After buying a new blue dress, she had her hair done at a hairdresser's, and a manicure and facial: she also had her first encounter with commercial rouge, having hitherto used a rose leaf from an old summer hat. Nellie never did feel the need to sacrifice any of the traditional "feminine" pleasures for what she called "common justice."

Although Nellie was now the wife of a prosperous young druggist with a full-time, live-in maid and a mother-in-law always willing to lend a hand, she never forgot the hard lot of the farm woman. "Woman power," she felt, was what ran the west.

At the same time this indomitable fighter believed that women had to overcome the martyr-complex that had been ingrained in them. "Women who place a low value on themselves," she once wrote, "make life hard for all women."

By 1910 Nellie had a fourth child, Horace, and

there were two assistants in the drugstore. But the hours were long, and Wes began to feel the strain. Nellie persuaded him to sell the store. In 1911 he became an agent for Manufacturer's Life Insurance Company, and the family moved to Winnipeg where Mark, the last son, was born.

The Winnipeg move caused the whole tide of her life to change. She joined the Canadian Women's Press Club, a group that was inspired by the 1912 visit of the British militant suffragettes, Emmeline Pankhurst and Barbara Wiley. When the press club later formed the Political Equality League to obtain the vote for women, they became involved in the fight to improve the working conditions for women in factories. It was this campaign that brought Nellie into her first confrontation with Sir Redmond Roblin, the Conservative Manitoba premier. She and Mrs. Claude Nash, a fellow press club member, persuaded this "gentleman of the old school" to make a tour of actual factories.

On his way to the factory in his pretentious car, his "plump hands resting on a gold-headed cane," Sir Redmond made light of women's working conditions, observing that most of them were immigrants who "did not expect to be carried to the skies on a flowery bed of ease!" But after struggling "down dark, slippery stairs to an airless basement," where he could witness at first hand the filth, the dreadful toilet facilities, and the poor health of many workers, the premier emerged choking and exclaiming that he "never knew such hellholes existed!"

Back in the security of his own car, however, Sir Redmond recovered enough to express his disapproval that women like Nellie and Mrs. Nash should "ferret out such utterly disgusting things." When Nellie spoke to him later about votes for women the premier assured her that "nice women don't want the vote."

"By nice women," she flared, "you probably mean selfish women, who have no more thought for the underpaid, overworked women than a pussycat in a sunny window has for the starving kitten in the street. Now in that sense I am not a nice woman, for I do care . . . and we intend to do something about it."

Unfortunately for himself, Sir Redmond unconsciously provided the league with the material for their greatest victory. In January 1914, a delegation of women appeared in the assembly to ask for female suffrage. At his "foamy best" the old orator assured the delegation that there was nothing wrong with a society that could produce such pure and noble women. How could he permit such purity to be sullied by politics?

The next night was to be the opening of the league's satire, *The Women's Parliament*. In a reproduction of the legislature, the women "MLAs" received a male delegation asking for the vote. In perfect imitation of Sir Redmond, Nellie addressed the delegation. "Any society that produces such glorious specimens of manly beauty is good enough for me."

The play won enormous success. Public opinion was now with the suffragists. Manitoba was the first to give women the vote, in January 1916. Alberta and Saskatchewan followed the same year.

Wes was made manager of his company's branch in Edmonton and the family moved there in the fall of 1914.

In Edmonton, which Nellie described as "city of glamour" with an atmosphere "young, hopeful and full of surprises," she had never felt better or more keenly alive and was able to work both day and night. But always at the back of her mind was the dread of her eldest son Jack's enlistment.

It was in this state of mind that she wrote her most fiercely antiwar and most intensely feminist work—*In Times Like These*. Inspired by the agony of women during wartime, the book has as its main theme women's common humanity—a humanity that demands justice, not chivalry.

When war was declared Jack was old enough to enlist and in December of 1915 he set out for Europe. After she said good-by to him at the CNR station Nellie wrote in her diary. "When we came home I felt strangely tired and old, though I am only forty-two. But I know that my youth has departed from me." Jack survived the war, and went on to a distinguished legal career. But Nellie knew after he came back that he had "seen the negation of everything he had been taught," and he would never be the same. "A wound in a young heart," she wrote, "is like a wound in a young tree. It does not grow out. It grows in."

The end of the war gave Nellie her chance in politics at last. On the ticket of the Liberals and United Farmers she was elected to the Alberta Assembly in 1921. In the next five years she sponsored such social legislation as dental and medical care for school children, married women's property rights, and mothers' allowances. She was one of the first Canadians who favored birth-control, for she felt that no family should have an unwanted child. But she preferred a "bonny fight" to the tedium of parliamentary debate, and was too independent to enjoy the "party line."

For this reason her defeat in the 1926 election was not too severe a blow, although she did need an "orgy of cooking" to overcome her immediate disappointment. She lost by only sixty votes.

"The middle years of life come on like thunder," Nellie wrote of this period in her life. The family had moved to Calgary in 1923 where Wes's company had sent him.

Nellie and Judge Emily Murphy, the first Canadian woman magistrate, were presently off on a new crusade, accompanied by three other brave women: Mrs. Irene Parlby, a member of the Alberta cabinet; Mrs. Louise McKinney, ex-MLA; and Mrs. Henrietta Edwards, author of a book entitled *Laws Relating to Women*. It was Judge Murphy who discovered that by an 1876 enactment in British law women were not legally persons. "Women," the law declared, "are persons in matters of pains and penalties, but are not persons in matters of rights and privileges." A petition was drawn up by the "Alberta Five" and presented to the federal Senate, from where it was referred to the Supreme Court of Canada. In April of 1928 this august body turned down their case, denying the personhood of one half of the human race. Undaunted, the Alberta Five pressed their suit on to the Privy Council in England, who in October of 1929 stated that women were, after all, persons—and therefore could even be appointed to the Senate.

Throughout this and her numerous other activities, Nellie proved with eminent success that she could combine family and career. When she had been at the height of her suffrage campaigning she telephoned home every night before going on stage and began each lecture with the words, "Settle down now and don't worry about my children. They are all well and happy . . ."

Nellie was aware that she was, as she put it, "vulnerable in five places." Even the children themselves were aware of this and Nellie liked to tell how Horace had once smuggled a disheveled Mark in the back way lest the *Telegram* get a picture of "Nellie McClung's Neglected Child."

In 1921 the Methodist Church of Canada had appointed her as a delegate to the Ecumenical Conference in London. And in 1938 at the age of sixty-five Nellie made another trip abroad, this time as a delegate to the League of Nations in Geneva.

Saddened by the league's inability to act and by the outbreak of yet another war, Nellie returned to Canada. Yet she never despaired, and even when she was an old lady her eyes twinkled with irresistible humor and hope. In her comfortable home, Lantern Lane, which she shared with Wes at Gordon Head near Victoria, B.C., the veteran of many struggles finally found time to devote herself more completely to her writing and to become acquainted with her grandchildren.

This sense of the continuity of human life, along with her belief in the "fellowship of the soil" and her deep religious faith, enabled Nellie McClung to live on with courage and good humor in spite of a series of severe heart attacks, until her death in 1951 in her seventy-eighth year.

"She is," Wes wrote to Mark, "tranquil in her mind—full of love for us all—She has fought a good fight and kept the faith."

> When Nellie spoke to him later about votes for women the premier assured her that "nice women don't want the vote"

# The Best Known Woman in Prince Edward Island

## L. M. Montgomery, after her first success

By Maud Petitt Hill

JUNE 1928

**S**PRING HOUSECLEANING nearly always brings some neglected thing to light. The snow was lingering on the hills of Cavendish when L. M. Montgomery decided to go up to the attic one wintry afternoon and do a little of what housekeepers call "ridding up," preparatory to the spring cleaning.

Back there, in the farthest corner of the store room under the gabled roof, was that old hat box. She pulled it out. Oh, yes, the manuscript of *Anne of Green Gables*! Poor Anne, child of her dream—spurned by five publishing houses!

Well, Anne was evidently not destined for the world of book shelves in a pretty coat of red or green cloth. One more hope to the ground! Small wonder if she felt as Anne herself did when she found they had really sent for a boy at Green Gables, and weren't likely to keep her: "My life is a perfect graveyard of buried hopes."

But, at any rate, she could cut the manuscript down to a six- or seven-chapter serial for a juvenile paper. It meant a good deal of work, and she would only get thirty-five or forty dollars for it. But she ought to do something with it. It had lain there neglected for a year.

She took it out and began to read from the beginning. She read on and on. The sun sank lower behind the hills—its rays were running level through the gable window across the attic floor. Suddenly she started up. Gracious! The afternoon had slipped away! Time to look after the tea. She had read nearly all the afternoon like a school girl and forgotten all about the work she came up to do!

But still she paused, a queerish new light in her eyes. "If your own story could interest you after you have laid it away, until it made you forget all about your work like this—wouldn't it interest other people if it were printed," whispered something.

A few days later the would-be authoress tied up *Anne of Green Gables* and sent her off again to Boston, this time to the L. C. Page Company.

It was natural for a Prince Edward Island girl to send her manuscript to Boston rather than Montreal or Toronto, even if she had been rebuffed there before. All Maritime-Province ambition turns to Boston. The farmer's daughter is educated for a teacher or trained for a nurse and goes to Boston. The fisherman's daughter goes to Boston to get high pay in housework. The sons everywhere go there to try their wings in the world of commerce. A very large percentage of the professional men of

Massachusetts are natives of our Maritimes. When the people of the Maritime Provinces take a long trip, they go to Boston—very seldom to Montreal or Toronto.

Nevertheless, it was well that, with its millions of readers, Boston should get *Anne of Green Gables* on her sixth excursion. She passed through the hands of the manuscript readers and came, finally, to the publisher himself. And then, one more perverse publisher decided to reject *Anne of Green Gables*. Possibly the manuscript was a little dog-eared after its five previous excursions, and its year in the hat box. Undoubtedly, it had a sort of hangdog look.

At any rate, over among the manuscripts to be tied up for return, went *Anne*. But there was one factor on which the publisher had not counted. One of his manuscript readers was a girl from Prince Edward Island. Now the "Islanders" are intensely loyal to one another. It is said they never quite learn to think of any other place as home.

Into the office of the chief, entered the irate young Island reader when she learned of the manuscript's fate. She had its points all down pat. She had made up her mind to camp right there by the desk of L. C. Page until he said he would publish *Anne of Green Gables*. And camp there she did, and argued and argued and argued, until the publisher, being only a man after all, surrendered!

L. M. Montgomery never knew the true story of her book's acceptance until years after, when she heard it through a travelling salesman. All she knew then was that one afternoon the sunshine at Cavendish became all aglitter, because she had opened a letter from Boston saying her book was accepted for publication.

In her journal at that time, she wrote: "The book may or may not succeed. I wrote it for love not money; but very often such books are the most successful, just as everything in the world that is born of true love has life in it as nothing constructed for mercenary ends can ever have. The dream dreamed years ago, at that old brown desk in school has come true at last after years of toil and struggle. And the realization is sweet, almost as sweet as the dream."

Her idea of the success of her book had been, from her own confession, a very limited one. She had thought it would be read by girls of teen age. She had never dreamed that its sale would, according to her present publisher, touch the million mark; that premiers and princes would one day seek her out and shake her hand. It was not until the year after its acceptance that the book was published. On June 20th, 1908, she wrote in her journal:

"To-day has been, as Anne herself would say, 'an epoch in my life.' My book came to-day, 'spleet new' from the publishers. I candidly confess that it was to me a proud and wonderful and thrilling moment. There, in my hand, lay the material realization of the dreams, hopes, ambitions and struggles of my whole conscious existence—my first book. Not a great book, but mine, mine, mine—something which I had created."

Nor did the thrills end with that moment. As the sales mounted there were letters coming to the young writer from all parts of the world, not only from the children, who believed that Anne was real, but from gray-haired grandfathers, boys at college, pioneers in the Australian bush. The English public particularly responded to this simple life-story of the girl on a Canadian farm. But, of course, it was the American

*Mrs. Ewan Macdonald, now of Norval, Ontario, the well-beloved "L. M. Montgomery" author of "Anne of Green Gables"*

sales that swelled her royalties. Mark Twain described Anne as "the sweetest creation of child-life yet written." Bliss Carman also voiced his appreciation. And, if the sight of the American copy of her story had thrilled its author, what must it have meant to see a Swedish and also a Dutch copy appearing. The *Truro Weekly* said of the book that it had definitely fixed its author's place "as the Jane Austen of Canadian literature."

In 1909, following her big success, L. M. Montgomery had no difficulty in publishing her second book, *Anne of Avonlea*, and the following year *Kilmeny of the Orchard*. This was really an earlier work of hers, first published as a serial. Consequently, she was rather amused when a reviewer remarked of it that the book showed "the insidious influence of popularity and success."

> **The best way to know a writer is not to read a biographical sketch of her life, but to read something she has written.**

The following year, came *The Story Girl*, a replica of Prince Edward Island scenery and life as it was around her, the last of L. M. Montgomery's books to be written there by her window under the gabled roof.

The writer had been continuing her quiet life in these pastoral scenes, playing the organ of the little church, teaching in the Sunday school, bearing her share of the little neighborhood doings as though the literary circles of big cities had never beckoned her. There came into her community one day to preach, however, one, the Reverend Ewan Macdonald. He, it was, who was destined, a little later, to lure her from her beloved island.

In the winter of 1911, Grandmother Macneill died at the age of eighty-seven. There ended thirteen years of faithful care of one who had herself cared for the author from babyhood.

In the summer of that year, Lucy Maud Montgomery was married from her uncle's house at Park Corner, a few miles away, to the Rev. Ewan Macdonald, then in charge of the Presbyterian church at Leaskdale, Ont. They left immediately to spend their honeymoon in the British Isles.

We get a little glimpse of how deeply embedded in Mrs. Macdonald's nature is her love of home, when speaking of walking on the Spittal Shore by moonlight, she says: "It was beautiful, but so like the Cavendish Shore that it made me bitterly homesick."

In a London antique shop she picked up a pair of spotted china dogs for her new home, which reminded her of a funny incident of her childhood.

In her uncle's house at Park Corner there were two spotted china dogs on the mantel. When she was a little girl her father had told her that whenever those dogs heard the clock strike midnight they would bounce down on the rug and bark. She had thenceforth pleaded to be let stay up till midnight. But her elders were obdurate in refusing.

However, one night she discovered that the dogs didn't bark at twelve, and her faith in her father's truthfulness was badly shattered. But he restored it somewhat by explaining that he had said "whenever the dogs *heard* the clock strike they would bark!" but china dogs never heard.

Back to their new home in the Manse at Leaskdale, Ontario, came the bride and groom some sixteen years ago. Mrs. Macdonald settled to her life in the village manse, where two little sons, Chester and Stuart, were born. It is perhaps for the best that her own children have been sons, not daughters. Girls would have had a hard time holding their own with these dream girls of her fancy.

The best way to know a writer is not to read a biographical sketch of her life, but to read something she has written. Some one once said to a young writer, of people who said they knew her through her writing:

"They know you as you write. We know you as you are."

"No," said the writer quickly, "they who read me know me as I am. You, who live with me, know me as I seem."

People find something refreshing in the stories from this land where, as we once heard the writer say, "nearly every family still hopes the eldest son will be a minister and it would be a disgrace to have company catch one without three kinds of cake in the house."

When I visited Prince Edward Island last summer, I watched for that three kinds of cake—and do you know, at every table where we sat down, we always found the three varieties?

Another of the keys with which L. M. Montgomery has unlocked the door of success is that she lives life as well as writes. Down there on the

Island where she spends her holidays every other summer, people tell you the kindnesses she has done in passing—the books given the schools; the pictures hung on the school room wall; the lecture given for the funds of the little church; the delicate girl taken from some farm home back with her to Ontario.

"How do you manage to write in a Manse?" we asked.

"Oh, it isn't any harder to write in a Manse than any other place," she said. "I set apart three hours a day for writing." "I don't think her home has ever known neglect from her writing," said one who knew her intimately.

Her sons, Chester and Stuart, are now fifteen and twelve years of age. When they were "wee bairns," a guest tells us, they used to shove flowers under the door into the room where their mother was writing.

There is a nice big furry cat named "Lucky" in the Manse. I recalled a simple sentence L. M. Montgomery had added, seemingly rather irrelevantly, to an address some years ago: "And I always like a cat in the room when I'm writing!"

Many honors have come to the writer since the publication of her first book. She was the first Canadian woman to be made a Fellow of the Royal Society of Arts and Literature of Great Britain. When Premier Baldwin and the Prince of Wales were making their Canadian tour last summer, the Premier requested that it be arranged for him to meet the Canadian writer whose stories he had so much enjoyed. In consequence, when the reception was held for the Premier and the Prince at the Lieutenant-Governor's in Toronto, he made her acquaintance. Nor had he forgotten his request.

But of all the honors paid her, perhaps the simplest and the sweetest is the way in which her own Island people welcome you to their homes. When you enter their houses, they thrust forward for you "the chair L. M. Montgomery sat in, when she was here."

# Mazo de la Roche

*The famous Canadian novelist, author of our new serial "The Thunder of New Wings"*

**JUNE 1932**

IT ISN'T OFTEN THAT THE personal stories of famous writers are half as romantic as the novels they write; but to hear about Mazo de la Roche is to listen to a glamorous fairy tale of genius—the kind of genius that has "an infinite capacity for taking pains."

For here is a story of a traditional lady of the pen, left without family or fortune, but with a fine old heritage of Canadian courage behind her, and an unquenchable desire to write.

Miss de la Roche, one of the most noted women writers of the day, hailed on three continents as a master craftsman in literature, winner of the *Atlantic Monthly* prize of ten thousand dollars and author of half a dozen much discussed novels, is a Canadian of Canadians. On her mother's side of the family are six generations of United Empire Loyalists, and while her father was a native-born Canadian, his people were descendants of an old French Royalist family. Mazo, herself, was born in Toronto.

When she was still a young girl, her parents died within a year or so of each other, and Mazo de la Roche, an only child, was left alone. She had already published the first story she ever wrote—inspired by her father's vivid description of a holiday trip to Quebec. She wrote her story in secret, and mailed it to *Munsey's* magazine. Within a month a cheque came back for fifty dollars; proving that such things do happen.

Unknown, and in very difficult financial circumstances, the young writer began to work doggedly. Writing has never been easy for her. Years later, when acclaimed by the literary world, she was tendered a magnificent banquet on her winning the *Atlantic Monthly* prize of ten thousand dollars, and said that "writing a novel gives one the sensation of a mole starting to burrow his way through a mountain."

Today, Miss de la Roche likes, best of all, to sit out-of-doors with a pad of paper on her knee and

*Mazo de la Roche, the author of* Chatelaine's *new serial, "The Thunder of New Wings," is acclaimed everywhere as one of the most brilliant women novelists of the day.*

write for hours, revising constantly. Her prose, born of such ardent labor, has an exquisite quality, for all its power. One noted English critic said of her novels that she "wrote with the terrific absorption of a child."

Through all the years Miss de la Roche has written her stories laboriously in longhand—Miss Carolyn Clement has typed them for her. Twelve years ago these two adopted each other as sisters, and they have lived together ever since, through the bitter days of disappointment and the brilliant years of success.

In 1922, her first book was published—*Explorers of the Dawn*. This is a delightful collection of chronicles of child life, which appeared originally in the *Atlantic Monthly* and other magazines. In

1924, Miss de la Roche's first novel, *Delight*, was published. This is the romance of a waitress in an old-time Ontario hotel, and showed some powerful character portrayals that began to arouse public interest in the young writer.

When sensational success came in 1927 with the winning of the *Atlantic Monthly* prize, it was only the result of many years of work. *Jalna*, the winning manuscript, was selected from 1,200 manuscripts from the best writers throughout the world. It was acclaimed everywhere as one of the most notable incidents in the history of Canadian literature, and told the story of a strangely assorted family living in an old house on the shores of Lake Ontario. Since the publication of *Jalna*, two sequels have been written, *Whiteoaks* and *Finch's Fortune*, which have won admiration from everywhere.

Miss de la Roche has always loved the country, and her favorite hobby for spare hours is walking. Her winters in Canada were spent in a studio flat in Toronto, and her summers in a little cottage about twenty miles outside the city, or as the *Atlantic Monthly* naively put it, "in the Ontario forest." Some years ago, as she had always loved Devon, she moved there with her adopted sister, Carolyn Clement, and lives now in a quaint, old gabled house set in a beautiful garden where she writes for hours. Since going to England she has adopted the orphaned children of some friends— Michael and Patsy, two happy little youngsters who bring love and laughter into the busy days. Miss de la Roche and her adopted family are planning a trip to Canada this year—they often come home to re-establish old friendships and are seriously thinking of coming home to live. For much as Mazo de la Roche loves the quiet of her old-world Devon home, she finds herself homesick for her own land and her own people.

*Kate Reid,* ACTRESS (OCTOBER 1977)

*Barbara Frum,* JOURNALIST
(JANUARY 1982)

*Nancy Greene,* SKIER (FEBRUARY 1966)

*June Callwood,* WRITER, TV PANELIST
(OCTOBER 1966)

*Maureen Forrester,* SINGER
(SEPTEMBER 1972)

*Adrienne Clarkson,* TV PERSONALITY
(OCTOBER 1966)

*Diane Dupuy,* THEATRE DYNAMO (DECEMBER 1981)

# The Rebel Queen of the Northwest

*Cowboys dream of her, miners swear by her, politicians cuss her and everybody loves her. Meet Ma Murray, salty sage of the Alaska Highway*

BY EARLE BEATTIE

IN THE FOOTHILLS OF THE Rockies where the Peace River pours out of the mountains, a wizened little trapper emerged from his bachelor shack in response to my knock and said in a voice squeaky with age:

"Yis, Ma Murray was here just a few weeks ago. She gave me a bottle a' rum and a massive kiss. I'm the correspondent up here for her paper. That's all the pay I want, too."

Some sixty miles down the river at Fort St. John, B.C., where Ma Murray publishes her *Alaska Highway News*, an official for Canadian Pacific Airlines said, "You should have been here yesterday when Ma spoke at a luncheon for the company president. She had 'em rolling out of their seats."

Over at the Fort St. John telegraph office the agent's eyes lit up at mention of Ma. "She's at her daughter Georgina's ranch," he said. Grabbing the telephone, he cranked the handle and sang out, "Hey, Ma, put some water in the soup. Fella coming out to see you!"

In the taxi on the way to the ranch the driver said, "Once you get 'er talking, she'll never stop. You won't get a word in sideways."

That's how I trailed the rebel queen of the northwest to her home in the prairie land of the Peace River, a 1,200-square-mile block that straddles the B. C.–Alberta border two hundred miles north and west of Edmonton. Along the way my every query brought answers in exclamation marks about the galvanic little woman of sixty-four who has become a legend in her own time.

I caught up with the legend herself at the Keddell ranch just outside Fort St. John. Ma Murray was seated in a dining-room chair, dandling a grandchild on her knee. She talked like the taxi driver said, the rapid-fire conversation animating her small pink face. Snapping blue eyes behind shell-rimmed glasses gave her a lively birdlike appearance, accentuated by a careless shock of white hair that topped her off at five-feet-five.

Ma Murray turned to me and, scarcely taking time out to say hello, launched into a nonstop story of the Peace River—"this inland empire," its history, geography, coal, oil and timber, its pioneering spirit . . . all told with a gleeful slaughter of the Queen's English just for the joy of the kill. Occasional bursts of indignation over governmental neglect of the Peace River sent her off on volleys of barrackroom invective that made big Jim Keddell, her ex–sergeant-major son-in-law, stop in his tracks. All attempts by daughter Georgina to tone her mother down were futile.

The morning after I met her at the ranch, Ma was up with the dawn and off on her news beat. She climbed into her little English car and churned off in a small dust-cloud along the Alaska Highway. She turned into the Marie Wilson farm where she interviewed some oil workers drilling a well in an alfalfa field. She stopped at the Wilson farmhouse where she heard about a new variety of sweet clover and black stem rust on the alfalfa, and came away loaded with six cabbages, a sample of the diseased grain and a handful of the new clover. She crossed the magnificent Peace River bridge and pulled into Joe's Place to have a cup of coffee and pick up a giant-size potato Joe had been saving for her.

Back at St. John, Ma kicked her way through the door of the *Alaska Highway News*, arms hugging her haul of cabbages, alfalfa, clover and the largest potato the Peace ever saw. Seating herself at a typewriter she banged out half a dozen news stories on oil and crops and an editorial about noisy juveniles.

That afternoon she bustled up and down the board walk of Fort St. John, covering the police beat, hotels, courts and stores, a brisk and colorful figure in her long wool dress and red blazer. After supper there was a hospital campaign meeting. The end result, a day later, was another edition of Ma Murray's salty, eight-page weekly, written in the same earthy take-it-or-leave-it language she talks.

Ma calls Fort St. John "this little burg" and old-timers "old crocks." When the Government sent her a list of persons missing in the north country, she began her story "Lost in the shuffle of life are several persons . . ."

Her *Alaska Highway News* carries Paul Bunyan–like reports that "rabbits are eating up telephone poles along the highway" (Ma means the bunnies are nibbling at the creosote) to folksy reminiscences of her own career. And she occasionally harks back to her girlhood days in Kansas.

There she was born Margaret Lally and at thirteen, with only a grade three education, went to work for a saddlery firm. An enterprising as well as a romantic young lady, she slipped notes into the saddles she shipped and started receiving letters from lonesome cowboys all over Alberta. Some of the replies contained proposals, so deciding "to go out and marry some of those cowboys," Margaret Lally took off north with her sister Bess.

They entered Canada via Vancouver and she met a newspaperman first. George Murray hired her as a bookkeeper for his paper, the *Greater Vancouver Chinook*, but although Margaret Lally had eyes for the boss "he was shy, Murray was." Even though he held her hand once and put notes in her typewriter, she decided "I can't tarry here— I'm going to Stettler and marry the good-looking cowboys with the lariats." In Calgary she found "big men, bigger than in Kansas, wearing big coon coats and with big, walrus mustaches that drooped with icicles."

But when the winsome Lally girl went back to Vancouver on a business trip for a farm paper she found a new George Murray. He met her at the train on a Sunday, took her to a hockey game on Monday, popped the question Tuesday, married her Wednesday. (Ma says now that Editor Murray was emboldened because she told him, "You need someone to look after you."—"But all I really meant was he had so many libel suits threatening he needed a lawyer.")

When Catholic Margaret Lally went to her bishop for permission to marry a Protestant she was met with the wrathful blast: "You not only ask me to bless you for marrying a Protestant, but you ask me to do it on the first day of Lent." However, the nimble-tongued Irish girl from Kansas talked the bishop himself into doing the deed and loaning them his housekeeper for a witness. Georgina arrived a year later while the Murray newspaper was strikebound. Danny came three years after that when his father was in jail, charged with criminal libel.

Ma thought Danny would be born with bars on his face, but her husband was simply bound over to keep the peace.

After her husband's own paper finally folded during

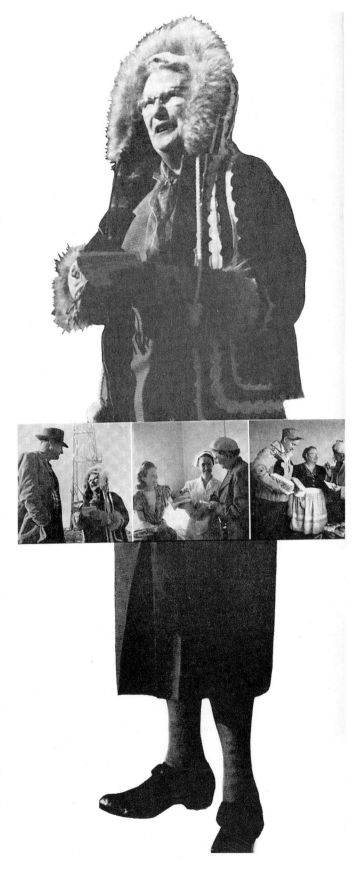

*Reporter Murray boosts Peace River oil, babies, wheat.*

World War I, he became managing editor of the *Vancouver Sun*. Becoming interested in politics, in 1933 George Murray was chosen Liberal candidate for the provincial constituency of Lillooet, 200 miles up the Fraser from Vancouver.

"We had an old Willys-Knight touring car," says Ma. "Besides us it carried a case of hooch, a typewriter, a feather bed, a washtub and seventy-five dollars in cash. A banner on the car said: 'Liberal Headquarters. Vote Murray.' We slept in the car."

Murray was elected.

The campaign excitement over, Ma itched to get her fingers back into printers' ink and, as quickly as another woman might whip up a cake she was putting out the *Bridge River–Lillooet News*. Hard-rock miners in the district gold mines found her editorials as sharp-edged as their diamond drills and loved her for it. At one stormy union meeting, during a strike in 1935, a big Scot began cussing violently and someone moved that "all ladies be asked to leave the hall." The offending miner objected, "There's only one lady here and she's Ma Murray and Mrs. Murray is no lady." Ma stayed.

> **"There's only one lady here and she's Ma Murray and Mrs. Murray is no lady"**

In 1937 Ma and George turned the paper over to Georgina and Dan, now experienced publishing hands of 19 and 17, and went off to China to write newspaper articles. The Murrays' nose for excitement brought them to Shanghai just as the Japs started dropping bombs in the preliminary round of World War II. From the Metropole Hotel they watched bombs destroy the Cathay Hotel which they had just checked out of, and began cabling their eyewitness stories to Vancouver papers before the smoke had cleared. Later they were evacuated down the Yangtse River in a British gunboat while Jap flyers rained death around the decks.

Memory of that occasion was all that saved Ma from an unspeakable catastrophe two years later when the Murrays were presented to the late King George VI and Queen Elizabeth at Victoria. As the provincial legislators and their wives moved in solemn procession toward the throne seat in the B. C. parliament buildings, Ma unaccountably began thinking of all her father had told her of the Irish famine and his hatred of the English.

She thought, "What would my father say if he could see me lining up to meet the English King!" and she had the horrible feeling that she was going to kick the King instead of curtsy to him.

Her heart was beating wildly as the queue carried her forward. "Then," says Ma, "I saw the King, and he so mild and with such a little sword that I began to cry. I thought of the British gunboat that took us down the Yangtse River. And I felt so proud of the British and grateful that instead of curtsying I pumped the King's hand so hard he weaved a bit on the platform—and the Queen's hand, too, and she with such a heavenly smile."

Ma Murray first showed up in the Peace River country in 1944. George Murray had traveled over the newly created Alaskan Highway the year before and inflamed Ma's mind with such glowing tales of the boundless northwest that she left Danny in charge at Lillooet and hied off to Fort St. John, determined to launch a new paper. Starting from scratch she sold the advertising, collected the news and boomed the circulation to a thousand with the slogan "Twenty-five cents a bushel more on wheat."

Just when things were rolling nicely for the Murrays another strange spell came over Ma. The scandal was born of frustration after Ma joined a rebel group at the B. C. Liberal Convention in Vancouver in 1945 in an attempt to end the Liberal–Conservative Coalition Government which had been in power four years. The rebels lost, the Coalition continued, and Ma arrived back in Fort St. John in too weak a state to resist the proposals of Social Crediters that she seek revenge as their candidate in the coming election.

"I started steaming up Social Credit in the Peace," says Ma. Most horrified of all were husband George, son Dan and daughter Georgina, to whom Social Credit was wilful heresy. Danny published a statement in the *Lillooet News* that Mrs. Murray was related to the other Murrays by blood only. Angered by Ma's defection, Premier Hart turned against *all* Murrays and demanded that Lillooet voters trounce George while voters in the Peace were trouncing his wife.

In the thick of the campaign Georgina arrived home from London, England, and her wartime radio assignment with the Wrens. "I was flabbergasted," she relates. "I asked Ma, 'What's Social Credit anyway?' and Ma said, 'Georgie, I don't know, but I'm running for it. If you want more information, ask headquarters.'"

When the election returns came in, both Murrays took a sound shellacking. Politically shaken, the family foursome redirected their joint energies to journalism and soon produced a new sensation which focused the attention of the entire world on the Canadian Northwest.

It was 1946, the war had been over a year and newspaper front pages were sadly lacking in color and excitement, when one day in October a prospector named Frank Henderson dropped into the office of the *Alaska Highway News*. Onto the counter he poured thirty ounces of coarse gold and with it a story. He had penetrated an area just north of where the B. C.–Yukon borders meet, known as the Nahanni Valley, where he had arranged to meet his partner, John Patterson. But his partner failed to show up and Henderson never saw him again.

The Murrays flashed the story to the outside world, drawing on local legend about the Nahanni as an amazing tropical valley roamed by prehistoric animals and head-hunting Indians and littered by the corpses of luckless prospectors. Had the mysteriously vanished Patterson suffered the curse of the Nahanni and been reduced to a torso?

A full-scale gold rush was averted only by stern RCMP warnings as to how cold, remote and unmysterious "Headless Valley" really was. Finally a letter reached Georgina from the Philippines, written by a man who said the missing Patterson had drowned unromantically when a raft the two of them were riding toward the Nahanni River broke up.

The Nahanni excitement ended, Ma Murray was all envy and frustration when her husband plunged back into the political wars as Liberal candidate for the federal constituency of Cariboo, which includes the B. C. section of the Peace River block. "Tainted by Social Credit," as she put it, Ma realized she daren't campaign for George. But on the excuse of visiting daughter Georgina, then living in Whitehorse, Ma set off for the Yukon where she promptly began campaigning for Liberal nominee Aubrey Simmonds.

Bespectacled, pink-cheeked and by then a grandmother, Ma "campaigned like mad up and down the gold cricks" haranguing miners wherever she found them, at work, at church, in movies, pubs and camp dining halls. At Mayo one evening she talked to men loading ore on a boat; sailed into a movie as the feature ended and turned the program into a double bill; took over a religious meeting in another hall; and pushed on to the local tavern where by buying beer all round she persuaded the manager to lock everyone in while she spoke.

Election night, Georgina was elated to get a wire from Ma saying: "Both my men got in." George Murray had been elected M.P. for the Cariboo, Aubrey Simmonds won the Yukon—and the taint was off Ma.

Ma Murray still keeps friends and family wrong-guessing where she'll head for next. And perhaps in the ranchlands around Calgary a few lonesome cowhands, now growing old, look at their worn Kansas saddles and wonder whatever happened to Miss Margaret Lally who was coming up to marry them.

> *"I asked Ma, 'What's Social Credit anyway?' and Ma said, 'Georgie, I don't know, but I'm running for it. If you want more information, ask headquarters.'"*

# Hit or Flop? The Truth about Barbara Ann

*Barbara Ann's bid to fill Sonja Henie's crown was obscured by a blizzard of conflicting headlines. Here's the lowdown from a* **Chatelaine** *reporter who followed her U.S. tour*

BY JAMES DUGAN

APRIL 1952

CANADA'S TINY OLYMPIC FIGURE-skating queen, Barbara Ann Scott, has recently won the biggest, toughest and most exhausting championship of her career—a smashing success at the U. S. box office.

The irony of this foreign triumph is that exaggerated and conflicting headlines so baffled Barbara's fourteen million Canadian fans that few of them fully appreciate the true size of her American victory.

It was away last August when headlines first blared that Barbara Ann Scott had deposed Sonja Henie as queen of the biggest skating spectacle on earth, the Hollywood Ice Revue, and optimistically estimated her season's salary at a million dollars. By mid-January one Toronto tabloid was trumpeting "Barbara Ann Scott Flops Badly," declaring that her show closed more than a week early in Indianapolis and played to less than 300 in the 17,000-seat Chicago Stadium. Other newspapers rushed special writers to cover the New York opening in Madison Square Garden, and triumphantly quoted the glowing acclaim given Canada's heroine by Manhattan critics. But buried in these stories were reports that the opener drew only 8,000 people to the 15,000-seat Garden, and this started the home folks worrying again.

There was a lot of nonsense in all of this. The Ice Revue *didn't* close early in Indianapolis and actually played two extra performances in Chicago. The critics everywhere raved about both the show and Barbara, but they didn't hesitate to point out that she still has a lot to learn. However, it was at the box office that Barbara Ann had to make or break, and it was here she scored.

For Barbara Ann Scott's new world record consists of topping last year's gross receipts and attendance figures in the show in which the famous Sonja Henie starred for fifteen seasons. This is a fact, for the large and normally affable Arthur M. Wirtz, producer of the Hollywood Ice Revue, was so angered by the clippings I showed him from Canadian papers that he brought out his box-office figures for my inspection.

**In a sparkling bodice and powderpuff ballet skirt, she came down the ice and flew**

This was after the Ice Revue had arrived in New York. I had been following the progress of Barbara Ann and her show across the U. S. since last December when *Chatelaine*'s editors told me they'd like to have a play-by-play on "BA's" invasion of these United States, by an American reporter. On your side of the border Barbara Ann Scott is a national attraction in a class with Banff and Niagara Falls. But to myself and other U. S. entertainment seekers, the harsh fact is that Barbara Ann is not a big-name draw. When she signed up with the Arthur

Wirtz show last fall we knew she was some sort of Olympic champion who had once done a couple of weeks on an ice-cube rink at New York's Roxy Theatre, and that she was nice and pretty. We take a show-me attitude toward alien fame.

Then we proceeded to make things just as hard for Barbara as we could. We had been flocking to see Sonja Henie for years and we used to buy out her show in advance. We knew she had departed in a shower of fireworks, and we did not besiege the box office ahead of time for tickets to see this Barbara Ann Scott. Catherine Littlefield, the brilliant choreographer and director who had staged the Hollywood Ice Revue for years, collapsed during final rehearsals and died. Still shaken, the company opened in Milwaukee to a poor first night in a city that had already seen five ice shows within a year. Press notices were good here and at all stops, but it's the box-office score that counts—and here it is in black and white:

- *Milwaukee:* Gate $250,000 for 14 performances—but Sonja gated that much in 10 performances in 1950. Verdict: Only fair.
- *Indianapolis:* Gate $297,000 for the 17 scheduled performances—and it had taken Sonja 20 to earn this much. Verdict: Made good money.
- *St. Louis, Missouri:* Gate $125,000. Verdict: "A stalemate," admits Wirtz, in which the Ice Revue almost lost money—but Sonja's show grossed $4,000 less a year ago!

The rumor that the show had to close early in Indianapolis was not only false; it apparently started when Barbara Ann turned up in Toronto and was reported as being "home for Christmas." The star had simply flown home for a day and a half (her first visit in six months) while the show's nine railway carloads of sets, lights, props and costumes were being trundled on to Chicago.

Barbara Ann reached Chicago in time for the opening show in the continent's largest indoor arena (17,000 seats) on Christmas night—and so did Chicago's worst blizzard in fifty years. A state of emergency was declared in the city, but Arthur Wirtz showed me box office records to prove that fully 10,000 people (instead of "less than 300") waded through three-foot drifts to attend the opener.

As the storm cleared and enthusiastic comment spread about the show, attendance grew till Wirtz scheduled two extra performances. The last five performances grossed $240,000—the biggest business ever done in the Chicago stadium by any ice show. Barbara Ann's Revue did 32% better than Sonja's last show for Wirtz. Chicago verdict: made BIG money.

All this time there was never any doubt that the show itself was terrific. *Variety*, the tough-minded trade paper of show business, declared after the Milwaukee opener: "Hollywood Ice Revue had everything. The big inning comes with the entry of Miss Scott, attractive and well-poised, unwrapping her unique skating style. The star, wholesome and elflike, leaves ducatholders a bit breathless with her leaps, spins and trick ballet. Backed by a full troupe, highlighting tribal beauts and Mounties, she garners heavy gloving at the bowoff."

Having looked up all this strange jargon in my pocketsize dictionary of Varietese (*ducatholders*—audience; *tribal beauts*—Indian girls; *heavy gloving*—loud applause; *bowoff*—exit), I arrived for my first look in Indianapolis with great expectations. But I was still unprepared for Canada's "Star of the North," as Barbara Ann's first spectacle number was named in her honor.

At the end of the ice, 9,000 goggling citizens of Indianapolis and I saw a revolving stage that looked like a king-size jukebox. It slowly turned a small regal figure into view. Your girl appeared draped in an $8,000 cape of silver fox, turquoise velvet and beadwork, above chorus girls dressed as Hollywood Indians and chorus boys in fire-engine red parkas with sequins. These I took to be *Variety*'s "Mounties," but although I've never seen anybody wear such fancy parkas in Canada's north country, I think the wearers were intended to be Eskimos. Worshipful courtiers removed Barbara Ann's robe, and in a sparkling bodice and powderpuff ballet skirt, she came down the ice and flew.

She flourished around the rink melding her famous repertoire of one hundred school figures into one flowing line of dance. She scored to a halt on tiptoe in centre ice in three spotlight rays reaching down from the girders. She began to spin. She was a bob-bin whirling in a dark mill, a centrifuge gone crazy, a dust devil, St. Elmo's fire. The audience strained forward, lost and gone. When the figurine stopped, resumed human shape and bowed, the audience was slow to realize it had been humanly done.

"The sitspin sequence is so unbelievable that a person attempting to review the show should not try to describe it, just skip over it quickly and pretend it didn't happen."

That's how the Star-of-the-North sequence bowled over Ed Wallace of the *World-Telegram* and *Sun*, when Barbara Ann finally reached New York. He called her display "the finest skating that has ever been done in Madison Square Garden," while John McClain of the *New York Journal American* murmured through a slight haze, "Barbara Ann Scott is a dream."

The Garden, as previously reported, was just a bit better than half full opening night—but night after night the crowds grew and grew. When the engagement ended the New York run had also beaten last year's figures—not by much, but enough.

*Cheesecake shot of the ice-show star by Bruno of Hollywood.*

Among the realistic people of show business, Barbara Ann Scott will probably always remain something of an oddity. Off the ice she has none of the airs and postures of the performer such as exhibitionism in restaurants, eye-catching clothes, obsessive trade talk and cries of "Darling!"

The simple truth is that she does not have their job insecurity. The trouper puts up a big front to battle the harsh facts of life in show business, where jobs are few and far between. The allowance doled out to Barbara Ann by her St. Lawrence Foundation is less than dozens of salaries in the Hollywood Ice Revue, but "everything is taken care of" for her.

There has been of late a notable withdrawal of Barbara's mother, Mrs. Ann Derbyshire Scott, from direct supervision of her affairs. It is apparent that Mrs. Scott has felt the criticism that she was mother-henning Barbara Ann too much, and she is making a determined effort to cut it out. She has stopped referring to her twenty-three-year-old daughter as "child"; and while she travels with the show when she feels like it, she does not live with Barbara.

But for all this Barbara Ann still lives in a protective nimbus of her fame and her well-entrusted wealth. In show business, Barbara Ann is a one-girl Utopia.

# Pauline McGibbon

## The woman behind all those "first woman" jobs

BY MARIAN ENGEL

*Novelist Marian Engel grew up beside her, in Sarnia, Ont. Here's a warm, close-to-the-bone profile no one else could possibly have written.*

**OCTOBER 1974** AT THREE O'CLOCK IN THE afternoon on April 10th, 1974, a neat woman in a long royal blue satin gown wearing as jewelry only rings and the Order of Canada medal, entered the parliamentary chamber of the Legislature of Ontario and, with a dignity that can only be called aplomb, accepted the office of Lieutenant-Governor of the Province of Ontario.

From high up in the visitors' gallery, she looked small. Her hair was wound, as always, in a braid around her head. When she spoke, her voice was low and clear.

Six weeks later, after *Chatelaine* assigned me to write about her, a black car stopped at my house. The driver wore no uniform, but confessed easily to being a member of the Ontario Provincial Police. Like everyone else who stops at my house, he wanted me to nip out quickly so he wouldn't get a ticket on the crowded street.

The day was green and golden. The absurd pink sandstone buildings of the Legislature looked as if they were made of strawberry ice cream (how could the government know, when it ordered the buildings washed, that they'd turn out not dignified beige, but pink?)

I went through a heavy door with a beveled-glass window pane. A maid took my coat. I sat down in a reception room where a table was already laid for two. It was a handsome room, furnished like a minister's (low Anglican, I think) parlor: good oak, sturdy patterned upholstery, an Empire looking-glass, chipped vases from China; paintings by an artistic aunt. I ask for an ashtray and am given a brass bowl.

A voice—*the* voice—behind me. "Well, hello, Marian."

I stand up to salute her. She is just the same—wide-smiling. She has always grinned that grin, moved with that almost awkward economy. She is compact, neat, efficient but never cold. She is wearing an apple-green suit as fresh as the day. "Well, hello, Pauline."

We are amused by this official meeting. The first time I met her I was the new kid who'd moved next door to her mother, Ethel Mills, chairman of the Sarnia Board of Education, and she was Mrs. Mills's glamorous thirtyish daughter, coming home for the weekend with her husband. On subsequent occasions, she was the thoughtful person who took me out for my first formal luncheon (at Winston's, in Toronto, when you still had to have a key to go), and the lady who saved my life when I was starving in England by taking me to a posh hotel in Piccadilly when I'd been fired from Foyle's bookstore.

She was born in Sarnia in 1910. Her father and his brother ran a department store for a while; by the time I moved down there Mr. Mills had gone independent in a dark glass-and-wood emporium where you went for good gloves, really fine yarn goods and linen-and-lace hankies.

"Ribbons were big business then, Marian" (she always interjects your name), "and I loved them. I used to go to the back of the store and loop them all around me when I was little. I loved the store. Come and see what I've done to my office."

Sunlight floods the red carpet, lights the marble fireplace scrubbed white. The new furniture is succinct, a big plain desk and credenza, a number of olive-green straight chairs (which the apple green of her suit sets off eerily, did she think of that? Yes.) a huge glass coffee table, and oh, my stars and garters, two shocking-pink corduroy settees.

After we moved to live beside the lady who looked like Queen Mary in Sarnia I became aware that there were two events for which our shared driveway must be cleared: the arrival of the coal-man with his jangling slides and the arrival of Pauline and Don from Toronto.

By 1947, they were already outstanding citizens. They had met in high school, both gone to Victoria College, University of Toronto, and married in 1935 after Don was transferred by Imperial Oil to Toronto. (A graduate in economics, he took the year's only opening at Imperial Oil in 1932, an office boy's job in Sarnia at $40 a month.) He's a handsome man with a turned-up nose and a benevolent smile. In his heart of hearts he wanted to be a professor, but there was no question of further education for him. The McGibbons were respectable, but not well off. Don's mother had died young, and his father, lucky in those days to have a job at all, clerked in the liquor store. The Great Day that Sarnia was put on the map by the shooting of bank robber Red Ryan outside that store, Mr. McGibbon was there. It was one of the things everybody knew about him: he was in the liquor store the day Red Ryan was shot, my my. That was fame.

Mrs. Mills held court on her glider all summer long. Long after her jolly husband died in the late forties, she was active in politics and music. On summer weekends Pauline and Don would come and sit on the big porch smoking du Maurier cigarettes, with their new bound books and boxes of Laura Secords. They were always a delight to see; plainly but immaculately dressed, car dark and polished, big handsome smiles. Pauline had her clothes made, just as her mother had her hair done by a woman who came each week to the house in Sarnia: they had a sense of their own value.

"Oh, I was a spoiled child, an only," Pauline recalls. "I went everywhere with them and got to love people. I weighed nearly eleven pounds when I was born. I was a monster. I never had any maternal urge myself; even when I played with dolls I made them into grown-ups. Maybe it was Mother's talking about her labor with me; I may have been subconsciously afraid. She went ten months and had a terrible time. They weren't much help to them then, and she said all the time she was stalking the halls trying to give birth there was a young male intern sitting on a table nonchalantly swinging his legs and saying 'Oh, it's always hardest with the first one.' When she was pacing desperately, trying to give birth to this monster, me, and my big head," says the Lieutenant-Governor of Ontario, also past chancellor of the University of Toronto, past IODE national president, and past chairman of the board of Women's College Hospital.

"There are those who say it's selfish not to have children, but I honestly don't think I've ever had the urge. It's always seemed to me there are other things you can do with your life. You know I was great friends with Dr. Marion Hilliard. She was a marvelous woman, residence doctor at Vic when I was a student. When later I went to her with a female complaint she thought I was there to sell her a war bond. She knew me. I was repelled by that waiting room full of enormous women, and I knew I wasn't cut out to be a mother, and she knew it, too. We were both sure childless-

*Pauline McGibbon and her mother, taken in January 1958.*

ness is not a tragedy."

It's easy to forget how recently married middle-class women have been allowed to work outside the home. In 1935, in the depths of the Depression, Pauline McGibbon, wife, got through her house-work in an hour and sat all day reading. No two-income families were allowed. She loved to read, but she was sociable, too, so when a new junior chapter of the IODE was started, she joined.

Ability rises. She became national president in 1963. Meanwhile, back in Sarnia, she had met a Sarnia lawyer a school generation older, who had been active in the formation of the Dominion Drama Festival, D. Park Jamieson. "Park phoned me in Toronto and said the DDF needed an unpaid secretary and would I do it. I was scared. I was film officer of the IODE and I didn't then know you could do two things at once. I asked Don about it. He said it would be very difficult because Park was such a perfectionist—and that sold me."

The Dominion Drama Festival is a world of its own. Pauline became president in 1957; Don has been president also. Where there is Canadian theatre, there are the McGibbons. She and Don like to bring artists commissions, help writers get plays put on and take hungry students to lunch in London and Paris, but they don't condescend. I've met people of grander origins who think that people who don't live like them are willfully grotty, but the McGibbons know what simplicity is.

They were the first people I knew who bought hard-cover novels and paintings. Once I remember taking a piece of pie to Mrs. Mills when she was oldish, and of course going in for a chat and six Laura Secords. She had a new artifact: a bas-relief of Pauline by Florence Wyle: a flat, round plaque, the perfect meeting of form and content, for who else in Canada has such a Della Robbia head? It faced the wedding picture on the mantelpiece that was always the ultimate in chic: tall smiling bride, column of satin, armful of roses and, instead of orange blossoms and a veil, an infinitely smart pointed almost military satin cap.

*Officer of the Order of Canada, 1967; LLD, University of Alberta; DU, University of Ottawa;*
*BAA, Ryerson; Dame Commander, Order of St. Lazarus of Jerusalem; Centennial Medal; Canadian Drama Award; Award of Merit: Canadian Public Relations Society.*

*Chancellor, University of Toronto 1971-1974; first woman president, Alumni Association, U of T; member, Board of Upper Canada College; past chairman, Board of Governors, Women's College Hospital; past-president, Canadian Conference of the Arts; former national president, IODE; first woman chairman, Board of Governors, National Theatre School, director of the Canada Committee. And a lot more.*

Two last questions: what would your mother have done if she were starting out now? What would you have done?

Deep, throaty laugh. "Marian, if Mother had had a chance she'd have been an excellent musician. When I was still small she practiced the piano three hours a day and went every week to lessons in Detroit. She was serious and talented and in another day she'd have been an excellent pianist-accompanist.

"Me: You know, I gave a speech at Simpsons to an employees' club, recently and I confessed an old ambition. At Christmas lots of my friends in Toronto worked in Eaton's and Simpsons but I had to go home and work at Mills' Brothers; I always wanted to work in a big Toronto store.

"They were enchanted when I said that. And I was sincere. You know I think I would have been a crackerjack at merchandising."

"I went downstairs with the head of the glove department and tried on kid gloves for ages. She admitted their new counter arrangements aren't as good as the old elbow stands, and was delighted to find someone who really knew how to work gloves on. We went through a whole shipment of them and had a wonderful time."

"Would you go into politics if you started again?"

"Marian, the traditional starting point in politics for women is the Board of Education. If you have no children in school you're out of touch with that."

Pauline McGibbon's career has been in volunteer work. She hopes that in spite of pressures to work professionally, women will continue to donate their time to volunteer organizations. "You can always get volunteers for the arts, or for the hospitals—but the other organizations? Difficult."

I remember a famous occasion of McGibbon charity. One Christmas when my family started out for Toronto, our car broke down in a blizzard. It took hours to find a tow-truck. Eventually, we took refuge in the jail in Strathroy while my father and a repairman put the car together again.

We returned woebegone to Sarnia late in the afternoon, having canceled our trip to Toronto. Just as my mother was getting the bacon and eggs out of the fridge, the rest of us called "Hold it!": coming from next door was a procession of McGibbons—Don, Pauline, Don's sister Margaret—carrying platters of turkey and big dishes of fixings through the snow. Even a pudding with holly.

"How did you get that way, Pauline? Who are you? Where did your drive come from?"

"I don't know. It helped to be spoiled. It helped to come from hard-working farming and merchandising stock, where no one was idle. I'm physically strong. And the women weren't weak in our family."

It is time to go. Old Home Week is over. I think of her in splendid golden and black robes being installed as Chancellor of the University of Toronto. Now she has bills to sign, fourteen convocations to get through in her last term as First Female Chancellor of the University.

I feel I have overstayed. She shows no sign. At the door, she continues to be gracious. "And listen, when it's not so busy in the summer, come back and bring the kids."

Now, does that sharp cardfile upstairs read "Marian Engel—always ask about her kids," or is she just like that?

No. All the world's a stage. The breeding house for that stage is the small town, where you know everyone. Widen the circles, slowly, slowly. Keep the warm smile, the interest in everyone, and if what your family sold was always all wool and a yard wide, you'll marry it, you'll be it, and you'll create it. Genius for anything, after all, is ninety percent hard work.

# The Kain Mutiny

*The Parisians adore her, Nureyev cossets her, the Bolshoi wants her. But here at home, well . . . Can good grey Canadians really love a star of dynamite talent, whose world includes punishing hard work, and also limos and luxury dinners, sexy dresses and devoted young men?*

By Barbara Amiel

JANUARY 1977

"IF YOU READ THE ADS PUSHING the current tour of Roland Petit's French ballet company across Canada, you'd think the only person dancing was Canadian Karen Kain. The National Ballet's leading dancer is a guest with the company, but the National reportedly has its collective nose out of joint that it is nowhere acknowledged that Miss Kain is dancing by permission of the National. According to one wag, that's because the National itself only appears these days by permission of Miss Kain."

—GLOBE & MAIL, OCTOBER 2, 1976

"By the standards of some committee women who support the ballet, Kain socially, is a flop. I have seen her at a diplomatic party in a dowdy, mauve formal gown. I have seen her in the streets in a frumpish fur-trimmed coat. At a luncheon with me recently, Kain wore a black velvet pantsuit with gilt trim, an outfit that resembled the costume of a magician's assistant. Kain lacks the grace of entertaining small talk. Asked about her recent season in Australia, she said: 'It was very nice.' Asked where she lived during her recent season in Paris, she said: 'I shared a place with another girl.'"

—MCKENZIE PORTER,
TORONTO SUN, SEPTEMBER 16, 1976.

As Pierre Berton observed to Gordon Sinclair during an exchange on *Front Page Challenge*: "I don't care what the press says about me, I just measure the number of inches I get." Karen Kain recognized the wisdom of the remark when I repeated it to her, a little smile flickering across the wide white oval of her face, before going back to explaining how *awful* it was to be dancing on the stage of the Forum at Toronto's waterfront Ontario Place, leaping high into the air and then noticing, *right there on the stage*, sitting taking notes, McKenzie Porter and *Globe & Mail* dance critic Lawrence O'Toole. At the open air Forum, decent seats in the audience couldn't be reserved for reviewers and so they were perched uneasily on little chairs on the side of the stage. She could see the glasses of Larry O'Toole glinting under the stage lights as she leaped high into an extended *entrechat* even though her own vision (never very good without glasses) was hampered by clouds of mosquitoes buzzing cosily around her face.

It wasn't, she explained, that she disliked reviewers, although O'Toole's occasional predilection for starting off perceptive ballet reviews with homilies like "Karen Kain is in an unholy mess" was disturbing. It was just that since her triumphant appearances in Paris (*Le Figaro*: "sparkling . . . inexhaustible vivacity"; *L'Aurore*: "What elegance of line . . .") there had been a sort of snippy feeling in the air as if everyone expected her to behave badly and act, well, like a star.

---

**The life of a dancer is not conducive to long-term relationships, and the life of a star even less so**

---

"People suddenly start waiting for you to get out of line so they can blame it on the fact that you think you're really good," she said. "If I ask for a new costume now, I'd have to be careful about the way I ask, the tone of my voice. People rarely change. It's just that everyone looks at them differently."

Oh Canada! It must be something in the water. No man is a hero to his valet and all that, but still in Canada our antipathy to homegrown excellence has gone beyond the checks and balances of natural debunking. All for naught. Because as Celia Franca wisely pointed out when she was accused of an antistar policy during her reign over the National Ballet, "You can't hold a star down. A star simply emerges and no policy will decide it."

∾

Backstage at Hamilton Place, Karen Kain is decked out in a very décolleté green-satin and black-velvet corselette. Although she has just this minute finished dancing *Carmen*, there is barely a sheen of perspiration on her skin.

Along the cramped corridor outside her dressing room, a retinue is forming. Her manager, David Haber, is at the head of the line. He is the first real confirmation of Karen's status. For a percentage of her guest-appearance fees, Haber makes deals and does Karen's nagging for her. He is a constant threat to the egalitarian, starless National Ballet—always circling, smiling, pushing for his client.

All the same, it takes Karen's mother to clear out the dressing room. Mrs. Kain is immaculately attired in tiers of black chiffon crowned by a perfectly bouffant head of grey hair. "Here's our little Carmen," she trills, quickly appraising her daughter's sluttish costume, matter-of-factly turning on the shower, and preparing to scrub all that horrid gold glitter off Karen's back.

"I didn't know you had to die in this ballet, dear," she says, looking fiercely at the silk jersey tunic Karen has put aside to wear to the reception being thrown for her. "Isn't it a little open at the sides?"

From Mrs. Kain's point of view—wife of an important Westinghouse executive, resident of the fashionable community of Mississauga, all chock-full of decent upper-income Middle Canadians—it *is* a little open. The armholes of the tunic are slit almost to the waist and when Karen moves and holds her arms at a certain angle, her breasts, naked under the tunic, are fully visible. It is, nevertheless, an elegant outfit, sophisticated and flattering, and Karen knows it. She opens her eyes wide. "I think it will be all right, Mother," she says, and begins gathering up her hair into the matching turban.

Outside, in the Studio Theatre of Hamilton Place, in the city where Karen was born, along with ruddy-faced Hamilton aldermen and distinguished guests, is McKenzie Porter. Only a week ago Porter labeled Karen's clothes "frumpish" in his newspaper column. As she walks into the large room crowded with Hamilton's finest all ready to proclaim Karen Kain Day in Steel City, Mrs. Kain makes a beeline for McKenzie Porter. "How do you do," she says holding an elegant hand just a fraction out of his reach. "I'm Mrs. Frump."

∾

Since almost the first moment Karen *grande jetée*'d onto a stage and into the public eye, ballet critics and audiences have exclaimed over her sensuality and sexuality. Ballet dancers have always seemed so relentlessly aseptic. Offstage their bodies are hideously bundled up in old woolies, feet disinfected and disfigured, their entire concentration spent in rapt appraisal of their mirror image. On stage they live in a distant world of exquisite lines and rippling beauty that is quite uninhabitable for anyone who doesn't care to *entrechat* into the omnipresent magic forest. Their faces are expressionless masks coated in chalk white powder and coal black points of emphasis. Only the men occasionally seem to exude sexuality, but even this was thought to be exclusively for one another.

Karen on the other hand seemed so *accessible*. Onstage her warmth and animation spilled over the footlights. Clearly she enjoyed men. Not like Pavlova, whose brief affairs were justified in terms of therapeutic value. "Sex is like medicine," Pavlova would explain, "it is nasty at first but good for you."

Still, the life of a dancer is not conducive to long-term relationships, and the life of a star even less so. At first Karen solved this problem by cutting a wide swathe through the eligible men in the National Ballet Company. First there was a choreographer and then a principal dancer and then a romance that sizzled all across the stages of North America when Frank Augustyn and Karen Kain began dancing together. It was not easy to explain to her middle-class parents that marriage was something far off in the future.

"I know my parents want to see me happy," explains Karen, "but I just don't have the courage to face up to them and fully explain my life-style. You know, in the old days a ballerina could be mistress of the tsar and it was all very glamorous." So, while Karen continues footloose and fretful about it, the admirers, young and old, continue to send notes backstage. ("Dear Miss Kain: Could you come to our grade 9 class and be my project for next Wednesday afternoon? Or Thursday. Please phone tonight.") Last time she was in New York, a chauffeured limousine waited outside the stage door to carry her off to dinner at the Beautiful People's Twenty-One club.

"It was sort of fun. He was a millionaire, and there were roses and presents. But it didn't work, you know. I didn't like him especially and the car and the roses couldn't change that."

Karen's home in the heart of Toronto's Cabbagetown, with the sagging porch, is set back a little from the street. The sand-blasting crowd, intent on spiffing up this neighborhood into rows of chic identical townhouses, hasn't caught up to Karen's street yet, which looks pretty much the way it has for the last 50 years.

Buying the house was a major decision for Karen, whose salary is very decent for a principal dancer in Canada—close to $25,000 including her guest appearances—but it isn't enough to support a very fancy way of life. Shortly after she moved into her new home she was burglarized. There wasn't much to steal. The house is pleasingly furnished with enough inexpensive Canadiana, pine chests and Karen's favorite rocking chair, but the thieves did make off with some jewelry of sentimental value and with it a bit of Karen's naïveté.

Because, in spite of her cosmopolitan lifestyle—jetting off to New York and Paris—Karen remains unaffected and strikingly unsophisticated. Her personal life has none of the trappings of stardom—not even a cleaning woman once a week.

Back in the early days when Karen first came to the National Ballet School in Toronto, all of 11 years old and already a veteran of two years of ballet lessons, her artistry was an unknown factor. By the time she was 17, Karen was close to 5 feet 7 inches, a thoroughly menacing height for a dancer, who gains a hefty five inches when she rises on her points. She had put on weight, too, pounds of it, and the one extant photo of her at the school during those years shows a solid-looking girl with thighs like tree trunks planted firmly in the floor with barely a hint of knee and ankle.

No one had time to worry about Karen's artistic ability: it was more a practical question of whether or not she could shed enough poundage to fade quietly into the *corps de ballet*.

"Betty Oliphant [director of the National Ballet School] lost a bit of faith in me, but she never really gave up entirely. Even when Miss Franca said, 'She'll never make it; she's too fat and too tall.'

Then Miss Oliphant came to me and said 'Miss Franca is coming in two weeks to audition for the company, which gives you 14 days to lose weight.' So I had nothing but lettuce for the next two weeks. Right after the audition I went out and had four dozen cookies."

Of course, they hadn't given up on her at all. Though artistic director Celia Franca was very taken with the delicate, expressive dancing of Veronica Tennant, who was already doing principal roles in the National Ballet Company, she had too tough and shrewd an eye to close it entirely to Karen Kain. But it's conventional wisdom that a curious blend of gnawing self-doubt and enormous ego is the stuff of stardom. From Karen's point of view most everything was wrong with her.

"My body is too long and my back is too loose and I can't get my legs up very easily because I'm so tight at the hip. People always think I have very high legs, but that's only because I'm so long. I guess you could say I'm not very loose in the right place and quite loose in the wrong ones!"

All the same, even Karen knew that when it came to certain aspects of dance she was gifted with natural advantages. Her *ballon*, that marvelous ability to jump high in the air and, while suspended there, knit a pair of socks, came as easily to her as hopscotching.

Back in 1970, after only one year in the ballet company, a chubby, nail-biting Karen Kain mustered up that indispensable aid to stardom—chutzpah—and decided she was ready for bigger things. Miss Franca was, as usual, several beats ahead of any member of her ballet company.

"Learn *Swan Lake*," she commanded. One month later in Arizona, when Veronica Tennant ripped her back, a shaky, slimmed-down Karen Kain tottered onto the stage as the Swan Queen. It took only three more years for the greatest impresario of them all, Rudolf Nureyev, to anoint Miss Kain officially and scoop her up for guest appearances all around the world. The kid from Steeltown, Ontario, was on her way.

"She's never been afraid of working hard," says Celia Franca, "and Karen's certainly got what you call 'the magic' that makes a great dancer. But she was always impatient with me when it came to working at a role intellectually. Dancing came so easily to her that she didn't understand that a role must be thought through, interpreted, worked at. She kept dancing Karen Kain."

Coming up is an appearance with the Bolshoi ballet in Moscow with partner Frank Augustyn, and an open invitation to dance with the prestigious Royal Ballet in London (the first such invitation for a Canadian dancer). She's made it to stardom and now she only has to come of age spiritually to release the mature artistry that will give Canada its very first *prima ballerina assoluta*.

# Woman of the Year: High-flying Roberta Bondar

*When Roberta Bondar soared into space, she became Canada's first female astronaut and an inspiration to every young woman who wants a science-oriented career. John Colapinto salutes her achievements and encounters a tough but oddly vulnerable person behind the bland P.R. mask*

BY JOHN COLAPINTO

**JANUARY 1993** WITH HER NINE-DAY space shuttle flight last January, Dr. Roberta Bondar made history as the first Canadian woman in space. At the time, she was portrayed as a kind of intergalactic Anne Murray—the wholesome, but decidedly bland, onetime Girl Guide, who actually listened to tapes of "O Canada" while orbiting the earth. The portrait bears a touch of the airbrush. With her short salt-and-pepper hair, chiseled facial features and laser-like gaze, Bondar, at 47, is one tough customer, who, as fellow astronaut Ken Money says, "isn't afraid to fight when there's a fight on." Bland she is not. "I don't suffer fools gladly," Bondar admits. Her older sister, Barbara, Roberta's senior by 15 months and co-owner of her own data management firm, amends this: "Bobbie doesn't suffer fools at all."

Which includes journalistic fools. Asked why she insists on being interviewed in an anonymous hotel suite, Bondar says bluntly, "No one comes into my home unless they're my friends."

A reporter whose agenda is to discover the real Roberta Bondar behind the public-relations mask has his work cut out for him. While ex-colleagues at the Canadian Space Agency (CSA) will admit that Bondar was well known for her sharp temper, none will offer any examples. Ask fellow astronaut Dr. Bob Thirsk and he says, "When Roberta focuses on a task, she's hell-bent. She can piss some people off." Everyone from Bondar's sister to her past professors will allude to her combative streak—but that's all they'll say.

Maybe no one wants to tarnish a newly minted Canadian hero's luster. But the decaffeinated portraits of Bondar do her an injustice. Her edge is what makes her both interesting and likable. She didn't beat out her male competitors for a space flight by being deferential. You sense, in Bondar, a pungent streak of rage-at-the-way-things-are; she's got something to prove, a chip on her shoulder that even the embrace of the nation's media has failed to dislodge. It's an anger that has been simmering since she was a child in Sault Ste. Marie, Ont.

Bondar's Russian and Ukrainian grandparents had settled in the Soo in the early 1900s. They were not accepted in the small, closed, predominantly WASP enclave, says Barbara. "In those days, immigrants were known as DPs [Displaced Persons]." Although Edward was born in Canada, the stigma of foreignness still clung to him. "There was a time," Barbara says, "when my dad wasn't allowed to play badminton in the local club." Roberta's mother, Mildred, an only child who was brought up in the Soo not by her own mother but by her English and Welsh grandparents, also grew up with a sense of being different, of not belonging. "My mother felt acutely alone," says Barbara, "*acutely* alone." They married a few years after high school, where Edward was known as Eddie Know-All Bondar, and Mildred was valedictorian. Neither could afford to attend college—a lack both felt keenly. Mildred eventually attended university at

age 48, earned her BA and became a schoolteacher. Eddie Know-All Bondar, who had the brains to become a doctor or scientist, instead worked as an office manager at the Sault Ste. Marie Public Utilities Commission. "My parents were determined that we would have the things in life that they didn't have," says Roberta. "They didn't stress accomplishment as much as they stressed being the best we could be," adds Barbara. "The *best* friend. The *best* sister. The *best* role model." The girls were pushed to excel in an array of after-school activities, which their parents hoped would knit the children into the community in a way that they, as young people, had not been. "We were involved every night and every day of the week doing something in the community," says Barbara. Perhaps a tad too involved from the point of view of Roberta's grades. Until her college years, Roberta worked just hard enough to get by. "That was fine with my parents," says Roberta. "They always stressed that you learn as much *outside* school."

When Roberta arrived home one day with the dreaded "L" (for Laggard), Mildred went ballistic. "She was furious," Barbara recalls. "She went to see the principal and said, 'How dare you! We don't want to see this ever again!'" When a guidance counselor suggested to Mildred that Roberta should change her mind about studying science because she didn't work hard enough, Mildred replied: "Roberta will do whatever she wants to do." Both stories suggest that Canada's favorite astronaut comes by her feisty temperament honestly.

Edward Bondar, meanwhile, instilled in his daughters the ability to handle tools, shoot guns, work a lathe and play sports. He encouraged Roberta's passion for building rocket models and nurtured her fascination with science by installing a chemistry lab in the basement.

By the time Roberta entered high school at Sir James Dunn Collegiate & Vocational School, she was known for her boyish appearance and interests. In high school, she recalls, girls deferred to boys, held back in class, yielded the front row desks, dropped out of the competition.

"I thought to myself: What is this nonsense?" Bondar says. "I'm as capable as a male!"

"She danced to a different drum," says Richard

Annett, a fellow student at Sir James Dunn, and now a geography teacher at the school. Describing Bondar as "the Peppermint Patty of Sir James Dunn," Annett says, "She never went out of her way to put on makeup or dress attractively. She always wore this green cardigan plastered with badges for her participation in every school activity, club, athletic event and house league." At dances, she was always the organizer—she took the tickets, did the decorating and helped with the clean-up crew. Annett says she did not escape the inevitable teasing: "I'm sure that she was called 'butchy.' It probably didn't bother her, though. Otherwise, she would've changed."

In fact, it did bother Bondar. She still speaks with palpable anger and hurt about those years. "My close friends were usually younger women on the basketball team because the ones who were older were into the prom, and I wasn't."

Her scholarly side emerged during her third year at the University of Guelph. Bedridden with a case of mumps, she had little else to do but study, relying on other people's notes because she could not be in class. Her marks soared into the 80s, and upon her graduation in 1968, with a B.Sc. in agriculture and zoology, she embarked on what would prove to be nine years of postgraduate studies, racking up a master's degree in experimental pathology from the University of Western Ontario in 1971, a Ph.D. in neurobiology from the University of Toronto in 1974 and an M.D. from McMaster University in 1977. Somehow, she also managed to find time to earn her pilot's licence.

At the same time, Bondar was beginning to question where all of her sometimes frantic intellectual and physical activity was taking her. Once qualified as a physician, she accepted a job as an assistant professor of medicine in neurology at McMaster in 1982. Then, just 18 months

after starting her job, she happened to hear over her car radio that the National Research Council's newly created Canadian Astronaut Program was looking for people to fly on the space shuttle. Bondar, then 37, immediately applied.

It's not hard to understand why Bondar was one of the six selected from the 4,300 applicants. The astronaut program drew together her eclectic skills and training, combining the cerebral rigors of science, the physical challenges of sports and the risk-taking of flying airplanes. Accepted into the program as the sole woman, her life suddenly took on a focus. There was, of course, no guarantee that she would be chosen to fly; the National Aeronautics and Space Administration (NASA) had promised just two flights for Canadians. But Bondar figured that even if she were not chosen, she could carve out a niche for herself in aerospace medicine. "Then," she says, heaving a deep sigh, "*Challenger* happened."

At the time of the explosion of the shuttle *Challenger* in 1986, Bondar thought only of the seven crew members who died—many of them her friends. "I just went into a cold sweat when I heard," she recalls. "I felt my stomach turn. I had sweat rolling down my armpits into my hands."

The disaster halted the entire program for two years, stranding Bondar and her fellow astronauts.

**WOMAN OF THE YEAR**

**High-flying Roberta Bondar, astronaut**

Only two months earlier, she had been faced with personal tragedy when Edward Bondar unexpectedly died of a heart attack. Roberta was in Ottawa at the time—a fact, Barbara says, that still haunts her. "My sister hasn't dealt with his death well yet." Father and daughter used to clean guns together, and she has been planning, ever since his death, to clean them one last time. "But I haven't been able to touch them, because you can smell the sweat from his hands on the gun. I feel . . . very sort of . . ." Her voice trails off.

When she speaks about her father and how her fame provided a kind of vindication for him, her eyes brim. "When I got into the astronaut program," she says, her tough exterior melting for a moment, "everyone in the Soo started saying hello to my dad. He was getting some of the respect he should have had all along."

After the *Challenger* explosion and her father's death, she threw herself with redoubled energy into the space program, which gradually showed signs of coming back to life. In 1989, it was announced that a mission, slated for early 1990, would include one of two Canadian astronauts: Ken Money, a then-54-year-old physiologist from Toronto, or Bondar.

"She trimmed all the excess fat off her daily life," says fellow astronaut Dr. Bob Thirsk. "She got involved in experiments on her own that filled the gaps in her experience. She was tireless." She also displayed her legendary temper, clashing often with the CSA's head of the astronaut program, Bruce Aikenhead. Ken Money recalls a meeting in which one of her space agency bosses used the expression "Just lie back and enjoy it"—an oblique allusion to the dirty joke about what to do when rape is inevitable. "Roberta said, without a smile, 'There's absolutely nothing funny about rape,'" Money recalls. "She wasn't gonna let that pass, even though this guy was in a position to do her a lot of harm or a lot of good."

Apparently, Bondar's outspokenness did not prejudice the CSA brass against her. In January 1990, she was selected to fly. Bondar's voice turns hard when discussing the inevitable rumors that being a woman helped to get her chosen. "I was more qualified than anyone else in the program. We had a diversity of experiments that ran all the way from basic science to things in zoology and agriculture. I had a degree in that. There were microscopic experiments. I had degrees in that. Everything that I studied was on this flight. Of the six people in the Canadian astronaut program, I was the most qualified." Her fellow astronauts say they agree—and that her qualifications went beyond academic. She possessed, they say, the Right Stuff.

"The Right Stuff is the ability to perform in spite of fear," says Money. "Roberta has enormous amounts of the Right Stuff. I have ordinary amounts." Physically, she was a match for her male crew members, rappelling down the side of the shuttle and being raised by a block and tackle and dropped four meters into a tank of water—all while wearing the 100-pound space suit. And when, after an interminable year and a half's delay, Bondar finally flew on the shuttle on January 22, 1992, she amazed her backup, Ken Money. "The launch is supposed to be the scariest part," he says. "But I honestly don't believe she felt fear. She seemed quite exuberant." "Of course, I had fear," Bondar counters. "But you don't express it on the morning of the launch, because that's not the time to do it."

*"The Right Stuff is the ability to perform in spite of fear," says Money. "Roberta has enormous amounts of the Right Stuff."*

During her speech last fall to the Canadian Club, Bondar spoke about the "depth and luxury of color" of the earth as viewed from the shuttle windows and of how such beauty, once seen, "becomes a part of you." Bondar's time aboard the shuttle didn't allow for much sight-seeing. As payload specialist, she worked at least 14-hour days and conducted some 55 scientific experiments while battling space sickness. Press Bondar for more philosophical reflections on her flight and she shrugs. "I'm such a realist," she says. "Since I've been back, people look in my eyes or touch me in some new reverent way." She shakes her head. "It's great going up and looking at the earth, but all I could think of was getting back and having a glass of cold skim milk."

Since her flight, Bondar has been celebrated as a role model for young women. It's a responsibility she takes seriously. She speaks often to schools, church groups, Girl Guides—and her message is always the same. Vividly recalling the teasing and rejection she faced in high school, she urges young women not to sacrifice their energy and spirit in the interest of fitting in.

But her professional accomplishments have carried a personal cost. Bondar and her sister offer a multitude of rationalizations as to why she has remained single, ranging from Roberta's curt, "It's none of your business," and "I was too busy," to Barbara's "There are no men good enough."

# Index

# Acknowledgment of Sources

**Cover**

Photographs: *back row, woman in glasses*: August 1997 © Robert Kenney. Reprinted by permission; *woman with flower*: March 1963 © Beverly Rockett. Reprinted by permission; *Karen Kain*: June 1997 © Cylla Von Tiedemann. Reprinted by permission; *front row, Roberta Bondar*: January 1993 © Alex Meyboom. Reprinted by permission.

**Chapter One: Herself: Woman's Changing Image**

*Page 16*: advertisement, courtesy Vogue. Copyright © 1929 (renewed 1957, 1985) by the Condé Nast Publications, Inc. Reprinted by permission; *25*: advertisement, June 1946 © Elizabeth Arden. Reprinted by permission; *27*: photograph, September 1977 © Richard Sharabura. Reprinted by permission; *28*: photographs, November 1966 © Murray Dutchak. Reprinted by permission; photograph, January 1996 © CCFTA Foundation. Reprinted by permission; *30*: photograph, March 1963 © Beverly Rockett. Reprinted by permission; *31*: photograph, November 1966 © Murray Dutchak. Reprinted by permission; *35*: photograph, December 1981 © Joy Von Tiedemann. Reprinted by permission; *36*: photograph, January 1946 © Stella Pharmaceutical. Reprinted by permission; *37*: photographs, April 1966 © Beverly Rockett. Reprinted by permission; *39*: photograph, February 1993 © Joseph Santos. Reprinted by permission; *40*: article, February 1993 © Eve Rockett. Reprinted by permission; *41*: photograph, February 1993 © David Gray. Reprinted by permission.

**Chapter Two: Partnerships**

*Page 42*: illustration, June 1981 © Dennis Noble. Reprinted by permission; *45*: article, November, 1928 © Madge MacBeth. Reprinted by permission of the estate of Madge MacBeth; *47*: illustration, November 1928 © R. W. Major. Reprinted by permission of the estate of R. W. Major; *51*: article,

August 1946 © Isobel Rappaport. Reprinted by permission; *59*: article, January 1972 © Catherine Breslin. Reprinted by permission; *61*: photograph, January 1972 © Catherine Breslin. Reprinted by permission; *62*: article, May 1981 © Philip Marchand. Reprinted by permission; *63–64*: illustrations, May 1981 © Christine Middleton. Reprinted by permission; *65*: article, April 1993 © Robert Collison. Reprinted by permission.

**Chapter Three: Her Home, Her Castle**

*Page 68*: illustration, April 1928 © James C. Snyder Furniture Inc. Reprinted by permission; *70*: illustration, November 1934 © Mather's & Haldenby, Architects. Reprinted by permission of the estate of Eric Haldenby; advertisement, June 1929 © Northern Telecom Ltd. Reprinted by permission; *73*: photograph, May 1981 © Paul McCarthy. Reprinted by permission; *76*: advertisement, June 1939 © Crane Canada. Reprinted by permission; *81*: photograph, December 1981 © Claude Noel. Reprinted by permission; *82–83*: illustrations, August 1934 © Mather's & Haldenby, Architects. Reprinted by permission of the estate of Eric Haldenby; *85*: photograph, September 1972 © Karol Ike. Reprinted by permission; *87*: illustrations, February 1952 © Gibson & Pokorny, Architects. Reprinted by permission of the estate of G. K. Pokorny; *88*: photograph, March 1972 © Karol Ike. Reprinted by permission; *89*: photograph, April 1972 © Clive Webster. Reprinted by permission; *91*: photographs, February 1996 © Evan Dion. Reprinted by permission.

**Chapter Four: Parenting**

*Page 96*: illustration, November 1928 © Stella Grier. Reprinted by permission of the estate of Stella Grier; *103*: illustration, July 1928 © J. S. Hallam. Reprinted by permission of the estate of J. S. Hallam; *104*: photograph, December 1972 © Don Newlands. Reprinted by permission; article, December 1972 © Robert Fulford. Reprinted by permission; *105*: article, April 1985 © Rona Maynard. Reprinted by permission; *109*: article,

February 1993 © Don Gillmor. Reprinted by permission; *111*: article, November 1993 © Barbara Wade Rose. Reprinted by permission.

## Chapter Five: Food & Entertaining
*Page 117*: photograph, May 1977 © John Reeves. Reprinted by permission; *119*: photograph, May 1932 © Lockwood Haight. Reprinted by permission; *121*: photograph, August 1981 © Ken Mulveney. Reprinted by permission; *123*: advertisement, November 1946 © Northern Telecom Ltd. Reprinted by permission; illustration, April 1981 © Val Lapsa. Reprinted by permission; photograph, September 1963 © René Delbuguet. Reprinted by permission; advertisement, March 1932 © Fridgidaire Canada Ltd. Reprinted by permission; *125*: photograph, May 1963 © Peter Croydon. Reprinted by permission; *127*: advertisement, October 1957 © RJR Nabisco. Reprinted by permission; *129*: photograph, July 1968 © Peter Croydon. Reprinted by permission; *132*: photograph, July 1966 © Normunds Berzins. Reprinted by permission; *133*: photograph, December 1963 © René Delbuguet. Reprinted by permission; *136*: photograph, November 1972 © Murray Dutchak. Reprinted by permission; *137*: photograph, February 1966 © Normunds Berzins. Reprinted by permission; *138*: article, September 1993 © Suanne Kelman. Reprinted by permission; photograph, September 1993 © Ruth Kaplan. Reprinted by permission.

## Chapter Six: Mating Rituals
*Page 152*: article, February 1956 © June Callwood. Reprinted by permission; *155*: article, September 1957 © Eric Nicol. Reprinted by permission; *158*: article, April 1977 © Beverley Slopen. Reprinted by permission; *161*: article, April 1993 © John Colapinto. Reprinted by permission.

## Chapter Seven: On the Job
*Page 169*: article, September 1934 © Nellie McClung. Reprinted by permission of the estate of Nellie McClung; *178*: article, August 1941 © Jack Mosher. Reprinted by permission of the estate of Jack Mosher; article, September 1943 © Lotta Dempsey. Reprinted by permission of the estate of

Lotta Dempsey; *181*: article, February 1977 © Joanna Morgan. Reprinted by permission of the estate of Joanna Morgan; *183*: article, May 1981 © Charlotte Gray. Reprinted by permission; *186*: article, July 1981 © Allan M. Gould. Reprinted by permission; *188*: illustration, April 1981 © David Craig. Reprinted by permission.

## Chapter Eight: Citizenship
*Page 193*: article, September 1928 © Helen Gregory MacGill. Reprinted by permission of the estate of Helen Gregory MacGill; *206*: article, May 1957 © George Bain. Reprinted by permission; *208*: photograph, August 1957 © Paul Rockett. Reprinted by permission; article, October 1971 © Barbara Frum. Reprinted by permission of the estate of Barbara Frum; *211*: article, May 1972 © Erna Paris. Reprinted by permission; *213*: article, January 1985 © Charlotte Gray. Reprinted by permission; *216*: article, January 1994 © Charlotte Gray. Reprinted by permission.

## Chapter Nine: Gender Wars
*Page 220*: advertisement, April 1928 © UCS Group, Ltd. Reprinted by permission; *234*: photograph, February 1963 © Beverly Rockett. Reprinted by permission; *235*: article, January 1974 © Michele Landsberg. Reprinted by permission; *238*: article, April 1974 © June Callwood. Reprinted by permission; *240*: article, September 1974 © Eve Rockett. Reprinted by permission; *241*: article, September 1981 © Myrna Kostash. Reprinted by permission; *243*: article, May 1996 © Deborah Jones. Reprinted by permission.

## Chapter Ten: Role Models
*Page 246*: photograph, March 1993 © Jim West. Reprinted by permission; photograph, March 1981 © Guy Dubois. Reprinted by permission; photograph, January 1966 © Robert Ragsdale. Reprinted by permission; *247*: photograph, January 1981 © Don Miller. Reprinted by permission; *248*: article, November 1974 © Gwen Matheson and V. E. Lang. Reprinted by permission of V. E. Lang; *257*: photograph, October 1977 © V. Tony Hauser. Reprinted by permission; photograph, January 1982 © Gordon Hay. Reprinted by permission; photograph,

October 1966 © John Sebert. Reprinted by permission; photograph, September 1972 © Don Newlands. Reprinted by permission; *261*: article, April 1952 © James Dugan. Reprinted by permission of the estate of James Dugan; *263*: photograph, April 1952 © Bruno Bernard. Reprinted by permission of Bernard of Hollywood Publishing; *264*: article, October 1974 © Marian Engel. Reprinted by permission of the estate of Marian Engel; *267*: article, January 1977 © Barbara Amiel. Reprinted by permission; *270*: article, January 1993 © John Colapinto. Reprinted by permission; *272*: photograph, January 1993 © Alex Meyboom. Reprinted by permission.

**SPECIAL THANKS TO:**
The National Library of Canada, reference services
The National Archives of Canada, reference services
Cancopy (Canadian Copyright Licencing Agency)